FOODSERVICE MANAGEMENT FUNDAMENTALS

DENNIS REYNOLDS, PhD

and

KATHLEEN WACHTER McCLUSKY, MS, RD, FADA

WILEY

This book is printed on acid-free paper.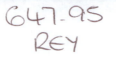

Cover Image Credits:

Top photo: Rob Melnychuk/Getty images, Inc.

Bottom photo: PhotoAlto/Jerome Gorin/Getty Images, Inc.

To my students, who make my career fulfilling, and to my family and friends, who make my life complete.

DR

To Reynard, my husband and biggest supporter, who gave me editorial and emotional support throughout this project.

KWM

CONTENTS

We find ourselves in an era marked by sweeping political, economic, social, and technological change. It would be easy in such an environment to overlook another sweeping change, a seemingly mundane transformation at the core of human experience: our eating habits. With increasing prosperity, human beings are embracing the convenience, epicurean pleasure, and value of eating meals outside of the home.

These changing patterns in expenditures and consumer behavior affect the foodservice business in many ways; the most fundamental is the manner in which operations are managed. This includes a better understanding of the role of foodservice in society, foodservice as a business, and general foodservice management. It also creates an ever-increasing need for sustainability and social responsibility.

Another change is the very nature of the foodservice business. At its inception, the foodservice business was unique in that it served as a delivery system where guests ordered and then received food—that in itself was unique. Today, the basic function is the same, but the business has evolved into a dynamic, service-based industry where key points of service often overshadow the core product (food). The management function has similarly evolved. Decades ago, managing in a corporate café or midscale restaurant was much simpler. Today, foodservice management calls for a variety of skills and abilities, including creativity, analytical skills, interpersonal skills, and operational acumen.

As foodservice industry revenues, reflecting these changing dining and business patterns, rise at an ever-increasing pace, so the number of college programs featuring foodservice-management courses—across the nutrition, dietetic, food science, and hospitality-management curricula—has grown during the last several years. More than ever, students need these programs to provide a strong foundation of conceptual knowledge, along with practical tools that are necessary for managing effectively in today's aggressive business environment. This is perhaps most true for students seeking successful careers in foodservice-related fields, given the considerable financial opportunities there are and the unprecedented business complexity of the entire service industry. This, then, is the impetus driving *Foodservice Management Fundamentals*.

Foodservice Management Fundamentals delivers critical information to help students learn how to position, manage, and leverage a successful foodservice operation. The compilation of management practices, tools, and techniques provided illustrates essential approaches that are applicable to operations in any segment of the foodservice industry. The overarching goal throughout the text is to focus on management-related topics that, when addressed properly, lead to a positive bottom line through innovation, global awareness, and social impact.

This is not just another clone of the typical textbook that students encounter. While *Foodservice Management Fundamentals* includes a historical perspective, it does not repeat outdated methods used by past generations of foodservice managers. Rather, it presents the latest, best practices in order to fully develop the future leaders of the global foodservice industry, introducing and explaining approaches that are appropriate for a foodservice operation in a resort, a corporate headquarters, a manufacturing plant, a ballpark, a hospital, or a university. Moreover, one could say that, in a way, this book—like the best restaurants—is menu driven. That is, the menu is the primary vehicle through which a successful restaurant implements its concept; in this book, the exposition and analysis of every segment covered is in one way or another connected to best management practices, which then relate to the menu. Indeed, the book is written in a style that an entrepreneur would appreciate. It includes theory and background as needed, but is focused on preparing the student to succeed in the foodservice industry—regardless of segment.

Finally, the book's genesis provides for a perspective that other foodservice texts lack. Specifically, the collaboration between a classically trained hospitality professor and a seasoned registered dietitian with years of experience resulted in a robust textbook, one with a fresh, innovative approach to foodservice management. In fact, these differing perspectives sometimes align yet sometimes call for very different approaches to foodservice-management issues. Thus, *Foodservice Management Fundamentals* is distinctive in that it offers multiple approaches to many common management issues. And it is these approaches that will ably prepare the next generation of foodservice and dietetic professionals.

Organization

The book is divided into four parts. **Part I, The Foodservice Industry,** is an overview, which includes a historical perspective as well as a critical analysis of what differentiates the foodservice business from other sectors of the service industry. This includes the following chapters:

- Chapter 1: The Foodservice Industry

- Chapter 2: The Foodservice Business

Part II, The Menu, provides the foundation for what every foodservice manager needs to know, beginning with menu development. Specifically, we address the philosophy behind menu formulation, the planning considerations, and the types of menus found in different segments. We then discuss recipe standardization, costing, and analysis, functions critical to an effective menu. Finally, we explore menu pricing, an aspect that is tied directly to profitability. These topics are divided into the following chapters:

- Chapter 3: Menu Planning and Development

- Chapter 4: Recipe Standardization, Costing, and Analysis

- Chapter 5: Menu Pricing

Part III, The Foodservice Operation, considers operational issues. These begin with planning, designing, and equipping the foodservice operation. This chapter includes such things as planning considerations, safety, and design. It even extends to corporate responsibility in terms of energy, water, and waste management. Relatedly, we then discuss food sanitation and safety, which is vital in every foodservice operation. This is followed by a discussion of supply chain management, encompassing everything from purchasing to how foodservice managers should work with suppliers. Part III concludes with food management, which addresses how food and other products are received, stored, inventoried, and ultimately combined to create menu items. Part III's chapters include:

- Chapter 6: Facilities Planning, Design, and Equipment

- Chapter 7: Food Sanitation and Safety

- Chapter 8: Supply Chain Management

- Chapter 9: Food Management

Part IV, General Management, addresses general management topics. We begin with financial management, including general accounting topics, and then move into the various financial statements, incorporating analyses and related cost concepts; this segues into budgeting. Next, we consider the various issues of customer service, not the least of which is service recovery. We then discuss what many consider the most important and sometimes challenging subject related to foodservice management: human resource management. The section concludes with a thoughtful presentation of leadership and management, including both theoretical and applied perspectives. In sum, Part IV features:

- Chapter 10: Financial Management

- Chapter 11: Customer Service

- Chapter 12: Marketing

- Chapter 13: Human Resource Management

- Chapter 14: Leadership and Management

Finally, **Part V, Advanced Management,** delves into advanced management topics. The first is internal control, including the related general principles. Next, we consider operational analyses. For example, we discuss revenue management and then explore both cost and operational analysis techniques. Beverage management is the next advanced topic. Here we address the unique aspects of beverage alcohol service, which includes such considerations as health, legal issues, and training. The text concludes with a look to the future. We first consider lessons from the industry's past and then explore the forces for change. In conclusion, we offer some predictions as well as a consideration of what technology will look like in 2050. The specific chapters are:

- Chapter 15: Internal Control

- Chapter 16: Operational Analyses

- Chapter 17: Beverage Management

- Chapter 18: The Future of the Foodservice Industry

Features

Foodservice Management Fundamentals offers a number of unique, interesting features for students, including innovative practical applications. For example:

- Each chapter begins with a chapter outline, followed by clear **learning objectives** to guide students through the material.

- Numerous **photos**, **illustrations**, and **tables** enhance the presentation of topical material, helping students visualize key aspects of the foodservice business.

- Many **real-world examples** reinforce and extend the learning opportunities.

Several special features extend the application of foodservice management principles to the next level. Each chapter concludes with learning tools:

- **Managerial implications** are designed to bring closure to these learning objectives.

- **Industry exemplars** provide useful information as well as real-world illustrations of the qualities that make them leaders in their segments.

- **Key terms** highlight the glossary terms introduced in the chapter.

- A short **case in point** underscores the main issue of the chapter.

- **Review and discussion questions** quiz students on the subject material covered in class, and may be used for class discussion or assigned as homework.

Supplements

The *Student Study Guide* (978-1-118-36334-8) provides additional material to aid in assimilating the concepts, vocabulary, and applications. Each chapter of the Student Study Guide includes

Learning Objectives; an annotated Chapter Outline; True/False, Multiple-Choice, and Fill-in-the-Blank questions; and a Case Activity.

The foodservice industry is very broad. Even an instructor who brings experience in a given segment into the classroom will be challenged to teach students foodservice management techniques that cover all areas and all segments. *Foodservice Management Fundamentals* makes this readily achievable through a comprehensive presentation of material. The accompanying *Instructor's Manual* (978-1-118-16232-3) includes several features to support teaching the material. For example, each section of the manual contains

- a brief overview of each chapter;

- the learning objectives;

- lecture checklist suggestions; and

- answer guidelines for end-of-chapter materials, which instructors can use to keep classroom discussions on track.

The **Instructor's Manual** also includes a **Test Bank** with hundreds of multiple choice, true/false, matching, and essay questions. The final section of the **Instructor's Manual** is the complete **Student Study Guide Solutions**. In addition, we have compiled a complete **Power-Point Presentations** that enhances the delivery of each chapter. In summary, these features facilitate teaching a high-quality course with very little additional preparation.

The **Test Bank** has been specifically formatted for **Respondus**, an easy-to-use software program for creating and managing exams that can be printed to paper or published directly to Blackboard, WebCT, Desire2Learn, ANGEL, and other eLearning systems. Instructors who adopt Foodservice Management Fundamentals can download the Test Bank for free. Additional Wiley resources can be uploaded into your LMS at no charge.

A companion website (www.wiley.com/college/reynolds) provides readers with additional resources, as well as enabling instructors to download the electronic files for the **Instructor's Manual**, **Study Guide Solutions**, **PowerPoint Presentations**, and **Test Bank**.

ACKNOWLEDGMENTS

This textbook is the product of great teamwork, and we are indebted to all of our team members who made producing this first edition a pleasure. Research assistants Scott Hagihara and Andrew Lombard were artful in helping build the foundation of materials used in writing the book. Imran Rahman (Washington State University) was instrumental in assisting with the supplementary materials. Colleagues at Morrison and other industry friends were actively involved. Their responsiveness when contributing pictures, stories, and suggestions (as seen throughout the text) helped us achieve our goal of making this book both robust and practical. Next, we applaud our colleagues in hospitality management and nutrition and dietetics programs around the globe—your collegiality and support were incredible. The staff members at Wiley, especially Julie Kerr and Christina Volpe, were encouraging, supportive, and patient. Finally, Bill Barnett of *WordCraft* once again made an indelible impact.

Many faculty members from hospitality management and nutrition and dietetics programs have provided helpful information and feedback in the preparation of the manuscript. Their comments and suggestions have helped us immensely. They are Patricia Bowman, Johnson & Wales University; Elisabeth Cochrane, Radford University; Emily Wilcox Gier, Cornell University; Gary Hoyer, George Brown College; Krista Jordheim, Normandale Community College; Dolores Kearney, Texas Woman's University; Miriam Nettles, Michigan State University; Natasha Pogrebinsky, Brooklyn College; and Lisa Trone, Florida State University.

Our families and friends have encouraged us throughout the lengthy development of this book. They provided us with emotional sustenance and graciously allowed us the time we needed to do this book justice. We are truly grateful for their support.

DENNIS REYNOLDS
KATHLEEN WACHTER McCLUSKY

ABOUT THE AUTHORS

DENNIS REYNOLDS, PhD

Dennis Reynolds proudly serves as the Wine Business Management Director and occupies the Ivar Haglund Endowed Chair of Hospitality Management at the Washington State University School of Hospitality Business Management. Prior to joining WSU's College of Business, Dr. Reynolds was the J. Thomas Clark Professor of Entrepreneurship and Personal Enterprise at the Cornell University School of Hotel Administration.

Dr. Reynolds speaks frequently before management groups in Asia, Europe, and North America and has been cited in broadcast media (including *Morning Edition* on National Public Radio) as well as newspapers and magazines around the globe. His lively speeches cover such topics as maximizing productivity in the workplace and understanding key value drivers in the hospitality industry. Dr. Reynolds also assists a variety of leading foodservice companies in maximizing their human capital. In particular, he offers assistance in implementing strategic human resource initiatives as well as enhancing management-development programs that are applicable to both the executive and middle-management ranks.

Professor Reynolds's research focuses on pathways leading to enhanced managerial efficiency and effectiveness, especially in service organizations. Recent papers have also addressed the related effects of management feedback on subordinate self-efficacy and a new approach to evaluating and enhancing operational efficiency for multiunit foodservice organizations using food and beverage menu-engineering techniques. His work, which has captured numerous awards from the Academy of Management and other organizations, has been published in leading journals, such as the *Academy of Management Learning and Education*, the *Advanced Management Journal*, the *Cornell Hospitality Quarterly*, the *Journal of Hospitality and Tourism Research*, and the *International Journal of Hospitality Management*. He is author or coauthor of five textbooks, with his latest advancing to its tenth edition.

Of greatest personal importance, Dennis and his wife, Julia, are proud parents of two wonderful daughters. The Reynolds family currently resides in Pullman, Washington.

KATHLEEN WACHTER McCLUSKY, MS, RD, FADA

Kathy McClusky has enjoyed a long career in foodservice management, holding several positions in a variety of professional organizations. Kathy has worked as a public health nutritionist, a dietetic internship director, and an adjunct faculty member, and has been a food and nutrition services director in a large medical center as well as in a statewide mental health system in New York, the latter position involving the development of a statewide cook/chill system. Kathy has served as president of the Missouri and New York State Dietetic Associations, an American Dietetic Association (ADA) site visitor, as a member of the ADA House of Delegates in several capacities, and as chair of the Management in Food & Nutrition Services Practice Group, as well as several ADA committees. She is currently Consultant for Patient Services with Morrison Management Specialists.

Kathy has received the ADA Medallion Award, was New York's Distinguished Dietitian, and was a member of the board of directors and treasurer of the ADA from 2009 to 2011. She is currently a member of the board of directors of the Academy of Nutrition and Dietetics (formerly the American Dietetic Association).

PART 1

THE FOODSERVICE INDUSTRY

We begin Chapter 1 by considering the foodservice industry from a general as well as a historical perspective. This includes a discussion of how our industry is segmented. In Chapter 2, we explore the ways in which this industry differs from other sectors of the service industry. As you might expect, Part I provides the necessary foundation for the remainder of the book.

THE FOODSERVICE INDUSTRY

LEARNING OBJECTIVES:

After becoming familiar with this chapter, you should be able to:

1. Identify key milestones and dates in the long history of the foodservice industry.

2. Appreciate the effects of culture on the evolution of the foodservice industry.

3. Gain a more thorough understanding that the foodservice industry is more than just "restaurants."

4. Describe the six segments of foodservice and know the factors that differentiate each one.

5. Recognize the potential for enjoying a fruitful career in foodservice management.

Restaurants are where we go for special-occasion celebrations, to grab a quick lunch, or to stage casual business meetings. Many people start the day with breakfast purchased from a drive-through restaurant. Adults in the United States report, on average, enjoying lunch at a restaurant at least once every week. And more people than ever eat more of their evening meals at restaurants than at home. Even in such nontraditional settings as hospitals or schools, foodservice is a mainstay for customers and employees alike. In short, the foodservice industry reflects our culture and anchors our everyday life.

How important is this industry? Perhaps it is only by coincidence, but it might tell us something that no two countries with McDonald's restaurants have ever gone to war with each other.[1] In economic terms, people are spending more money than ever on food that is

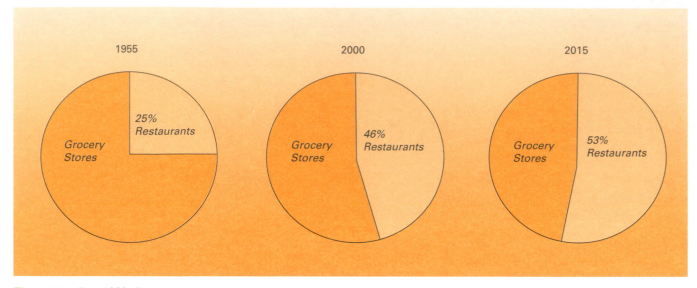

Figure 1.1   Food $$$: Grocery stores vs. restaurants.

purchased or consumed outside of the home. In the 1950s, for example, Americans spent some 25 percent of their food dollars at restaurants. According to the National Restaurant Association, we will soon spend more than 50 percent of our food dollars at foodservice establishments![2] (See Figure 1.1, the comparative chart.) And where are these expenditures taking place? The scope of the foodservice industry is broader than ever. From quick service to fine dining, from college eatery to corporate cafe, the breadth of offerings makes the competition for consumers' **stomach share** more intense than ever. From Lexington, Kentucky, with about 1,000 restaurants for its 301,569 residents (about one restaurant for 300 people), to San Francisco, where there are 5,369 restaurants for 791,684 city dwellers, to Seoul, South Korea, where there are more than 331,025 foodservice outlets serving 10,356,000 residents (that's about one restaurant for every 31 people!)—foodservice is everywhere!

So what does this mean for you? The most important point is that the foodservice industry can take you anywhere, whether you are just starting a career in hospitality or are moving into the higher management ranks. And your career does not have to follow the traditional progression that previous generations experienced. Today, we see chefs leave jobs in five-star hotel restaurants to work in healthcare foodservice; dietitians now may move from a traditional hospital foodservice operation to manage fast-casual restaurants that are positioned to offer healthier fare than their fast-food competitors do; and managers in school foodservice may find positions as multi-unit managers in any one of the various segments. Indeed, foodservice today offers a huge range of settings, which means more career options than ever before.

■□ HISTORY

Roots and Ancient Origins

So how did the foodservice business arrive at its currently lofty status? What set its evolution in motion? The story begins around 25,000 BC with the appearance of the first oven.[3] It is unlikely, however, that prehistoric bakers used their newly created ovens to sell food. In truth, it wasn't

Lettuce Entertain You Enterprises

Lettuce Entertain You Enterprises (LEYE) is an empire of approximately 70 restaurants founded by Rich Melman and Jerry A. Orzoff in Chicago in 1971. The company had five restaurants by 1976 and, by the mid-1980s, employed over 2,000 people with annual revenues of more than $40 million. The restaurants they operate are unique and vary in price, theme, and cuisine. LEYE currently owns, licenses, or manages more than 60 establishments in Illinois, Arizona, Maryland, Virginia, Georgia, Minnesota, and Nevada, including Ed Debevic's, Wildfire Grill, Petterinos, Shaw's Crab House, and Everest. Also among their creations are the Eiffel Tower Restaurant and Mon Ami Gabi in the Paris Las Vegas Casino Resort. 2011 revenue exceeded $300 million, with net profit of more than $50 million.

Photo courtesy of Lettuce Entertain You Enterprises, Inc.

until around 3,500 BC that humankind began to think of food as a commodity that could be prepared and exchanged or sold. But from that time through the age of ancient Greece, people generally produced food to prevent starvation, not to capitalize on its potential as a medium of exchange.

There is some evidence of restaurants in ancient Roman times, but they were more like bakeries from which locals could buy bread and other food items. There is also evidence in Pompeii of meeting places where food was served. The seeds of the foodservice industry were, however, more likely sown by early *caterers,* people who would provide food and drink to accompany religious celebrations.

Do you really need to know about Babylonian eating habits or the origins of the modern cafeteria if you want to become the next Wolfgang Puck or Richard Melman (founder of *Lettuce Entertain You Enterprises*)? The answer is yes. The leaders of today's top foodservice companies (e.g., Compass Group PLC—see the industry exemplar at the end of this chapter—McDonald's, or Panera Bread) acknowledge the importance of understanding how eating, drinking, and cooking have evolved in different parts of the planet and how trends began with the very first restaurant. After all, to understand these aspects of its evolution is to understand the importance of cultural influences on the foodservice industry. The saying is, "You are what you eat," but *how* you eat is how you live!

Evolution and Culture

Since the dawn of time, we have experienced food on a very personal level. When food is scarce, we seek sustenance for self-preservation. In times of plenty, food helps us to celebrate—often to excess. And across cultures, food has reflected various perspectives and values, satisfying our desires nutritionally, spiritually, and, of course, hedonistically. Consider that it was the nutritional perspective that led our ancestors to use heat to alter food: Heat allows nutrients to be released from some foods and makes otherwise inedible foods palatable. Most of the world's religions have developed food guidelines, often reflecting engagement with religious symbolism but originating over food safety concerns that are still practiced today. Finally, the hedonistic approach to food—eating for the taste of it—spans all cultures and dates back to when we first hunted game and gathered the fruits of the land.

Yet these observations do not explain why the foodservice industry did not truly burgeon until the nineteenth century. The industry could not flourish until societal norms surrounding food underwent their own evolution. Simply put, throughout the Middle Ages people did not pay—and did not expect to pay—for their own food when eating away from home. This *food is included* ethic was evident, for example, in hotels (known as inns at the time). Yes, the traveler was expected to pay, but for the respite from travel that was offered, which included a place to rest, sometimes a place to bathe, and food. Most often, such inns were extensions of an innkeeper's home. It was inconceivable for a host to charge extra for a meal! Such an interpretation of hospitality was seen in recent times for many years in the airline industry. It was unthinkable that airline passengers would be expected to pay for food when they were, in essence, guests of the airline. (This has changed dramatically, of course, in the last decade.)

When not traveling, folks throughout the Middle Ages would eat away from home only when invited to a special event such as a wedding or a royal affair. Such occasions, or others put on by the wealthy who could afford to stage large parties, involved hiring caterers who would, in turn, employ the area's leading chefs. People expected the finest food when attending such parties, but would never consider paying for their own food. There was some reciprocity in that if you were invited to a family's wedding, the expectation was that you would invite that family when your family celebrated a marriage.

This phenomenon was most prevalent in Europe prior to the French Revolution (see Figure 1.2). Some of the rich families did hire chefs, but this was more akin to hiring an

Figure 1.2 *"Dinner for Louis XIV at the Hôtel de Ville de Paris, January 30, 1687."* Fêtes pour le rétablissement de la santé du Roi (Festivities in the Honor of the Recovery of the King's Health).

exclusive caterer—they simply cut out the middleman. People would also hire chefs to entertain business associates or politicians.

What changed this understanding of foodservice? As is common in our species' history, it was war that changed it—in this case, the political and social upheaval of the French Revolution (1789–1799). French nobles fought to protect their lands but could not afford to also keep chefs on the payroll. The caterers, too, folded, putting hundreds of chefs out of work. The big parties and the expectation that others will provide food and drink at no charge came to an end.

What did the legions of chefs do? They did the only thing they could to make money: They cooked food and sold it to anyone who would buy it. Thus was the modern restaurant industry born. The instant availability of many small restaurants created a market shift that required people to reorient their idea of foodservice from one that reflected a host-provided system to one involving a commodity exchange in which food was traded for currency.

Foundation of Current Operations

The French style of restaurant spread quickly across Europe (there were more than 500 in Paris by 1804). Still, such eateries were considered **public dining rooms** as there was no effort to brand or differentiate the operations. Eating out was expected to be very much like eating at home, except that here one pays for one's meal. And the offering was simple: A chef would prepare one large batch of a single item and everyone would dine together at the same time.

It remained essentially that way until a man known to us only as **A. Boulanger**, a chef who specialized in soups, opened a business in Paris in this same time period. The sign above his door advertised "restoratives," for he saw his soups as providing more than just sustenance. In French, this is *restaurer*. Thus, *restaurant* now denotes an eating place—but one that provides something more than just eating at home—in English, French, Dutch, Danish, Norwegian, Romanian, and many other languages, with some variations. For example, in Spanish and Portuguese the word becomes *restaurante*; in Italian it is *ristorante*; in Swedish, *restaurang*; in Russian, *restoran*; and in Polish, *restauracia*.

Boulanger's restaurant was also unique in another very important way: it was the first public dining room where a guest could order from a menu offering a choice of dishes. Again, until then, inns and public dining rooms offered meals only for the host's table—**table d'hôte**. Innkeepers, for example, made their family meals in bulk, serving the same fare to their guests. The entrepreneurially minded Mr. Boulanger knew the benefits of providing choices!

Other chef-operators quickly recognized the benefit of differentiation and the rest, as they say, is history. The newly evolved business model moved beyond Europe quickly, with the first restaurant in the United States opening in Boston in 1794. Its cuisine? French, of course!

Thus did the evolution of restaurants redefine foodservice for the world's inhabitants. **Robert Owen**, a British utopian socialist, saw the benefits of offering foodservice to employees using the restaurant model and in 1805 built a kitchen within his textile mill that was designed to provide wholesome meals to his employees. Located in Scotland, the mill included an onsite dining room that was open to employees and their families where meals could be purchased for a nominal price. Thus, we had the first onsite eatery in a factory. Extending this idea, 1891 witnessed the birth of the onsite cafeteria, in the YWCA of Kansas City, Missouri, where the club served meals cafeteria style to its members. It was also at this time (the transition from the nineteenth to the twentieth century) that onsite foodservice operations began in previously unheard-of locations such as hospitals.

Other common features of restaurants appeared periodically as the business continued to evolve. For example, in 1834, **Delmonico's** in New York City offered something never seen before: a printed menu! (See Figure 1.3.) The Delmonico brothers were entrepreneurial pioneers

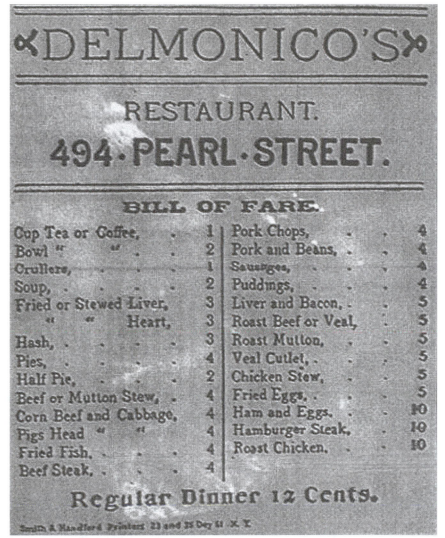

Photo courtesy of Delmonico's.

Figure 1.3 Delmonico's first menu (circa 1850).

in other ways as well, extending their restaurant concept to other cities and establishing the first chain, with units in Philadelphia and Boston.

Underscoring the co-evolution of the foodservice industry with modern society, the first **drive-in restaurant** opened in Glendale, California, in 1936 in response to the proliferation of automobiles. The drive-in concept peaked in the early 1950s, which coincided with the emergence of a new concept: **fast food**. **Ray Kroc**, founder of the McDonald's organization, revolutionized the restaurant industry (again) by systematizing the production of hamburgers, french fries, and milkshakes. The first branded McDonald's (the original McDonald's restaurants were started by Dick and Mac McDonald in California) opened in Des Plaines, Illinois, in 1955. The first day's revenue totaled $366.12 (approximately $3,000 in today's currency).

Has the evolution of the foodservice industry reached full term? Most agree that there is still much to bring to the guest's table. While we discuss the future of foodservice at length in later chapters, there are recent developments that illustrate how technology, globalization, and merging cultural norms are coalescing to further shape the foodservice landscape. A great example of this is a new, fully automated restaurant that opened in Nuremberg, Germany, in 2008. Named 's Baggers, the restaurant completely redefines service—it removes employees from the service exchange (see Figure 1.4). Patrons order their meals from touchscreens and the food and drinks are delivered to the table via a system of metal tracks that look like a miniature rollercoaster

McDonald's

Use with permission of McDonald's Corporation.

Considered iconic by many, McDonald's continues to shape the global foodservice industry. While its sales, penetration, and global reach are well known, the company has done other things that set it apart. For example, McDonald's has provided comprehensive nutrition information for several decades, one of the first quick-service restaurants to do so. Similarly, McDonald's was one of the first quick-service restaurants to offer nutritional information to help consumers make informed eating choices. More recently (2005), *Fortune* magazine awarded McDonald's its "Best Place to Work for Minorities" Award. Underscoring its dedication to its employees, McDonald's believes in lifelong learning, providing ongoing training and development at all levels. Finally, McDonald's has made Ronald McDonald Houses its charity of choice; these homes-away-from-homes provide temporary housing for families with seriously ill children in hundreds of communities around the world.

Photo © 's Baggers GmbH, Nuremberg, Germany.

Figure 1.4 's Baggers restaurant in Nuremberg, Germany.

system. The notion that the guest experience can be completely altered is underscored by another novel feature: The touchscreens that customers use to place their orders can also be used to send e-mails and text messages!

SEGMENTATION

Although European restaurants immediately following the French Revolution were different in chef only, modern foodservice outlets operate and are positioned in distinctly varied ways. Different types of restaurants serve the varying needs and tastes of an increasingly diverse public. These segments of the industry differ in style of service, price point, and value proposition (discussed in greater detail in Chapter 2). Thus, we can categorize the foodservice industry into the following: quick service, fast casual, family or midscale, moderate or theme, fine dining, and onsite.

Quick Service

Perhaps the most pervasive segment in terms of number of units globally, **quick-service** restaurants (QSRs), often called "fast food" because of the speed of service, are unique in many ways. Of course, they offer food at a low price. But this is only possible because they feature mostly standardized products combined with an efficient delivery system. Additionally, the limited menu facilitates the uniformity that is a mainstay of QSRs.

Changes in supply-chain management (discussed in later chapters) have also led to the penetration of QSRs. For example, when the first McDonald's restaurants began adorning the American landscape, add-on items such as tomatoes and lettuce were delivered to each unit by the case and sliced at that unit. Today, these items are delivered prewashed, precut, and, in some cases, preportioned, thereby allowing for less food handling (and handling by less-skilled workers). Such an approach to internal distribution helps lowers costs, contributes to standardization, and increases efficiency.

The final unique feature of QSRs is the common brand affiliation. Most toddlers are quick to spot the golden arches and make the connection with Happy Meals. Moreover, the preponderance of McDonald's, Burger King, Wendy's, and Jack in the Box (to name only a few) has inevitably (and in some ways unfortunately) shaped other countries' views of American culture.

Fast Casual

Fast-casual restaurants, which evolved from the QSR segment in response to customer demand for a little higher quality and better ambiance (accompanied by a willingness to pay a premium for such features) combine the convenience of QSRs with the fresh ingredients of traditional sit-down restaurants. Fast-casual restaurants are value driven, to be sure, but the style of preparation and the quality of the basic ingredients are better. Typically, the food involves longer preparation time, and in some cases the guest orders and pays at a counter but the food is delivered to the table when ready.

Fast-casual operations also offer more amenities than QSRs. For example, it is not unusual to find plants or even aquariums and similarly interesting features at a fast-casual restaurant. The lighting is usually softer, and the seats and tables are more conducive to a relaxing meal. There is also a greater emphasis on service than there is in the QSR segment.

Panera Bread

anera Bread's bakery-cafe concept highlights everything good about fast-casual restaurants. The bread is baked at each location daily, which is paired thoughtfully with made-to-order sandwiches and tossed-to-order salads. The soups are served in freshly baked bread bowls. The company has garnered many culinary and guest-service awards including recognition by the *Wall Street Journal*. Publicly traded, the company had more than 1,300 units in 2008 with sales exceeding $1 billion.

Finally, menus at fast-casual restaurants are more flexible and offer many more options. At a Panera Bread outlet, for example, a sandwich can be customized almost without limit, as you can choose your bread type and preparation (toasted or not), toppings, and temperature (hot or cold). At a Panera Bread, it would not be surprising for the order taker to make recommendations, guiding your decision far beyond the stereotypical, "Would you like fries with that?"

Family/Midscale

Midscale restaurants, or those considered family friendly, offer table service but at a relatively low price point given the tableside service. In this segment, foodservice operators seek to build brand loyalty with customer-friendly programs such as a children's menu, children's table activities (e.g., crayons and puzzle books), drinks, and dessert specials. Furthermore, menus offer many more choices than are offered in other segments with operators looking to capture the broadest possible audience. Typically, the listings in each category, such as appetizers and entrees, are quite numerous.

Midscale restaurants are also positioned for a specific dining purpose. In other words, they seek to entice diners for a family breakfast or dinner with family or friends. They market themselves as community friendly. Finally, they attempt to align with what they see as family values, which means that they market themselves as places where families can experience a meal together.

In terms of pricing, the common element in midscale restaurants is their focus on value. Large portions at reasonable prices prevail. Food quality, while slightly better than what is found at QSRs or even most fast-casual restaurants, is underplayed—again, the emphasis is on value. (We discuss value and the associated value proposition at greater length in Chapter 3.)

Moderate/Theme

Moderate or theme-style restaurants market themselves by creating a tie between the customer and a concept based on type of cuisine or time period or some other easily captured cultural phenomenon. This is most evident in the ambiance, where décor is more thematic than in the previously discussed segments. For example, a moderate-theme restaurant in an

American urban neighborhood might feature an Australian theme, tapping into the allure of the Australian outback with food that also aligns with that theme (think, for example, of steaks and shrimp "on the barbie").

The choices in theme restaurants, while not as plentiful as those found in midscale restaurants, are ample enough to appeal to a broad market. To increase such a restaurant's appeal, the menu often offers greater flexibility—guests can readily make substitutions, modifications, or special requests. A knowledgeable service staff can also make recommendations to suit differing dietary restrictions and preferences.

Menu prices at moderate-theme restaurants are notably higher than those in the midscale segment, but customers arrive knowing that the meal will be priced a little higher and that the portions may be smaller than those featured at midscale eateries. The quality of the food should, however, be higher. The service, too, is expected to be a bit more refined.

Fine Dining

The epitome of epicurean accomplishment is found in **fine dining** restaurants. Here, both the theme and product offering are unique, underscoring the specialness of the restaurant. Food quality and menu complexity are extremely high. The emphasis on the value or price of the food itself is gone; instead, fine dining operators look to maximize guests' overall dining experience. Guests pay not only for the food but also for the total dining experience, from the hospitality exhibited by the staff to the beauty or uniqueness of the décor to the elegance with which the meal is arranged on the plate.

Thus, in addition to serving high-quality, sophisticated meals, foodservers must understand all aspects of the offerings, including typically lengthy wine lists, and be prepared to offer advice or to elaborate on menu descriptions. They must also place a greater focus on the graciousness of the service; much more is expected of them than simply taking the food order and delivering the food when it is ready. Servers must anticipate each guest's every need and strive to exceed that guest's expectations.

Fine dining restaurants provide, then, the ultimate in ambiance: linen napkins and tablecloths, fine silverware and glassware, richly appointed restrooms, and aesthetically pleasing lighting, seating, background music, and decorations.

The systematic approach to food production that homogenizes one's experience at all QSRs of the same brand is not apparent to guests in fine dining restaurants, but a standardized system of order taking, food production, and service delivery is nevertheless found in these operations. The difference is that here these activities are transparent to the guest!

Onsite

Onsite foodservice is too often considered the poor stepchild of the foodservice industry. Yet it is one of the most dynamic and growing segments and can encompass features found in any of the previously described segments. For example, one of the highest grossing Outback Steakhouse restaurants is located at PNC Stadium in Pittsburgh. Another example is the McDonald's located in Elmhurst Hospital Center—the busiest healthcare facility in Queens.

Onsite foodservice operations are defined as food outlets in **business and industry** (B&I), schools, universities and colleges, hospitals, skilled-nursing centers, eldercare centers, childcare centers, correctional facilities, and recreation facilities such as stadiums. Some would include military and transportation-related foodservice (e.g., in airlines) in this segment, but these subsegments have become so highly specialized and distant from the core onsite businesses that they are now considered separate and distinct. Moreover, providing a specialized service such as airline food is now more akin to commodity production than foodservice.

Onsite foodservice is particularly noteworthy because of its points of differentiation from the other segments. For example, the emphasis on nutrition (which consumers are beginning to demand in the other foodservice segments) is deeply embedded in onsite operations. Consider foodservice in a hospital: The nutritional and even therapeutic value of the food is today considered a vital component of the holistic process of patient care. In schools, too, dietary requirements—often mandated by governmental agencies—must be met.

Another differentiator of onsite foodservice firms is that they must adapt to the requirements of the institutions within which they operate. In a B&I cafe, for example, the operation is open only for breakfast and lunch, Monday through Friday. Thus, the quality of life for their managers is considerably different from that of typical restaurant managers, who must cope with longer hours and weekend crowds.

While some speak of the captive patronage of an onsite operation as an attribute—its patrons have no other option unless they are able to leave the institutional setting—onsite operations also require meticulous forecasting and attention to standards. In a correctional facility, for example, the foodservice manager knows exactly how many meals she must produce every day. Yet controls must be in place to ensure that food production (including the related processes that are discussed later) is matched to these forecasts.

The same is true in a college setting. Students today have more food choices than ever and are more discerning as well. Thus, the foodservice manager must consider nutrition, menu-item appeal, value, and appropriate production of each item at each of the various outlets on campus.

Management in onsite foodservice can also feature different structures. For example, a hospital may manage its foodservice operations by hiring a foodservice director who will staff the unit accordingly. Such an operation is considered self-operated because all of the employees including the management team are hospital employees; this is typically referred to as **self-op**. By contrast, a hospital might choose to outsource the foodservice operation. In such a case, a contract foodservice company is hired to run the foodservice operations. Such companies specialize in onsite foodservice and add value through standardized practices.[4]

INDUSTRY LEADER PROFILE

Sodexo

© Sodexo.

Sodexo, based in Paris, is a leading onsite foodservice company operating in more than 80 host countries. Its healthcare division deserves special mention, however, because of its reputation as a leader in providing a high-quality patient experience by providing healthcare institutions with a range of offerings such as foodservice, reception, information, hygiene, environmental management, free-time activities, and medical equipment maintenance. The division represents approximately 20 percent of the parent company's revenues, with healthcare-related-services revenue of more than $3.5 billion.

Finally, menus in this segment must mirror those from the other segments relative to the operational focus. They must also, however, offer enough variation to keep the captive patronage satisfied with their offerings. In the B&I subsegment, for example, suppose that 50 percent of the business employees at a particular site eat breakfast or lunch onsite at least 50 percent of the time; here the foodservice operator must employ cyclical or rotational menus and also offer frequent specials to keep its patrons from trading the convenience of the onsite meal for the allure of the competing nearby restaurant. So consumer demand plays its role here as well, as operators must contend with the opportunity some patrons have to eat outside of the complex.

It is worth noting that the onsite segment must also contend with a host of changes that affect the global foodservice industry, such as nontraditional work scheduling, telecommuting, increased focus on dietary preferences and restrictions, increased interest in healthy eating, demand for culturally based cuisines, focus on new flavors, and more. In fact, Sodexo, a global leader in onsite foodservice and the world's top provider of healthcare foodservice, has made it a priority to respond to changes and trends that are shaping the future of foodservice (see sidebar).

INDUSTRY STATISTICS

Students looking for a career in the hospitality industry typically imagine working in hotels. But did you know that the foodservice industry generates three-and-a-half times the revenue of the lodging industry? Another noteworthy statistic is that the number of foodservice managers is projected to increase by 11 percent between 2008 and 2018. Moreover, the foodservice industry is the largest nongovernment employer in the United States. Sometime between 2010 and 2015, the number of foodservice outlets will exceed 1 million in this country alone!

In recent years, foodservice sales have increased by around 4.1 percent and currently equal 4 percent of the US gross domestic product. The foodservice industry employs 9 of every 100 working American citizens, and, according to the National Restaurant Association, total employment in this hospitality sector will top 15.1 million people by 2018.

In an era marked by a changing workforce and growing variety in corporate composition, the foodservice industry is a leader in workplace diversity. During the first decade of the new millennium, women and minorities represented three of five owners of eating and drinking establishments. The foodservice industry also employs more minority managers than any other industry. Finally, women and minorities are finding increasing ownership and management opportunities in both independent and chain restaurants.

Speaking of independent and chain restaurants, the foodservice landscape today is also changing rapidly. For example, of the more than 900,000 foodservice outlets in the United States today, approximately 25 percent are chain restaurants. Sales statistics suggest, however, that chains command an even greater share of the market: Chain outlets capture half of all restaurant revenues in the United States. Moreover, more than nine out of every ten hamburgers eaten away from home are purchased from a chain restaurant.

This preponderance of chains appears to be increasing. Revenues at the top 25 chain restaurants have in recent years grown by approximately 5.1 percent (versus the 4.1 percent noted earlier for the industry in general). Global chain restaurant growth is also increasing faster than growth in the foodservice industry in general, a phenomenon that is projected to continue long into the twenty-first century, creating even more management opportunities!

MANAGERIAL IMPLICATIONS

The role of foodservice operations continues to evolve, with people spending more money than ever on food purchased for consumption outside of the home. Within the next few years, Americans will spend over half of their food dollars at restaurants and onsite foodservice establishments. Although this creates unprecedented opportunities for managers and entrepreneurs, it also results in a hugely competitive marketplace.

Although this evolution has occurred within a relatively short time, the roots of the foodservice industry run very deep. Understanding the influences on the industry's evolution better prepares the next generation of foodservice leaders to move the industry forward. In particular, it facilitates an appreciation of cultural influences—and appreciating the industry's history helps us to anticipate future trends.

An excellent illustration of how the past links to foodservice today is the story of the first chef who advertised his foodservice operation as a place where patrons could be restored by the healthful qualities of his signature product, soup. As we see today, the trend toward healthful fare is pervasive across all segments, not just in healthcare foodservice. Even QSRs today are responding to this market pressure, offering nutritional information either on the premises or online.

Consider also how menus came into place. The first restaurants served only a few items; the choices were communicated to the guest by the server or, more commonly, the kitchen staff. Then, less than 200 years ago, the printed menu emerged as the vehicle for communicating with the guest.

The history of foodservice is also the history of segmentation. Even within segments, new concepts continually emerge. In onsite foodservice, for example, organizations find their foodservice operations competing with offsite operations and in response have developed new models that keep their personnel in house for work-time or even after-work meals. Again, this creates unprecedented opportunities for foodservice managers and those who have a vision of a new concept.

INDUSTRY EXEMPLAR

Compass Group PLC

Compass Group is a market leader, providing food and support services to organizations in B&I, healthcare, recreation, and education in 55 countries, totaling revenue in excess of $20 billion. Based in Surrey, United Kingdom, the firm is the largest employer of foodservice workers on the planet.

What makes Compass Group unique among onsite providers globally is that the company was built by acquiring other leading onsite companies and—rather than blending these acquisitions into a uniform organization—operating them largely autonomously. In other words, the company looks for great companies, buys them, and then lets them continue to grow and do what they do best.

This innovative approach in a world in which everything trends towards globalizing, commoditizing, and homogenizing has made Compass Group the leader it is.

Identifying opportunities in vending, for example, Compass Group acquired Canteen Vending in 1994. Then, after recognizing opportunities in healthcare foodservice in North America, it acquired Morrison Management Specialists (now named simply Morrison), a leading North American onsite foodservice company specializing in healthcare. Subsequently it sought to enter the higher-end cafe and catering markets, especially in the B&I and education segments, with its purchase of Bon Appétit Management Company, a renowned leader in this sector.

According to Mark Swenson, regional vice president of Bon Appétit, the acquisition has been smooth. Having joined the firm after graduating with a hospitality degree from Washington State University in 1975, Swenson met the founder of Bon Appétit and joined the company in 1977. The company's success is attributable largely to its ongoing ability to focus on culinary expertise, a commitment to socially responsible food sourcing and business practices, and strong partnerships with respected conservation organizations.

Has this changed since Bon Appétit became a part of Compass Group? As Swenson notes, "Compass has integrated many of our practices such as sourcing local food products but has not forced its operating practices on us. In fact, they have helped us grow thanks to their depth of resources and knowledge of global business practices."

If Compass Group serves as a model for consolidation in the foodservice sector, it could expand the global reach of many companies. What does this mean for future foodservice leaders and managers? According to John Tuomala, Director of College Relations for Compass Group North America, "It means that all of our associates have a great opportunity to advance in their careers with one global organization. Our year-on-year success in growing all of our lines of business both organically and through acquisitions has created a worldwide demand for high potential management talent—and is the reason why internal talent management, training, and college recruitment tops our list of HR priorities."

KEY TERMS

Case in Point

The College Experience

Both of Katlin's parents had graduated from Central State University, so they were very excited when Katlin listed it as her first choice for college. They were also ecstatic about visiting the university for a tour. Katlin's mom, Kathy—a graduate of the university's hospitality program—had been reminiscing almost nightly about her college days and was curious to see how things had changed. Her father, an architect named Sam, was also curious about the changes they would see on campus.

Because the visit to her parents' alma mater would include meetings with some of the faculty and the hospitality program's adviser, Katlin began preparing a list of questions in anticipation of her encounters with potential future professors. Although she was curious, of course, about the curriculum, she was somewhat familiar with the general program thanks to the hours she had spent perusing the various CSU online sites. She wondered which companies typically recruited new graduates. How much money could she anticipate making as a new hire? What other choices would she have after graduation?

Katlin knew what she wanted to do with her college degree but she was worried that her goal might disappoint her parents, so she kept it to herself. This made the last few weeks leading up to the college visit a little awkward during family dinners. Sam and Kathy assumed that her silence meant that Katlin didn't know what she wanted to do. They were worried that she wouldn't seem focused on a clear goal during the meetings at CSU.

Throughout the drive to the small college town, Kathy talked about all her college friends who had gone on to work in hotels when they finished college. Kathy herself had started at a large hotel chain with which she had worked for many years before starting her own travel agency. Sam had just finished designing some high-end restaurants, so his mind was more on Katlin's opportunities in the foodservice sector. Katlin's parents dropped subtle hints (well, maybe some were not so subtle), hoping to elicit from Katlin some indication of her desired career path, but Katlin just nodded and smiled politely.

After meeting two of the professors and the academic adviser, the trio met with the hospitality school's director. The conversation was casual at first, but the small talk soon gave way to a more pointed inquiry when the director looked Katlin square in the eye and asked, "So what do you want to do after you graduate from CSU with a degree in hospitality management?"

Sam and Kathy held their breath. Katlin, meanwhile, inhaled loudly and said, "Last year in school I found Fannie Merritt Farmer's *Boston Cooking School Cook Book,* which my English teacher described as 'the Bible of the American kitchen.' He said that it changed the way cookbooks were written forever by listing exactly how much of each ingredient would be needed at the top of every recipe. Then she gave the instructions for making the dish. I thought that was amazing. But what I found even more amazing is that many of the dessert recipes from this book, which was written way back in 1896, are a lot like many of today's recipes."

Katlin continued: "That got me interested in baking—especially in trying new things, using new ingredients, and applying different approaches. And I do enjoy this, but my passion isn't only for baking. I want to redefine bakeries as a *business*. So, my goal is to start a chain of high-end bakeries, starting maybe with my first one in New York City and then adding a few more each year. I'm hoping this program will enable me to do that."

Sam and Kathy just stared at Katlin. They had no idea that she was so focused or that she had such an ambitious goal. On the other side of the desk, the director grinned widely. He then responded, "Well, I must tell you how refreshing this is. Too often, students look at managing a single restaurant or hotel, or working with an event-planning business. You, on the other hand, want to be an entrepreneur. And that is exactly what we're designed to foster. In fact, our collective mission in the school is to craft our best and brightest into the leaders of the global hospitality industry. I have a feeling that you will be at the front of our next cohort of these leaders."

Did you have a similar experience when you were considering which college to attend or maybe deciding if dietetics or hospitality was in your future? How would you have responded to the same director if you were Katlin? And now that you're in a hospitality or dietetics program, how would you respond today?

REVIEW AND DISCUSSION QUESTIONS

1. What is surprising about countries in which McDonald's operates?

2. How much has Americans' behavior changed in terms of food dollar spending over the last 50 years?

3. When was the first oven created? When did humankind start thinking of food as a commodity?

4. Explain how catering served as the founding father of the modern foodservice industry.

5. What is a modern example of incorporating food into the hotel experience that was common in the Middle Ages?

6. What role did the French Revolution play in the evolution of today's foodservice industry?

7. What kind of restaurant (in terms of cuisine) was the first to open in the United States, and when and where did it open?

8. Why was Robert Owen's approach to factory design so novel?

9. Where and when did the first modern cafeteria open?

10. What did the Delmonico's founders do that was so unique but that changed the foodservice industry forever?

11. Name the six foodservice segments and describe two unique features of each one.

12. What is the projected increase in the need for food-service managers between 2008 and 2018?

13. In the United States, which industry is the largest nongovernment employer?

14. What proportion of the gross domestic product in the United States does the foodservice industry represent?

15. What is the status of diversity in the foodservice industry?

16. In the United States, how many units form a chain? How do these chain restaurants compare in terms of annual sales?

17. Which is growing more rapidly: independent restaurants or chain restaurants, both domestically and globally?

ENDNOTES

1. Friedman, T. L. *The World Is Flat: A Brief History of the Twenty-first Century.* New York: Farrar, Straus, & Giroux, 2005.

2. National Restaurant Association. *Restaurant Industry 2008 Fact Sheet.* www.restaurant.org/pdfs/research/2008factsheet.pdf. Accessed March 29, 2008.

3. Tannahill, R. *Food in History.* New York: Three Rivers Press, 1988.

4. For more information, see Reynolds, D. *Onsite Foodservice Management: A Best Practices Approach.* Hoboken, NJ: John Wiley & Sons, 2003.

CHAPTER 2

THE FOODSERVICE BUSINESS

LEARNING OBJECTIVES:

After becoming familiar with this chapter, you should be able to:

1. Understand the unique aspects of the foodservice business, including its characteristics and distinct segments.

2. Relate current trends to foodservice operations' evolution throughout the business lifecycle.

3. Appreciate the importance of site selection and the value of environmental scanning in terms of the foodservice marketplace.

4. Describe value as it is perceived by guests, integrating the various components of the overall dining experience.

5. Discuss value drivers, along with the role of capacity constraints and the importance of understanding the service-value chain.

In the first chapter we considered the evolution of the foodservice business and identified the various segments—including onsite foodservice. We now consider the foodservice business within a competitive setting. In light of the importance of market position to financial success in the new economy, we need to appreciate fully how a foodservice operation is related to others both within and outside of its segment within the larger framework of competing foodservice enterprises.

WHAT MAKES THE FOODSERVICE BUSINESS UNIQUE?

Many who consider entering the foodservice business think that this industry is bulletproof—or at least recession proof—citing the old adage, "everyone has to eat." Yet while we do need to eat, our choices are almost limitless. If you are in a large office building, there is likely a cafe on the premises and there are probably several restaurants within walking distance. Then, of course, the office denizen can always have food delivered or choose from a variety of snacks stocked in vending machines.

Thus, the foodservice business and the accompanying business landscape are incredibly diverse. In fact, there are few other industries, even within hospitality, that have so many differing elements. For example, during what **dayparts**—breakfast, lunch, dinner, late night—does the foodservice operation offer service? What type of service is offered (table service, grab-and-go, etc.)? Does the operator provide takeout or delivery? Is alcohol served?

There are other unique features, too, that pertain to décor, lighting, ambiance, parking, seating, employee uniforms, training, and the management approach. What about the type or quality of serving ware? Each of the decisions related to these basic operating issues can have a direct impact on the financial success of a foodservice operation, underscoring the unique, multifaceted nature of the foodservice business. Consider the restaurateur who selects extremely ornate silverware complete with the restaurant logo embossed on each piece, only to find that customers all too frequently take them home as souvenirs! Or a university foodservice manager who provides oversized trays hoping to boost sales; the hope is that students might buy more items in order to fill a tray. Unfortunately, some students learn quickly that the oversized trays make great snow sleds and the cost of replacing the trays compromises the operation's profitability. These are simple examples but they remind us of the many nuances of the foodservice industry.

KEY CHARACTERISTICS

Building on these points, it is useful next to consider the key characteristics of the foodservice business. These include sales volatility, product perishability, labor intensiveness, and the ease with which one operation can replicate another's food offerings. The most complex of these, sales volatility, can be analyzed into four distinct types. The first is tied to the economy. For example, in early 2008, the world experienced a severe recession, which affected the economy for several years. This resulted in a precipitous decline in sales for fine-dining restaurants. Restaurants in hotels also suffered—as business travelers were forced to reduce travel, hotel occupancies declined, and so did hotel restaurant sales. However, the economic downturn and the resulting unemployment caused many either to go back to school or to stay in school instead of entering the workforce. As university attendance increased, so did sales at campus eateries. Similarly, sales in quick-service restaurants increased. Customers still wanted to eat in restaurants, but instead of paying fine dining or even family restaurant prices, they opted for more price-friendly quick-service fare.

Another type of volatility results from seasonality. For example, restaurants located in tourist destinations are subject to periods of high tourism-related traffic. Sales suffer in college and university towns when most students leave for the summer. These seasonal effects are particularly problematic for foodservice operations, as they must maintain a certain number of employees in order to remain open even if sales are inadequate to cover the associated expense. This means that foodservice managers must ensure that cash surpluses resulting from busy seasons cover the potential deficits created during the offseason.

A third type of volatility is seen in day-to-day sales. A restaurant located in the financial district or a cafe in a corporate headquarters, for example, may enjoy strong weekday sales but may not be able to justify staying open on weekends. Some operations may also see strong Friday and Saturday night sales, only to experience much lower sales earlier in the week. As a result, accurate sales forecasting becomes critical, in terms of food purchasing, inventory management, and staffing.

The fourth type of volatility is intraday volatility. Restaurants that are open during multiple dayparts may experience very different sales levels, say, in lunch and dinner business. Such variation may be extreme even within a given daypart. Responding effectively to such contingencies often requires managers to adopt innovative pricing and promotion strategies. Daypart volatility lays the foundation for such familiar offerings as early-bird and happy-hour specials.

TRENDS

Every industry sees trends, whether in clothing styles or products that affect lifestyles (think of the impact of the iPod). For the foodservice industry, understanding and identifying lasting trends is paramount. First, savvy foodservice professionals must distinguish the short-lived fad from the lasting trend. For example, many pizza concepts have shunned delivery, failing to acknowledge the consumer trend toward wanting the associated convenience. Others have embraced it, and—in the case of Domino's—capitalized on this trend.

One trend in years past had foodservice operations providing large portions. The trend today is for more serving size options, including small plates. McDonald's capitalized on this trend with its three-dollar mini meals. Other operators have seen this and converted their menus to include only **tapas**—a tapa (a term borrowed from Spain) is a small portion, usually a quarter of a full-size menu offering. Customers like this because it allows them to try a wider variety of dishes and to dictate what counts as one "serving."

Another pervasive trend is found in the evolution of children's menus. Decades ago, foodservice operators added kid's menus to attract families. These were generally a good value and catered to what children wanted, typically fried items. Today, children's menus offer truly unique menu items—no longer just chicken fingers and grilled cheese sandwiches with fries. This trend is a response to several cultural changes, including our renewed awareness of the problems associated with obesity and the benefits of healthy eating.

What other trends are emerging? Only time will tell, but the important thing is to ensure that you are aware of what has been popular in the past in order to identify what may now be just a fad but will later become a trend. A good source for related information can be found in trade magazines; one of the most widely read is *Nation's Restaurant News*. Finally, understanding trends requires that you monitor new and innovative features that operators at each of the various lifecycle stages are offering.

BUSINESS LIFECYCLE

In studying the foodservice business, it is critical to understand the **business lifecycle** and its associated stages. As shown in Figure 2.1, these stages include introduction, growth, maturity, and decline. In the introductory stage, as the name implies, an entrepreneur considers entering the industry and looks for opportunities. During this stage, inexperience often leads to losses or

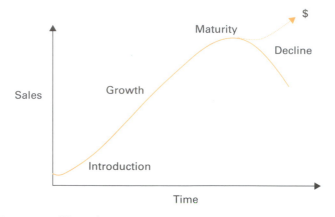

Figure 2.1   Restaurant life-cycle stage.

even business failure. Yet it is at this stage that an operator must determine an establishment's price-value position (which we discuss fully later in the chapter). At this stage, there should be a strong investment in advertising in order to penetrate the market. Also, management tends to be highly centralized so there is an intense focus on resource management (especially food and labor).

At the growth stage, where the operator typically expands the number of units, operations are streamlined. In order to facilitate growth, standardization becomes critical. Also, as the popularity of a given concept increases, the emphasis on localized markets for each of an establishment's units heightens. Menu refinements continue at this stage, but the emphasis is generally on high-profit items. There also is a balance now between consistency in the delivery of food and service and consistency in expansion. During the growth stage, problems that were present in the introductory stage will, if they are not already solved, become even more difficult to address as they will replicate across units. Also, competitors are more likely to attempt emulating popular menu item concepts offered at the growth stage in order to leverage their success.

In the maturity stage sales stabilize and the brand becomes fully leveraged—meaning it is now the market leader. The operator continues to gain market share, steadily but more slowly. Typically, the foodservice company will now begin branching out, harnessing its experience and sometimes launching new brands. Too often, however, the maturity stage finds operators focused more intently on profit than on standards. At the same time, competitors continue to try innovations and new concepts—sometimes the most effective ones are much like what the mature foodservice establishment already offers—to steal market share.

Finally, when an establishment enters the stage of decline, its concepts either reinvent themselves or die. Sometimes, management simply drifts into complacency or is uncertain how to retool to adapt to a changing marketplace. This problem is exacerbated by customers who are looking for the next big thing and begin shifting to foodservice operations that are in the earlier stages. Employees, too, sometimes want to be associated with new concepts and fresh management. The related lack of growth and reduced revenue can lead to financial problems, which, in turn, negatively affect operations.

The most effective strategies to pursue during the decline phase are based on facing reality—management cannot simply wait for things to change, because it is unlikely that they will change for the better. Also, management must renew its knowledge of the market and its customers' consumer preferences. At the same time, it takes a concerted effort to keep unit management fresh and motivated—but there is little choice when customers want something new! Finally, management must assume a new perspective and consider establishing new brands, entering new markets, and capitalizing on past successes with a fresh perspective.

UNDERSTANDING THE MARKETPLACE

Having introduced the key characteristics of the foodservice business, achieved a fuller understanding of how trends shape concept development, and considered the effects of the business lifecycle on foodservice operations, we now delve further into the specifics of a given market. We will explore here processes that are critical to many scenarios: an entrepreneur who is planning to open her first restaurant in a suburban area, an onsite foodservice company that is contemplating adding a new cafe to a college campus's dining facilities, and others within the almost limitless range of situations facing foodservice operators in every segment. Such considerations require several analytic techniques.

Environmental Scanning

The most useful first step in understanding a market comprised of various foodservice operations is a process known as **environmental scanning**. Environmental scanning is the acquisition and use of information about business trends and relationships in an organization's external environment. Although the process is usually applied broadly to the macroenvironment, for our purposes we focus on the competitive set, the marketplace itself. This scanning process provides a general impression of a given marketplace and potentially offers a sustainable competitive advantage to a firm looking to enter that market.

First, we consider an area's economic situation. Is the economy strong? What are the demographics—the general characteristics of and statistics on the human population? For example, are there enough people in the area to support new foodservice concepts? What other industries are operating in the area? What other types of hospitality businesses are in the area (e.g., hotels, tourism outlets)? Finally, how much turnover has occurred in recent years, and where? How many restaurants have failed, and what types of restaurants were they?

Several factors determine the appropriate depth of such an analysis, the most important of which are the size of the market and the resources available to the entity seeking entry. For large suburban areas, such information may be commercially available and already packaged as a readily accessible database. In other cases, a prospective business must acquire such information through a variety of data-gathering approaches. In either case, the cost can be daunting. Yet the cost of *not* analyzing accurate data or, even worse, of not completing the environmental scanning process can be much, much higher.

Concept Mapping

Having employed environmental scanning to evaluate the competitive marketplace, the next logical step, **concept mapping**, is taken to identify possibilities and exploit untapped opportunities. As defined in the *International Encyclopedia of Hospitality Management*, concept mapping is a technique that provides the fullest possible understanding of relationships among ideas, concepts,

Figure 2.2   Quality of food served vs. average check.

and even business operations.[1] The traditional approach to concept mapping involves linking related ideas unidirectionally and expanding their number while brainstorming or investigating complex clusters of interrelated ideas. Concept mapping is also instrumental in analyzing units based on dimensional attributes.

It is this latter application that offers utility to foodservice operators. Having collected data on the types of operations that exist in a given market during environmental scanning, an entrepreneur looking for a niche in that market then expands the data collection to include information about cuisine style and average entrée price while also considering the size of each restaurant in the analysis. Note that this is true regardless of segment; a healthcare center considering adding a new cafe should also adopt this practice. As shown in Figure 2.2, which includes actual data from a US suburb with a population of approximately 100,000 and some 250 restaurants, such a map readily identifies gaps in the market. Here, the size of each unit is depicted by the diameter of the associated data point and the color represents the type of cuisine. (The types of cuisine to be represented in a concept map are dictated by the competitive marketplace being studied; this example includes only the six represented in this locale.)

The second step in concept mapping, which is critical in further differentiating the new business from its competitors, is integrating the quantity of food. For example, what if some of these restaurants serve only tapas? Thus, the concept map requires the addition of another vector to permit analysis based on all characteristics under consideration: average check, quality of food, quantity of food, type of cuisine, and restaurant size. Rotated accordingly, the concept map depicted in Figure 2.3 on a two-dimensional basis (due to the limitations of printed media) offers an ideal example.

With all the data entered, we can now proceed to the most important—and most valuable—step in the concept-mapping process. For this we use the three-dimensional model and explore the competitive marketplace by individual type of cuisine. For example, in separating the data for Mexican restaurants, Figure 2.4 illustrates with graphical clarity a very apparent gap in the given market. For an entrepreneur with expertise in high-end Mexican cuisine, the opportunities here are considerable.

Of course, concept mapping does not integrate every market condition (owing largely to constraints associated with multidimensional analysis). For example, a depressed economy would dictate prudence in the type of concept to be launched. Moreover, the socioeconomic, demographic, and psychographic profile of potential customers must also be weighed. But

Figure 2.3 Quality of food served vs. average check.

Figure 2.4 Identifying gaps in the Mexican restaurant marketplace.

these are tertiary steps; performing environmental scanning and concept mapping provides a wealth of information that has many applications. Furthermore, it can be refreshed routinely to provide an operator with the information necessary for repositioning a given unit or for adding new ones.

It is important to note that concept mapping performed routinely over time in the same marketplace often reveals an interesting phenomenon, **mimetic isomorphism**, the tendency of firms in a market to become more like each other. In this context, mimetic isomorphism occurs when foodservice operators adopt practices—such as menu innovations, pricing structures, and marketing—that mirror those already employed by others. An example of this is the 99-cent-per-item menu that became common across quick-service chains in the early 2000s. In healthcare foodservice, many operators today offer food, such as unbaked pizzas, for employees to purchase at the end of their shifts to take home for dinner. Still another innovation is the trend among mid-scale operators to offer take-out service, along with dedicated ordering kiosks and parking for customers picking up their to-go orders. Thus, markets that were at one time heterogeneous become homogeneous on one or more of the vectors used in the analysis. Such a development in a market generates opportunities for savvy operators with accurate information to capitalize on these conditions, but it also serves as a cautionary warning to those who allow their existing operations to become too much like others in their marketplace.

■■□ VALUE FROM THE CUSTOMERS' PERSPECTIVE

Prospective operators, we have seen, need not enter into markets blindly. Even with an understanding of where opportunities exist within a given market, a potential entry must next consider what value it can bring to that market, particularly in light of what other operations are doing. The logical next step, then, is to evaluate existing enterprises in terms of their **value propositions**. A value proposition is a clear statement of the tangible results a guest receives from engaging the services of the enterprise. It doesn't matter whether the outlet offers burgers and fries, a quick snack at a grab-and-go kiosk in a hospital, or gourmet-quality fare at a fine-dining seafood restaurant perched over a gorgeous beach. Each has a value proposition that speaks—sometimes only implicitly—to the customer.

Think of your most recent restaurant meal. Before you left your residence, you likely had a general idea of how much you would spend on the meal, how long you might have to wait for a table, and what you might order. More than anything, however, you made the conscious decision to patronize that foodservice operation with a general idea of the *value* it offers you. The challenge for operators, then, is to provide value to customers with differing perceptions of what makes the experience worthwhile to them. Hence, we need to understand value from multiple stakeholder perspectives. Additionally, we need to appreciate which value propositions are critical and the limitations associated with each.

Originally value, particularly for restaurateurs, was understood as a simple function of price. As shown in Figure 2.5, this limited definition suggests that customers will evaluate a restaurant highly if they receive the quantity or quality of food that they desire at a price that they perceive is a good value. This was convenient for operators, as it made it easy for them to articulate a simple value proposition. For example, in 1921 the first White Castle restaurant opened in Wichita, Kansas. The operator's value proposition was simple: hamburgers at the unbelievable price of $.05 each (see Figure 2.6).

Soon, however, a more holistic definition of value developed, incorporating other variables that contribute to what ultimately defines the restaurant experience for guests. The expectations that we discussed previously are represented by one such additional variable, adding greater specificity

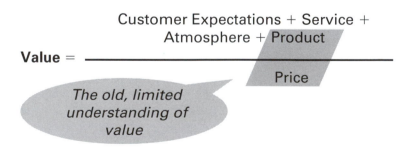

Figure 2.5 The components of value.

Figure 2.6 A White Castle unit (circa 1921).

to the value definition. Service is also critical, since food quality can easily be undermined if not delivered appropriately. Atmosphere, which we discuss at length later in the text, is equally important. Take, for example, a hole-in-the-wall burger joint that offers no white tablecloths but plenty of Superman-sized burgers and bathrooms with comic-book wallpaper. Returning customers may never mention the food but instead will tell others about the atmosphere—in this case, the unique toilet facilities. The product, too, is pivotal. After all, it is the *food*service business! Finally, price—as the central element to all value perceptions—must be considered.

With this more robust definition of value, operators can better—that is, more accurately and for a broader audience—define their value propositions. For example, Domino's Pizza learned early on that one of the key elements related to customer expectations was speedy delivery. This led to the chain's "30 minutes or it's free" guarantee, which ran from 1979 to 1993. Operators integrated state-of-the-art equipment and employees were trained to make pizzas as quickly as possible. This value proposition later evolved (owing largely to lawsuits involving pizza-delivery drivers who potentially compromised safety for the sake of speed) to the chain's "Total Satisfaction Guarantee," which said: "If for any reason you are dissatisfied with your Domino's Pizza dining experience, we will re-make your pizza or refund your money."

The evolution of Domino's value proposition underscores the importance of understanding all the components of value. Even in a situation where the atmosphere and service are not defined in a traditional way, the importance of identifying and assessing the key variables remains critical. Take, for example, a delivery driver who is dressed in a slovenly way. The customer is likely to see the driver's personal presentation as a sign that the restaurant is similarly unconcerned about taking care of the details of cleanliness and service.

Value Drivers

Entrepreneurs and corporate executives alike understand that businesses now see creating value as essential to their success. But which elements of a concept venture are capable of creating value? And which elements, if not properly managed, are capable of destroying value? Building on our previous definition of value, we need to consider many elements of value, all of which must be regarded in light of price and market conditions.

In order to understand—and leverage—value effectively, then, we draw on **value drivers**. These are organizational capabilities that can be used to enhance value to the guest. Considered in this context, value drivers offer varying operational effects. Suppose, for example, that an operator selects a site that she believes will generate strong walk-by traffic. This may be a value driver *if* ease of access is perceived as important by potential customers.

A study conducted by the Hospitality Sales & Marketing Association International (HSMAI) underscores well how this conditionality applies to a hotel application. HSMAI surveyed hotel operators and found that most considered price points, location, and personal service to be the key value drivers affecting customer choice. In surveying their customers, however, the study showed that these considerations represented only about 70 percent of the purchasing decision. Other value drivers, embraced by customers but understood only by the leading operators, included in-room technology, loyalty programs, and room and meeting customization options.[2]

Thus, the proper identification of value drivers is paramount. For Papa Murphy's, which is the subject of this chapter's industry exemplar, the initial value driver was the uniqueness of its concept focusing on **home meal replacement** in the form of pizzas that customers bake at home. This has changed dramatically since the original store opened! Today, the chain is known for its quality as well as reasonable prices with products that include calzones, lasagna, salads, and cookie dough.

The Service-value Chain

Value drivers can be identified best through an understanding of the **service-value chain**. First posited as the service-profit chain in the 1990s by Harvard University Business School professors, the linkages in question underscore the key elements in creating value.[3] As shown in Figure 2.7,

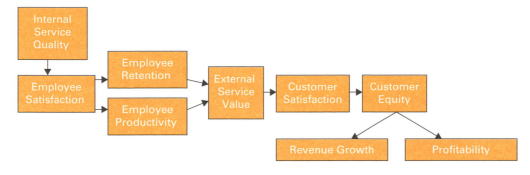

Figure 2.7   The service-value chain.

each variable bears a unique relationship to value creation. This understanding is particularly important in studying the competitive marketplace, as it demonstrates how some concepts may provide more opportunities for value creation than others may offer.

The left side of the model involves the operating strategy and service-delivery system. Within that domain, the value elements lead to external service value by creating incentives for employees to commit to excellence in job performance. For example, service workers are most satisfied when they are able to offer *quality* products (and are empowered to do so). Establishing such a connection is easily achievable in a fine-dining setting but can prove to be frustratingly elusive in a quick-service setting.

In turn, employee satisfaction leads to better retention and productivity, which plays directly into external service value. It is no surprise, then, that one leading mid-scale chain found recently that units with the highest reported employee satisfaction represented the top 20 percent in terms of profitability. This same chain also found that dissatisfied employees are 300 percent more likely to leave the organization, representing extraordinary costs related to the management of human resources (as well as creating negative ramifications with respect to the chain's value proposition).

Referring back to the components of value shown in Figure 2.5, it is clear that the variables incorporated into the service-value chain integrate all aspects of the holistic definition of value. This integration is underscored by the linkage connecting external service value with customer satisfaction. Regardless of industry segment, customer-perceived value is the single-most important determinant of satisfaction!

Continuing across the service-value chain, customer satisfaction—stemming from perceived value assessments—leads to **customer equity**. Customer equity is the strength (and value) of the relationship between the customer and the organization or brand. According to the researchers who coined the term, customer equity has three drivers:[4]

1. *Value equity*: The customer's objective assessment of the utility of a brand, based on perceptions of the value of what is given up relative to the value of what is received.

2. ***Brand equity***: The customer's qualitative assessment of a brand, above and beyond its quantitatively perceived value.

3. *Retention equity*: The tendency of a customer to stick with a brand independently of that customer's objective and subjective assessments of the brand.

The customer equity construct is central to our discussion of the competitive marketplace because returning customers, those who demonstrate their loyalty by repeating their product purchase, shape how the market will perform. Additionally, given the earlier discussion of mimetic isomorphism, the importance of understanding customer equity is difficult to overestimate: With leading restaurant chains within a given segment becoming more like one another, a clear evaluation of your current customers' equity commitments makes it possible to discern differences and select new operating strategies. A recent study of US restaurants highlights the importance of customer equity by showing that customers with high levels of reported equity in a given chain were 60 percent more likely to patronize the same brand again!

The service-value chain ends, not surprisingly, with revenue growth and profitability, two key attributes of realized brand value. The statistics firmly support these final linkages. For example, a 5 percent increase in customer loyalty can boost profit by 25 to 85 percent. Chains in the pizza segment have measured the effects of customer loyalty and concluded that the lifetime value of just one loyal pizza eater can exceed US$8,000 in net profit.

Although the utility of the service-value chain extends beyond its application to analyzing the competitive marketplace, in that context it is especially valuable, as it helps foodservice managers understand value from many perspectives. Of greater importance, however, is that it paints a fuller picture of the ways in which restaurant concepts differ from one another. We're all familiar with the enormous range of these concepts, taking us, as they say, from the sublime to the ridiculous.

Capacity Constraints

The final consideration in addressing the foodservice business pertains to **capacity constraints**. We alluded to this earlier in the discussion of environmental scanning, where it was noted that the market must be evaluated in terms of its demand function. Thus, the first obvious constraint to be considered pertains to how many potential consumers there are in a given market. As noted in the discussion of concept mapping, another constraint reflects the number of players in the same subsegment. In any market there is a limit to the number of restaurants that can coexist while featuring the same type of cuisine with the same value proposition.

There are, of course, many other capacity constraints to consider. By definition, a capacity constraint is a physical or systemic limit on capacity (such as equipment, people, or other resources). The most obvious capacity constraint in the restaurant business is in the number of seats (which is why this variable was included in the earlier concept-mapping example). Much as a room night in a hotel is perishable, so are restaurant seats. Operators understand this more clearly today, and we explain the management of this perishability fully in Chapter 10.

In terms of marketplace assessment, the list of capacity constraints starts with the number of potential customers. To determine this figure the basic approach is to calculate the number of seats available versus the number of potential guests in a given subsegment. A restaurant's product offering may also face constraints. If you're contemplating opening a seafood restaurant where seafood availability is limited, this could represent a constraint. The question, then, is whether you can increase supply and thereby reduce the potential constraint.

Still another capacity constraint involves labor. When assessing the competitive marketplace, then, it is critical to understand whether an adequate number of appropriately qualified staff employees are available. The first indicator may be a market environment's unemployment rate. Low unemployment may signal a short supply of potential employees. Moreover, it may indicate that higher payroll costs should be expected with such a constraint on labor.

The final high-capacity constraint lies in the availability of real estate. In mature markets, the most likely location for a new operation is an existing restaurant. As any restaurant manager knows, another constraint associated with real estate involves parking. In places such as Seoul, Korea, for example, even mid-scale restaurants must offer valet parking since space comes at a high premium.

The amount and types of capacity constraints depend on the marketplace being analyzed. Still, any thorough market assessment must include such constraints in the analysis in order to understand fully the opportunities and threats associated with launching a new operation in that locale. Furthermore, when determining the most prudent course of action, such a capacity-constraint analysis must be considered as only one among the several other evaluative procedures we have outlined.

MANAGERIAL IMPLICATIONS: MAXIMIZING OPPORTUNITIES IN THE COMPETITIVE MARKETPLACE

Restaurateurs need to know as much as possible about the competitive marketplace to understand where the potential exists for future business. This begins with environmental scanning, which is complemented by the robust process of concept mapping. Together these approaches yield much useful information about the marketplace and paint a very definitive picture of business possibilities.

Expanding this knowledge base includes understanding value, which helps the operator position a concept—or redefine one—in a way that aligns more completely with guests' needs. Understanding value propositions and appreciating value drivers is therefore critical. Additionally, the service-value chain provides a valuable tool for identifying each of these value drivers. An often-unrealized advantage of this approach is that it creates opportunities through which a newcomer to the market can generate added value. The service-value chain can be reapplied during any stage of a restaurant's lifecycle.

Finally, accurately identifying capacity constraints is particularly important to existing operations that are reevaluating their value drivers. For example, a manager might identify an unrealized value driver but be able to harness it only partially due to a constraint created by a restaurant's location, situation, or even the concept itself. Similarly, certain constraints may be endemic in a given marketplace, such as insufficient physical space for new entries.

In this chapter, we have demonstrated that operators with a comprehensive understanding of competitive marketplace assessment have a much greater likelihood of success than those who enter without such knowledge. In the next chapter, we build on this discussion and address *concept development*—the next stage in our survey of foodservice management fundamentals.

Papa Murphy's

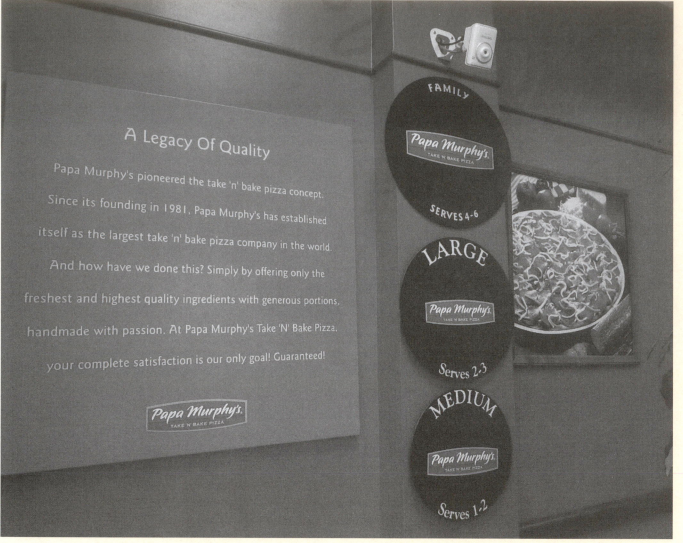

Courtesy of Papa Murphy's.

n the 1950s, pizzerias were independent operations that took advantage of the pizza craze that had developed after World War II. Then, in 1958, Frank and Dan Carney opened the first Pizza Hut in Wichita, Kansas. A year later, they incorporated and opened their first franchise unit in Topeka, Kansas. While Pizza Hut was devoted to in-house dining for pizza, Detroit native Tom Monaghan founded Domino's Pizza in 1960 and pioneered the delivery concept. A short time later, Michael Hitch, also from Detroit, founded Little Caesars, which focused on the carryout segment for inexpensive pizza.

These were distinct concepts but, with all three, pizza is prepared in the restaurant. In 1981, Papa Murphy's took

pizza in a new direction with the concept of preparing pizzas to order but packaging them to be cooked at the customer's home. This *take-and-bake* notion allowed for broad customization of pizzas while giving customers the freedom to cook them at their convenience. A customer could pick up a pizza, freshly made before her eyes, on the way home from work, and save it in the fridge until dinnertime. The result was a fresh product, served hot.

The take-and-bake concept had another key advantage. Because there are no ovens needed, the capital cost to open a franchise specializing in unbaked pizzas is very low, particularly compared with the cost of equipping other foodservice franchises. This feature also allows for a broader range of locations, since venting and other traditional cooking features are not required.

Yet another advantage is that, since the pizzas (and now calzones, lasagna, and cookies, as well) are sold uncooked, many states allow them to be purchased with food stamps. This is, after all, no different from buying uncooked or frozen pizzas with food stamps in supermarkets. Estimates for some Papa Murphy's units show that such purchases represent 5 to 10 percent of sales.

Under the leadership of Terry Collins, Papa Murphy's was voted Best Pizza Chain in America by *Restaurants and Institutions* magazine and was named Top Food Franchise by *Franchise Business Review in 2011*. There are currently over 1,100 stores in 34 states, plus 14 stores in Canada. It is the fifth largest pizza chain in North America, with nearly all of the stores franchised. In 2010, the privately held company was sold to Lee Equity Partners of New York for $180 million.

KEY TERMS

daypart   22

tapas   23

business lifecycle   23

environmental scanning   25

concept mapping   25

mimetic isomorphism   27

value proposition   28

value drivers   30

home meal replacement   30

service-value chain   30

customer equity   31

brand equity   31

capacity constraints   32

Case in Point

Restaurant No. 2

Kris Mueller had already realized considerable success with her first restaurant in a bustling suburb of Orlando, Florida. But she had been lucky. Since she had very limited resources, she had not been picky about the location and had accepted an offer from a family friend to launch her concept in the strip mall he owned. To be sure, she realized that most locals went to the new mall with the high-end anchor stores just a few blocks away, but she really didn't have much choice. Besides, it had worked out fine. After 15 months of operation, she was showing a profit and already had an investor interested in helping her launch a second unit.

The investor was, however, rather restrictive regarding his offer to help. He would cover all start-up costs, but would terminate the relationship if Kris could not show strong cash flow from the new operation within the first two quarters of operation. Furthermore, he wanted her to open the new unit in Tampa, a very different setting from the one she had chosen and one about which Kris knew very little. The investor explained that he selected Tampa because that was the location of his main office and he felt the convenience of being nearby would help him entice investors to launch the concept as a national chain.

Even with her limited experience in restaurant ownership, she knew this meant that she needed more than luck to start the second unit. She had been to Tampa once and even had a distant aunt who lived there. How could she learn about the market quickly to assess whether her concept would make it?

Around that time, Kris remembered a college friend who had joined a hospitality consulting firm after graduate school. She called Lucy, and, after reminiscing with Lucy about the good old days, she posed the question: Can you help me assess the area of Tampa where I'm hoping to open the new restaurant?

Kris was rather startled by Lucy's response. Lucy explained that her company used complex analytical tools designed for various types of service-based businesses that could provide useful information. Furthermore, she had just completed a similar analysis for another client with surprising results. As a friend, Lucy disclosed to Kris that she had recommended to her client that he not open a restaurant there! Lucy went on to say that this client's value proposition was similar to the one offered by Kris's concept.

After thanking Lucy with a guarantee of free desserts for life at her restaurant, Kris called her potential investor. Without divulging the confidential information she had received from Lucy, she explained to him that she thought it was a bad idea to open in the area near his office. She added that she would be interested in considering another location.

The investor reiterated that he needed the new restaurant to be near his office. "Kris, don't you want me to take all my wealthy clients there?" he asked. The conversation ended with a clear message to Kris: If you want my money, you'll open the restaurant near my office. If not, then consider this relationship ended.

Kris stared out the window, gripped by a sense of impending doom. Should she take the shot and gamble on success? Or, should she listen to her friend's free advice and wait for another chance—one that might never materialize?

REVIEW AND DISCUSSION QUESTIONS

1. What is a day part?

2. Name the four ways to consider sales volatility.

3. What is a current trend in the foodservice industry that is not mentioned in the chapter?

4. Identify the four stages of the restaurant lifecycle and provide a characteristic of each one.

5. What is environmental scanning? When would a foodservice company typically use it? What are the various steps?

6. Why should an entrepreneur who is considering entering a new market perform concept mapping?

7. In the simplest terms, explain *mimetic isomorphism*.

8. Think of your favorite foodservice outlet (it could be anything from an eatery on a college campus to a fine-dining restaurant). Name two of its value propositions and two of its value drivers.

9. Describe the notion of value as discussed in the chapter.

10. Which step in the service-value chain do you think is the most important, and why?

11. What are the three drivers associated with customer equity?

12. Why is the consideration of capacity constraints important?

ENDNOTES

1. Pizam, A. (Ed.) (2005). *International Encyclopedia of Hospitality Management*. Oxford: Elsevier.

2. *HSMAI Marketing Review* (Fall 2002).

3. Heskett, J. L., Sasser. W. E., & Schlesinger, L. A. (1997). *The Service-profit Chain*. New York: Free Press.

4. Rust, R., Zeithaml, V., & Lemon, K. (2000). *Driving Customer Equity: How Customer Lifetime Value is Reshaping Corporate Strategy*. New York: The Free Press.

PART 2

THE MENU

Building on the general and historical information discussed in Part 1, we begin Part 2 by looking at the business much as an entrepreneur views a potential foodservice venture. Specifically, in Chapter 3 we explore menu planning and development, often the first step in creating any new foodservice entity. This leads into a discussion of recipe standardization, costing, and analysis in Chapter 4. In Chapter 5, we consider the various issues related to menu pricing; we also address menu psychology and introduce menu engineering.

MENU PLANNING AND DEVELOPMENT

LEARNING OBJECTIVES:

After becoming familiar with this chapter, you should be able to:

1. Appreciate the importance of menu philosophy.

2. Understand the basics of menu planning and review the importance of the menu in the operation of any foodservice operation.

3. Recognize how menus differ in the various segments of onsite foodservice.

4. Be able to explain the art underlying menu development.

5. Identify and explain differences in menu philosophy as they apply to sustainability.

Having covered the industry's history, segmentation, and the nature of the business, we now shift our focus internally to the heart of any foodservice operation—its menu. Any discussion of the fundamentals of foodservice must start with the menu, because the menu is *fundamental* to any foodservice operation.

◾◽ PHILOSOPHY
◽◾

Since the latter part of the twentieth century, foodservice has undergone major changes. For example, restaurants and onsite foodservice operations originally had little in common, except that they both served food. The similarity ended there—menus and menu items bore little resemblance to one another; staff were trained differently and worked under different philosophies and often with very different kinds of food products. Restaurant foodservice and onsite foodservice were almost considered "distinct industries." This has all changed.

In any foodservice operation today the menu is a printed or wall-mounted display of the food and beverage choices available to a guest. A menu may be **à la carte** or *table d'hôte*. *À la carte* (pronounced "ah-la-kart") is a French expression meaning "from the menu," and it is used in foodservice operations in two ways:

- To refer to a menu of items priced and ordered separately rather than selected from a list of preset multicourse meals at fixed prices.

- To designate the option to order a main course item along with a side dish that is included with the dish at no extra charge.

As introduced in Chapter 1, *table d'hôte* is a French phrase that literally means "host's table." Restaurants use this term to indicate a menu that offers multiple-course meals with limited choices at fixed prices. Such a menu may also be called **prix fixe** (fixed price, pronounced "prefix"). Even with these two simple types of menu structure, the fundamental and philosophical importance of the menu is apparent.

Mixed Birthday Message?

Sonya and Jim wanted to go out for dinner to celebrate Jim's birthday—they chose a new "steak" restaurant near their house and thought they were going to a nice, sit-down steakhouse. The restaurant's advertising featured grilled steaks and showed a menu typical of an upscale steakhouse but with lower prices. They entered to find that customers walk up to a beautifully appointed counter and are expected to select from a large, brightly lit board behind the counter. They were astounded to discover that the choices consisted mainly of variations on the steak sandwich, mostly using ground or sliced steak, along with chicken and fish sandwiches, fries, etc. There were some steak-related items on the menu, the food looked tasty, and the atmosphere was cheerful and friendly. But it just was NOT what they thought—and hoped— it would be.

How did Sonya and Jim likely feel about this experience? They formed their expectations based on the menu they saw in the advertisement, while the actual menu was more akin to what one sees in a quick-service restaurant (QSR). This emphasizes how customers associate menu style with specific types of foodservice operation.

The menu translates the overall philosophy of a foodservice operation to the customer. It is the center, the heart, the core of the operation. The style of food, the design of the building or kitchen area, the employees, the ambiance, and even financial outcomes—all flow from the menu.

Because the style of the menu they encountered did not meet Jim and Sonya's expectations, they were confused—and ultimately disappointed.

PLANNING

It is important to understand that most diners enjoy a wide variety of dining styles and price points as well as having many items from which to choose at a given establishment. At the shore in a little place on the water, diners happily eat in the open from paper plates. People at the beach are content to enjoy the "catch of the day" with fries and slaw and a very limited range of other choices. But when vacationing at a beautiful resort by the sea, people expect restaurants to serve a wide variety of seafood, all prepared in interesting and unique ways, with fresh vegetables and salad options—not to mention some very impressive and irresistible desserts and wines. These respective menu styles suit particular situations and also drive many other decisions about restaurants. In this case, while both styles of restaurant feature seafood, little else will be the same. It's obvious that the menus will differ significantly. But the restaurants themselves will also feature differing building styles and décor, contrasting service standards and pricing, and equipment and service ware that fit the respective restaurant menu styles. It is also very likely that the wait staff in the more elegant restaurant will not be dressed as pirates, while that attire would be acceptable in the seafood shack by the shore.

Planning and Development Phases

Today's foodservice menu requires careful strategic planning because it must be aligned with an operation's concept and it is critical to the execution of that concept. As always, the menu must make the diner feel comfortable with the available choices while always meeting or exceeding the diner's expectations. The menu must be flexible, too, as changes are sometimes necessary. When a QSR chain begins to serve gourmet coffee drinks, for example, this very likely will impact its local market. Such changes can necessitate menu modifications to nearby foodservice operations competing for the same customers.

Fortunately, the factors that predominately influence menu planning can be summarized by reference to type of foodservice operation. Figure 3.1 provides a summary table associating each type of restaurant with these factors.

Another planning issue that applies to all segments is the menu label requirements attached to Section 4205 of the **2010 Patient Protection and Affordable Care Act**. The Act requires restaurants and similar retail food establishments with 20 or more locations to list calorie content information for standard menu items on restaurant menus and menu boards, including drive-through menu boards. Other nutrition information such as fat, saturated fat, cholesterol, sodium, total carbohydrates, sugars, fiber, and total protein must be made available in writing upon request. (The Act also requires vending machine operators who own or operate 20 or more vending machines to disclose calorie content for certain items.)

Categorization and Menu Policy

As introduced in Chapter 1, the foodservice industry can be segmented into several categories. Here we discuss how those categories drive the menu policy.

Menu Concepts	Quick Service	Fast Casual	Family/Midscale/Theme	Fine Dining
Environment/ Ambiance	Clean, bright, immediate access to menu & service, tempting pictures of food, fast service	Clean, crisp, adult-oriented and family friendly; food is in forefront (not ordering system), relaxed café atmosphere	Table dining in warm, adult-oriented but family friendly area, may feature an ethnic menu or a theme; service is the main goal with traditional table service from friendly staff	Professionally designed lighting, flooring, tables, fabrics welcome diners into a world of elegance and excitement
Customer Wants/ Needs	Limited choices, easy to understand, little waiting, easy access to food & payment, simple but tasteful surroundings	High quality, shows food being freshly prepared or assembled in view, often "perceived" as healthy	High quality, often with chefs visible to dining area, customer requests can be honored for many times	Multiple, high-trained wait staff attend to customer's expressed and observed needs
Menu Policy/ Philosophy	Simply prepared food served quickly & courteously, reasonably priced	Made or finished on site, signature items not found elsewhere wide variety with minimal daily changes in soups, etc.	Chef-prepared ethnic authenticity, may feature daily specials, menu changes periodically, variety of choices in all menu areas	Chef-designed prepared, original recipes or ethnic perfection are trademarks, may feature unique items, pastry chefs, wine sommeller
Menu Presentation	Light board with pictures for easy accessibility & understanding	Available at door on paper, displayed on menu board above ordering area, customer walks past food display before ordering	Attractively presented menu delivered to table—look and feel of menu invites guests to explore new items or multiple courses, may feature children's items	Attractive, artistic menu delivered to table, may change daily, multiple courses; separate and extensive wine list and dissert list from pastry chef
Ordering/Receiving food	Counter service with immediate payment	Customer orders & pays at registers, but goes to a table to await fresh preparation of food; may be called to pick up or it may be delevered to table	Customer formally orders from knowledgeable wait staff, food is prepared to order, service ware is attractive, appropriate flatware, linens, etc.	Food prepared after customer order, artistically plated and served; preparation may be extensive and require time; served in courses
Price	Low	Low to moderate	Moderate	Expensive (and beyond)

Figure 3.1 Menu factors by foodservice category.

QSRs

Facilitated by the menu, both the service and eating are "fast" in a QSR. QSRs feature multiple locations for ordering, including walk-up counters both inside and outside (where appropriate) and drive-through windows preceded by lighted outdoor menus. For indoor ordering and dining, customers approach the counter, read the menu display, order, receive and pay for the food—all in a matter of minutes (the procedure is nearly identical for drive-through ordering). The customer then eats and leaves—or leaves and eats!

It is also interesting to note that this same menu approach is found in nontraditional foodservice settings. For example, many supermarkets have introduced QSR-style dining, offering items

BURGER KING®

BURGER KING® is the second-largest fast-food hamburger chain in the world. Every day, more than 11 million guests visit a BURGER KING® somewhere in the world. For over 50 years, BURGER KING® restaurants have been serving high-quality, great-tasting and affordable food around the world. The BURGER KING® website says, "Our commitment to the food we serve is what defines us as a company and is at the center of our HAVE IT YOUR WAY® brand promise." BURGER KING® restaurants feature a variety of burgers—beginning with the WHOPPER® Sandwich, but also other beef, chicken, and fish sandwich items—as well as breakfast items, side items, dessert items, and a wide variety of soft drinks, coffee, and shakes.

The full menu for BURGER KING®, as well as extensive nutritional information, is available on the company website.

The physical environment in a QSR truly focuses interest on the menu display (see Figure 3.2). Always brightly lit, often with very appetizing (and likely enhanced) pictures, the display is the focal point of the facility and is usually found immediately above the preparation area. The companies who plan these restaurants have targeted the customer who's in a hurry—most customers know the menu from both experience and television ads and often know their choices before they enter. Customers neither expect nor welcome frequent menu changes. When changes or additions do occur, they are accompanied by prominent advertising campaigns. Although the rest of the décor and design are important, the restaurant's success is based almost entirely on the structure and function of the menu.

The BURGER KING® trademarks and images are used with permission from Burger King Corporation.

Figure 3.2 Family enjoying lunch in a BURGER KING®.

Courtesy Wegman's Food Markets.

Figure 3.3   Diners in a Wegman's Market Café.

ranging from sandwiches to stir-fry. Guests like this dining option since they can eat lunch and go shopping in the same location. (See Figure 3.3.)

Fast-Casual

The fast-casual menu expands on the QSR concept by enhancing each of the key features of a QSR while still providing value for the dollar. Although the food is prepared to order, it is still served quickly, whether to be retrieved by the customer when notified that it is ready or delivered to the table. See the Industry Leader Profile in Chapter 1 of Panera Bread for an example of a fast-casual restaurant.

Like QSRs, fast-casual restaurants feature limited menu choices but lead the way in offering or encouraging the selection of food preparation options. Many fast-casual restaurants are marketed as health-conscious: Healthful items may occupy a much higher proportion of the menu than in a QSR, and high-quality ingredients such as free-range chicken and freshly made salsas are not unusual. Customers at most fast-casual restaurants expect the food to be higher in quality than traditional fast food, which utilizes more centralized pre-preparation of food, described in Chapter 1. Some ethnic restaurants provide fast-casual dining, while many fast-casual restaurants feature one or more ethnic cuisines on their menus.

According to *Fast Casual*, a magazine covering contemporary ideas and trends, fast-casual design often displays a nontraditional look.[1] For example, Baja Fresh features fish tacos but does not look like a traditional Mexican restaurant. Note the pictures in Figure 3.4 showing the modern upscale look.

Family/Midscale

In general, the structure of a family/midscale restaurant menu will follow a pattern something like this:

- Appetizers
- Soups and salads
- Entrees
- Side dishes (starches and vegetables)
- Desserts
- Beverages, including at least beer and wine

The offerings within these categories will be quite varied, but this is the standard menu structure in the United States. Even many ethnic restaurants have adopted this format, or a modification of it, since it is easy to interpret and matches the typical North American eating pattern.

Courtesy Baja Fresh.

Figure 3.4   Baja Fresh.

Romano's Macaroni Grill

Committed to its vision of serving "Fresh, Simple and Authentic™" food, Romano's Macaroni Grill offers an extensive menu featuring the Italian Mediterranean way of cooking. Its simple recipes require the finest ingredients, such as vine-ripened tomatoes, colorful vegetables, imported artisan pasta, extra virgin olive oil, fresh lemons, pan-seared fish, select seafood, grilled meats, and fresh, fragrant Italian herbs. (See Figure 3.5.) At Romano's, it is customary to start your meal with a glass of wine poured on the "honor system" while enjoying a bowl of Mediterranean olives along with their warm peasant bread. The dining experience is reminiscent of the Italian Mediterranean, where chefs prepare dishes in open kitchens and fresh bouquets of gladiolas welcome guests into each restaurant. The festive atmosphere also encourages kids and adults to draw on the white paper tablecloths with crayons.

Courtesy Romano's Macaroni Grill.

Figure 3.5   One of Romano's Macaroni Grill's new pasta dishes.

A selection of breads is almost always offered in restaurants in the United States and is expected to be included in the price. It is also not unusual for soup or salad to be included with an entrée, but this is less likely to be the case in a more expensive restaurant. The salad bar became very popular several decades ago and was usually included in the meal price as well. Salad bars have since become more common in family-style restaurants. They have declined in popularity somewhat, as we will see later when we discuss sanitation and safety in Chapter 7.

Moderate/Theme

Although some theme restaurants are designed to evoke a historical era or a style of food like country cooking, ethnic themes comprise the largest segments in this sector. Ethnic choices might offer food from Afghanistan to South Africa to a variety of South American cuisines. They can include English pubs and intimate French restaurants. Asian food is represented by Szechuan, Cantonese, Hunan, Japanese, Korean, Indonesian, Malaysian, Indian, Thai, and Vietnamese cuisines, among others. The entire global spectrum is available in almost any large city, and some segments can be found in most small cities and even some small towns. There is a small town in Central Florida with an Icelandic restaurant! Figure 3.6 shows just a few of the major flavor characteristics (sometimes referred to as flavor profiles) that define the variety of ethnic cuisines.

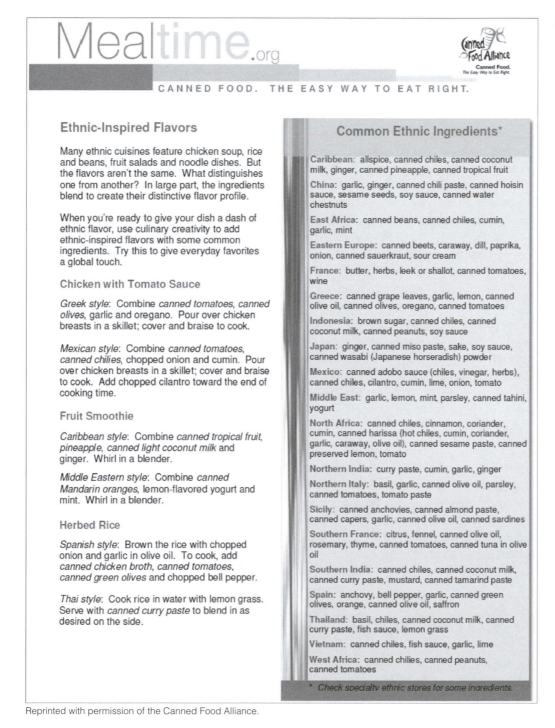

Figure 3.6 Flavor characteristics.

Bobby Flay's Mesa Grill

B obby Flay opened the Mesa Grill in New York in 1991. As a celebrity chef and Food Network star, Flay developed a signature style of American cookery, featuring the flavors of the Southwest with his fondness for grilling. The menu features hot and spicy items and cool and sweet items, with special rubs for meats, and very bold and spicy sauces. Menu items include, for example, black bean soup, blue corn pancakes, and yellow cornmeal crusted oysters. There are featured plates of the day, while the spice-rubbed New York strip steak with house-made MESA Steak Sauce has been a favorite for years. In addition to its New York City location, there are now two more Mesa Grills, one in Las Vegas and another at the Atlantis Paradise Island resort in the Bahamas.

As chefs develop new approaches to recipes and menu structure for these varied cuisines, they often begin to combine influences and sometimes refer to the offerings as **fusion cuisine**. The menu planner who adds ethnic influence to the basic menu will often use these flavors for interest or variety. As discussed in the previous chapter, many restaurants are adapting the small bites or tapas concept, especially for desserts, on their menus.

Looking at the menu concept checklist in Figure 3.1, note that these types of restaurants share characteristics with the family/midscale profile, except that the ambiance may be very authentically ethnic, reflecting the nation of origin of the food. The menu may show items in the original language side-by-side with English translations as well as ingredient listings, to make choices more understandable to a wide audience.

Some themed restaurants emphasize "family fun." Whether featuring a jungle setting or a prehistoric environment, such restaurants often serve as entertainment venues that feature food; the menu may include cleverly titled items such as T-Rex burgers or Gator Bites. Sometimes patrolled by animated animals or other characters that interact with guests, such entertainment offerings only add to the fun. As noted earlier, however, the theme must begin with the menu-planning process.

Fine Dining

The concept of fine dining has been traditionally associated with French cuisine, and then the American love for beef began to find expression in some very high end steakhouses. Today, however, due in part to the popularity of several television shows featuring food and one network entirely devoted to food, the fine-dining concept has expanded to encompass many food and, correspondingly, menu approaches. An examination of the menu on the Mesa Grill website will clearly demonstrate the blend of American, Southwest, and creative cuisine that has been delighting diners for almost 20 years.

MENUS IN ONSITE FOODSERVICE

In terms of categorization and menu policy, some of the biggest changes in the foodservice industry during the past few decades have occurred in onsite foodservice. This would be interesting if for no other reason than that onsite foodservice is provided for people whose purpose for being at the particular site has nothing to do with food. Taking its cue from restaurants—where customers *choose* to go—the challenge for onsite foodservice is to have the guests feel that they are eating there by choice. Fortunately, the onsite industry has responded to the vast expansion of choices and cuisines available to all diners today, and has become equally innovative in its menu-planning approach. This has driven the development of many changes in menu structure and offerings— the old factory-style cafeteria cannot survive in today's onsite world.

Wellness, sustainability, and nutritional content are among the driving factors that have shaped the development of onsite foodservice menus and operations. We will consider all of these menu types as we now examine the main segments of onsite operations.

Healthcare

Modern-style hospitals have been around since the latter part of the nineteenth century, and by the early twentieth century they had became highly organized, formal treatment facilities. As hospitals progressed from places where people "went to die" to places where people "went to get better," food became more important. At first, this meant cooking up big vats of soups and stews that were considered healthy, were inexpensive, and could be ladled into smaller containers for each patient. Patients were in beds; the beds were arranged in rows in large wards. It was simple, but in this case the foodservice "customers" were glad to be alive and eating.

The next innovation brought menus to hospital foodservice, typically listing a soup or salad, an entrée, a beverage, and a dessert. Patients were not given choices, but there was usually something palatable enough to eat. By the 1940s and 1950s, people began to expect a bit more—and there were now dietitians on staff who knew a lot more about vitamins and the role of nutrition in recovery from disease or injury. The concepts of nutrition and specialized diets began to drive menu design and content. The following is a listing of the major types of hospital diets and menu-planning considerations:

- Regular or house or general menu

- **Special or modified menu** (ordered by the physician, planned by registered dietitians, and usually controlled with respect to one or more nutrients such as calories, fat, sodium, etc.)

- Consistency modifications (fluid restrictions, clear liquid, full liquid, ground, chopped, pureed)

Unfortunately, the modifications made to hospital menus to coordinate the patient's diet with the treatment of a specific condition (such as heart disease) or to prepare a patient to undergo a specific procedure (such as a test or surgery) are rarely pleasing to patients. People don't want to be sick and they don't want to change their eating habits. They are afraid of being in the hospital and uncomfortable with having little control over their daily routines. Such diets may be necessary for a patient's well-being, but they make eating "hospital food" an unpleasant and unfamiliar experience.

Healthcare menus reflect the patient-care philosophies of their institutional hosts. Often, a hospital will use its menu to help demonstrate its customer or patient focus. In today's competitive healthcare environment, such a customer focus often differentiates one hospital from another. The following story will illustrate this idea.

Restaurant or Hospital?

Tom and Lena, two college athletes, undergo knee surgery at different hospitals in the same town. Both are 250-bed community hospitals with great reputations for good care and impressive orthopedic surgery units. The athletes each spend three days in their respective hospitals after surgery. Both eat "regular" diets for the last two days. But the similarity ends there. In hospital A, Tom is given a printed menu that changes daily with two entrée choices—the vegetables and starchy side dish are part of the selection. He can choose his beverage (iced tea, a soft drink, coffee, or hot tea) and fruit or a sweet dessert. Tom accepts this, but unfortunately, most college students do not eat roasted boneless chicken breast with green beans and rice for lunch.

Lena calls to tell Tom about the great lunch she had at hospital B—a roasted ham and asiago cheese sandwich on a hard roll with her choice of toppings, crisp shoestring potatoes, Caesar salad, and gelato. She was able to order a cappuccino as well. She says the menu looks "just like a restaurant's" and that she can always find something she likes.

Hospital A is serving just what Tom expected—"hospital food." It tasted good and Tom ate it, but he was certainly looking forward to his first meal at home, since it would definitely not be "hospital food." But Lena describes a menu that sounds more likely to have come from a restaurant. She was genuinely excited about the choices she could make, although the menu offered the same 12 entrées every day.

When a restaurant menu does not meet the customer's expectations, it makes the customer uncomfortable. In Lena's case, she expected "hospital food" but got much more. Hospital A offers a **selective-cycle menu** while Hospital B offers a **restaurant-style menu** in a format called **room service** (which we explain later in the chapter). It was a pleasant surprise in the healthcare setting and made Lena feel good about her eating experience. It also exceeded expectations, even though she would have preferred not to have had surgery in the first place.

Healthcare menus are structured to reflect both an institution's commitment to food and service quality and its size and operational organization. The key factor is that diners are usually housed and fed far from the site of food preparation. The two most common healthcare institution menus follow a cyclical scheduling and planning scheme.

Selective-cycle Menu

A **cycle menu** is a menu on which the offerings are planned for a period of from 6 to 30 days and then are repeated at the end of that period. When such a menu is served "as is, with no variation," it is called **nonselective**. (Note: The longer the cycle, the more difficult is the task of planning all those varied menu items. Unfortunately, the eater often feels that "chicken is chicken, no matter what it is called," so lengthening the cycle often does not prevent the customer from noticing the repetition.) Short cycles entail frequent repetition, an unpleasant situation for a captive hospital patient.

A cycle menu includes choices, usually two entrées paired with various sides and perhaps a choice of fruit or dessert and a beverage. The diner receives the menu for the next day and indicates his choices. (As noted above, the risk of repetition is even greater when the planner must include at least two items for every meal.) Even with the choices offered under this scheme, it is often the case that the diner does not like any of them!

In any kind of cycle menu planning, the planner must consider many aesthetic variables: Variety, color, type, temperature, texture, and preparation style must all be included to avoid boredom. A restaurant-style menu offers foods chosen by the diner, so if she wants tomato sauce on pasta with sliced tomatoes and cooked beets, she can eat this "red" meal as long as her diet permits it. However, if such a meal is not chosen but simply "received" by the customer, it would not be considered acceptable, so the healthcare menu planner must carefully consider how to provide variety both within and across meals.

Sunday Week 1 Breakfast	Monday Week 1 Breakfast	Tuesday Week 1 Breakfast	Wednesday Week 1 Breakfast	Thursday Week 1 Breakfast	Friday Week 1 Breakfast	Saturday Week 1 Breakfast
Tomato Juice Cold Cereal Oatmeal French Toast Scrambled Eggs Sausage Margarine Syrup Prunes Milk Cofee/Tea	Orange Juice Cold Cereal Cream of Wheat Hard Boiled Egg Bacon White Toast Margarine, Jelly Fruit Cup Milk Cofee/Tea	Apple Juice Cold Cereal Cream of Rice Egg Casserole Wheat Toast Margarine, Jelly Orange Wedges Milk Cofee/Tea	Cranberry Juice Cold Cereal Oatmeal Breakfast Sandwich (Ham/Egg/Cheese) Bran Muffin Margarine, Jelly Cantaloupe Cubes Milk Cofee/Tea	Orange Juice Cold Cereal Cream of Wheat Blueberry Pancakes Sausage Patty Toasted Bagel Margarine, Syrup Sliced Bananas Milk Cofee/Tea	Grape Juice Cold Cereal Oatmeal Ham Cheese Omelet Hash Browns Glazed Doughnut Margarine, Jelly Prunes Milk Cofee/Tea	Apple Juice Cold Cereal Cream of Wheat Waffle Bacon White Toast Margarine, Syrup Canned Apricots Milk Cofee, Tea
Lunch	**Lunch**	**Lunch**	**Lunch**	**Lunch**	**Lunch**	**Lunch**
Cream of Mushroom Soup Garden Salad w/Italian Drsg. Roast Turkey w/Gravy Bread Dressing Green Beans Roll -or- Chefs Salad w/Italian Drsg. Dinner Roll Chocolate Pudding Angel Food Cake Milk	Turkey Veg. Soup Mixed Greens w/Italian Drsg. Baked Pork Chop Mashed Potatoes Sliced Beets Garlic Toast -or- Chicken Salad Sandwich Chips German Chocolate Cake Applesauce Milk	Tomato Soup Carrot/Raisin Salad Baked Fish Rice Pilaf Sugar Snap Peas -or- Grilled Cheese Sandwich Rye Roll Peach Crisp Canned Apricots Milk	Cream of Potato Soup Pear and Cottage Cheese Beef Brisket w/BBQ Sauce Steamed Carrots Corn Casserole -or- Spaghetti with Meat Sauce Wheat Roll Mixed Fruit Cup Orange Cake Baked Apple Milk	Cream of Celery Soup Calypso Salad Glazed Ham Mashed Sweet Potatoes Steamed Broccoli Dinner Roll -or- Caesar Salad w/Grilled Chicken Chocolate Ice Cream Fresh Grapes Milk	Chicken Rice Soup Calypso Salad Pot Roast w/ Vegetables Roasted Potatoes Brussels Sprouts -or- Vegetable Lasagna Italian Roll Chocolate Brownie Cinnamon Applesauce Milk	Tomato Vegetable Soup Baked Chicken Scalloped Potatoes Steamed Spinach -or- Greek Salad Rye Roll Butter Pecan Ice Cream Pound Cake Fresh Banana Milk
Dinner	**Dinner**	**Dinner**	**Dinner**	**Dinner**	**Dinner**	**Dinner**
Chicken Noodle Soup Ruben Sandwich Spring Garden Slaw Vanilla Ice Cream Butter Cookies Hot Tea	Corn Chowder Cheese Enchilada Spanish Rice Sliced Tomatoes Flan Oatmeal Cookies Hot Tea	Onion Soup BLT Club Sandwich on Toast Stewed Tomatoes Tossed Salad Fresh Strawberries Chocolate Cookie Hot Tea	Egg Drop Soup Stir Fried Chicken and Vegetables Steamed Rice Sliced Cucumbers Bread Stick Butterscotch Pudding Canned Peaches Hot Tea	New England Clam Chowder Meatball Sub. Sandwich Tater Tots Tossed Salad w/Creamy Italian Drsg. Pecan Pie Fresh Apple Hot Tea	Bean Soup Tuna Salad Sandwich Green Beans Confetti Slaw Cheese Bread Chocolate Chip Cookie Lemon Cream Pie Hot Tea	Split Pea Soup Four Cheese Pizza w/Sausage Garden Salad w/Ranch Drsg. Blueberry Crisp Pear Half Orange Italian Ice Hot Tea

Figure 3.7 Typical cycle menu for one week.

REGULAR/NO ADDED SALT BREAKFAST (DAY 1 - SUNDAY)		REGULAR/NO ADDED SALT NOON (DAY 1 - SUNDAY)		REGULAR/NO ADDED SALT EVENING (DAY 1 - SUNDAY)	
Chef Special	Scrambled Eggs Bacon Biscuit Grits Margarine *NAS-bacon not allowed*	Chef Special	Chicken w/Julienne Veg. Seasoned Green Beans Rice Pilaf Dinner Roll w/Margarine Cake w/Strawberry Glaze	Chef Special	Chopped Steak w/Gravy Whipped Potatoes w/Gravy Steamed Carrots Dinner Roll w/margarine Chilled Fruit Cup
Alternate	Rice Krispies Banana Fruit Muffin Margarine	Alternate	Beef Vegetable Soup Roast Beef Sandwich w/Lettuce & Tomato Cake w/strawberry glaze	Alternate	Tomato Bisque Turkey Sandwich w/Lettuce and Tomato Coleslaw Chilled Fruit Cup
Beverages	Coffee Decaf Coffee Hot Tea Decaf Tea 2% Milk Skim Milk Orange Juice Apple Juice Grape Juice	Beverages	Coffee Decaf Coffee Iced Tea Hot Tea Decaf Tea 2% Milk Skim Milk	Beverages	Coffee Decaf Coffee Iced Tea Hot Tea Decaf Tea 2% Milk Skim Milk

Figure 3.8 Typical hospital selective menu for one day.

Restaurant-style Menu

Many hospitals have moved increasingly toward restaurant- or hotel-style service, sometimes called *room service*. Figure 3.9 shows a restaurant-style hospital menu where the patient sees choices for the entire one-week cycle, but a server reviews today's choices plus possible substitutes at the bedside and takes the order for meals. Figure 3.10 shows a hotel-style room-service menu, where the customer has a menu in his room and calls his order in for each meal. The same menu is available every day. Room service is a growing trend in healthcare foodservice; it is more akin to hotel room service, which is appealing, and it allows patients greater flexibility in eating what they want when they want. This approach reduces food waste that results when patients are served food at pre-specified times that are not necessarily when they want to or can eat.

When the state of a patient's health or another clinical factor drives the menu that can be offered, the baseline healthy diet is the foundation of a specialized variation that fills specific patient needs. The composition of a healthy diet is summarized in the USDA's **MyPlate** (Figure 3.11), which in 2011 replaced the longstanding reference known as the **Food Guide Pyramid**.

The original Food Guide Pyramid was produced in 1992 and served as a mainstay for almost two decades, depicting how foods fit together to provide an adequate diet. Since the science of nutrition is always changing based on current research, the Pyramid needs periodic revision. The new MyPlate, which was conceived as a crucial part of First Lady Michelle Obama's campaign against obesity, is intended to remind consumers about the basics of a healthful diet. Instead of emphasizing grains as the foundation of a diet, the USDA, among other points, emphasizes filling half the plate with fruits and vegetables and is clearer in suggesting that consumers reduce their intake of salt and sugary drinks. The website provides extensive information about how to apply the guide to individuals and groups of various ages and in various languages and ethnic food types.

Catering to YOU

breakfast

SUNDAY
- **Denver Style Scrambled Eggs** — Served with Strips of Bacon, Oatmeal and a Biscuit
- **Rice Krispies with Milk** — Served with a Peaches & Cream Parfait and a Blueberry Muffin

MONDAY
- **Orange Scented French Toast with Syrup** — Served with a Sausage Link and Grits
- **Homestyle Scrambled Eggs** — Served with Strips of Bacon, a Biscuit and Special K with Milk

TUESDAY
- **Homestyle Scrambled Eggs** — Served with Strips of Bacon, Cheese Grits and a Biscuit
- **Baked Zucchini & Tomato Frittata** — Served with Cheerios and Milk and a Blueberry Coffeecake Muffin

WEDNESDAY
- **Blueberry Pancakes with Syrup** — Served with Sausage Patty
- **Breakfast Casserole** — Served with Oatmeal and a Biscuit

THURSDAY
- **Homestyle Scrambled Eggs** — Served with O'Brien Potatoes, a Turkey Sausage Link and a Biscuit
- **French Toast with Syrup** — Served with Strips of Bacon and Oatmeal

FRIDAY
- **Ham and Cheese on Croissant** — Served with Breakfast Potatoes and a Chilled Fresh Fruit Cup
- **Bacon, Eggs & Cheese Burrito with Salsa** — Served with Oatmeal and a Chilled Fresh Fruit Cup

SATURDAY
- **Homestyle Scrambled Eggs** — Served with Strips of Bacon, Grits and a Biscuit
- **Cheerios with Milk** — Served with Cantaloupe and a Banana Muffin

lunch

Meals are served with a choice of dessert and a roll.

SUNDAY
- **Chicken Marsala** — Served with Rice Pilaf and Dill Carrots
- **Cottage Cheese and Fresh Fruit Plate** — Served with Chicken Noodle Soup and Banana Bread

MONDAY
- **Italian Style Meatloaf with Marinara Sauce** — Served with Red Skin Whipped Potatoes and Steamed Broccoli
- **Cobb Salad** — Served with Minestrone Soup

TUESDAY
- **Roast Pork Loin with Pineapple Salsa** — Served with Sweet Potatoes & Escalloped Apples and Green Bean Almondine
- **Grilled Chicken Caesar Wrap** — Served with Beef Vegetable Soup and a Garden Green Salad

WEDNESDAY
- **Braised Pot Roast of Beef with Gravy** — Served with Red Roasted Potatoes and Whole Baby Carrots
- **Turkey Club Wrap** — Served with Vegetable Soup and a Garden Green Salad

THURSDAY
- **Roast Turkey with Dressing and Gravy** — Served with Cut Green Beans
- **Tuna Salad on Wheat Bread** — Served with Tomato Bisque and Carrot & Raisin Salad

FRIDAY
- **Pasta with Peas & Shrimp** — Served with a Mixed Greens Salad
- **Turkey & Roasted Red Pepper Sandwich** — Served with Chicken & Rice Soup and a Garden Green Salad

SATURDAY
- **Rotisserie Turkey Breast** — Served with Mashed Sweet Potatoes and Seasoned Peas with Pearl Onions
- **Italian Hoagie Sandwich** — Served with Potato Soup

Some foods may be restricted due to your diet prescription

dinner

Meals are served with a choice of dessert and a roll.

SUNDAY
- **Stuffed Fish Florentine** — Served with Garlic Mashed Potatoes and Cut Green Beans
- **Charleston Chicken Wrap** — Served with Cheddar Corn Chowder and a Garden Green Salad

MONDAY
- **Oven Fried Chicken** — Served with Baked Macaroni & Cheese and Seasoned Mixed Greens
- **Bistro Sandwich** — Served with New England Clam Chowder and a Garden Green Salad

TUESDAY
- **Tilapia with Roasted Cherry Tomatoes** — Served with Yellow Rice and Broccoli Florets
- **Roast Beef & Cheddar Cheese Sandwich** — Served with Ham & Vegetable Soup and Creamy Coleslaw

WEDNESDAY
- **Stuffed Chicken Jennifer** — Served with Buttered Bowtie Pasta and Sugar Snap Peas
- **Chef Salad** — Served with Chicken Noodle Soup

THURSDAY
- **Asian Beef Pepper Steak over Steamed Rice** — Served with a Garden Green Salad
- **Crispy Fried Chicken over Salad** — Served with Cream of Broccoli Soup

FRIDAY
- **Honey Apple Roast Pork** — Served with Garlic Roasted Potatoes and a Medley of Corn, Red Pepper & Green Beans
- **Bacon, Lettuce & Tomato Sandwich** — Served with Beef Barley Soup

SATURDAY
- **Roast Sirloin Strip Steak** — Served with Potatoes Delmonico and Yellow Squash with Red Onions
- **Tuna Salad Wrap** — Served with Roasted Onion and Mushroom Soup and a Tomato & Cucumber Salad

Courtesy of Morrison.

Figure 3.9 Restaurant-style menu.

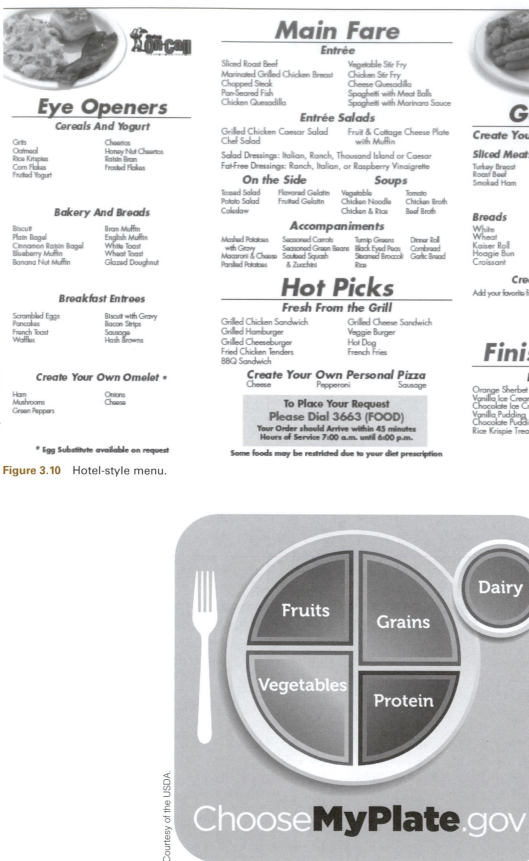

Courtesy of Morrison.

Figure 3.10   Hotel-style menu.

Courtesy of the USDA.

Figure 3.11   MyPlate.

Our bodies need food in order to obtain nutrients, so it is important to know which nutrients are necessary to be healthy and in which quantities. The definitive guide to daily nutrient needs is found in the **Recommended Daily Allowances** of the Food and Nutrition Board of the National Research Council of the National Academy of Sciences.[2]

That is a very long name, but the members of this highly sophisticated group of nutrition researchers review all pertinent research to determine how much of each major nutrient is necessary for healthy people. The resulting information provides the basics of nutritional needs for most hospital dietitians. It is revised as the science underlying it develops. It is used by registered dietitians and other professionals to compare the analyzed nutrient content of a meal. In this way it can be determined whether a diet is "adequate" or not.

Many hospitals today consider foodservice an attractive feature for prospective patients, and they are constantly looking for ways in which to make it a positive part of the patient experience. Writing in *Food Management* magazine,[3] Tom Monetti, Food Service Director at New York's Mt. Sinai Medical Center, commented: "Whether it's a sit-down black tie banquet for 1,000 at the Waldorf Astoria or daily lunches and dinners delivered bedside to 1,000 patients, the objective is the same: to produce quality food that meets the expectations of a diverse customer base and to deliver it in a small window of time."

In addition to variety, healthcare menus (and residential care menus, which will be discussed next) must include foods to fit many dietary restrictions. Example: If ham is the entrée choice, people on low-sodium (salt-restricted) diets would need a different item; if fried chicken is the entrée, people on calorie-controlled and low-fat diets would need an item that is not fried. Hospitals can find themselves having to offer 50 or more variations on the regular diet, but common sense and current practice often reduce this number to as few as five or six. Joyce Scott-Smith, MS, RD, LDN, is director of Food Service at the University of Pittsburgh Medical Center, Shadyside Campus. She has written extensively on the subject of liberalized diets. Smith notes: "The **patient-controlled liberalized diet program** (PCLDP) . . . respects the individual values and choices of patients and families."[4] This concept was clearly spelled out by the Academy of Nutrition and Dietetics in its 2002 Position Paper on liberalized diets.[5]

In concluding this lengthy discussion of healthcare menus, we must address the differences in long-term care menus found in residential care facilities and nursing homes. The major principle of menu planning for any residential care facility has long been that this was the major (or only) source of nutrition for the individuals living there. The menu became very important because residents were there not just for an evening out or even a short stay. Regulations centered on ensuring the nutritional welfare of these residents, particularly since many were also victims of ill health and often could not function independently. Such extended-care facilities were once obligated to serve a 30-day cycle menu that usually did not offer choices. The principle behind the 30-day cycle was to ensure variety while also providing adequate nutritional intake, meaning that variety is not only the spice of life but also the key to good nutrition. Unfortunately, regulations on these foodservice operations grew so cumbersome that the menus offered often were too difficult to change and residents became very dissatisfied and bored. Today, regulations allow for selection, as long as a facility can demonstrate that intake is carefully monitored and residents have a variety of foods from which to choose.

It is still common to find four-week cycle menus at residential care facilities, which are very similar to the cycle menu shown in Figure 3.7, but today such facilities' menus often incorporate some type of choice. As members of the baby boomer generation age and require residential care, they refuse to accept the idea that they cannot control their dining choices. Therefore, restaurant-style menus such as we have discussed are also being used in some residential care facilities. When a restaurant-style menu is used, the same level of care is expected by regulatory agencies regarding the provision of nutritional adequacy.

In addition to these mechanisms for regulating nutritional adequacy, the **Center for Medicare Services** *(CMS)* of the US Department of Health and Human Services publishes a highly detailed manual of "Operational Guidelines" for Residential Care. Such guidelines ensure that food is prepared in a palatable manner, meets all nutrient needs, follows all prescribed diets, and can be adjusted to the individual needs of the patient. There is also a set of regulations that cover the timing of meals. These regulations are quoted here because they have an impact on menu structure:

Frequency of Meals

1. Each resident receives and the facility provides at least three meals daily at regular times comparable to normal mealtimes in the community.

2. There must be no more than 14 hours between a substantial evening meal and breakfast the following day, except as in point 4.

3. The facility must offer snacks at bedtime daily.

4. When a nourishing snack is provided at bedtime, up to 16 hours may elapse between a substantial evening meal and breakfast the following day if a resident group agrees to this meal span, and a nourishing snack is served.[6]

Schools

Foodservice that is provided in schools at the elementary, middle, and high school levels is highly regulated in all areas of operation, but especially in menu development. The **National School Lunch Program** (NSLP) is a federally assisted meal program operating in public and nonprofit private schools and residential childcare institutions. It provides nutritionally balanced, low-cost or free lunches to children each school day. The program was established under the National School Lunch Act, signed by President Harry Truman in 1946.[7]

Today the program provides not only lunches but also in some cases breakfast, snacks, and a special milk program. Foods are provided at a specified cost, or at free or reduced cost. In 2007, the program provided lunches to over 30.5 million children each day. The **US Department of Agriculture** (USDA) Food and Nutrition Service administers the program at the federal level. At the state level, the National School Lunch Program is usually administered by state education agencies, which operate the program through agreements with school food authorities.

How does the National School Lunch Program work? Generally, public or nonprofit private schools at the high school level or lower and public or nonprofit private residential childcare institutions may participate in the school lunch program. School districts and independent schools that choose to take part in the lunch program get cash subsidies and donated commodities from the USDA for each meal they serve. In return, they must serve lunches that meet federal requirements, and they must offer free or reduced-price lunches to eligible children. School food authorities can also be reimbursed for snacks served to children through age 18 in afterschool educational or enrichment programs.

What are the nutritional requirements for school lunches? School lunches must meet the applicable recommendations of the 1995 Dietary Guidelines for Americans, which recommend that no more than 30 percent of an individual's calories come from fat, with less than 10 percent coming from saturated fat. Regulations also establish a standard for school lunches to provide one-third of the Recommended Dietary Allowances of protein, Vitamin A, Vitamin C, iron, calcium, and calories. School lunches must meet federal nutrition requirements, but local school food authorities decide what specific foods to serve and how they are to be prepared.[8]

The regulations section of the USDA website explains a flexible option that has greatly improved the program for foodservice directors and students. **Offer versus serve** or *OVS* is a concept that applies to menu planning and allows a wider range of lunches to be considered reimbursable under NSLP guidelines. *OVS* allows students to decline some of the foods offered in a school lunch or school breakfast and is applicable to all menu-planning approaches. The goals of OVS are to reduce food waste in school meals programs and to permit students to select the foods they prefer. Schools must implement OVS in high schools, and local school authorities can choose to implement OVS in elementary and middle schools.[9]

The MyPlate guide (Figure 3.11) and its accompanying guidelines (which have replaced the Food Guide Pyramid) are the basis for menu planning for the NSLP. When the program began, the emphasis was jointly on providing meals to school children *and* utilizing surplus agricultural commodities. Thus NSLP menus in the past had guidelines for specific amounts of butter, raisins, peanut butter, and processed cheese (among other commodities) that had to be served daily. Today's guidelines are solidly based in the latest nutrition guidelines, and often emphasize local produce purchases as well. While school foodservice is still very highly regulated, it now allows for several reimbursable variations. The complicated regulations are best reviewed in detail on the NSLP website, but general information is outlined in Figure 3.12.

	3 MENU-ITEM MEAL	4 MENU-ITEM MEAL	5 MENU-ITEM MEAL
Entrée:	**Choose 1:** Baked Fish Nuggets with Macaroni & Cheese and Garlic Bread Sausage Pizza with Broccoli Spears Vegetarian Chili with pinto Beans & Bread Sticks	**Choose 1:** Baked Fish Nuggets with Garlic Bread Sausage Pizza Vegetarian Chili with Bread Sticks	**Choose:1** Baked Fish Nuggets Sausage Pizza Vegetarian Chili
Side Dishes	**Group 1: Choose1** Orange Slices & Brownie Garden Salad with Dressing & Grapes Coleslaw & Raisin Cup	**Group 1: Choose1** Broccoli Spears Cole slaw Pinto Beans Garden Salad with Dressing Grapes Orange Slices **Group 2: Choose1** Macaroni & Cheese Banana half Raisin Cup Brownie	**Group 1: Choose1** Broccoli Spears Cole Slaw Pinto Beans Garden Salad with Dressing Grapes Orange Slices **Group 2: Choose1** Garlic Bread Bread Stick Macaroni & Cheese Brownie Banana half Raisin Cup
Milk	**Choose 1:** Fat-free Milk Low-fat Milk	**Choose 1:** Fat-free Milk Low-fat Milk	**Choose 1:** Fat-free Milk Low-fat Milk
Number of Menu items Required for OVS:	This is a 3 menu-item meal. Students must select a minimum of two items.	This is a 4 menu-item meal. Students must select a minimum of two items.	This is a 5 menu-item meal. Students must select a minimum of three items.

Figure 3.12 Variations in lunch structure for nutrient-based menu-planning approaches.

Courtesy Washington State University Dining Services.

Figure 3.13   Campus dining venue A.

In summary, menu planning in any environment that is regulated by government program guidelines or law will be complicated. The menu planner or foodservice director should carefully study the regulations; considerable guidance is available on the appropriate government websites. These regulations usually address nutritional adequacy as the primary consideration; however, additional regulations can and will emphasize serving times, preparation methods, cost, and purchasing guidelines.

Colleges and Universities

Since college students are adults, foodservice operations and the menus in higher education environments are not regulated beyond applying the same standards that apply to restaurant foodservice. Individual universities may have strong philosophies regarding how their foodservice operations should be managed, parents who pay the bills may have strong feelings about the cost and availability of foodservice for their children, and students themselves will have their own

Courtesy Washington State University Dining Services.

Figure 3.14   Campus dining venue B.

preferences. The task in the university setting is to satisfy all of these preferences while providing good nutrition, effective cost control, and high levels of flexibility and originality in terms of menu planning and scheduling. See Figures 3.13 and 3.14.

The **National Association of College & University Food Service** (NACUFS) is composed of member foodservice operations. The NACUFS website contains the Council for the Advancement of Standards for Higher Education (CAS) Standards and Guidelines for College and University Food Service. This set of standards is quite lengthy, but the philosophy they embody is best described by reference to the mission of such operations:[10]

■   A dining environment that encourages both individual and community development

■   Engagement of students in learning about sound nutrition practices

■   Safe and secure facilities that are clean, attractive, well maintained, and comfortable

■ Management services that ensure the orderly and effective administration and operation of all aspects of the program

■ Reasonably priced, quality, safe, diverse, and nutritious food offerings

Such a mission describes the basics of foodservice in a higher education environment. This is, however, only the beginning when it comes to achieving the mission. College foodservice menus must acknowledge the needs of students to have some level of foodservice available at almost any time of the day—and night. It must acknowledge that many of today's students are vegetarians—it no longer suffices simply to point out the yogurt or salad bar or the daily macaroni and cheese. Nutritious and creative meatless items must be available for those who prefer to eat no animal products at all (**vegans**), those who eat dairy products (**lacto-ovo vegetarians**), and those who eat all foods except meat and poultry (some vegetarians eat fish, others do not). No matter what type of vegetarian diet one may follow, every foodservice facility must offer options for those who choose to eat this way.

> It is the position of the Academy of Nutrition and Dietetics that appropriately planned vegetarian diets, including total vegetarian or vegan diets, are healthful, nutritionally adequate, and may provide health benefits in the prevention and treatment of certain diseases. Well-planned vegetarian diets are appropriate for individuals during all stages of the life cycle, including pregnancy, lactation, infancy, childhood, and adolescence, and for athletes. A vegetarian diet is defined as one that does not include meat (including fowl) or seafood, or products containing those foods.[11]

Researchers, dietitians, and chefs have contributed the following convenient Vegetarian Pyramid (Figure 3.15) to help individuals who follow this pattern of eating to meet all their nutritional needs.[12]

Vegetarian preferences are not the only dietary restrictions university foodservice operators must consider in developing their menus. For example, some students today prefer or require a gluten-free diet. Others avoid dairy products. Thus, the menu planner and university foodservice director must consider some of the same issues that challenge the healthcare foodservice director: allergies and dietary modifications to accommodate food intolerances, diabetes, and even renal disorders. While university dining facilities need not plan specific menus for these situations, foods that meet the dietary needs of such students must be available. The special dietary needs of students are usually in a student's file; the importance in such cases of flexibility and responsiveness on the part of the foodservice director cannot be overemphasized.

Menus in university foodservice operations today must also reflect environmental and sustainability issues. This trend was reflected in a panel presentation at the 2008 National Restaurant Association Show in Chicago.[13] Several university foodservice directors acknowledged a range of eco-friendly practices, including the following:

■ Using the Monterey Bay Aquarium's Seafood Watch list (www.montereybayaquarium.org/cr/seafoodwatch.aspx) when deciding which fish to buy; avoiding anything on the "endangered list" by purchasing farm-raised fish such as tilapia or wild-caught salmon (Yale University)

■ Harvesting food from "certified organic gardens" run by staff and students to "raise awareness of sustainability" (Bowdoin College)

■ Using a state's department of agriculture to find local producers (University of Oklahoma)

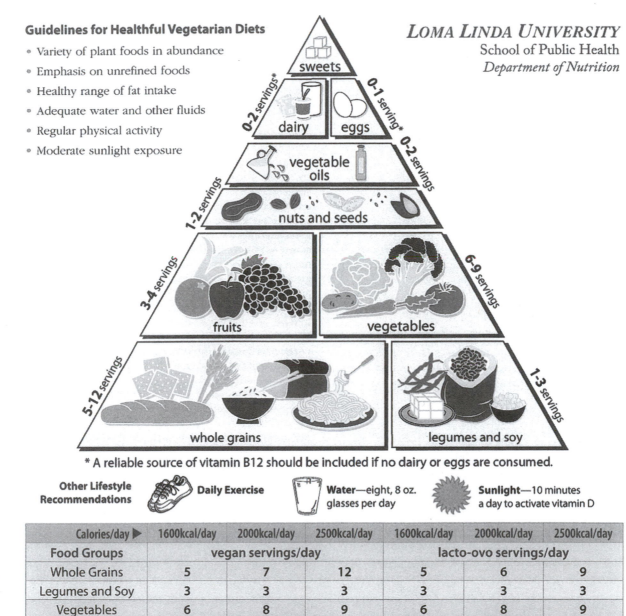

The Vegetarian Food Pyramid

Guidelines for Healthful Vegetarian Diets

- Variety of plant foods in abundance
- Emphasis on unrefined foods
- Healthy range of fat intake
- Adequate water and other fluids
- Regular physical activity
- Moderate sunlight exposure

LOMA LINDA UNIVERSITY
School of Public Health
Department of Nutrition

sweets

0-2 servings* dairy   eggs   0-1 serving*   0-2 servings

vegetable oils   1-2 servings

nuts and seeds

3-4 servings   fruits   vegetables   6-9 servings

5-12 servings   whole grains   legumes and soy   1-3 servings

* A reliable source of vitamin B12 should be included if no dairy or eggs are consumed.

Other Lifestyle Recommendations   **Daily Exercise**   **Water**—eight, 8 oz. glasses per day   **Sunlight**—10 minutes a day to activate vitamin D

Calories/day ▶	1600kcal/day	2000kcal/day	2500kcal/day	1600kcal/day	2000kcal/day	2500kcal/day
Food Groups	vegan servings/day			lacto-ovo servings/day		
Whole Grains	5	7	12	5	6	9
Legumes and Soy	3	3	3	3	3	3
Vegetables	6	8	9	6	8	9
Fruits	3	4	4	3	4	4
Nuts and Seeds	2	2	2	1	1	2
Vegetable Oils	1	2	2	1	2	2
Dairy Products	0	0	0	2	2	2
Eggs	0	0	0	1/2 egg	1/2 egg	1/2 egg
Sweets	Optional					

Figure 3.15   Vegetarian pyramid.

Sustainability as it applies to menu development will be discussed in greater detail at the end of this chapter and in later chapters as it applies to various other aspects of the foodservice operation.

Today's students have learned to enjoy a wide variety of menu items. To please the eclectic and flavor-of-the-month tastes of today's college students, popular ethnic dishes as well as regional specialties from across the country and the world should be offered to reflect the ethnic backgrounds or predilections of the student population. And while many students still desire classic "fast food menu items," there is a strong emphasis on health and fitness. Thus low-calorie, organic, and fresh foods are in high demand.

Earlier in this chapter, menu development was discussed from the point of view of one organization: one restaurant, one hospital, one high school, and so on. University foodservice differs significantly from these operations both in its typical hours of operation and in the many styles and types of food and foodservice options that must be available.

Business and Industry

Not all workplaces are conveniently located near eating establishments, nor do most workers have the time to enjoy a leisurely meal, including the travel necessary to obtain it. Historically, these challenges brought food vendors to the gates of factories, providing simple food for purchase. Over time, large companies began to offer onsite foodservice to employees, providing a benefit to employees while also helping to control time spent traveling to and from lunch.

As in the case of college and university dining, the customers of workplace foodservice operations are adults, expecting some kind of restaurant-style foodservice. The difference is that usually only one meal a day is offered—lunch. In certain manufacturing and healthcare settings, however, the onsite foodservice operation may need to accommodate at least three meal periods or sometimes remain available on a 24-hour basis. The most common format for many years was the cafeteria-style operation, and this format remains in place in many facilities today. The menu in such a case is dictated by customer preferences for both pricing and menu items; pricing might or might not reflect subsidization by the company. Beyond that basic framework, the workplace philosophy of the individual company comes into play. When a large company decides to offer onsite dining to its employees, it may also want to consider sustainability and healthy lifestyle issues, and ensure that nutritionally sound choices are available.

In recent years a more interesting trend has developed in B&I foodservice. Rick Post, CEO of the Compass Group, North America, recently discussed developments in workplace dining with John Law of *Food Management* magazine.[14] He noted that many operations have employees who increasingly bring food back to their desks or work areas. This seems to call for a new foodservice model instead of the traditional cafeteria style operation.

One solution is to provide a kiosk-style, walk-up-and-order operation with a limited menu—such operations can be installed in multiple locations in a large workplace and offer take-out foods and take-home dinners. This kiosk concept is also being used in other settings, such as healthcare and university foodservice operations. Its roots are in fast food, but typically the menu offerings are pre-prepared and packaged to go, and often feature salads and sandwiches or chilled or frozen items to take home and reheat.

Once again, the decentralization of foodservice operations has brought onsite menus closer in concept to those found in fast-food or fast-casual restaurants, and this influence can be seen throughout the onsite foodservice industry, including sports and entertainment.

Sports and Entertainment

The amazing evolution of foodservice and menu development we have noted previously applies to the sports and entertainment segment, too. Originally, menus in ballparks were simple: beer and hot dogs. Today, menu planning is key because customers' expectations demand a broad range of choices whether the setting is a marina cafe in a national park or a kiosk in a stadium.

Although sports and entertainment foodservice facilities are subject to the same regulatory restrictions as all restaurants are, limited space and equipment present unique challenges. Moreover, the use of these facilities, particularly in stadiums, is limited. This means that menu items should not require elaborate or expensive equipment; the product flow for menu items must also be short.

One other critical issue in this segment is pricing. And while we discuss the various pricing strategies in a separate chapter, we mention it here because in this segment we have a very unique feature that applies to menu planning, and that is the amount of money that goes to the sports team involved with the specific venue. Many people complain that prices at stadiums are inflated simply because the operator knows the customer has no other alternative. (The lack of alternatives is particularly relevant today as most stadiums and ballparks prohibit fans from bringing bottles and coolers into the facilities.) In reality, however, operators must charge the seemingly outrageous prices because in many cases as much as 50 percent of the menu item price goes to the team or stadium management—not the foodservice provider.

Operators planning menus for sports and entertainment foodservice facilities must therefore identify items that create value in virtue of unique attributes or exceptional quality because the customers know the food will be expensive. This explains why items such as foot-long hot dogs were developed by menu planners—they were unique, enabling customers to rationalize paying a high price. While foot-long hot dogs are no long considered unique, the pizza with smoked duck breast or tenderloin sushi found at leading stadiums push the boundaries.

Correctional Facilities

While standard menus are not typically found in correctional facilities, foodservice operators in this segment must nevertheless plan meals thoughtfully. Moreover, in some instances food selections *are* posted for inmates. In either case, a process that is similar to menu planning and execution for schools must also be carried out in correctional facilities.

Originally, there were no guidelines regarding correctional foodservice. However, the bloody 1971 Attica Prison riot in New York, which was fueled largely by inmates' dissatisfaction with the food, changed all that. In 1977, the American Correctional Association developed standards for foodservice in correctional facilities. These standards include nutritional guidelines as well as quality and portion control.

▪▫ THE ART OF MENU DEVELOPMENT

We have discussed several aspects of the incorporation of aesthetic and cultural influences on menu planning and design, as well as the use of menus to communicate such factors to the customer. This section adds a few more of these less measurable concepts in menu development.

As a chef begins to plan a menu using the principles described in this chapter, she can clearly locate and use any of the factors listed. The "art" of menu planning is expressed through psychology, communication, aesthetics, and cultural influences to make the final decisions about a menu. All these factors must be woven together; they cannot be clearly measured or checked off on a list, and they apply to all foodservice segments. We discuss several psychological factors that influence menu planning in Chapter 5.

Some establishments have emphasized comfort foods on their menus, or have added items consistent with this aesthetic when the weather is cold. Some have argued that these items become more popular when the economy is in difficulty. Such issues are not always clear-cut, however, since everyone has his own list of favorites that serve as comfort foods. In North America, however, one can be sure that meat loaf and fried chicken will be popular in most places, while turnip greens and grits had better be on most menus in the South, in some form. But those comforting, huge pastrami sandwiches in New York delis will probably be not seen as "comforting" in Texas ranch country.

The art of menu development is also largely shaped by the foodservice operation's target market. For example, if the intent is to attract customers who are looking for healthy cuisine, the menu might include nutritional information. If the theme centers on a wine bar, then wine pairings should be included in the menu item descriptions. Again, we discuss menu psychology at length in Chapter 5 but the point here is that each foodservice concept and the market it serves will require unique menu aspects.

Finally, the adoption of new and old technologies must be addressed in menu development. In an era when customers pay for their Starbuck's coffee by using their smartphones and students order pizza on campus from their computers, foodservice operators must also embrace technology to exceed their guests' expectations. In some settings, online menus are used more often than in-house menus are. For example, Domino's pizza generates a growing percentage of sales through it online ordering system. Thus, we cannot offer a prescriptive method where font, design and layout, and color scheme can be specified. As we've demonstrated, the design must match the theme, which is different for every concept in every segment.

SUSTAINABILITY IN MENU PLANNING

We address sustainability as well as corporate responsibility where it is relevant throughout this book. For menu planning and development, sustainability means including ingredients and menu items that are procured from renewable sources. According to the website of the Division for Sustainable Development of the United Nations Department of Economic and Social Affairs, the goal of such an approach should be to "meet the needs of the present without compromising the ability of future generations to meet their own needs."[15] In a discussion of sustainability in large foodservice operations, a researcher interviewed several registered dietitians who are foodservice directors and who are considered pioneers in adopting sustainability in their foodservice operations.[16] These individuals have led their organizations to adopt a more eco-friendly approach by following a few basic steps:

■ Buy local when possible; buy items produced within a radius of a few hundred miles of your operation (of course, one will still have to keep the price competitive, although in a profit-making organization such as a restaurant, customers may choose to pay more for locally grown products).

■ Buy organic when it comes from a trusted source and the price is competitive.

■ Keep in close communication with suppliers to insure safety, reliability, and compliance with transportation goals.

■ Use products in season—this practice often provides a favorable price from local vendors or producers.

■ Use terminology such as "seasonal vegetables" or "seasonal fruits" on the menu to indicate the use of what is immediately fresh and available.

■ Be careful when using small suppliers that might not be inspected by local authorities. In some cases, visit these providers to ensure that correct practices, safe water sources, and safe handling practices are being used.

The related concept of **food miles** has been used to describe the distance that food has to travel before purchase by the end customer. One measure of food miles is the distance from farm to fork, or where the item is harvested to where it is consumed. Considering food miles in selecting menu-item ingredients also encourages the use of local ingredients, which can ensure freshness, purity, taste, community cohesion, and preservation.

In an August 7, 2007, article in the *New York Times*, James McWilliams noted that considering food miles is not always a simple matter:

> Scientists at Lincoln University in New Zealand have expanded their equations (for food miles) to include . . . water use, harvesting techniques, fertilizer outlays, renewable energy applications, means of transport, the kind of fuel used, the amount of carbon dioxide absorbed during photosynthesis, disposal of packaging, storage procedures and other inputs. They found that lamb raised on New Zealand's clover-choked pastures and shipped 11,000 miles by boat to Britain produced 1520 pounds of emissions per ton, while British grown lamb produced 7280 pounds of carbon dioxide per ton, in part due to poorer pastures . . . in other words, it is four times more efficient for Londoners to buy New Zealand lamb.[17]

What Does This Mean?

Shawn wants to be sure that his nursing home foodservice is using "environmentally sound" practices. He and his employees plant a small organic garden and the residents who can do so enjoy working in the garden. Shawn carefully integrates the produce into his menu. This is an excellent practice and everyone wins. Shawn then decides to purchase beef from a local farmer. But because Shawn's operation is in a large metropolitan area, he must travel frequently to the ranch, which is 250 miles away, to ensure proper practices that meet his green requirements, and he must then go to the packing company to select his meat and the packing company is another 150 miles away. The small packer must then travel in a smaller truck to Shawn's operation several times per week. The travel that Shawn and the small packer's truck must undertake to accomplish this green practice results in a larger **carbon footprint** (greenhouse gas emissions caused by an organization, event, product, or person) than receiving a shipment from a large truck that was making fewer trips would. This does not mean that Shawn cannot find a more environmentally friendly source of beef—he simply must consider more than just the "appearance of eco-friendliness."

One of the best guidelines for sustainability is the Monterey Bay Aquarium's Seafood Watch Guide. It clearly helps the consumer and foodservice operator identify which seafood choices are "sustainable" and which are not (Figure 3.16).

To use your pocket guide: 1. Cut along outer black line
2. Fold on grey lines

Monterey Bay Aquarium® Seafood Watch | The Monterey Bay Aquarium Seafood Watch program creates science-based recommendations that help consumers and businesses make ocean-friendly seafood choices. Carry this pocket guide with you and share it with others to help spread the word.

BEST CHOICES

Arctic Char (farmed)
Barramundi (US farmed)
Catfish (US farmed)
Clams (farmed)
Cobia (US farmed)
Cod: Pacific (US non-trawled)
Crab: Dungeness, Stone
Halibut: Pacific (US)
Lobster: California Spiny (US)
Mussels (farmed)
Oysters (farmed)
Sablefish/Black Cod (Alaska & Canada)
Salmon (Alaska wild)
Sardines: Pacific (US)
Scallops (farmed)
Shrimp: Pink (OR)
Striped Bass (farmed & wild*)
Tilapia (US farmed)
Trout: Rainbow (US farmed)
Tuna: Albacore (Canada & US Pacific, troll/pole)
Tuna: Skipjack, Yellowfin (US troll/pole)

GOOD ALTERNATIVES

Basa/Pangasius/Swai (farmed)
Caviar, Sturgeon (US farmed)
Clams (wild)
Cod: Atlantic (imported)
Cod: Pacific (US trawled)
Crab: Blue*, King (US), Snow
Flounders, Soles (Pacific)
Flounder: Summer (US Atlantic)*
Grouper: Black, Red (US Gulf of Mexico)*
Herring: Atlantic
Lobster: American/Maine
Mahi Mahi (US)
Oysters (wild)
Pollock: Alaska (US)
Sablefish/Black Cod (CA, OR, WA)
Salmon (CA, OR, WA*, wild)
Scallops (wild)
Shrimp (US, Canada)
Squid
Swordfish (US)*
Tilapia (Central & South America (farmed)
Tuna: Bigeye, Tongol, Yellowfin (troll/pole)

AVOID

Caviar, Sturgeon* (imported wild)
Chilean Seabass/Toothfish*
Cobia (imported farmed)
Cod: Atlantic (Canada & US)
Crab: King (imported)
Flounders, Halibut, Soles (US Atlantic, except Summer Flounder)
Groupers (US Atlantic)*
Lobster: Spiny (Brazil)
Mahi Mahi (imported longline)
Marlin: Blue, Striped (Pacific)*
Monkfish
Orange Roughy*
Salmon (farmed, including Atlantic)*
Sharks* & Skates
Shrimp (imported)
Snapper: Red (US Gulf of Mexico)
Swordfish (imported)*
Tilapia (Asia farmed)
Tuna: Albacore*, Bigeye*, Skipjack, Tongol, Yellowfin* (except troll/pole)
Tuna: Bluefin*
Tuna: Canned (except troll/pole)

Support Ocean-Friendly Seafood

Best Choices are abundant, well-managed and caught or farmed in environmentally friendly ways.

Good Alternatives are an option, but there are concerns with how they're caught or farmed—or with the health of their habitat due to other human impacts.

Avoid for now as these items are overfished or caught or farmed in ways that harm other marine life or the environment.

Key
CA = California   OR = Oregon
WA = Washington
* Limit consumption due to concerns about mercury or other contaminants.
Visit www.edf.org/seafoodhealth
Contaminant information provided by:
ENVIRONMENTAL DEFENSE FUND

Seafood may appear in more than one column

Why Do Your Seafood Choices Matter?

Worldwide, the demand for seafood is increasing. Yet many populations of the large fish we enjoy eating are over-fished and, in the U.S., we import over 80% of our seafood to meet the demand. Destructive fishing and fish farming practices only add to the problem.

By purchasing fish caught or farmed using environmentally friendly practices, you're supporting healthy, abundant oceans.

You Can Make A Difference

Support ocean-friendly seafood in three easy steps:

1. Purchase seafood from the green list or, if unavailable, the yellow list. Or look for the Marine Stewardship Council blue eco-label in stores and restaurants.

2. When you buy seafood, ask where your seafood comes from and whether it was farmed or wild-caught.

3. Tell your friends about Seafood Watch. The more people that ask for ocean-friendly seafood, the better!

Learn More

In addition to the recommendations on this guide, we have hundreds more available from our scientists.

To see the complete and most up-to-date list visit us:
• Online at **seafoodwatch.org**
• On our free app
• On our mobile site
• Or join us on Facebook or Twitter

MONTEREY BAY AQUARIUM

Seafood WATCH®

MONTEREY BAY AQUARIUM

YELLOWFIN TUNA

National Sustainable Seafood Guide January 2012

MONTEREY BAY AQUARIUM®

Figure 3.16 Monterey Bay Aquarium Seafood Watch Guide.

One researcher summarized the complexity of issues surrounding sustainability as follows: "Whether you believe that organic and sustainable foods are good, bad, or neutral, the fact remains that the trend is here to stay and that culinary professionals, registered dietitians, and the entire food industry must become familiar with these concepts and trends. There are many ways to connect to local communities . . . food co-ops, community cooking groups using whole foods and farmers markets all offer opportunities to connect to those who want to promote healthy, enjoyable foods."[18]

MANAGERIAL IMPLICATIONS

A foodservice operation's menu, regardless of the industry segment, communicates the philosophy and represents the source for all other operational decisions such as décor, staffing, pricing, and marketing. In planning and developing a menu, a chef or manager must anticipate changes that may make alterations to the menu necessary. Such changes may be caused by competitors, trends, or economic conditions.

Menu policy is dictated largely by the respective industry segment. In a QSR, for example, the menu is the focal point for customers and its items designed for quick, efficient preparation. In family/midscale restaurants through fine dining restaurants, the structure of the menu is more systematized and is separated by categories such as appetizers, soups and salads, and entrees. Also in these segments, menu items can be adapted using a variety of ethnic ingredients and preparation styles.

In onsite foodservice, menu planning and development have evolved such that menus are very similar or the same as in traditional restaurants. Still, the unique nature of the onsite sector requires extra steps in the menu-planning process. For example, in healthcare the menu planner must design menus or modify menu items to suit the various dietary restrictions and delivery styles. This is also true in long-term care settings. In schools, foodservice is highly regulated and thus the menu must be planned carefully to assure adherence. Participation in the National School Lunch Program also adds a level of care and complexity to menu planning. In colleges and universities, the regulatory issues are replaced by the need to plan menus that provide good nutrition, allow for effective cost control, and offer high levels of flexibility and originality. Also, accommodation must be made for a range of diet preferences and restrictions including vegetarian diets. In business and industry, menus must be developed that reflect local preferences but that also entice the organization's employees to dine in house versus buying food elsewhere. This may include offering food that employees can take back to their desks to eat. Finally, in sport and recreation, menu planning must be performed to meet customers' increasing expectations and offer unique attributes that can offset the perception of unnecessarily high prices.

The art of menu planning is achieved by using psychology, aesthetics, and cultural influences. It means using the menu to communicate the foodservice operation's philosophy. Menu planning also requires attention to sustainability. Designing menu items that use local, organic, responsibly grown or raised, and seasonal ingredients is important and represents a growing trend.

Seasons 52

Seasons 52 is a small, regional restaurant group operated by Darden Restaurants. Originally confined to Florida and Atlanta, it is gradually branching out to other parts of the country. It features the follows:

- Seasonally inspired dining choices expertly designed to excite and surprise the palate
- An award-winning international wine list featuring diverse wines that personalize the dining experience

- Knowledgeable, approachable service that inspires confidence
- A casually sophisticated adult ambiance that feels inviting
- Extensive menu information and detailed nutritional analysis on its website

Courtesy of Darden Concepts, Inc.

KEY TERMS

à la carte   42

prix fixe   42

2010 Patient Protection and
Affordable Care Act   43

fusion cuisine   50

special or modified menu   51

selective-cycle menu   52

restaurant-style menu   52

room service   52

cycle menu   52

nonselective   52

MyPlate   54

Food Guide Pyramid   54

Recommended Daily Allowances   57

patient-controlled liberalized diet
program   57

Center for Medicare Services   57

National School Lunch Program   58

US Department of Agriculture   58

offer versus serve   59

National Association of College &
University Food Service   61

vegan   62

lacto-ovo vegetarian   62

food miles   67

carbon footprint   67

■■■■■■□ Case in Point ■■

The Handwritten Menu

This chapter has looked at the menu as a management tool. The menu is, however, also a marketing tool for any foodservice operation. There is a small chef-owned restaurant in a coastal town in the Northeast. At this small restaurant, the chef shops every morning at the docks for fresh fish and at local markets for produce and other items. He then handwrites four or five menu items on a plain piece of paper. He will do this ten times—there is no copy machine or typed menu. The server brings one of the handwritten pieces of paper to the table—since there are few copies, diners have to make their choices quickly so the menu can be passed on to others. There are no additions or substitutions allowed by the chef, and the menu is rather messy and hard to read. Despite the chef's rather unusual personality, the locals flock to the door at dinner. Oh yes, the phenomenal view of the ocean probably attracts them as well!

How does this chef follow or ignore the principles of menu planning outlined in this chapter? What unusual factors can you identify in this scenario that could account for his success? Would you suggest that this chef/owner change his menu style or philosophy? If so, why? If not, why not?

REVIEW AND DISCUSSION QUESTIONS

1. Are traditional restaurant menus and menus found in onsite operations more or less similar to what they were decades earlier? Explain your answer fully.

2. Briefly explain the differences as they apply to the menu among the various foodservice segments. Be sure to include the segments of onsite foodservice.

3. For full-service restaurants, what is the typical categorization of menu items?

4. Using your preferred search engine, find an ingredient that is now being used that has not been found previously in domestic restaurants.

5. Why has hospital food had such a negative reputation? What are today's foodservice operators doing to change this?

6. Name and describe two menu styles found in healthcare settings.

7. What prompted the National School Lunch Program, and when did it begin?

8. What are the nutritional requirements of school lunches?

9. What are three important issues that a foodservice operation should address in planning a menu for a university foodservice program?

10. Why are menu-item prices in stadiums so high compared to those paid in other settings?

11. What is the most unusual food item you've eaten in a sports and recreation setting? Where were you?

12. What are three steps a foodservice manager might take to make her restaurant more eco-friendly?

13. What are food miles, and why is this concept important?

14. Look at the Monterey Bay Aquarium's website and use the link to the most recently updated Seafood Watch Guide. Name three items that represent good choices and three that you should avoid.

ENDNOTES

1. Coomes, S. "Restaurant Design: Fast-Casual Look Attracts Customers." *Fast Casual* (August 18, 2008).

2. National Research Council, *Recommended Dietary Allowances*, 10th ed. Washington, DC: National Academy Press, 1989.

3. Monetti, T. "From Caviar to Comfort." *All Business*, www.allbusiness.com. Accessed July 18, 2008.

4. Horace, L. "A bold step: Liberalized Patient Diets, an Interview with Joyce Scott Smith." *Market-Link* (a newsletter of the Food Service Management Dietetic Practice Group of the Academy of Nutrition and Dietetics) (Fall 2006).

5. Academy of Nutrition and Dietetics. "Position Paper: Liberalized Diets for Older Adults in Long-Term Care." *Journal of the Academy of Nutrition and Dietetics* 102 (2002): 1316–1323.

6. "State Operations Manual, Appendix PP—Guidance to Surveyors for Long Term Care Facilities." www.cms.hhs.gov/manuals/downloads/som107ap_pp_guidelines_ltcf.pdf.

7. USDA. "National School Lunch Program." www.fns.usda.gov/cnd/Lunch. Accessed September 10, 2012.

8. Ibid.

9. USDA. "School Meals." www.fns.usda.gov/cnd/Governance/regulations.htm. Accessed September 10, 2012.

10. National Association of College and University Food Services. www.NACUFS.org. Accessed September 10, 2012.

11. Academy of Nutrition and Dietetics. "Position of the Academy of Nutrition and Dietetics: Vegetarian Diets." *Journal of the Academy of Nutrition and Dietetics*, 109 (2009): 1266–1282.

12. Messina, V., V. Melina, and A. Reed-Mangels. "A New Food Guide for North American Vegetarians." Revue Canadienne de la practique et de la recherché en dietetique, 64 (2003): 82–86.

13. Walkup, C. "College Foodservice: Learning to Live Green." *Nation's Restaurant News* (June 30, 2008).

14. Lawn, J. "Viewpoint Interview: A Conversation with Compass Group's Rick Post." www.food-management.com. Accessed August 13, 2008.

15. Division of Sustainable Development. United Nations Department of Economical and Social Affairs. www.un.org/esa/dsd/index.shtml. Accessed September 2012.

16. Mills, L. "From Local Chow to Green Machines." *ADA Times* (January/February 2008).

17. McWilliams, J. E. "Food That Travels Well." *The New York Times* (August 6, 2007).

18. Barkley, W. "Organics and Sustainable Foods." *Market-Link* (a newsletter of the Food Service Management Dietetic Practice Group of the Academy of Nutrition and Dietetics) (Summer 2007).

CHAPTER 4

RECIPE STANDARDIZATION, COSTING, AND ANALYSIS

LEARNING OBJECTIVES:

After becoming familiar with this chapter, you should be able to:

1. Understand and appreciate the importance of recipe standardization.

2. Explain the basic methods for recipe standardization.

3. Explain the methods used to calculate a recipe's cost.

4. Appreciate the purpose and use of recipe analysis.

5. Identify what issues are involved in accurately costing recipes.

6. Understand the role of computer software in all of these processes.

The correct costing of a recipe underlies the subsequent process of menu pricing since cost must be known in order to proceed with pricing structure. In fact, both steps are key to financial success. But before cost calculations, it is important to discuss recipe standardization and the major information necessary to develop a standardized recipe, which is how we begin this chapter.

■□ RECIPE STANDARDIZATION
□■

Definition

Most people have heard the same story from a mother, sister, brother, or uncle. It goes something like this. "When I was a kid, Grandma made the most perfect gingerbread I ever tasted. When I became a dietetic student, I asked her where she got the recipe. She said it was not from a cookbook—she got it from her mother. I asked her to write it down for me and she said she couldn't—you just had to learn how to do it right. So I watched her make it and carefully wrote everything down. A few weeks later I decided to make some of my own. To this day, I can't make that gingerbread!!!"

This story could be about anything—pie crust, rye bread, noodle pudding, or cracklin' cornbread. The art and science that is applied to menu development, discussed in Chapter 3, is not unlike the art and science of cooking—but cooking involves actual chemistry with the added fun of artistic expression. Unfortunately, some see this as a conflict, but it need not be. Many years ago, a recipe was called a *formula,* a term borrowed from the chemistry lab because cooking involves a series of chemical reactions. A correct formula should produce the same "reaction" every time, if followed exactly, in the same sequence, with the same ingredients. After all, food consists of compounds composed of many, many chemicals. There is not just one possible reaction to a combination of these variables . . . there are many. Try moving from Denver, Colorado, and its altitude to Tampa, Florida, and see if your bread recipe makes the same loaf. The noodle maker in a small room in Hong Kong will have difficulty producing the same product in St. Louis, Missouri.

Yet everyone knows that recipes can be standardized to produce uniform products, because a burger at a famous national chain in Maine will taste the same as one at the same chain in Utah. All large foodservice operations must rely on what are known as **standardized recipes**, and most others utilize the principle in some way. Without "standardization" a manager cannot determine what foods to purchase to produce a given recipe, she cannot determine how long it will take to produce the item, nor can she be sure that it will be correctly prepared. There is no consistency without standardization. That may sound uncreative, but it's really the key to customer satisfaction. Grandmother's gingerbread was always perfect and tasty, a comforting and satisfying holiday treat. Everyone has the same expectation for the meatloaf at his favorite diner or the BIG BAD BURGER at his favorite chain. A customer may be happy to experiment with the chef's special in his favorite restaurant, but the orange glazed chicken that is always on the menu had better taste the same each time he orders it.

Recipe standardization provides this consistency. Simply stated, a recipe is a list of ingredients and a set of instructions about what to do with them. A standardized recipe is more than a recipe. A standardized recipe has been tested in the facility where it will be used and it does not count as "standardized" until a consistent product and a standard amount of product are produced every time the recipe is used. To achieve this level of consistency, more is needed than a list of ingredients and amounts. Alton Brown, host of the Food Network's *Good Eats* program, provides a great listing of what should be included in a standardized recipe:[1]

- Food items, listed in order of use

- Amounts of each item (preferably by weight)

- Action for each as a raw ingredient: drained, soaked, cleaned, peeled, chopped, diced, canned, fresh, etc.

- Necessary tools: knives, measuring tools, mixer, pots, pans, etc.

- Methods for combining (fold, mix, whip, stir, etc.)

- Amount of time for each preparation step: mixing, heating, reducing, etc.

- Total time for recipe preparation and cooking time

- Required temperatures for cooking: oven, sauces, etc.

- **Subassembly**: separate steps for combining groups of ingredients before all are combined for the finished product (example: combine milk, eggs, and water)

- Final yield and/or number of servings and the size of each serving

- Serving suggestions or directions for how to plate or present the prepared item

- There are two additional steps included in standardized recipes in all foodservice organizations today:

  - ☐ Nutritional analysis

  - ☐ Additional instruction for safe food-handling practices

Advantages and Disadvantages

Using standardized recipes involves more than simply listing the ingredients and processing steps. The process of standardization serves many functions beyond food preparation alone. The use of correctly standardized recipes facilitates foodservice operations in many ways:

- *Procurement planning*: A correctly standardized recipe can be used as an ordering guide that specifies how much of each ingredient is needed for every item on the menu.

- *Fiscal planning*: To develop a foodservice operation's food and labor budget it is necessary to calculate the cost of producing every menu item, which means knowing how much of each ingredient is needed and how much preparation time is involved.

- *Scheduling*: The operator who knows processing times can properly schedule preparation cooks to ensure that items with long prep times are prepared when needed.

- *Teaching*: Employees in training or those who wish to advance in rank will be able to learn how to prepare basic items such as white sauce and know which utensils to use to obtain the best results.

- *Nutritional analysis*: Precise data on ingredient portions is essential in calculating nutritional values.

- *Chemistry*: Following the exact order of and techniques used in each step in a recipe ensures that its ingredients combine together to produce the desired result. If mixed in the wrong order, foods can interact incorrectly and the result is lumpy gravy, curdled custard, a tough pie crust, or stringy cheese sauce.

- *Extensions*: In many large food service operations, standardized recipes include **recipe extensions**, which make it easy to calculate the amounts needed to increase serving yield by regular increments—if a recipe serves 10, for example, it might include instructions for extending it to produce 25 or 50 servings as desired.

- *Mise en place*: A French culinary term that denotes the process of preparing and arranging all the ingredients in a recipe so that they are ready to be combined efficiently to produce the desired item.[2] This is also known as pre-preparation. Onions must be chopped, tomatoes seeded, peppers diced, and so on, to create a food item in which they are ingredients. Utilizing **mise en place** also makes it possible to prepare in a single processing task items such as chopped onions for use in many recipes. Example: If stew requires 1 cup of chopped onions and meatloaf requires 2 cups, then 3 cups of chopped onions can be prepared ahead. In addition to the items requiring chopping or other techniques, *mise en place* also includes measuring all other ingredients in the correct amounts for the recipe and having them ready. It is obvious why there is no simple, one-word translation for this culinary term! Standardized recipes make *mise en place* possible.

On the one hand, after considering all of the advantages of standardized recipes, it is clear they are a powerful tool. Yet they do not guarantee success unless they are followed consistently. On the other hand, they challenge foodservice operators and chefs in several ways:

- *Cost*: Creating standardized recipes is time consuming and therefore costly, but they represent an investment that should pay off in terms of cost savings on ingredients, labor, and so on.

- *Training issues*: Without proper training, employees may take it upon themselves to come up with their own variations on ingredients or processing steps. Managers must utilize standardized recipes as training aids and not assume that proper use is self-evident.

- *Creativity issues*: Beware of cooks who pride themselves in their "secret recipes," who always think they "know better" than a recipe, or who insist that, "If you need a recipe, you can't cook!" When these attitudes prevail in a foodservice operation, inconsistency and error soon follow. The result can sometimes be a very expensive disaster.

- *Communication*: The consistency that only standardized recipes ensure is essential, but it is also important for a chef or manager to maintain an open line of communication with the cooking staff. Sometimes a staff member comes up with a better way of doing something, and this needs to be communicated to management. Without effective two-way communication, this could have bad consequences. First, it might cause staff members who know about the innovation to ignore the standardized recipes because they think they are written in stone and can't be revised. Second, if the innovation truly enhances the operation in some way, the chef or manager should know about it and see that the recipe is revised. There must be a way to continually communicate information about standardized recipes. New ingredients, new equipment, new techniques—all are essential to the continuous evolution of good recipes. Standardized recipes should not be allowed to take the "art" out of cooking.

- *Computers*: Before computers became commonplace in foodservice operations, standardized recipes had to be created and stored in print media, usually collected in notebooks or file boxes. They were easy to misplace and difficult to revise. Today's chef can print out daily *mis en place* items separately and send them electronically to prep cooks. The final recipes for each item can be printed afresh every day. Revision requires only a few keystrokes before everyone who needs it has an updated copy of a recipe (access to standardized recipe files should be controlled to ensure that only knowledgeable, authorized staff can make changes).

- *Quality*: The quality of the products produced by even the best standardized recipes is only as good as the quality of the ingredients that go in them. Therefore, an operation that uses standardized recipes must ensure that the ingredients provided to the cooking staff are of the requisite quality on a consistent basis.

- *Sustainability*: Related to procurement (and quality), a standardized recipe can integrate specific product attributes such as tomatoes from a local farm. Such a feature facilitates sustainable sourcing and serves to enhance the menu item while also reducing food miles (a concept described in the previous chapter).

There are many "sets" of standardized recipes available for purchase, such as the one put out by the Army Quartermaster.[3] Such recipes have been developed over many decades, but are designed to feed thousands quickly, efficiently, nutritiously, and cheaply. Still, recipe sets designed for such large-scale operations as a military installation cannot simply be dropped into, say, a hospital foodservice operation. The army's recipes are designed very specifically to suit a military or government environment. As we have noted, recipes must be developed for each specific operation, depending on its type, location, size, and so on. It is perfectly acceptable to use several recipe sources as references for recipe standardization, but every organization, operation, or individual must consider the very specific needs of a particular operation if standardized recipes are to be effective. The Quartermaster's website, for example, references numerous other websites that are resources for standardized recipes.

Several textbooks feature standardized recipes. For example, *Food for Fifty* has recently been updated with more than 400 standardized recipes for large-scale foodservice operations.[4] This has been a standard resource for over 60 years. In addition, many individuals have posted websites featuring recipes designed to feed large numbers of people. An example of one of these is Becky Dorner's website.[5]

Chefs and Dietitians

Standardized recipes are most commonly the work of chefs and dietitians, and most of them earn credentials by seeking certification from professional trade associations. The American Culinary Federation (ACF)[6] is the largest professional chefs' organization in North America, with more than 22,000 members who belong to more than 230 chapters in four regions in the United States. The ACF offers certification in five categories of cooking, and in the "Cooking Professionals" category there are five credentials based on education and work experience requirements. These range from Certified Culinarian® (CC®) at the entry level to Certified Sous Chef ™ (CSC™) and Certified Chef de Cuisine (CCC) at the intermediate levels to Certified Executive Chef® (CEC®) and Certified Master Chef® (CMC®) at the highest levels.

The CEC® is the department head and, in the case of some restaurants or hotels, the owner. This person is usually responsible for all culinary units in a restaurant, hotel, club, hospital, or foodservice establishment. The CEC® is also responsible for budget preparation, payroll, maintenance, cost control, finance, and inventory.

The CMC® is the consummate chef. A CMC® has demonstrated the highest degree of professional culinary knowledge, skill, and mastery of cooking techniques. A separate application for this level of certification is required, in addition to successfully completing an eight-day testing process judged by peers. Certification as a CEC® is a prerequisite.

The Academy of Nutrition and Dietetics is the world's largest organization of food and nutrition professionals.[7] Nearly 75 percent of its 70,000 members are registered dietitians (RDs) and 4 percent are dietetic technicians, registered (DTRs). Nearly half of all ADA members hold advanced degrees.

A **registered dietitian** must have an undergraduate degree in nutrition or dietetics—or the equivalent in coursework—from an accredited institution as well as have completed a 1,200-hour supervised dietetic internship and must pass a standardized exam developed by the Commission on Dietetic Registration (CDR).[8] The CDR currently awards seven separate and distinct credentials: Registered Dietitian (RD), Dietetic Technician, Registered (DTR), Board Certified Specialist in Renal Nutrition (CSR), Board Certified Specialist in Pediatric Nutrition (CSP), Board Certified Specialist in Sports Dietetics (CSSD), Board Certified Specialist in Gerontological Nutrition (CSG), and Board Certified Specialist in Oncology Nutrition (CSO). Dietitians working in clinical settings are generally licensed by the states in which they practice. This is currently true in 46 states and usually involves sitting for a licensure exam.

These two groups of professionals, chefs, and dietitians, have occasionally misunderstood each other's roles. Now, however, increased interest in nutrition on the one hand and in the culinary arts on the other has brought the two professions into an excellent working relationship in many settings. Local professionals from both groups often cooperate as chef/dietitian teams in culinary competitions. More importantly, at the restaurant or onsite level, recipes are often developed by chef/dietitian teams, resulting in finished recipes that are beautiful, tasty, *and* nutritious. Bryan Roof wrote of the "Perfect Pairing" of chefs and dietitians that some chefs may perceive dietitians as "evil stepsisters" who slap their hands on the way to a generous pat of butter or a healthy pinch of salt while dietitians may perceive chefs as "dietary outlaws."[9]

Today, the two professions recognize and acknowledge that each brings something to the table that the other needs. A dietitian in a hospital setting might once have instructed a patient to "just leave out the salt" when using a favorite recipe, but many patients would rather ignore such an instruction than eat tasteless food. The patient needed to be able to discuss what could be added to restore flavor, not just what to leave out. A chef may appear on a TV program and proclaim that there is NO substitute for salt, leaving thousands of viewers feeling that they are doomed to a lifetime of tasteless food because they are sincerely trying to live without salt to assist in controlling their high blood pressure. Dietitians and chefs can address this dilemma only by working closely together, and they are making considerable progress in undertaking cooperative activities.

Partnerships that are now developing throughout the United States between chefs and dietitians have allowed for a greater understanding of the role food plays in health and well being. It's got to taste good before we are going to eat it—and "healthy" can also taste good! So take that recipe for mother's beef stew, use unsalted beef broth and omit the salt, and add generous amounts of fresh parsley, garlic, onions, and rosemary, along with some red wine. At serving time, add freshly chopped basil and a bit of toasted garlic to the top of each steaming bowl. As Schaeffer says wryly, "You *can* teach an old tongue new tricks."[10] She cites research that reminds us that our preference for sweet and aversion to bitter is with us from birth. We learn to appreciate more complex flavors as we age; hence, our liking for marmalade or beer! If we can learn to appreciate bitter, we can certainly learn to appreciate the taste of a wonderful sauce made with fresh herbs and a chicken breast sautéed in olive oil rather than lard. Schaeffer goes on to point out that we have also trained ourselves to enjoy highly processed foods and their (often) salty taste—most snackers do not realize that it is not the potato in the potato chips that they like. It's the salt and the fat.

As dietitians and chefs continue to work together to broaden the tastes of eaters, the education process has produced individuals credentialed by both groups. There are a growing number of RD/chefs who are developing new approaches to cooking and recipes. There is an example of a chef/dietitian partnership in the industry exemplar at the conclusion of this chapter.

Applying Yields

When considering recipe standardization, one of the first concepts that must be understood is that of **yields** A food yield is an equivalent measure of a specific food. Here are four easy-to-follow examples:

1. How many strips of bacon will give you one cup of bacon crumbles?

2. What volume of apple slices do you get from an apple?

3. How many pounds of beef will serve 15 people after it is cooked?

4. If I have a pound of flour, how many cups is that?

All of these questions could be answered by putting on that apron and frying and crumbling bacon, slicing apples into a cup, and so on. But it's a lot easier and more accurate to consult a reliable table of food yields, since a recipe could include many ingredients and it is preferred that a standardized recipe include both a volume measure and a weight for each component, when possible. There are many food yield tables available. Websites such as About.com include comprehensive and easy-to-use yield tables for southern cooking.[11]

Here now are the answers to the yield questions:

- 1 slice of cooked bacon = 1 tablespoon crumbled bacon

- 1 medium apple = 1 cup diced or sliced apples

- 1 pound of flour = 4 cups of sifted flour or 3⅓ cups of unsifted flour

- 5 pounds of beef tenderloin will produce 12 to 16 servings

Yield tables are valuable tools when applied to developing or changing a recipe. Today's food service software programs include such data; once a recipe is in a computer database, yields can be calculated by the program.

Since the purpose of a standardized recipe is to achieve a certain product quality and consistency, the examples given above clearly show why accurate yields are important. If a recipe called for a tablespoon of bacon crumbles and the cook used three slices of bacon, this would be wasteful. In addition, the nutritional analysis of the recipe ingredients would be calculated for 1 tablespoon of crumbles, but there would actually be 3 tablespoons, adding significant amounts of calories and fat. And if another item called for bacon, there might not be enough remaining if too much was used in the first recipe. Such an error would be multiplied by many times over if the cook were preparing food to yield a large number of servings.

The concept of yields is clear enough when it is applied to bacon, apples, and flour. What is different about the beef? Calculating yield or equivalents for meat gets a bit complicated. This is because meats "shrink" when they cook. Consider the previous beef example:

- 1 pound of beef = 16 ounces of beef

- 5 pounds of beef = 80 ounces of beef

The average serving of beef is 4 ounces. Dividing 80 ounces by 4 ounces should produce a 20-serving yield, but the yield chart says that 80 ounces of beef yields only 12 to 16 servings. The reason for this is shrinkage. Cooking removes water and fat from meat, and the amount of edible material left after cooking is sometimes significantly less than the raw amount. Therefore, yield charts are even more important for meats than for most other foods because in order to calculate yields for meats you must include a factor of 25 to 35 percent in shrinkage. No one wants to run out of the burgundy beef in the middle of a party!

Yield tables are important for one more reason. It is generally more accurate to weigh ingredients than to measure them. But liquid ingredients, although they can be weighed, will rarely be packaged with an equivalent weight displayed on the container. Thus, it can simply be more efficient to use a volume measure, such as 1 gallon of milk. However, weight ounces are not always equivalent to fluid ounces, so these measures must be distinct. The computer can easily calculate both measures, so if possible it would be best to include both measures for each item. It should be noted that the average home recipe usually includes only volume measures for liquids, but in an environment in which many servings of the same item must be prepared, weight is more accurate and can help control food cost as well.

Development and Standardization

Many people enjoy collecting cookbooks and food magazines. The Internet has made hundreds of recipes for any given item available to everyone. Chefs search continually for new ways in which to prepare and present the dishes they serve their customers. There are millions of recipes out there, with millions more to come. One reporter, marveling at the lengths to which chefs will go to push the envelope of creativity, mentions a few who are making dishes that resemble dirt, rocks, and soil. He notes that this seemingly crazy approach is "fueled by a focus on farm-to-table cuisine" as well as on using new technology to make chocolate cookie crumbs, beets, and mushrooms look like dirt and rocks.[12]

When Brittany decides to look up a recipe for macaroni and cheese, the first thing she noticed is that not all recipes are set up in the same way, or written in the same formats. Recipe formatting decisions provide answers to the following questions:

- Is the recipe name at the upper left, center, or upper right?

- Is there a category (entrée)? Or a number (356) for ease of location?

- Is the ingredient listed first, with the amount following?

- Is the procedure set off to the side, or do all instructions follow the ingredient list?

- Can you immediately find the yield and portion size?

Go back to the list of items a recipe should contain at the beginning of this chapter. It might not bother Brittany to have three or four recipes in several formats when she is preparing for a small dinner party of three. But for Juan, the cook in a hotel restaurant, it will quickly become discouraging if none of the recipes he uses look the same and he has to look in five places to find the number of servings yielded. Figure 4.1 shows a recipe format as it is produced by a software program. In the early days of computer use, recipes had to be typed and then printed out in a very difficult-to-use format. Today's software programs produce user-friendly formats with pictures to show the final product, and can produce recipes on request so that huge files of recipe cards are no longer necessary. The recipe in Figure 4.1 was developed and tested by a chef to offer excellent flavor; it was reviewed by a dietitian to be low in sodium and fat; and it was extended by the computer software from 5 to 300 servings.

The particular software used allows for as many as four extensions, selected by the user. This is important because increasing the number of portions systematically and reliably has been a major problem in recipe standardization. Recipes designed to be used in foodservice operations would often include extensions to 25, 50, 100 servings or more. As can be seen in Figure 4.1, the software now does this automatically. In fact, a manager is no longer limited to any specific number of servings, although one might rarely need to produce 18 rather than 20. We should add one note of caution regarding extensions whether calculated manually or by dedicated software: It is more than just multiplying each ingredient in equal proportion based on the number of servings. When changing from small to very large number of servings, the resulting menu item should be tested in increments to ensure consistency and quality.

Many related reports are available for the user of this and other such software programs. Among those are:

- A list of items needed to purchase to make the recipe

- A cost report for the recipe

- A nutrient analysis for one serving

- A production worksheet for cooks

- A taste and temperature report for recipe evaluation

Braised Beef with Brown Sauce, Great Living (20898.1)

Slow cooked tender sirloin steak in a rich brown Sauce

Revision Date: Dec 08, 2009

Minimum Batch: 1
Maximum Production:

Portion: 4 oz (p)

Step	Ingredients		5 Servings	300 Servings	Servings
1	Beef Sirloin Flap Meat, Raw	AP	1 lb, 10–1/2 oz	98 lb, 12 oz	
2	Onions, Fresh, 1/2" Diced	EP	5–3/4 oz	21 lb, 4 oz	
	Celery, Fresh, 1/2" Diced	EP	2 oz	7 lb	
	Carrots, Fresh, 3/4" Diced	EP	2 oz	7 lb	
	Garlic Cloves, Peeled, Fresh	AP	1–1/2 tsp	1–3/4 cup, 3/4 tsp	
	Tomatoes Diced in Juice, No Added Salt	AP	3–3/4 oz	14 lb	
	Olive Oil	EP	1–1/2 tsp	1–3/4 cup, 3/4 tsp	
3	Burgundy Cooking Wine	AP	3 tbsp, 2–1/4 tsp	3 qt, 2 cup, 2 tbsp	
4	Water	AP	3–3/4 cup, 3/4 tsp	14 gal, 2 cup	
	Thyme, Fresh	EP	1–1/2 tsp	1–3/4 cup, 3/4 tsp	
	Rosemary, Fresh	EP	1–1/2 tsp	1–3/4 cup, 3/4 tsp	
	Kitchen Bouquet Flavoring	AP	3/4 tsp	3/4 cup, 2 tbsp, 1/4 tsp	
	Worcestershire Sauce	AP	1/4 tsp	1/3 cup, 1 tbsp, 2–1/8 tsp	
	Low Sodium Tomato Juice, Canned	AP	1/4 cup. 2–1/8 tsp	1 gal, 1–3/4 cup	

Step	Method
1	**HACCP** Refer to HACCP Plan Form: HFS #001: Prepared Hot for Hot Service; or HACCP Plan Form: HFS#002: Prepared Hot, Chilled for Cold Storage. Thaw beef overnight under refrigeration. Trim beef flap meat of most all visible fat
2	**Braising Sauce** Preheat oven to 475F. Toss all the onions, celery, carrots and garlic together. Lightly spray large sheet pan(s) with cooking spray. Spread vegetables out on pans. Roast for 15–20 or until browned. Stir in tomatoes.
3	Lightly spray a large stock pot with cooking spray and heat over medium high heat. Add roasted vegetables. Deglaze the pan with wine; reduce wine 75%.
4	**Braising Sauce** Stir in remaining ingredients. Bring to a boil, turn heat to simmer and reduce for 1 1/2 hours or until liquid is reduced by half. Internal temperature must reach 165F. Remove sauce from heat, strain through a china cap. Discard solids.

Figure 4.1 Extended standardized recipe.

In summary:

- One 4-ounce serving (131 grams) of this braised beef dish provides 225 calories.

- These calories come from 13 grams of fat, 2.6 grams of carbohydrate, and 22.5 grams of protein.

- There are also 61.6 grams of cholesterol and 123.3 milligrams of sodium—both very good from a nutritional point of view.

In the final analysis, a foodservice organization must pick a recipe format that is best for its food production staff, whether it involves a single chef in a sit-down restaurant or 50 cooks working in a tent on a battlefield serving 3,000 hungry soldiers.

Earlier in the chapter, we reviewed the advantages and disadvantages of standardized recipes, as well as the major elements each recipe should contain. Standardized recipes must be tested many times and revised throughout the process based on the outcome of each use. It is perfectly acceptable for an organization to serve such products during the testing phase, but careful evaluation should be performed at every step and clear notes recording the changes should be kept. The status of a recipe should be noted after each test. For example, a note could read: "Burgundy beef, version 4, changed dried parsley flakes to fresh chopped parsley." The recipe-testing process should continue until at least three batches of acceptable quality and yield have been produced. Batch evaluation should be performed by either a panel of staff (which might include chefs, dietitians, and servers) or by customers. Customers often love it when the server tells them that the day's special is a new recipe and the restaurant would really appreciate feedback. After the recipe is fully evaluated and tested, it is advisable to have a new cook or a cook from another area prepare the item. That final test will show that the directions and methods are clear. The recipe is then standardized—until someone decides to change the burgundy beef to teriyaki beef.

It is also important that not all ingredients can be mathematically extended with equal ease. First, it is not practical to require chefs to work with unwieldy fractions or decimal places, so most software will include "rules for rounding." Cooks rarely have highly refined chemical scales or spoons that measure less than a quarter teaspoon. The computer can eliminate such anomalies using rules, and such rules are included in most standardization software. Yet the software must reflect the complexity of extensions. Not all spices, for example, can be extended in the same way as main ingredients can be. Thus, extended recipes must be carefully checked for seasoning, since ½ cup of chili powder for 25 servings does not always extend to 1 cup for 50 servings. Many spices will be too strong if simply doubled or tripled along with other ingredients. Only tasting can confirm the correct amount.

Very few establishments open with completely new recipes. As explained in Chapter 3, the menu is developed first, followed by the recipes to support it. Recipes can come from many different sources, and then can be further developed through testing and evaluation to find those that produce the best product for your restaurant or onsite establishment. Fondue is a great item, and it may be your favorite recipe, but it is not practical to serve it on the line in a school cafeteria (think of arming children with all those tiny forks and the logjams that will result when the dexterity of a six-year-old goes up against a vat of hot cheese). When considering a new recipe or thinking about changing an old one, a chef or manager always needs to consider these factors:

- Will the change in the item be acceptable to customers? If they expect meatloaf with tomato sauce, will the switch to brown gravy be accepted even if it is cheaper?

- Will the change in the item increase the price to the point where the item will no longer be popular with your customers? Caviar might be a great addition as a new garnish, but not if the item cost goes from $8.00 to $25.00.

- Can a vendor provide what is needed? Sweet potato fries may need to come from a specialty vendor, and, for a small restaurant, this could be a problem.

- Is there a reasonable amount of preparation time for current staffing levels and talent?

- Is staff sufficiently trained to prepare a particular sauce without curdling it?

- Is the proper equipment available?

- Is there a "convenience" ingredient (such as bagged, frozen chopped onions) or a "convenient" food item (such as ready-to-use pastry puffs) that can appear more costly at first glance but make up for a shortage in staff or a piece of equipment?

Only after considering all of these factors can the cost of a recipe be determined. It may be perfectly acceptable to purchase a pressure fryer if fried chicken is on your menu every day, but not if you were planning to serve that dish as a special only once a month.

RECIPE COSTING

Earlier in this chapter we compared the listing of ingredients by weight and volume measures. This becomes very important when considering costs. Let's take a partial recipe for beef stew as an example:

- 25 pounds of stew beef @ $2.95/pound = $73.75

- 10 pounds of Yukon gold potatoes @ $0.50/pound = $5.00

- 10 pounds of carrots @ $ 0.75/pound = $7.50

- 5 pounds of onions @ $0.90/pound = $4.50

In this oversimplified example, the total food cost of the recipe would be the sum of the above totals, or $90.75. If this standardized recipe makes 40 servings, the cost per serving will be equal to the total cost of the recipe ($90.75) divided by the number of servings (40), or $2.27. In the following chapter we discuss various ways for determining the selling price of an item using such cost information.

There is one other important aspect in recipe costing and that is the **unit of measure**. A unit of measure provides a basis on which a person or a computer can calculate the price of an item correctly. Consider the carrots in the example: These carrots come in 5-pound bags, so each bag costs $3.75. Since that is how carrots are purchased from the vendor, the purchase unit for cost calculations is a 5-pound bag. If someone were to think mistakenly that the unit of measure being used is a 1-pound bag and then entered the price for a 5-pound bag, the computer or the manager would see an incorrect price of $3.75/pound, rather than the correct per-pound price of $0.75. Thus, the pricing of the recipe would be incorrect.

Product identity is another major issue in pricing. Since any foodservice organization uses hundreds of items, even a few minor errors can have dramatic effects on costing and pricing. Consider the simple green bean:

- Green beans can be fresh, canned, or frozen.

- Each of the above kinds of green beans can be whole, cut, or french cut.

- Green beans can be available breaded and fried.

- Green beans can be dried or dehydrated.

- Green beans are available in cans in low sodium and regular versions, or even seasoned with bacon.

- Every one of these green bean products is available in multiple sizes of cans, bags, cartons, or boxes.

Here we have one food product readily available in over 15 forms. If Jenny is looking up pricing in a catalog and selects french-cut frozen green beans in a 5-pound bag but uses this product in a recipe that actually calls for canned green beans in a no. 10 can, then the yield, cost, and quality of the recipe will be wrong. In a large foodservice operation, such errors can occur with hundreds of products and can be very costly indeed. Computers often come to the rescue again with printed lists identifying the product configuration, but errors can still be made.

Since most cost calculations today are done by computer, it is extremely important that the initial data used include the correct purchase unit for the item. A recipe might specify 10 pounds or two 5-pound bags and the calculation will still be correct as long the manager or the computer uses the correct price: either $0.75 per pound or $2.75 per 5-pound bag. Without an accurate cost of the food as purchased, the cost of the ingredients cannot be calculated. Without an accurate and predictable amount of servings for a given recipe, the cost of the recipe cannot be calculated. Major errors can occur if such important information is incorrectly calculated. Note that the cost data for the recipe in Figure 4.1 are based on exactly the items listed for that recipe, in the exact amounts listed.

In summary, the development of a standardized recipe, through several steps of testing and adjustment, is known in management as an **iterative process**. The repeated cycle of testing and evaluation is necessary as the recipe becomes more and more accurate with each iteration. The purpose of this iterative process is to achieve predictable results that the manager, the staff, and the customers can trust.

RECIPE ANALYSIS

In addition to their use in calculating accurate cost information, standardized recipes form the basis for three other important types of analysis.

Nutritional Analysis

Nutritional analysis is the process of determining the major nutrients in one serving of an item, which is accomplished by determining the amount of each nutrient in a given quantity of each ingredient. If a recipe produces 10 servings, for example, then all quantities are divided by 10 and the nutritional composition of each ingredient is then listed for that amount, such as 1 cup of soup or 3 oz. of roast beef. In the past such calculations were carried out painstakingly by hand by finding ingredients listed on large tables of nutrient content. This provided considerable opportunity for error and the labor involved was so extensive that, even in a hospital, extensive nutrient information was calculated only in highly sophisticated research units. For all other hospital patients, only the major nutrients were calculated and then only on the basis of averages. For example, all meat might be assumed to provide 7 grams of protein per ounce, even though the amounts of protein in various types of meat may vary.

Today no one would perform this task by hand. There are applications for cell phones and websites that provide nutritional analysis. Software that provides the basis for all aspects of food-service management includes or links to nutrient databases. Thus, once the standardized recipe for braised beef shown in Figure 4.1 was developed and tested, the nutritional analysis was automatically available.

Earlier in this chapter, we mentioned partnerships between dietitians and chefs. Nutritional analysis is one of many areas in which practitioners from these professions work together to reduce the amount or type of fat in a recipe, for example, or to reduce the amount of salt, or to substitute fresh items with greater nutritional value for salty canned items. As discussed in Chapter 3, restaurants are now expected (or in some areas required) to display or make readily available to customers the amounts of calories, fat, sodium, and carbohydrates that are in their dishes. Computers make this possible.

Intake Analysis

In a healthcare or residential care setting, **intake analysis** is essential to ensure that residents are consuming adequate amounts of essential nutrients daily. Intake analysis determines the content of foods that are actually consumed by individuals. The dietitian and the medical team must plan for care based on intake analysis data, adding nutritional supplements or offering alternatives that might be more easily consumed.

HACCP

The final component of standardized recipes we introduce here is a set of instructions for handling food safely. Food safety is achieved through the application of a system known as **HACCP** or Hazard Analysis Critical Control Point. This system is designed to prevent food-handling errors and thereby optimizing food safety. It was originally used by NASA to protect astronauts' food from biological contamination, but today it is used in virtually all foodservice organizations. The US Food and Drug Administration (FDA) includes HACCP guidelines in its regulations covering foodservice facilities. Examples of critical control points are storage temperatures, hand-washing and food-washing timing and techniques, and the handling of food as it is transformed from raw into cooked products. It is important to note that the standardized recipe has become the major tool with which to incorporate steps that identify and respond to these control points and thus it is a major food safety tool as well.

MANAGERIAL IMPLICATIONS

Foodservice operations today rely on standardized recipes to produce uniform menu items. This uniformity is critical for day-to-day consistency, as well as consistencies across units in a chain setting. Standardized recipes are the result of lengthy testing and include a formalized set of information extending far beyond just the list of ingredients. The advantages of standardized recipes, in addition to the aforementioned consistency, include applications in procurement planning, fiscal planning, scheduling, and training. The main disadvantage is the time and cost required to produce standardized recipes. Moreover, if a recipe is not followed, it loses its value. Finally, standardized recipes should be updated as needed, and any changes communicated to all appropriate individuals.

Most of the main creators and users of standardized recipes, chefs and dietitians, are represented respectively by two organizations in the United States: the American Culinary Federation (ACF) and the Academy of Nutrition and Dietetics. The ACF offers a range of certifications including certified executive chef and certified master chef. Nearly 75 percent of Academy of Nutrition and Dietetics members are registered dietitians, a designation granted by the Commission on Dietetic Registration. More than ever, chefs and dietitians are working together to create food that is both tasty and healthy.

Every standardized recipe should reflect expected yields. A food yield is an equivalent measure of a specific food, such as the amount of beef that a five-pound roast will produce after it is cooked. The associated yield tables are valuable when developing standardized recipes and are typically part of recipe-management computer programs. Finally, yields are best expressed as a weight, as this is more accurate.

The format of the standardized recipe is also important. Typically, it includes a number of extensions so that it can readily be used to create dishes to produce, say, 25, 50, or 100 servings. A standardized recipe is also accompanied by a variety of reports based on the information listed. These can include a report on the ingredients that must be purchased (to assist in the ordering process), a cost report (to assist in financial accounting), a nutrient analysis (for consumer information), a production worksheet (for the cooks), and a taste and temperature report (for evaluation purposes). The usefulness of a given type of report depends on the nature of the foodservice operation in question.

Recipe costing is performed once the recipe is standardized. By adding together the cost of every item in a recipe and then dividing by the number of servings produced, the manager knows the cost of each item. This information can then be used as part of the menu price calculation.

The final aspect is recipe analysis. Such analyses include nutritional analysis, intake analysis, and hazard analysis critical control point, or HACCP. The latter is designed to prevent food-handling errors and is commonly used in every segment of foodservice today.

Morrison

Several years ago, Morrison Healthcare Food Services began a major project to integrate all of its computer systems for purchasing, recipe development, food production, nutrition, costing, inventory, and serving and selling food into one Web-based system. In order for this project to be successful, it had to be built so that each segment could draw information from every other. Thus, the same cost data that helped build a budget also drove the cost of a recipe and formed the basis of the selling price. Every foodservice director in hundreds of hospitals and senior living facilities throughout the country would be able to access and use these systems, but this meant a significant amount of training would need to be delivered to hundreds of staff members. It also required installing the proper network access infrastructure and computer hardware.

It was determined that the return on this investment in development, training, and organization would indeed be worth the effort. The result was a series of Web-based "e-systems" covering everything from finance to nutrition. Webtrition® is the recipe- and nutrition-based part of this program.

Figure 4.2 shows the login page of a secure system with tightly controlled access levels based on rank. When

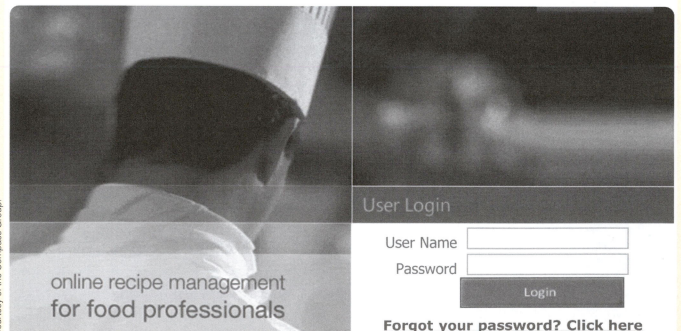

Courtesy of the Compass Group.

Figure 4.2 Computerized recipe system.

an executive chef develops or approves a recipe received from a hospital chef or food service director, the recipe is then reviewed for nutritional content by a registered dietitian, and only certain individuals can enter or change recipes once they are entered. Some staff may be granted access to look up and print out recipes, while others can use a recipe development tool in the system. This completely integrated system will then provide nutrient data that can be used to modify diets or to print out nutritional information on the tray ticket that accompanies a tray going to a patient's room, individualized for his or her particular choices. Testing, approval, and continuous evaluation of recipes means that the same great braised beef is enjoyed in a hospital in San Diego and in a senior living center in Baltimore.

Information provided by this system has also been helpful in the production of the **Great Living Starts Here**© video series (Figure 4.3). Each video features a chef and a registered dietitian providing specific information about a prescribed diet and explaining how to prepare tasty and healthy food within the limits of a dietary restriction. The series covers diabetes, heart health, gluten-free food, kidney disease, and heart disease. Each video offers specific information about making foods come alive with flavor. By enhancing the taste experience for patients, it should be possible to bring about positive changes in how and what they eat for a healthier life. The videos can be shown in classes or given to patients and residents, and they can also be distributed via a closed-circuit television system or intranet.

Image © Morrison Management Specialists 2010.

Healthcare | Senior Living | Financial eTools | Client Testimonials | Careers | Continuing Education
Overview | Patient Experience | Retail Experience | Nutrition and Wellness

Nutrition & Wellness ▸   Great Living Starts Here ▾

Morrison has created a collection of healthy eating videos to help our patients and customers with their daily eating habits. These videos focus on the most common modified diets and provide smart and easy tips and cooking preparation tools for the viewers. At Morrison, great living starts here!

Lisa Roberson
Corporate Wellness Development

great
starts here

great
people

great
service

great
food

great
responsibility

Figure 4.3   Screen shot from **Great Living Starts Here**® video series.

KEY TERMS

■■■ Case in Point ■■

Recipe, What Recipe?

Having just graduated with a college degree, Tim was excited about his new job at the city's newest dinner house. Tim had interviewed with the two owners—Bill and Bonnie, a husband and wife team—and knew he could make a difference managing their small dining room. The owners made it clear that their strength was in the kitchen (both were experienced chefs) and that what they needed was someone who could take care of the front of the house. Bill and Bonnie were honest with Tim and explained that, not long after the restaurant had opened only a few weeks earlier, they realized that they couldn't manage all aspects of the operation themselves. They hoped to divide the kitchen duties so that while one was cooking, the other could focus on administrative matters such as paying invoices, processing payroll, and compiling financial information. Ultimately, the owners wanted to open a chain of restaurants with the same menu, décor, and so on.

Tim's first few nights managing the dining room were great. The customers raved about the food and generally enjoyed the dining experience. There was the occasional glitch with food coming out of the kitchen a little slowly when all the tables were full, but after the initial rush everything was running pretty smoothly. At the end of each night, Tim sat with Bonnie and discussed how they could change things to improve the speed of service and coordination between the kitchen and the dining room staff.

On the fourth night, Tim began hearing complaints about the food. Some complained that the portions were too small; one couple who had been at the restaurant the week before asked why they had changed menus.

Tim couldn't understand what was happening. He made it through the night, but ended up not charging several guests for their meals in response to their numerous complaints.

This was the first night Tim had worked with Bill only (it was Bonnie's night off). As soon as Tim began to explain the nature of the complaints, Bill became defensive. Tim was careful not to criticize the food or the preparation but tried to explain that he had received no complaints during the previous evenings. Bill and Tim agreed that it was probably a fluke and that they would consider the evening a learning experience. Unfortunately, the next night was exactly the same. The main complaint was about portion sizes; guests felt they were being overcharged for the small portions and many told Tim that they would not return.

Finally, at the end of that night, Tim asked Bill the fateful question: "Are you using the same recipes that Bonnie uses?" Much to Tim's surprise, Bill didn't get upset. In fact, his first reaction was a big smile. Bill said, "My wife and I have different styles, but we agreed on menu items that complement both our talents. We don't always see eye to eye on some of the sauces, so these might change from night to night. She also tends to use more meat than I do. Between you and me, I think she's trying to give away the house with her large portions, but I figure we balance each other out doing it this way."

Tim drove home wondering what to do. He certainly didn't want to create problems between Bill and Bonnie, but he knew that without consistency, the restaurant would not be successful.

What should Tim do?

REVIEW AND DISCUSSION QUESTIONS

1. Why is the term *formula* a good alternative to *recipe*?

2. Name two advantages and two disadvantages of standardized recipes.

3. What information should be included in a standardized recipe?

4. Using your choice of search engine, find three recipes and identify anything that is missing in each that should be included in a standardized recipe.

5. What are the five credentials that the American Culinary Foundation offers?

6. In addition to a registered dietitian, what other types of dietetic professionals are there?

7. Why might a chef and a dietitian disagree when developing a recipe together?

8. Explain the concept of *yields* and discuss why they are important in recipe development.

9. Take your favorite family recipe, extend it (to the best of your ability) to make 50 servings, and then standardize it. (Note: You don't have to cook it, but do make the necessary calculations so that a cook could follow it. For example, you need to adjust measurements; including "75 teaspoons of ginger" would not be appropriate.)

10. Using the recipe you just standardized, cost the recipe such that you calculate the cost per serving.

11. In your opinion, should restaurants provide a nutritional analysis? Provide an example of a restaurant chain that provides this information and one that does not.

12. Using the Food and Drug Administration site, find five examples of hazard analysis critical control points.

ENDNOTES

1. Brown, A. *I'm Just Here for the Food*. New York: Stewart, Tabori, and Chang, 2002.

2. Pryor, H. www.cooksrecipes.com. Accessed February 2010.

3. US Army Quartermaster. www.quartermaster.army.mil. Accessed February 2010.

4. Molt, M. *Food for Fifty*, 13th ed. Upper Saddle River, NJ: Prentice Hall, 2010.

5. Dorner, B. www.beckydorner.com. Accessed March 2010.

6. American Culinary Federation. www.acfchefs.org. Accessed February 2010.

7. Academy of Nutrition and Dietetics. www.eatright.org. Accessed February 2012.

8. Commission on Dietetic Registration. www.cdr@eatright.org. Accessed February 2010.

9. Roof, B. "Perfect Pairing: Chefs and Dietitians Unite for Healthy, Flavorful Cuisine." *Today's Dietitian* 12 (2010): 8–10.

10. Schaeffer, J. "Taste Better, Live Better." *Today's Dietitian* 10 (2008): 54–58.

11. "Ingredient Equivalents." http://southernfood.about.com/library/info/blequivb.htm. Accessed September 2012.

12. Thorn, B. "Slinging Mud: Chefs Create Dishes That Look Like Dirt." *Nation's Restaurant News* (July 20, 2009).

MENU PRICING

LEARNING OBJECTIVES:

After becoming familiar with this chapter, you should be able to:

1. Understand the major menu pricing approaches.

2. Explain the methods used to calculate a menu item's price.

3. Appreciate the importance of menu psychology and understand how it applies in the menu development process.

4. Recognize the importance of menu engineering and understand how various approaches can be applied.

This chapter addresses the most important part of the menu-planning process not covered in the previous chapters—pricing. Building on the notion of value discussed in Chapter 2 and using the recipe-costing methodology addressed in Chapter 4, the goal in pricing is to convey to the customer that the price for a given item is reasonable while also ensuring that the foodservice operator profits from the sale of that item. To this end, we present six approaches to menu-item pricing in this chapter and then address the psychological aspects of menu pricing. We conclude with a discussion of menu engineering, which allows operators to optimize menu pricing.

◨ PRICING APPROACHES

Pricing is fundamental to a foodservice operation and can quickly equate to financial success—or failure. A menu item's price may be too high for the guest (that is, the guest does not perceive it to represent a good value) or too low to cover the associated costs and produce an adequate profit. (As you will recall, we address item cost calculation in the previous chapter.) In addition, while customers are typically willing to spend more money when dining out to eat something they could fix at home, most will shop around for a restaurant or eatery and base the resulting decision on a combination of price, location, past experience, reputation, the nature of the dining occasion (e.g., a business lunch or a quick meal before a movie), and other related factors.

In general, menu-pricing decisions result from two primary drivers: market and demand. Prices are **market driven** insofar as they must be responsive to the competition, particularly for menu items and delivery methods that are common across multiple providers. **Demand-driven pricing** can be adopted more robustly for customers who want items or service styles for which there are few providers or alternatives in the marketplace.

Beyond these considerations, the traditional pricing approach is to apply one of a handful of menu pricing models. The first of these is the nonstructured approach, known also as seat-of-the-pants pricing. The various quantitative approaches that are widely used include the factor method, the prime-cost method, the actual-cost method, the gross-profit method, and the stochastic-modeling approach.

Nonstructured

Nonstructured pricing is the simplest approach to menu pricing. It consists of little more than a cursory examination of the competition's prices with no consideration of other factors. A restaurateur might, for example, visit two restaurants with themes similar to his and price his menu to approximate prices charged for similar dishes at the other restaurants. Needless to say, this method is completely inadequate. Every foodservice operation is unique and pricing must reflect the costs associated with each specific operation. Surprisingly, however, some operators still follow this approach.

Factor Method

The **factor method** is the most common pricing tactic and dates back more than 100 years to hotel-restaurant operators in Europe. A *factor* is established by dividing 1.0 by the desired food-cost percentage. For example, if an operator wanted his or her food cost to be 37 percent, the resulting factor would be $1 \div 0.37 = 2.7$. The raw food cost of an item would then be multiplied by the factor to produce the menu price. An item with a food cost of $2.25 would therefore be represented on the menu at a cost of $6.08 ($2.25 \times 2.7$). This is a popular method owing to its simplicity. (As many readers might note, one could also calculate a menu price by simply dividing the raw food cost by the desired food-cost percentage.) The downside is that not every item should be marked up by the same proportion, since high-cost items would be priced beyond market value. Also, low-cost items such as coffee that normally produce higher-than-usual **contribution margins** (sales less all variable costs or, put another way, the amount of sales that is contributed toward fixed costs and profit), would be priced too low to generate an adequate return. Finally, this method does not reflect the potentially differing labor costs associated with dissimilar menu items. (A price of $6.08 also does not reflect the psychology of pricing, which we address later in the chapter. The purpose here is to explain the quantitative components.)

Prime-Cost Method

The **prime-cost method** is a variation on the factor method and integrates both raw product and labor costs. This method requires that labor costs be separated into direct labor costs (labor used for the preparation of a specific menu item) and indirect labor costs (labor used to finish the item, such as grilling, frying, etc.) for each menu item. The biggest advantage of the prime-cost method, then, is that it reflects cost differences that distinguish labor-intensive items from prepared foods. The challenge of the prime-cost method lies in accurately making such allocations, particularly since these may vary with the volume of items sold.

Here is a simple example using a single menu item: Assuming that the total direct and indirect labor costs for a steak sandwich (including the cost of benefits) is $2.60, the desired food cost is 37 percent, and the desired labor cost is 38 percent, the price of the item is calculated as:

$$\frac{(\$2.25 + 2.60)}{(37\% + 38\%)} = \$6.47$$

Actual-Cost Method

The **actual-cost method** accomplishes the vital goal of including profit in the price of every item on a menu. It uses food cost dollars, total labor cost per guest, a related variable cost percentage (covering such items as paper goods), a fixed cost percentage (critical when the fixed costs associated with an operation, say rent or fees for using a franchised brand, are substantial), and the desired profit percentage. Although calculating costs by this method limits an operator to information found on the operation's pro forma statement, this method has the advantage of incorporating a more inclusive set of inputs. An actual-cost calculation, using fictitious numbers for a generic item, is:

EP cost ($)	Selling price = X
+ Labor ($)	Var., fixed & profit = 34%
+ Variable cost (%)	Food & labor = $4.85
+ Fixed cost (%)	Food & Labor = 100% − 34% = 0.66
+ Profit (%)	0.66X = $4.85
Menu Price	X = $4. 85/0.66 = $7.35

Therefore, the menu price is $7.35.

Gross-Profit Method

The **gross-profit method** is intended to determine a specific amount of money that should be made on the basis of the number of guests who patronize the foodservice operation. Although this method represents an advance over these other methods insofar as it focuses on **gross profit** (sales less the cost of food), it is predicated on the accuracy of prior data and on serving a specific number of guests, so last-minute fluctuations in the numbers of guests served can affect the pricing structure dramatically.

Assume, for example, that a certain menu item, say a roast beef sandwich, is a leading seller and, in the same month last year, the restaurant sold 100. The desired gross profit is 63 percent. Suppose that, during that month last year, sales from this dish produced average revenue of $1,368. Thus, the targeted gross profit is $862 ($1,368 × 63%) or $8.62 per sandwich sold. Assuming that the food cost for this menu item is $4.25, the price would be set at $12.87 ($4.25 + $8.62).

This method underscores the importance of pricing menu items on the basis of how many are expected to sell. The risk here is that popular items do not always remain popular from one year to the next; seasonality also affects sales of certain items (for example, more people order soup when the weather is cold). Thus, forecasting accurately is vital if the gross-profit method is to work properly. Situations such as catered events are ideal for this approach as the operator charges by the number of guests and can readily calculate the optimum price for items on the menu.

Stochastic-Modeling Approach

Stochastic-modeling is the only pricing method that integrates internal and external variables, including demand functions such as item popularity and market position. In the event that a foodservice operation is new but nearby dining choices are plentiful (think of a new kiosk in a food court), for example, an operator's pricing approach might need to reflect these competitive forces. Conversely, if an eatery is already recognized in its marketplace (e.g., the chef is well-known) or it offers products that are unavailable elsewhere, market position is strong and should be reflected in the pricing algorithm.

The data necessary to price a menu using the stochastic-modeling approach are:

- Oc = Percentage of sales allocated to costs other than food and labor (sometimes referred to, somewhat incorrectly, as occupation costs)

- Lc = Percentage of sales allocated to labor

- Pm = Percentage of menu price (MP) desired for profit markup (which may vary by item)

- EP = Raw food cost (also known as the edible portion)

- Mc = A subjective determination of market sensitivity; the variable that represents promotional discounts or premium

- MP = Menu price

The menu price calculation, then, is:

$$Menu\ price = \frac{EP}{(100\%\ MP) - [Lc + Oc + (Pm \times Mc)]}$$

As an example, assume a foodservice operator has a signature dish at her Italian-themed cafe. Since she plans this to be one of her best-selling items and knows that it is unique to Italian restaurants in the area (and conveniently consists of a large amount of pasta but little meat), she wants it not only to produce a profit similar to that of the other entrées on the menu, 10% (Pc), but if possible to boost her profit, and decides to add a promotional premium of 2.5% net profit ($Mc = 1.25$). The resulting calculation, assuming 38 and 25 percent for Lc and Oc, respectively, and a raw food cost of $6.95, is:

$$Lc + Oc + [Pm \times Mc] = 0.38 + 0.25 + [0.10 \times 1.25] = 76\%$$

therefore, food cost is 24%.

$$MP = \frac{EP}{(MP\%\ available\ for\ food)} = \frac{\$6.95}{24\%} = \$28.96$$

The foregoing list of menu-pricing approaches is not exhaustive but it provides the basis for most approaches used today. Some computer packages simplify the process, and some integrate a variety of other variables. The important thing is to understand how each of these variables functions in producing individual menu prices. And as is the case with most management functions, menu pricing is both science and art; failure to embrace both aspects will result in less-than-optimal operating results.

MENU PSYCHOLOGY

So what part of menu pricing is art? Many would argue that the answer is menu psychology, which supports strategies that operators use to entice customers to purchase items and can inform category layout, menu item placement, menu merchandising (such as pictures), and price-rounding strategies. It is this last component that applies most directly to menu pricing.

Retailers have long understood that customers tend to round down a price of $9.95 to $9 rather than $10. **Odd pricing** suggests that menu prices should end in 5, 7, or 9—often referred to as *magic numbers*. This is a practice long seen in gas stations; the price is displayed in bold numbers followed by 9/10. The notion, again, is that $3.22 9/10 is perceived by the consumer as $3.22, not as the more accurate $3.23.

But does this work? Some restaurant chains embrace it wholeheartedly. For example, P.F. Chang's China Bistro, the popular full-service upscale casual-dining restaurant, prices all of its food items ending in a 5 (see Figure 5.1). Moving up a segment, many fine-dining restaurants, including the niche-positioned restaurant Black Cypress in Eastern Washington, simply price everything in whole dollars (as shown in Figure 5.2). The belief is that odd-pricing at these price points is unnecessary.

P.F. CHANG'S.

STARTERS/SMALL PLATES	SOUPS/SALADS	SIDES	LUNCH BOWLS	CHICKEN/DUCK
BEEF PORK/LAMB	SEAFOOD	NOODLES/RICE	VEGETARIAN	P.F. CHANG'S FOR TWO
	GLUTEN FREE	KID'S MENU	DESSERTS	

STARTERS/SMALL PLATES

CHANG'S CHICKEN LETTUCE WRAPS	CRAB WONTONS	DUMPLINGS
Quickly-cooked spiced chicken served with cool lettuce cups 7.95	Crunchy wonton filled with rock crab meat and served with a side of spicy plum sauce 6.95	Handmade every day in our kitchen steamed or pan-fried Pork 5.95 Vegetable 5.95 Shrimp 7.25

☀ CHANG'S VEGETARIAN LETTUCE WRAPS	SALT & PEPPER CALAMARI	CRISPY WONTONS
A vegetarian version of our signature appetizer with tofu instead of chicken 7.95	Calamari tossed with scallions and our salt and pepper mix 7.25	Our pork wontons served crispy with a sweet & sour sauce 4.95

(a)

Source: P.F. Chang's.

Figure 5.1   P.F. Chang's menu.

CRISPY GREEN BEANS
More addictive than potato chips
5.95

SICHUAN CHICKEN FLATBREAD
Chinese scallion flatbread grilled with Sichuan marinated chicken, layered with melted cheese and served with creamy Asian Slaw
6.95

EGG ROLLS
Hand-rolled with marinated pork and vegetables. Served as a pair (2), this flavorful tradition is perfect with our special sweet & sour mustard sauce
4.95

SPRING ROLLS
Crispy spring rolls filled with shredded vegetables
(4) 5.95 (2) 3.95

NORTHERN STYLE SPARE RIBS
Tender wok-braised ribs served with a five-spice salt
8.95

CHANG'S SPARE RIBS
Wok-seared with Chang's barbeque sauce
8.95

SEARED AHI TUNA *
Sushi grade for the sushi fan. Served cold with spicy mustard and fresh mixed greens
8.95

火 **DYNAMITE SHRIMP**
Crispy shrimp tossed in a flavorful sauce… smoky with a little kick
8.95

(b)

火 SPICY   素 VEGETARIAN | VIEW OUR NUTRITIONAL INFORMATION |

All entrees are served with a choice of steamed brown or white rice.

Before placing your order, please inform your server if a person in your party has a food allergy. Additionally, if a person in your party has a special dietary need (e.g., gluten intolerance), please inform your server at the beginning or your visit. We will do our best to accommodate your needs. Please be aware that our restaurants use ingredients that contain all the major FDA allergens (peanuts, tree nuts, eggs, fish, shellfish, milk, soy and wheat).

For parties of 8 or more, an 18% gratuity will be added to your check. Please feel free to increase or decrease this gratuity at your discretion.

*These items are cooked to order and may be served raw or undercooked. Consuming raw or undercooked meats, poultry, seafood, shellfish or eggs may increase your risk of foodborne illness.

Restaurant #9818 - July 12, 2010

(c)

Figure 5.1   *(continued)*

B.C.
HOUSE
SMOKED
BACON
FOR SALE
1½ LBS PKG
$16

APPETIZERS

Monday: all menu apps half-off, until 7pm

SOYA 5
boilt soybeans, lemon, extra virgin olive oil, sea salt

CHEESE PLATE 11
please see our board or ask your server

OUR DAILY BREAD 7.50
bruschetta with toasted panhandle bread

CYPRIOT SANDWICH 8
haloumi cheese, date jam, mint

CLAMS 11*
bacon, garlic, greens, grilled bread

BLACK CYPRESS DIPS 11
tsatsiki, skordalia, briam, grilled bread

SOUVLAKIA 7
pork skewers, lemon, mountain oregano, shredded romaine salad

OLIVES 3
(olives)

SALAD

HOUSE 5/8
greens, red onions, green apples, blue cheese, bacon, candied walnuts, balsamic mustard vinaigrette

TURNIP THE BEETS 5/8
pistachios, blue cheese, parsley, extra virgin olive oil

BC CAESAR 5/8 *
romaine, bacon, parmigiano-reggiano, croutons

TODAY'S SOUP 5
please see our board or ask your server

PASTA

POMODORO 11
W/MEATBALLS 14
plum tomatoes, basil, parmigiano-reggiano, extra virgin olive oil

PAPPARDELLE BOLOGNESE 14
ribbon pasta, meat sauce, grana padano

KIMA 13
orecchiette, greek style meat sauce, myzithra cheese

CARBONARA 13 *
bacon, garlic & onion confit, cream, egg, parmigiano-reggiano

DAILY PASTA
see server for details

GRILL & SKILLET

LAMB CHOPS 21*
seasonal side, tsatsiki

PORK CHOP 19 *
seasonal potato side, shredded cabbage and carrot, mountain oregano jus

ROASTED CHICKEN 20
bread salad, seasonal greens, fresh herb pan jus

SHISH KEBAB 21*
grilled strip loin, mushrooms, zucchini, seasonal side

NEW YORK STEAK 24 *
RIBEYE STEAK 24 *
seasonal side and vegetable

GRILLED TOFU 14
briam, tsatsiki

DAILY FISH
please see our board or ask your server

All dietary restrictions and children's portions can be accomodated upon request.
*Eating raw or undercooked foods may increase your risk of food borne illness. 18% Gratuity may be added to tables of six or more.
Please ask about our catering services.

215 E. MAIN STREET, DOWNTOWN PULLMAN · (509) 334-5800

Courtesy of Black Cypress.

Figure 5.2   Black Cypress menu.

BLACK CYPRESS DRINKS

NON-ALCOHOLIC:

Draft Root Beer, Aranciatta, San Pellegrino 250mL (2) or 500mL (3.5)
Coca Cola and Sprite de Mexico in Bottles, Henry Weinhards Cream Soda (3), Diet Coke Can (1.50)

WHITE WINES *by the glass*

Cava, *Codorníu*, Brut, Spain (187mL)	8
Riesling, *KungFu Girl*, Columbia Valley, Wa '10	8.5/32
Chardonnay, *Alois Lageder*, Alto Adige, Italy, '09	8/30
Pinot Gris, *Maryhill*, Columbia Valley, '09	7/26
Sauvignon Blanc, *Oyster Bay*, Marlborough, NZ, '11	8.5/32
Moschofilero, *Boutari*, Mantinia, Greece '09	10/38
Viognier, *Zefina*, Horse Heaven Hills, Wa '07	8/30

RED WINES *by the glass*

Pinot Noir, *3°*, McMinville, OR '09	8/30
Merlot, *Kennedy Shah*, Rattlesnake Hills, WA, '09	7/26
Cabernet Sauvignon, *Chateau Smith*, WA	9/33
Zinfandel, *Artezin*, Mendocino Co., CA '09	8.5/32
Malbec, *Finca Sophena*, Argentina, '09	8/30
Syrah, Milbrandt *"Traditions"*, Wahluke Slopes, '08	9/34

LARGE FORMAT BEER
(750ML)

Chimay Premiére, Belgium	22
Omegang 3 Philosophers, NY	16

HOUSE WINES:

White or Red - *$3 for a 5 oz. glass,*
$6 for a 12 oz. carafe

DRAFT BEER 4.50
Ask your server for current selections.

GUILTY PLEASURES 3

Pabst Blue Ribbon Tallboys
Budweiser & Corona Bottles
Redbridge (gluten-free)
Beck's (Non-Alcoholic)
Abbeye de Leffe Belgian Blonde (5)

WHITE WINE BOTTLES

	PRICE
Sparkling	
Grüner Veltliner, Szigeti, Austria, NV	34
Prosecco, Adami Garbél, Italy, NV	26
Champagne, Veuve Clicquot Ponsardin, Brut, NV	75
Extended Tirage Brut, Argyle, OR, 2001	80
Pacific Northwest	
Whidbey Island White, WA	26
Riesling, Jones of Washington, Columbia Valley, '08	22
Pinot Grigio, C. Smith, Evergreen Vineyard, '08	30
Chardonnay, L'Ecole no. 41, Columbia Valley, '09	39
Carménère Rosé, Wawawai Canyon, Walla Walla, '09	25
California	
Sauvignon Blanc, Duckhorn, Napa Valley, '09	36
Viognier/Marsanne, Treana, Paso Robles, '07	37
Caymus Conundrum, Napa Valley, '08	41
Chardonnay, Rombauer, Napa Valley, '08	56
Far Away	
Chassagne le Cailleret 1er Cru, Girardin, FR, '06	81
Riesling Auslese, Wallhausen, Johannisberg, GER, '04	65
Retsina, Kourtaki, Greece, NV	24
Vermentino, Solosole, Toscana, Italy '09	32
Chardonnay, Errazuriz, "Wild Ferment," Chile, '10	42

RED WINE BOTTLES

Pacific Northwest	
Carmenére, Wawawai Canyon, Walla Walla, '08	30
Pinot Noir, Amity, "Eco-Wine," Willamette Valley, '08	34
Pinot Noir, Adelsheim, Willamette Valley, '09	41
Pinot Noir, Bethel Heights, Willamette Valley, '07	65
Merlot, Basalt Cellars, Columbia Valley, '05	28
Merlot, Abeja, Columbia Valley, '08	52

RED WINE BOTTLES *continued...*

Malbec, Milbrandt "Estates", Wahluke Slopes, '08	44
Cabernet Sauvignon, Amavi, Walla Walla, '08	39
Cabernet Sauvignon, L'Ecole No. 41, Columbia Valley, '08	40
Cabernet Sauvignon, Abeja, Columbia Valley, '08	57
Cabernet Sauvignon, Januik, *Champoux*, Col. Valley, '08	71
Syrah, Amavi, Walla Walla, '08	42
Syrah, Charles Smith, "Royal City," Royal Slopes, '08	140
Zinfandel, Thurston Wolfe, Prosser, '09	39
PNW Blends	
Merry Cellars, "Crimson Red," Pullman, WA, '09	32
Andrew Will, "Sorella," Walla Walla, '06	88
Helix, "Pomatia," Columbia Valley, '07	38
Dunham Trutina, Walla Walla, '07	44
JM Cellars, "Tre Fanciulli," Columbia Valley, '08	54
Woodward Canyon, "Artist Series," Columbia Valley, 08	64
California	
Bordeaux Blend, Araujo Altagracia, CA, '03	82
Cabernet, Stag's Leap Cellars, "Artemis," Napa, '06	75
Zinfandel, Rosenblum, "Monte Rosso," Sonoma, '05	62
Far Away	
Côtes Du Rhône, Kermit Lynch, France, '08	32
Chateauneuf-du-Pape, Dom. Roger Perrin, France, '07	61
Chambolle-Musigny, Lechenaut, France, '04	90
Priorat, Pasanau, "Finca La Planeta," Spain, '06	65
Nebbiolo, Aldo Conterno, "Il Favot," Italy, '01	120

DESSERT WINES (3OZ)

Chocolate or Hazelnut Porto	7
Dunham Late Harvest Riesling, CA	7
Warres Nimrod Porto, CA	7

Figure 5.2 *(continued)*

Whatever your approach to the psychological aspect of pricing, the key is consistency. Restaurant guests like consistency, and a menu with mixed pricing strategies that reflect conflicting menu psychology principles can be detrimental to sales. Moreover, the design of menus and the ways in which the qualities of menu items are communicated to the customer are also vital elements of menu psychology, as we consider next.

Design

As introduced in the previous chapter, the menu is the primary marketing vehicle for a foodservice operation. Thus, its design should align with the operation's theme. In a hospital, for example, the cover of the patient menu might show the healthcare provider's logo and its mission statement. In a restaurant that has a long history in a community, the cover might describe the restaurant's history.

Successful menu design doesn't stop at the cover. For example, the medium on which a menu is presented also merits design consideration. Shula's Steak House, founded by the famous football icon Don Shula, features a menu printed on an actual football. Other unique menus are one printed on cleavers that servers whack into tables or wine lists printed on wine bottles.

Whatever the setting, the design must also allow for readability. Notice the P.F. Change Bistro menu, discussed earlier and shown in Figure 5.1; it has ample white space, allowing the customer to read it easily. On a related note, the graphics should reflect décor and ambiance. As everything must stem from the menu, its design must be consistent with everything else the customer experiences while dining.

Entrepreneurs have taken great liberty with menu design today. For example, David Overton, founder of the popular Cheesecake Factory, offsets the cost of his voluminous menu by selling advertising space on it. As a result, a patron can not only select an appetizer to start a meal but she can also find the address of the local sunglass shop (see Figure 5.3).

Communication

We discussed the importance of how and what the menu communicates in Chapter 3. Here we apply communication principles to pricing. On the one hand, if pricing provides a competitive advantage to a foodservice operation, then prices should be displayed prominently on the menu. On the other hand, some operators are better off emphasizing unique menu offerings and downplaying price.

Consider the examples in Figures 5.4 and 5.5. In Figure 5.4, the price is shown very prominently. As we find in many restaurants, this is a traditional approach that acknowledges customers' natural curiosity about an item's price. In Figure 5.6, however, the operator places greater emphasis on the item itself, displaying the price more subtly. By including price as simply an unremarkable aspect of the menu item, the operator implies that the price is about what should be expected for such an item.

Figure 5.5 also integrates a smaller portion option. This is a popular menu strategy in an environment in which restaurants stand to benefit from minimizing the extent to which eating out is associated with the much-lamented obesity epidemic in the United States. Of greater importance, however, is the psychological impact of offering a smaller portion with a lower price that suggests to the diner that this menu item is a great value. The server will likely ask the guest if she would prefer the "regular" size version of the item, but even if the guest switches to the larger portion, she may very well continue to think of the dish as one that costs less than $10.

Item description is another key element of menu communication. Menu verbiage should be clear and the description should make the item desirable. For example, a menu item description ideally includes the method of preparation and essential ingredients (and accompanying

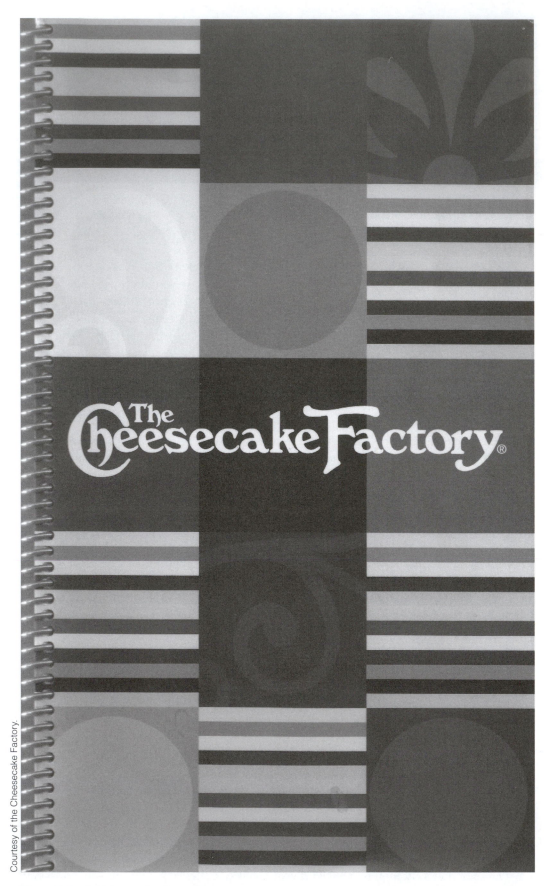

Courtesy of the Cheesecake Factory.

Figure 5.3   A Cheesecake Factory menu.

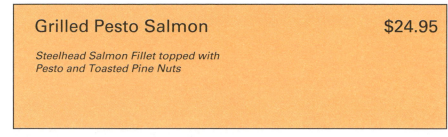

Figure 5.4   Menu item with prominent price position.

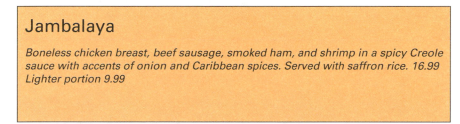

Figure 5.5   Menu item with more subtle price position.

side dishes). If a restaurant's marketing strategy emphasizes quality over value, an operator may include quality claims (such as fresh vs. frozen), information pertaining to specific varieties of produce and meat, or identification of geographic origin, which can be particularly helpful in underscoring the availability of locally sourced ingredients.

Many foodservice operators err by including item descriptions that are too long. The customer usually does not need to know everything about how an item is prepared. Similarly, a menu should not overuse words that are not typically associated with food and beverages. It simply doesn't make sense to advertise the meatloaf as accompanied by two *majestic* mountains of mashed potatoes or a steak with a *pristine* sauce. What is that supposed to mean? Another issue is overpromising. Superlatives such as "cooked to perfection" should not be used. After all, how else should something be cooked? Finally, the description should not state the size of a meat portion unless it is extraordinary. For example, if the filet mignon is a modest six ounces, there is no reason to advertise this. On the other hand, if the main attraction is the item's size (say, a three-pound lobster) then this may well be important to communicate.

Another strategy to consider when using the menu to communicate is to include humor. Referring again to our discussion of menu development in Chapter 3, the menu can help portray the fun atmosphere that the foodservice operator is trying to communicate. Rather than including information about how an item is prepared, it might have unique descriptions about the source or how the items were obtained, as shown in Figure 5.6.

The last word on menu communication is *honesty*. If a restaurant advertises "fresh" salmon, this means that it can't substitute frozen salmon. As we discussed earlier, the menu is an advertising vehicle and as such, falls under the same legal restrictions as other printed advertising. Therefore, no matter how creatively one crafts a menu's communication strategy, truth and accuracy must be considered.

Truth and Accuracy

Earlier in the text we addressed some of the regulations governing healthcare, long-term care, and school foodservice operations. Because such operations involve captive audiences with special nutritional requirements, the need for such regulation is obvious. Except for safety

Figure 5.6   A menu with humorous descriptions.

regulations (covered in Chapter 7), the restaurant industry has been relatively free from legislative involvement.

This observation does not, however, apply to truth and accuracy in menu descriptions. In the 1970s consumer groups began noticing inconsistencies between menu descriptions and the actual items served in some restaurants. For example, at one time McDonald's included placemats on serving trays that implied that real maple syrup was used on its pancakes and that the orange juice was fresh. In truth, the syrup was not pure maple syrup and the juice was frozen, not fresh. As a result, the California Superior Court fined the QSR operator $10,000 for violating the state's truth-in-menu regulations. McDonald's did not contest the charges and quickly redesigned the placemats.

More recently, regulatory efforts have begun to address all aspects of foodservice operations, including restaurants. First, all menus must comply with the Food and Drug Administration's (FDA) food-labeling regulations. There has been a lengthy history of debate over the proper way to apply these regulations to restaurants, but the first rule is that whenever a foodservice operation of any kind makes a claim regarding the healthiness, freshness, or source of a food, the operator must be prepared to demonstrate to a customer or inspector that the claim is true. The easiest rule to follow is, "Don't say it if you can't prove it," or, alternatively, "If you say it, serve it."[1] If an item is claimed to be low in fat, it must be. In addition, it is important today to include warnings about potentially harmful items that may not be obvious, such as "contains tree nut oil" or "includes shellfish broth." Documentation is needed if a menu uses any of the following words or symbols representing these words:

- Free

- Low

- Reduced

- Light/Lite

- Provides/Contains/Good Source of

- High/Excellent Source of/Rich in

- Lean/Extra-Lean

- Fresh

- Natural

- Healthy

- Trans-fat free

The FDA and the National Restaurant Association offer reference publications to assist operators in their efforts to understand food labeling laws.[2]

Another example of a possible problem in menu truthfulness involves dishes that are advertised to appeal to vegetarians. For some individuals, vegetarian choices are a matter of strict religious practice, while others avoid meat to be socially responsible or to eat a healthy diet. Still others have intolerances to certain food, and suffer if the food is not what it is billed to be. Whatever the consumer's rationale, she has a right to believe that if an item says it does not contain meat, that is accurate information. Inaccuracy in labeling can greatly disturb a customer who has ordered an item that says it contains no meat but has chicken broth in the sauce.

The next area of regulation for the restaurant menu, which is continually evolving at the local, state, and national levels, involves nutritional information that must be provided on or with restaurant menus. We discussed the related 2010 Patient Protection and Affordable Care Act's Restaurant Nutrition Menu Labeling Requirement in Chapter 3. (Recall that the Act requires restaurants and similar retail food establishments with 20 or more locations to list calorie content information for standard menu items on restaurant menus and menu boards, including drive-through menu boards.) Even prior to such legislation, several localities moved to regulate public access to the nutritional content of restaurant menus. New York was the first to require that this information be printed with the item on the menu, while other localities simply required that it be posted clearly or be available in a readily accessible place. Whatever the local adaptation, associated regulations are based on increasing consumer awareness of nutrition coupled with concerns about obesity, heart disease, or diabetes, which are often linked to nutritional factors.

The authors of an article in the May 2007 issue of the *American Journal of Preventive Medicine* discussed "How Major Restaurant Chains Plan Their Menus." In connection with profit-making organizations, these researchers noted that profit was the primary focus on restaurant menus. "Without an increase in consumer demand, it is unlikely the restaurant industry will increase their offering of healthy food choices."[3] Time changes things quickly. Writing in *Tastings* in Spring 2008, S. C. Weiss observed that National Restaurant Association data indicate that 76 percent of adults report that they are trying to eat healthier fare in restaurants than they did just two years earlier.[4]

Nevertheless, the move to force restaurants to provide such information has been resisted by many although, as noted earlier, some have long ago embraced the ethic of providing nutritional content, particularly in the QSR segment. Peter Romeo writes for *Nations Restaurant News* and recently noted that "a study just released by the Los Angeles County Department of Public Health said the implementation of menu labeling . . . would change the eating habits of just one in ten patrons."[5]

While there is certainly reason for restaurants to be proactive and work against unreasonable regulation or enforced uniformity, it is probably true that these regulatory efforts will continue and perhaps ultimately result in healthier choices on many menus.

■□ EXTENDING MENU PHILOSOPHY

The final menu psychology issue pertains to applying an operator's menu philosophy to more than one menu element at a time. The most basic example is found at any QSR outlet and is known as **bundling**. For the customer, bundling represents discount pricing and convenience. For the operator, bundling facilitates increased sales. As current practice shows, most QSR behind-the-counter menus dedicate the majority of space to bundled packages. Gone are the days when a customer would order a cheeseburger, fries, and soda from separate areas of the menu. Today, they are more likely to enter the drive-through lane and order a "number three."

A related aspect of bundling is the "upsizing" of a bundled package. Once referred to commonly as "supersizing," the idea is to upsell the customer to a larger side dish, typically french fries, and a larger beverage, at an incrementally increased price.[6] This strategy is consistent with our understanding of menu psychology because—just as we noted about offering smaller portions—large QSR menus typically display the prices of bundled menu items very prominently while adding the upsized serving price as a footnote. Thus, the customer subconsciously thinks of the lunch as costing $5.95 whereas the actual upsized price might be $7.45. As we discuss later, the profit on items such french fries and sodas is proportionately much greater than it is on QSR items such as hamburgers. So, it is in the operator's interest to offer upsized side dishes and drinks at a "discount" as a means to increasing profit.

Another variation on menu psychology is the children's menu. As people with children can attest, their kids often drive the decision about where to go when the family is looking to dine in a restaurant. As a result, restaurants in every segment typically offer some sort of children's menu. These range from very elaborate presentations meant to attract a child's eye to a basic black-and-white paper menu on which children can draw with crayons supplied at the table. Leading restaurant chains such as Chili's Grill & Bar are particularly aware of the importance of special children's dishes and have capitalized on the associated menu design and use (see Figure 5.7).

In designing children's menus, it is important to note that the pricing methods discussed earlier can be applied but the profit expectation on such items should be lower. Children's menu items are often considered **loss leaders**—they may not produce a substantial profit but they rather effectively achieve the primary objective of selling food and beverages at profit-producing prices to adults. In fact, many restaurant operators intentionally price children's menu items at a loss, knowing they will recoup the money from the sale of items to other family members.

Another nontraditional menu offered along with the main menu is the cocktail menu. A cocktail menu provides the restaurateur with an opportunity to market high-profit alcoholic beverages in a way that suggests their uniqueness in execution or presentation. A diner who is handed a cocktail menu is likely to assume that there must be something special about that restaurant's beverage offerings. Yet while any fine dining restaurant is expected to have a wine list, a restaurant with a cocktail menu runs the risk that consumers will perceive it as promoting alcohol and as a result lose some appeal to families. Still, cocktail menus can be very effective at increasing beverage sales.

Having made the decision to create a cocktail menu (which may include beer and wine as well as nonalcoholic options), the operator should focus on specialty drinks—particularly

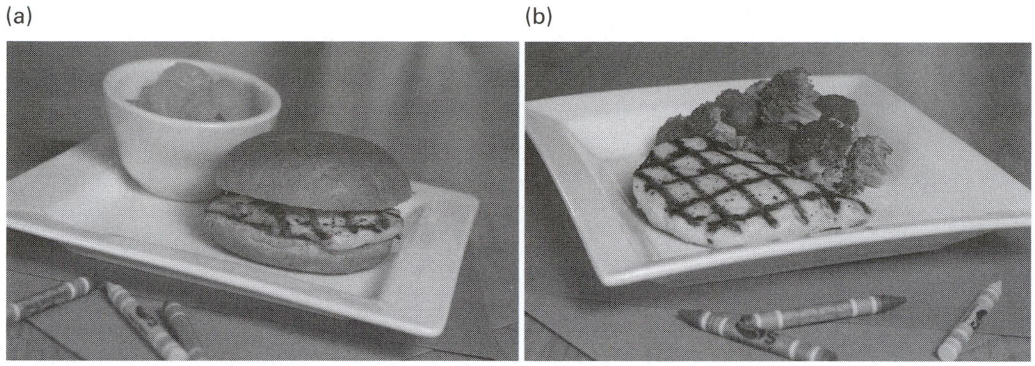

(a)

(b)

Courtesy of Chili's.

Figure 5.7 Two children's menu items.

those with a high profit potential. For example, a beach cafe might feature California Lemonade, which could be a fun twist on lemonade with the addition of pureed strawberries and rum. The presentation would be impressive, and the profit potential, if priced correctly, very strong. However, cocktail menu designers should not feature basic drinks such as gin and tonics, unless they offer unusual combinations of ingredients (as in the proliferating offerings of specialty "martinis" that contain neither gin nor vodka). After all, what else is going to be in a gin and tonic except gin and tonic? Moreover, it is generally not possible to price such a basic drink in a manner that produces a greater profit than other standard fare drinks. (Other issues concerning beverage sales generators, merchandising, and the associated liability are discussed in Chapter 17.)

Still, it is worth discussing the use of menu psychology to increase beverage sales or, more specifically, beer and wine sales. One of the best ways to do this is to include pairing suggestions on the food menu (even if a separate wine list is offered). Such suggestions allow the foodservice operator to identify compatible combinations (for example, grilled salmon with a nice, fruity Pinot Noir), and make it easy for the customer to make a dependable wine selection.

Unfortunately, many people do not know what food goes with what wine, and as a result, don't want to experiment in a restaurant setting. Others simply don't want to make a "wrong" decision in terms of food and beverage pairing. The inclusion of wine and beer options with paired food items removes these worries and can enhance beverage sales dramatically. A customer who might not have considered ordering wine with, say, a specialty sandwich is much more likely to break with tradition when the pairing suggestion is included with the item description.

MENU ENGINEERING

Once you have a solid understanding of menu pricing approaches and an appreciation of menu psychology, you are ready to assess how each menu item contributes to a foodservice operation's bottom line. The best way to accomplish this is through what is known as **menu engineering**. Menu engineering includes a broad range of analytical techniques that enable foodservice operators to optimize the **menu mix** (the type and number of offerings in each menu category—such as appetizers, entrées, and desserts) and menu pricing to enhance efficiency, increase guest satisfaction, and maximize profit.

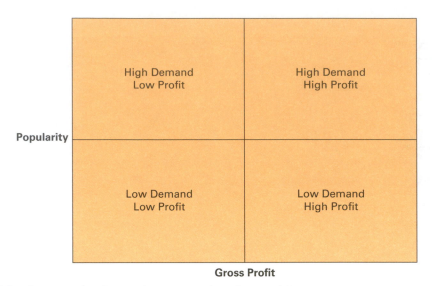

Figure 5.8 An example of an early menu engineering model.

Origins

The earliest menu engineering models focused on two key variables: gross profit (menu price less food cost) and popularity (sales of a given item).[7] All menu items are analyzed collectively using each of these two variables displayed on a two-dimensional grid, as shown in Figure 5.8.

The High Demand/High Profit items in the upper-right quadrant are clearly the menu "stars" and should be kept, while the Low Demand/Low Profit items in the lower left quadrant are "dogs" and should be replaced or changed (in cost or price). The High Demand/Low Profit workhorses of the upper right quadrant bring in customers and make them happy—they are probably keepers in most situations. The puzzling items are the Low Demand/High Profit items in the lower right quadrant. These merit careful reconsideration, since they may be favorites with a small group of important customers, particularly if they routinely also buy expensive wine.

Using these early models, operators were able to subject the menu mix and pricing to quantitative analysis, eliminating or changing items or prices. For example, they could identify items that appeared to be popular but that in reality hurt profitability, and they could adjust the menu price accordingly. Also, so-called signature dishes that didn't sell well could be readily modified. Similarly, dishes with low popularity and high gross profit might be promoted by the foodservers or repositioned on the menu.

While this and related approaches are still used by many operators, they exhibit several analytical deficiencies. For example, menu analysis models based on gross profit cannot reveal the true profitability of a menu item if other operating costs are not considered. First and most seriously, the models fail to address labor costs, arguably the greatest expense category in restaurant operations. Additionally, matrix models assume that all direct costs are equally related to all menu items. Finally, these models share the common shortcoming of variable interdependency. In other words, as the gross profit for a single menu item increases, the mean gross profit used as the normalizing factor changes. This fluidity in the convergence of primary vectors, while useful for mapping purposes, makes it impossible to quantify the actual performance of a single item objectively.

Advanced Techniques

In response to these issues, researchers have begun to integrate other fundamental variables into menu analysis. Furthermore, they now apply sophisticated statistical approaches, adapted for operators in easy-to-use software packages. While explaining the mathematical underpinnings for these is beyond the scope of this book, it is worthwhile to provide some examples.

One provocative menu-engineering model incorporates labor attributes expressed in categorical terms. This new process—data envelopment analysis—is used to construct a more complex menu analysis model that allows an operator to incorporate multiple input and output variables in the menu item evaluation process. Such variables include but are not limited to difficulty in preparation, duration of preparation time, number of employees required, and costs associated with inventory management. This approach also allows for comparison against the best-performing rather than average menu items.

Interestingly, results obtained using this new approach have differed from those produced by a similar analysis using the traditional matrix approach, suggesting that this area of foodservice analytics is still evolving.[8] In addition, many foodservice companies, in their quest to be socially responsible, are attempting to use more local ingredients and source items that require fewer food miles (discussed in the previous chapter). This variable should also figure into the menu engineering approach as part of an operation's overall strategic plan. The optimal mix of variables to test and the best analytic approach, as we now understand, varies by type of operation, industry segment, and operator sophistication. Thus, just as well-trained foodservice operators use advanced approaches for labor and inventory management (discussed in later chapters), future industry leaders will be able to apply promising new techniques to menu management.

MANAGERIAL IMPLICATIONS

To thrive in today's highly competitive foodservice industry, operators must be sensitive to many factors when developing their strategy for menu pricing. The simple menu-pricing models of yesterday are simply not adequate. Today, foodservice managers must understand the difference between market-driven and demand-driven pricing. Another critical tool involves employing price optimization science, such as using the stochastic pricing model. Moreover, menu-item pricing cannot yield accurate information by testing the same set of variables across menu-item categories. An operation's menu-pricing strategy must also be reviewed periodically, particularly as costs change over time.

In addition, foodservice managers must understand how psychology can affect customers' purchasing decisions. In some cases, odd pricing might be effective; in others, adopting a nontraditional approach such as rounding to whole dollars might strengthen sales. Using several menu types, such as specialized drink menus or children's menus, can also help to entice customers to order additional menu items. Finally, a menu's design and the message it communicates must be carefully orchestrated, as illustrated by the practice of including wine and food pairing recommendations.

With the most advanced pricing strategies in place, managers must constantly assess how each menu item performs in terms of profit and quantity sold. The old menu-engineering approaches that involve comparing the gross profit and popularity of individual items, while useful, must be understood by the industry's next generation of foodservice leaders but should be supported or replaced by newer, more sophisticated approaches. These new approaches make it possible to leverage technology in testing a host of variables such as profit, labor cost in terms of the complexity of menu-item preparation, and the sources of ingredients. Using food items that travel fewer food miles, such as those sourced locally, contributes to the local economy while also adhering to socially responsible practices.

Applebee's

Applebee's is the largest casual dining chain in the world, with locations throughout the United States and worldwide. Since the beginning, Applebee's has achieved its popularity by marketing itself as a neighborhood restaurant focused on serving good food to good people. The first restaurant was opened in 1980, and the company went public in 1989. In 1992, there were 250 Applebee's outlets in operation. By 1999, the chain had 1,168 restaurants with record systemwide sales of $2.35 billion. In 2007, the company opened its first location in China. In November of that same year, the chain was acquired by IHOP Corporation, creating the largest full-service restaurant chain in the world. Today, Applebee's (and the IHOP Corporation) are part of DineEquity, Inc., which is traded on the New York Stock Exchange under the symbol DIN. More than 1,990 Applebee's restaurants are now operating in 49 states, 15 countries, and one US territory. Widely considered to be a leader in this segment, the Applebee's system employs more than 28,000 employees.

KEY TERMS

Case in Point

The $47 Burger

Los Angeles, California, is arguably one of the leading destinations for those seeking the quintessential hamburger. California is known as the birthplace of many of today's most-popular drive-through QSR chains, including regional leader In-N-Out Burger. But it is also home to independent QSRs. Tommy, the second-generation owner of one of these independent restaurants, went on a quest to see what was new in the hamburger market.

What he found surprised him. At the time, he was selling a deluxe half-pound cheeseburger topped with chili and onions for $6.95; he thought it was expensive but he had been meticulous in applying advanced menu-pricing and menu-psychology approaches and his strategy was paying off—in the last several months it was his best-selling item. The first stop on his quest was the Fleur de Lys, a traditional French restaurant located in Las Vegas' Mandalay Bay Resort and Casino. Here he saw on the menu the FleurBurger—priced at $75! Tommy noted that the burger was unique: It was made of Kobe beef and garnished with foie gras—that's duck or goose liver—and black truffles. While his restaurant does not serve beer or wine, he also noticed that for a mere $5,000 you could get the FleurBurger 5000. This is the same FleurBurger, but it is served with a bottle of Chateau Pétrus 1990 in Ichendorf Brunello stemware, specially imported from Italy, which you take home.

Next, he visited the Old Homestead Steakhouse in Boca Raton, Florida, where he found the tri-beef burger.

This is made of a blend of three kinds of beef—American Prime, Japanese Wagyu, and Argentinean. The hamburger is served with its signature chipotle ketchup made with truffles and champagne. The restaurant's owners even donate $10 of every sale of the $125 burger to the Make-A-Wish Foundation.

Thinking he'd found the most expensive burger, he excitedly anticipated a visit to New York City's Wall Street Burger Shoppe. On the menu he found the Richard Nouveau burger—for $175. The ten-ounce Kobe beef burger is topped with black truffles, seared foie gras, aged Gruyere cheese, wild mushrooms, and flakes of gold leaf. But then he heard that Burger King—the same Burger King chain discussed in the previous chapter—had created the world's most expensive hamburger. Served only at the West London Burger King Restaurant, one can pay a whopping $186 for the menu item named simply "The Burger." The Wagyu beef patty is accompanied by white truffles, onion tempura prepared in Cristal champagne, and some of Spain's finest Pata Negra ham. It is presented in an Iranian saffron and truffle bun.

While he was not able to visit London, his explorations had given him much food for thought. He flew back to California and thought to himself, "I could build a burger that, by Los Angeles standards, would be hugely expensive. I could use unique ingredients and charge a nice $46.95—exactly $40 more than my current big seller costs. Would people buy it?"

Should Tommy try it? Would people buy it? What do you think of his pricing approach?

REVIEW AND DISCUSSION QUESTIONS

1. What is the difference between market and demand drivers in menu pricing?

2. Why would an operator use nonstructured pricing?

3. What is the advantage of using the actual-cost method over the prime-cost method?

4. Which of the pricing approaches would be desirable for a caterer, and why?

5. What is the advantage of using the Mc variable in the stochastic-modeling approach to menu pricing?

6. What is odd-pricing, and why would a foodservice operator use it? Be sure to provide examples.

7. Using a restaurant other than the one cited in the chapter, provide an example of a restaurant that prices its menu items in whole dollars.

8. We provided examples of unique menus such as the one printed on a football and another on a meat cleaver. Find a restaurant that has some other kind of unique menu aspect.

9. List two advantages in offering two portion sizes for entrees.

10. Search some restaurants' websites and provide (1) an example of a good menu item description and (2) one that needs improvement (be sure to include your recommendations for improving it).

11. We discussed the importance of truth and accuracy in menu verbiage. Would this also apply to pictures on a menu? For example, if the picture shows a fillet of halibut, can the restaurant serve halibut steak instead?

12. Provide four examples of words that if used on a menu must be supported by documentation if requested.

13. What is bundling? Give examples of its use in at least two restaurant industry segments.

14. Name one advantage and one disadvantage of offering a children's menu.

15. What is menu engineering, and why should a foodservice operator use it?

16. Identify at least one shortcoming of earlier menu-engineering models.

17. In terms of the multivariable menu engineering models discussed, what is one variable or foodservice attribute that you might include (other than those already discussed)?

ENDNOTES

1. Barth, S. "Truth in Menu: If You Say It Serve It." *Global Chefs*. www.globalchefs.com.

2. National Restaurant Association. "Guidance for complying with menu guidelines." www.restaurant.org.

3. Glanz, K., et al. "How Major Restaurant Chains Plan Their Menus." *American Journal of Preventive Medicine* (May 2007).

4. Weiss, S. C. "Registered dietitians in the restaurant and foodservice industry." *Tastings* (newsletter of the Food and Culinary Practice Group of the Academy of Nutrition and Dietetics) 2 (Spring 1008): 2.

5. Romeo, P. "Rather Than Wait with Bated Breath for Next Menu-Labeling Mandate, Operators Should Get Proactive." *Nation's Restaurant News* (May 26, 2008).

6. The use of the word *supersize* became unpopular following the 2004 American documentary film, *Super Size Me*, which implied that the QSR industry was partially at fault for increasing obesity. Following the film's release, McDonald's, the chain that made the term popular, stopped using it.

7. Kasavana, M. L., and Smith, D. I. *Menu Engineering: A practical guide to menu analysis*. Lansing, MI: Hospitality Publications, 1982.

8. Reynolds, D., and Taylor, J. "Validating a DEA-based Menu Analysis Model Using Structural Equation Modeling." *International Journal of Hospitality Management* 30 (3) (2011): 584–587.

PART 3

THE FOODSERVICE OPERATION

Following our overview of the foodservice industry and a thorough introduction to the vital role menus play in every segment, we now set our sights on the operation of restaurants and other foodservice establishments. We begin in Chapter 6 with a discussion of planning, design, and equipment, providing a step-by-step introduction to the processes involved in creating a working foodservice entity. We address food sanitation and safety, essential processes in any foodservice operation, in Chapter 7. In Chapter 8, we address supply chain management, including such functions as purchasing, distribution channels, supplier selection, methods of buying, and forecasting. We conclude Part III with a comprehensive introduction to food management, including receiving, storage, inventory management, and production management.

FACILITIES PLANNING, DESIGN, AND EQUIPMENT

LEARNING OBJECTIVES:

After becoming familiar with this chapter, you should be able to:

1. Understand the planning considerations that are vital to creating a successful foodservice operation.

2. Appreciate how safety and productivity pertain to facilities planning.

3. Identify the key elements in design and layout, particularly as they pertain to space allocation, dining room design, and kitchen design.

4. Understand what is involved in selecting food preparation and serving equipment.

5. Explain how to procure equipment for a new or remodeled foodservice operation.

6. Utilize practices that lead to enhanced corporate responsibility.

In earlier chapters, we talked about site selection and identifying a foodservice concept that best fits a particular marketplace. We then addressed the role of the menu as the foundation of any foodservice operation. Now, we are ready to discuss the steps that lead to creating such an operation. How this is done properly depends on the type of foodservice operation that is to be created.

For example, the physical structure of a beer garden at a ballpark is dramatically different from that of a hospital cafe or fine dining restaurant. There are, however, general considerations that apply regardless of industry segment.

PLANNING

Like any business venture, developing a foodservice operation starts with planning, and this entails determining several basic building blocks. If you are creating a restaurant or other operation, you must know how much space is needed in the kitchen and dining room areas (if applicable), how food will move through the kitchen, and how much room for storage is needed. The planning phase also takes into consideration regulatory and safety issues, location-specific restrictions (such as venting in a kitchen that is in the basement of a four-story building), and unique concept requirements. Once these general parameters of a foodservice operation are in place, the actual design and layout can be determined.

Planning Considerations

The scope and scale of a foodservice operation dictates which planning procedures deserve more attention and time, but, regardless of the complexity, the process begins with identifying the decision makers, understanding the expectations or goals of the planning process, and then ensuring that the outcomes address the needs and desires of all stakeholders, including owners, managers, employees, and guests.

Who makes the decisions? Answering this question is paramount at the outset, as the final responsibility for planning, design, and execution must rest with specific individuals. In some cases, primary or sole decision-making authority is assumed by the owner or owners. In others, the opening general manager or managerial team assumes this authority. (In foodservice chains or firms that involve multiple units owned and operated by the parent company or managed services company, the opening general manager and her team might be on location prior to opening and remain onsite for the first several months, after which they are replaced with a permanent team; the opening team then moves on to open the next location.) Failure to assign responsibility at the beginning of the planning process can result in miscommunication, which ultimately can jeopardize the operation's well being.

The list of decisions to be made is a long one, but it begins with articulating the details of any project under consideration. While everyone with important responsibilities should have input on the plan for a foodservice operation, there should be a single person or if necessary a small cohort of individuals who understand the big picture and who can ensure that every detail has been considered. (The chapter's Case in Point underscores this well.) The resulting plan, often termed a **prospectus**, should begin with a general description of the foodservice operation. It should then address the intended customer base, including demographic information such as age and income, and then determine operation-specific parameters such as hours of operation and number of seats. A sound foodservice operation plan should include every conceivable detail about the intended physical and operational characteristics of the foodservice operation, including staffing needs. To develop a thorough prospectus for smaller, simpler operations such as coffee kiosks requires little effort, while completing a prospectus for a large full-service restaurant will likely require considerable effort and many productive labor hours.

In some instances, a **feasibility study** is undertaken prior to developing a prospectus to objectively evaluate the strengths and weaknesses of the proposed business as well as the opportunities and threats in its marketplace (often referred to as a SWOT analysis), determine the resources required to make the foodservice operation a reality, and calculate the prospects of financial success. In other cases, although it is less common, the prospectus is used to execute the feasibility study. Either way, the information that supports both a prospectus and a feasibility study often comes from the same sources.

When the information provided in a feasibility study demonstrates that a proposed food-service operation is financially viable and a detailed prospectus is complete, the next decision—or set of decisions—pertains to the **timeline** for the actual construction or remodeling that is needed to create the new operation. In many settings, this is drawn up by a **project manager**, a person responsible for executing and completing a project as planned. In the foodservice business, the project manager may be the decision maker as well, but in many cases the project manager is a third party who reports to the owner or general manager. In either case, the timeline is critical for coordinating construction and managing costs.

As shown in Figure 6.1, a timeline has two major components: timing and tasks. Note that some tasks share the same blocks of time with others; this makes sense since many things can be done concurrently. However, optimizing the flow of tasks is critical. For example, before installing kitchen equipment, the floor and floor drains must be completed. The complexity that must be managed with a timeline is indicated by a list of the tasks that are entailed by such a project:

- Introductory meeting with management team
- Planning meeting with management team
- Kitchen equipment design
- Space and storage specifications
- Architectural design
- Architectural design review
- Signage design
- Landlord design review
- Signage procurement
- Architectural design permit submittal
- Kitchen equipment review
- Kitchen equipment procurement
- Mechanical, electrical, and plumbing design
- Mechanical, electrical, and plumbing design review
- Mechanical, electrical, and plumbing permit submittal
- Signage installation
- Mechanical, electrical, and plumbing procurement
- Kitchen equipment procurement
- Onsite construction
- Furniture, fixtures, and non-kitchen equipment procurement
- Kitchen equipment installation
- Furniture, fixtures, and non-kitchen equipment installation
- Facility review
- Move-in and training

Again, the duration and order of these tasks depend on the type of foodservice operation for which the plan has been devised.

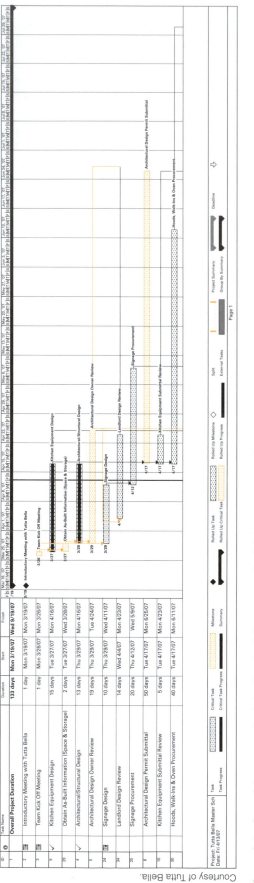

Courtesy of Tutta Bella.

Figure 6.1 A partial master schedule. For the full master schedule, go to www.wiley.com/college/reynolds.

Safety and Productivity

In planning any foodservice operation, there are two other overarching concerns that ultimately relate to the aforementioned issue of profitability: safety and productivity. In this context, safety pertains to the guests, the employees, and—to be addressed later in the chapter—the environment. In terms of guest safety, the biggest concern for foodservice operators is typically sanitation. This concern is so great, in fact, that the entire following chapter is dedicated to food sanitation and safety. In the planning phase, food sanitation and safety can best be addressed through the layout and selection of kitchen equipment.

Other guest safety issues that need to be considered during the planning process pertain to the foodservice operation's physical characteristics. For example, floors, ramps, stairs, and entryways should be covered in nonslip material. Selection of furnishings such as tables and chairs must be thoughtfully executed to ensure guest safety. Lighting, which varies considerably by type of operation, must nevertheless be adequate to ensure that guests can see where they are going within the foodservice establishment.

Abiding by legislation that pertains to both guest and employee safety is another key planning consideration. For example, the 1970 **Occupational Safety and Health Act** (OSHA) was created to ensure safe and healthful working conditions by setting and enforcing standards. According to the OSHA website, "Employers must provide their employees with a workplace that does not have serious hazards and follow all relevant OSHA safety and health standards." In terms of facilities planning, this means that owners and managers must plan a safe workplace, ensuring, for example, proper wiring of equipment, adequate kitchen lighting, and including or installing functional safety features on potentially dangerous equipment. Even the level of noise to which personnel are exposed must be considered. Most OSHA violations in the foodservice industry today are due not to management error but rather to poor design.

Productivity is the other critical concern relative to planning. A properly designed foodservice operation in which **workflow** has been carefully planned will likely incur lower labor costs by enabling employees to complete their tasks more efficiently. This principle applies not only to kitchen design but also to the dining room, where workflow is also important. Dining area workflow determines, for example, how food is delivered to the guest and how dirty dishes are returned to the dish room. Imagine the calamities that would befall a restaurant in which a single swinging door is the only access point from the kitchen to the dining room. Foodservers with hot plates would have to push the door from the kitchen into the dining room while bussers would have to return dirty plates by pushing the door from the dining room into the kitchen. That is the epitome of poor workflow planning!

These same flow concerns must be applied to the dining room. Often referred to as **traffic flow**, the paths over which guests move around a dining room or cafe should be carefully planned. This extends to considering how guests move from one area to another, such as from a bar to a dining room or a waiting area to tables. Again, thoughtful planning can result in operational efficiencies and greater guest satisfaction.

Other Concerns

In addition to general regulatory concerns, including those related to OSHA, still others associated with the **Americans with Disabilities Act** (ADA) must be considered in the planning processes. The ADA was enacted in 1990 and amended in 2008; it "prohibits private employers, state and local governments, employment agencies, and labor unions from discriminating against qualified individuals with disabilities in job application procedures, hiring, firing, advancement, compensation, job training, and other terms, conditions, and privileges of employment."

In essence, the ADA requires employers to make a reasonable accommodation to any known disability of a qualified applicant or employee. For a foodservice operation, such modifications could be simple, such as modifying a training program for an employee who has a learning disability but is otherwise perfectly capable of performing the requisite duties. Others, however, can be more difficult. Again, anticipating such potential accommodations during the planning process can save a lot of time and money.

The ADA also stipulates that public spaces—including dining rooms—must be accessible to people with disabilities. The ADA requirements are very specific, particularly pertaining to wheelchair access. For example, aisles in the dining area must be at least 36 inches wide. Similarly, the **Internal Revenue Code** includes several provisions aimed at making businesses more accessible. It is generally easier to add a wheelchair ramp to a new foodservice operation than to convert an existing building, for example, one that had been used for storage only, particularly if it involves making up for a considerable difference in height between the ground and the entryway. Still, this must be considered early in the planning process.

DESIGN AND LAYOUT

When all steps in the planning process are completed, attention shifts to the foodservice operation's design, creating a portrait of how the final product will look. Typically, a design consultant is included in this phase. One approach is to outsource the design and then have the team identified earlier review the results. However, it is better for the team to work directly with the designer during the process so that all functions of the foodservice operation can be addressed.

The first step in the design and layout process involves allocating space to functional areas. The next is designing the functional areas. Here we focus on the kitchen and dining room, but many advanced texts addressing foodservice layout and design are available, covering every aspect of an operation.

Space Allocation

Earlier in the chapter, we explained that the planning phase includes identifying all of the operational parameters beyond just the number of seats in the dining room. Such comprehensive planning makes the allocation of space to the various functional areas much easier. Still, some considerations related to space allocation are not often addressed in the prospectus. The first of these is the delivery schedule, which depends on the operators' preferences as well as the availability of suppliers. (We address food management, including inventory turnover, in Chapter 9.) The second consideration, which is more difficult to manage, is the length of time over which the foodservice entity will operate. In a segment such as university foodservice, this is generally not an immediate problem, as most universities can anticipate a very long horizon of operation. At the other end of the spectrum is the first-time restaurateur who may be optimistic regarding the long-term viability of her concept and who finds solace in the feasibility study's positive results but who cannot predict what external influences, such as local market trends or broader economic forces, might mean to the restaurant's prospects for success.

With that in mind, we should also add a caveat, similar to the one addressed in the discussion of menu development. Most of the processes associated with design and layout, including space allocation, are quantitative in nature. That is, we have years of experience and thousands of foodservice operations from which we can ascertain specific parameters such as space allowances per seat. However, every concept incorporates at least one or two unique design parameters. Even in onsite foodservice, the nuances of a specific hospital or school might dictate unexpected or nonstandard layout features in the kitchen or dining room. Thus, design and layout benefit from the right blend of science and art.

Dining Room Design

Dining room design begins with space allocation per seat. As you might expect, this depends almost entirely on the type of restaurant being designed. For example, a banquet room in a hotel would require less space than would a fine dining restaurant that offers tableside food preparation (e.g., Caesar salads or cherries flambé prepared at the table). Similarly, a QSR is not intended for leisurely dining where a guest will remain at the table for more than an hour. An onsite operation in education would require less space than in correctional foodservice, where greater separation among individuals in the dining area is advisable.

Furnishings can be differentiators for some guests. If a concept targets family-style dining parties of varying sizes combined at long bench tables, less space per seat will be needed than with a traditional dining arrangement. With variations in seat space requirements come corresponding choices in table and seat configuration. A dining room's furnishing arrangement must facilitate the concept, but most operators will also strive for optimal efficiency. For example, situating booths along the outer perimeter can result in a more efficient use of seating space. The key here is to identify the average group size at your foodservice operation. An Asian-style tearoom, for example, would cater to a greater number of individuals or couples; hence, it would require more **two tops** or **deuces** (tables for two people). A family-style restaurant, on the other hand, would require more **four tops** (tables for four people) and other larger tables. Similarly, kid-friendly foodservice must allow space for highchairs. Accommodating space for wheelchairs, as discussed earlier, must also be considered.

In the course of planning with all these variables in mind, foodservice operators can also turn to general guidelines that serve as standards based on foodservice segment. As shown in Table 6.1, standard square footage by segment falls within a range but serves as a good baseline for dining room design. Some of these figures may surprise you. For example, one might think that a cafe in a hospital would need less space per seat since it is used for short dining periods by both visitors and staff. However, because visitors might be visiting a sick relative or friend and possibly grieving, providing adequate space to ensure privacy is important.

In addition to creating a layout, the designer will create a **rendering**, which is a drawing or a computer-generated illustration of what the foodservice operation will look like once it is built or remodeled. A rendering helps the designer and foodservice planning team to ensure everyone is on the same page while also providing a better idea of how the layout schematic translates into an actual foodservice operation. Figure 6.3 includes three renderings of a proposed upscale/theme restaurant planned for a major city in the Pacific Northwest region of the United States.

TABLE 6.1 Dining Room Space Allocation per Seat by Foodservice Segment

Industry Segment	Sq. Ft.
QSR	10–15
Fast-Casual	12–18
Family/Midscale	15–18
Upscale/Theme	16–20
Fine Dining	18–20
Onsite Foodservice	
Business & Industry	12–18
Schools	8–11
Universities and Colleges	12–15
Healthcare	15–18
Sports and Recreation	10–18
Corrections	15–20

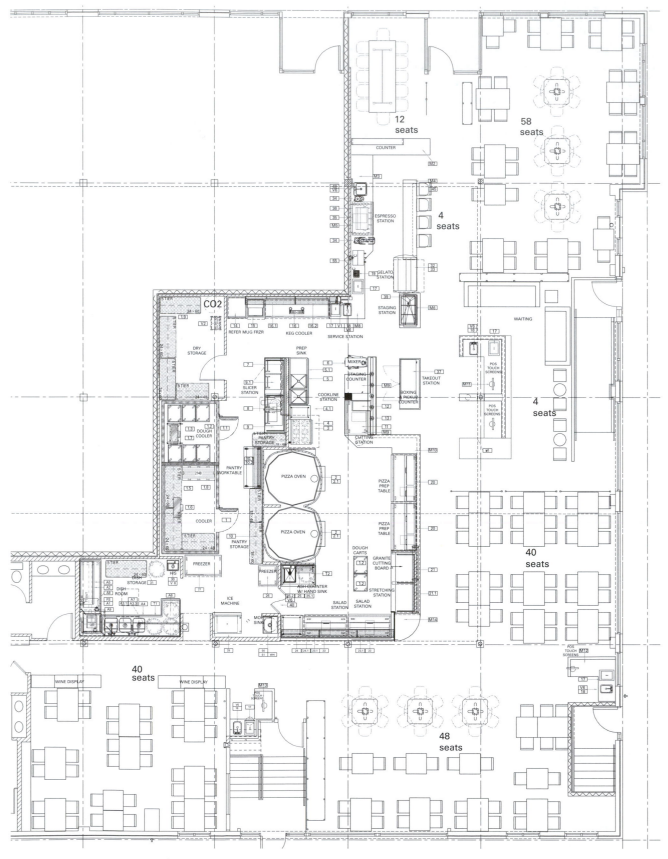

Figure 6.2 A sample layout for a midscale restaurant.

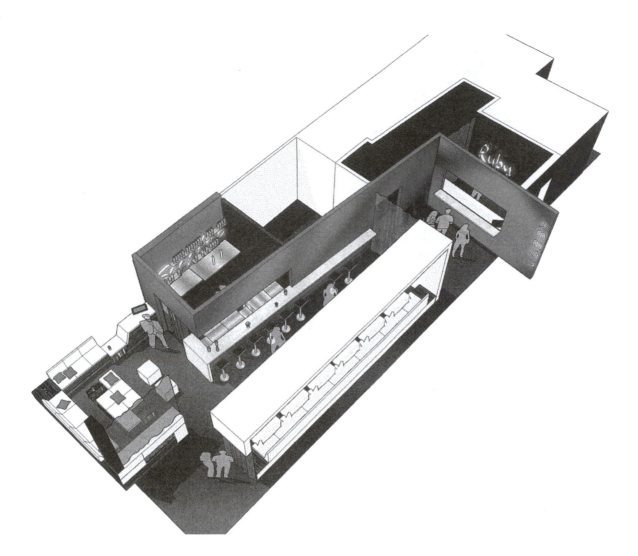

Courtesy of Nystrom|Olson Architecture.

Figure 6.3 Renderings of an upscale/theme restaurant.

Figure 6.3   *(continued)*

Kitchen Design

Although the essential factor in dining room design and layout is square feet per seat, kitchen or production area design cannot be so easily generalized because of the need to accommodate preparation and cooking techniques involved in the vast range of cuisines, concepts, and food that characterizes today's foodservice industry. The traditional rule of thumb has been to allocate 30 percent of a foodservice operation's space to the dining room, leaving the remaining space to production, a greeting area, restrooms, and so on. Today, however, we understand that revenue is generated in the dining room and therefore every effort is made to maximize dining space (and seats). Still, the production area must be large enough to support the operation's menu, sales volume, and staff.

Most modern designers now devote 25 to 40 percent of the space traditionally used for the dining room to the production area. (Look again at Figure 6.2 to see the space allocations for the dining room and kitchen.) Again, this depends on the type of operation to which the design applies. To understand the issues that designers address, we offer ten questions that, although often answered in the prospectus, are specific to production area design:

1. What type of food preparation is dictated by the menu? For example, a steakhouse that ages its meat in a display case in the lobby might buy entire sides of beef and prepare cuts of meat in the main production area. This would obviously require a large amount of space.

2. Will some food items be purchased in prepackaged form, requiring little preparation? Returning to our steakhouse example, an operator might choose to buy the three cuts of meat featured on the menu from a local cattle ranch, thereby requiring little extra preparation space.

3. Can some of the food preparation take place at another location? In a university or large healthcare setting, for example, all cold-food prep might be done in a central kitchen and then delivered to satellite dining centers. This would mean that the kitchen in the new dining hall on the edge of campus could be much smaller than it would have needed to be without centralized food production.

4. What volume of meals will be produced in a given daypart (discussed in Chapter 2), and how many dayparts are serviced? Consider a large Italian restaurant that is open only for dinner and typically serves 300 meals during an evening. In this situation, much of the day can be used to prepare sauces, dough, and other meal components for service that evening, thereby requiring only modest production space. But if the operator decides later to also open for lunch, he might find that the kitchen is too small to prep for dinner and execute lunch service properly.

5. How many distinct courses will likely be served (as indicated by the menu)? For a sandwich shop, the production area is designed primarily only to make sandwiches. However, a family-style restaurant might serve appetizers, salads, entrees, and desserts. Thus, multiple stations would be needed in the production area to prepare the various hot and cold items.

6. How elaborate is the menu in terms of food variety? For example, a typical outlet of The Cheesecake Factory must keep more than 1,000 items in inventory in order to create the dishes on its menu, requiring a large production area and extensive storage space.

7. Are there unique service or logistical aspects to consider? A kitchen in a school cafeteria must be prepared to produce all menu items in batches, whereas in a fine dining restaurant many if not most items are made to order. In many large operations, the kitchen is located on a separate floor from the main dining area. This would likely necessitate modification in the kitchen design—for example, installing plate warmers.

8. How much item customization is needed? Today's foodservice guests are more sophisticated and trend conscious than those from previous generations are, and most expect food items to be modified to fit their dietary preferences. Think of a local coffee outlet: The consumer today must decide between regular or decaffeinated coffee, not to mention facing a range of choices in cream and sweeteners. Greater customization typically requires more prep space in the kitchen and more storage space throughout the production area.

9. What equipment is available to reduce kitchen space (or require more space)? Specialized equipment, such as a wood-burning oven, may require extra production space. By contrast, a pizza restaurant operator might opt for a conveyor oven that cooks pizzas more quickly and often in a smaller space. There is a considerable variety of equipment available today—you can even install a sushi machine to save space and increase productivity in the kitchen (see Figure 6.4).

Courtesy of AUTEC, Inc.

Figure 6.4 The Maki Maker by AUTEC.

10. What changes might be required or desired in the future? This is probably the toughest question to consider, as it can rarely be answered with complete accuracy. Yet a little thought can go a long way. For example, have you considered adding catering to your operation in the future? This would likely require more space in the production area and certainly more storage space. Will you add menu items down the road? Again, it's hard to predict fully what trends will affect any foodservice operation but it is always better to plan ahead as much as possible.

In concluding our discussion of design and layout, we offer one other critical recommendation, one that is dismissed all too often by many restaurateurs who are doomed to fail. The old adages *function before fashion* or *form follows function* cannot be overstressed. It is very easy to become consumed with featuring the latest trends in a dining room design or deploying novel equipment in the kitchen. Such a strategy should be adopted only if it contributes to operationalizing the concept (again, beginning with the menu). A massive aquarium in the dining room might impress the guests, but if the aquarium is nothing more than a decoration, one that does not promote the concept, it is a waste of money. Similarly, a state-of-the art induction cooktop will perform beautifully, but if the menu does not specifically call for items prepared on such a cooktop, it is an expensive accessory, not a value enhancer.

▪▫ EQUIPMENT

While successfully completing the planning, design, and layout of a foodservice operation might seem daunting, selecting the proper equipment adds another layer of complexity to the process. Moreover, obtaining the right equipment through an effective procurement process can increase guest satisfaction. Fortunately, many of the decisions made during the planning and design phases will anticipate most of those pertaining to equipment.

Equipment Selection

Once again, we begin with the menu. What kitchen equipment do we need to prepare all the menu items? It is useful, also, to consider the answers to the ten key questions posed earlier relating to kitchen design. Another consideration is whether **stock equipment**, which is equipment produced in large quantities in standard configurations, can be used. This is usually desirable as stock equipment is cheaper than **custom-built equipment** that might be necessary to meet special food production requirements, concept requirements, or resolve design and layout issues. Furthermore, equipping a foodservice operation means more than procuring kitchen equipment, and similar principles aimed at lowering cost apply everywhere equipment is needed. For example, mass-produced glasses and silverware are much less expensive than are the same products created for a specific foodservice operation, perhaps sporting unique design features or the restaurant's logo.

Above all else, equipment selection should reflect real needs. If you don't need a specific piece of equipment and don't foresee needing it, then it is best not to add it to the operation. The cost of building or even remodeling a foodservice operation is so formidable that adding equipment that is not applicable is just a foolish use of resources. This applies as well to overe-quipping, which means purchasing equipment that far exceeds the needs of the operation. For example, a dish machine should be purchased to handle the level of volume projected. Buying one that has double the capacity "just in case" not only costs more in terms of purchase price, but also raises operating costs and maintenance expenses.

Food Preparation Equipment

As we discussed earlier regarding kitchen design, the equipment needed in the kitchen varies considerably, owing to the wide range of concepts and sizes of operations in the foodservice industry. Moreover, some decisions, such as selecting among gas, electric, or steam equipment, may be made for you in the event that only certain utilities (e.g., electricity but not natural gas) are available. Regarding others, the cost of installation may determine such answers.

While providing an exhaustive list of possible kitchen equipment is unnecessary, it is useful to consider the most typical types of kitchen equipment found in foodservice operations:

- Ovens: The type depends on the use, such as dedicated pizza ovens or proofing ovens for breads

- Convection ovens: quick baking

- Salamanders: finishing or browning

- Griddles: eggs, pancakes, bacon, etc.

- Deep fryer or fry kettle: deep-fat frying

- Warming ovens or built-in warming drawers: holding food or warming plates prior to service

- Wok ranges: stir-frying (some newer models include an induction cooktop, which is considered safer than a gas unit and is much easier to clean)

- Mixers: mixing dough, sauces, etc. (some have built-in heating units so that a menu item can be mixed and cooked in the same piece of equipment)

- Toasters: toasting bread and sandwiches

- Tilting skillets or braising pans: pan frying, grilling, simmering, and braising large quantities of food

- Steam kettles: soups and stews

- Charbroilers: grilling meats (see Figure 6.5)

Figure 6.5 Charbroiler.

Courtesy of Julia Reynolds.

Serving Equipment

Here again, the equipment used for serving depends on the concept and dining room design. In fine dining, guests expect multiple forks and knives for use with the various courses. In addition to nice tableware, they also expect wine glasses that match the various wine varietals they might order. On the other hand, a fast-casual concept will likely have plastic **flatware** (forks, knives, and spoons).

Even something as seemingly trivial as plastic forks merits an appropriate level of attention. For example, at a QSR known for its extremely low prices, guests would not be surprised to find very inexpensive plastic flatware. At a pricier fast-casual restaurant however, one might expect a fork and knife that will not easily break.

Equipment Procurement

When the time comes to make the actual purchase, the designer will often suggest where to find some of the equipment, particularly very specialized equipment that is unique to the operation (which may have to be custom built). For other items, however, the choices involve considerable variety in quality, versatility, and so on, so the foodservice operator must know exactly what she wants or needs. Some find utility in an **equipment specification sheet** for each piece of equipment. The equipment specification sheet is a compilation of all the pertinent information related to a particular piece of equipment. This might include the gauge of the stainless steel, the size, the capacity, and even the brand. A high degree of specificity will make it easier to compare prices among vendors and will result in equipment that precisely matches the needs of the foodservice operation.

◾ CORPORATE RESPONSIBILITY

Corporate responsibility, or corporate social responsibility, has been a concern to companies for a long time. Today, however, this notion of protecting the environment by engaging in sustainable, responsible practices is pervasive—and is certainly seen in many sectors of the foodservice industry. In terms of facilities planning, design, and equipment, it is vital that we embrace this responsibility, particularly regarding environmental issues, which entails more effective handling of energy, water, and food waste.

Environmental Concerns

The trend toward sustainable practices makes sense; foodservice operations that employ sustainable practices enjoy reduced energy and water use, less waste, lower emissions, and lower operating and maintenance costs. So how does this apply to facility design? The answer is simple: Smaller kitchens result in reduced energy consumption (which we address more fully in a moment). Also, equipment that is selected for its efficiency saves natural resources. And building a foodservice operation so that it conforms to **LEED** (Leadership in Energy and Environment Design) standards ensures that the building and the carbon footprint that it represents are *green*.

Energy and Water

US energy and water consumption equates to 9 percent of the world's greenhouse emissions and 12 percent of the fresh water consumption on a yearly basis. Energy consumption in this country is at an all-time high, and the cost is expected to rise 3 to 4 percent annually until new energy platforms are developed. An even more staggering statistic shows that people in the United States use more than three times the energy that the Chinese use on a per capita basis and twice that of the world average.

We mentioned earlier that foodservice operators and designers can help reduce energy consumption through reducing kitchen size and integrating high-efficiency production equipment. There are, however, many other areas in which to save energy. For example, better insulation can save heating and cooling costs, natural lighting can reduce the electricity used for interior lighting, and recapturing heat for other uses is becoming more commonplace. Similarly, low-flow faucets and spray valves as well as dual-flush toilets can reduce water usage.

Building to Reduce Food Waste

While we discuss sustainable practices in the production and preparation of food later in the book, we note here that creating a foodservice operation with the intention of reducing food waste is vital to managing foodservice in a sustainable fashion. Consider recent Environmental Protection Agency reports that show waste in the United States now exceeding 31.7 million tons per year, which accounts for 12.5 percent of the waste stream.[1] Thus, foodservice operations that integrate composting and related **bioconversion** approaches (using live organisms to reduce food waste) can divert food waste from landfills and contribute to a healthier environment. Finally, integrating a food pulper into dishroom workflow can dramatically reduce the volume of food that would otherwise enter the waste stream.

MANAGERIAL IMPLICATIONS

Planning a new foodservice operation is in many ways similar across all industry segments. However, a concept's size and complexity dictate the time and effort required to develop a comprehensive plan, often called a prospectus. The goal is to ensure that outcomes address the needs of all stakeholders, including owners, managers, employees, and guests. The planning stage also integrates key considerations pertaining to safety and operational efficiency. Other considerations extend to regulatory requirements, including those specified in OSHA and the ADA.

The first step in planning is to identify the decision maker, the person (or persons) with the final say in design and equipment selection. A feasibility study can help these individuals in making related decisions as it provides a wealth of information regarding the viability of the business venture. Following this step, a timeline is created that outlines the order of the requisite tasks and the duration of each step of the project.

The foodservice operation's design and layout begins with allocating space for the dining room and the kitchen as well as for other areas that are necessary to execute the concept successfully. Designers can appeal to general guidelines regarding the square footage needed per seat by industry segment to lay out the dining room. Kitchen design is not as programmatic and varies considerably based on the concept.

Effective, thoughtful equipment selection is equally important. Owing in no small part to the expense involved, the objective is to purchase only what is needed or what is anticipated for use in executing the concept. To this end, it may be useful to develop an equipment specification sheet for each major piece of equipment, which helps to ensure that unnecessary equipment is not obtained.

Today's (and tomorrow's) foodservice entrepreneur and manager must embrace corporate responsibility in order to succeed. This begins with planning, designing, and equipping the new business to meet a range of safety and environmental standards. Respecting the environment and adhering to LEED standards is a great first step. Using equipment and water controls that are efficient and reduce both energy and water use is another. Finally, designing the operation with the explicit intent of minimizing food waste is vital in creating an environmentally friendly business.

INDUSTRY EXEMPLAR

Tutta Bella Neapolitan Pizzeria

The inspiration for Tutta Bella Neapolitan Pizzeria stems from a passion for the authentic, fire-roasted pizzas born in Naples and found throughout Italy. For a century and a half, the pizza makers of Naples (or "pizzaioli" as they are known in their hometown) have produced unique, mouth-watering pizzas using the freshest ingredients available. It is estimated that nearly 7 million of these pizzas are produced in Italy every day.

Prior to opening Tutta Bella in January 2004, Joe Fugere, the owner, received his certification as a pizzaiolo and traveled to Naples to continue his training and refine his skills. Since Associazione Verace Pizza Napoletana (VPN) regulations do not require that every pizza be made in Naples to be authentic, any restaurant in the world has the opportunity to receive the VPN certification mark provided that their pizzas and the production process used to make them meets the Association's strict requirements. To date, only a handful of pizzerias in the United States have chosen to do so—Tutta Bella Neapolitan Pizzeria is the first restaurant in the Northwest to receive the coveted VPN certification.

While in Naples, Joe also cast a keen eye on the design of pizza restaurants in Naples. He was particularly taken by how each one seemed to fit perfectly into the area in which it was located. In fact, in each neighborhood, the pizzarias looked like they were part of the landscape, not just restaurants randomly located. So, when he opened his first Tutta Bella Neapolitan Pizzeria in Seattle, he vowed that it (and all those to follow) would be unique, with each location sporting its own look and feel. Achieving such local uniqueness isn't cheap—it means hiring an architect to design each location to match the locale and making every decision about food flow, layout, and so on anew. Not surprisingly, Joe believes this is part of what makes his restaurants special (see Figure 6.6).

To understand this unique approach to the foodservice business, it is best perhaps to consider Tutta Bella's guiding principles:

1. Provide the definitive Pizza Napoletana experience.
2. Treat customers, co-workers, and vendors with integrity, respect, and love.
3. Protect and promote the VPN and its charter.
4. Build a fun, profitable, and continuously improving business that provides opportunities for personal and professional growth.
5. Impact positively the environment and the communities in which we operate.

Courtesy of Tutta Bella.

Figure 6.6   Tutta Bella on a typical night.

KEY TERMS

prospectus   114

feasibility study   114

timeline   115

project manager   115

Occupational Safety and
Health Act   117

workflow   117

traffic flow   117

Americans with Disabilities Act   117

Internal Revenue Code   118

two tops   119

deuces   119

four tops   119

rendering   119

stock equipment   124

custom-built equipment   124

flatware   126

equipment specification sheet   126

LEED   126

bioconversion   127

◻◼◼◻ **Case in Point** ◼◻◼◼◼◻◼◼◻◼◼◻◼◼◻◼◼◻◼◼◻◼◼◻◼◼◻◼◼◻◼◼◻◼◼◻◼◼◻

Trash Cans

Julio had worked for many years as a line cook at a series of restaurants, but his eyes were always focused on owning his own. He saw every job he took on as preparation for his eventual real career as a restaurateur.

A few years ago, he started writing down his ideas and potential concepts that might be successful. He soon landed on what seemed like a great idea: A pizza restaurant that specialized in unique combinations and pizza by the slice. He also knew that in the Midwestern college town in which he lived, there was no competition for such a concept.

The day finally came for Julio to quit his day job and start his own business. While he had saved for this venture, his funds were limited and he was intent on building the pizza restaurant, preliminarily named "Julio's Pies," as inexpensively as possible. So, he opted not to hire an architect, attempting to design the place himself. The building he had leased had previously been a furniture store so it was little more than an empty box, which Julio viewed as a benefit, allowing him to create the type of interior that would best fit his concept without having to worry about structural limitations.

His first task was the kitchen. He had learned in his years of cooking that efficient food flow was critical, from receiving to storage to preparation and straight through to delivery to the guest. Looking at his design, he believed that, in spite of his having no professional design experience, his kitchen would be expertly efficient.

He also put considerable time into designing the dining area. The seating was comfortable but not too wasteful in terms of open space and the layout was appropriate for a pizza place. Even in the entry area, the space allowances and relationships were impressive, although it was his first attempt at restaurant design.

Next, he hired a contractor and construction began immediately. The contractor, Bob, had some experience working with drawings and plans created by nonarchitects and, thanks to the simplicity of the design, remodeling the space to create Julio's Pies proceeded quickly. The only glitch was that Bob had made several suggestions to improve the operation, but Julio wouldn't hear of any changes. At one point, Bob even had his wife, Lori, call Julio to appeal to his good sense and make a few modifications. Julio had one word for Lori: "No." He was determined to be the master of his destiny.

So Bob finished the job, for which Julio paid him immediately, and they parted ways. Julio was so excited that he could barely sleep that night. He was already thinking about whether he should open a second unit or franchise the concept.

A few days later, the food began arriving. Almost immediately, Julio realized that he had a problem. He had forgotten all about garbage! There wasn't a single garbage receptacle built into the kitchen or any of the side stations in the dining area. And, because he had created such a compact kitchen, there was no room even for a free-standing trash can.

Remodeling the kitchen would require every dollar he had left, leaving nothing for the initial food orders or payroll.

1. What advice would you give Julio?

2. What could he have done to avoid all of this?

REVIEW AND DISCUSSION QUESTIONS

1. What groups should be considered when planning the foodservice operation?

2. Which is better—to have one person make the decisions or have a large group (in order to spread the responsibility)?

3. Name five distinct elements included in a prospectus.

4. What does a feasibility study provide?

5. Why is a timeline important?

6. In terms of guest safety, what is the biggest concern for foodservice operators?

7. Why and when was the Occupational Safety and Health Act created?

8. Go to the American with Disabilities Act website. Name two requirements mandated by the act that are not discussed in this chapter.

9. Why would a restaurant intentionally have more deuces than larger tables?

10. What are two reasons that a designer would strive to keep a kitchen as small as possible?

11. In this chapter we have seen that equipment can often be used to save space and increase productivity. (The example used was the sushi machine.) Complete a Web search and find another example.

12. What is meant by the phrase *function before fashion*?

13. In general terms, which is preferable, stock equipment or custom-built equipment? Explain your answer.

14. Find a restaurant in your area that is LEED certified. What level of LEED certification does it have? What does that mean?

ENDNOTE

1. EPA. *Municipal Solid Waste in the United States: 2007 Facts and Figures*. Washington D.C.: US EPA, November 2008.

CHAPTER 7

FOOD SANITATION AND SAFETY

LEARNING OBJECTIVES:

After becoming familiar with this chapter, you should be able to:

1. Identify the major foodborne illnesses as well as their symptoms and growth conditions.

2. Recognize the other hazards that may be present in food and describe their effects.

3. Determine how foodborne illness can be prevented.

4. Understand how the safety of the work environment is linked to food safety.

Building on the earlier discussion of foodservice planning, design, and equipment (and the related safety issues), we now turn toward food sanitation and safety. As a future manager and leader in the global foodservice industry, you need to appreciate the importance of food safety and understand the possible risks involved in the food-preparation process. To this end, we define foodborne illness and then talk about the associated hazards. Finally, we discuss prevention and workplace safety.

■ FOODBORNE ILLNESS

There are millions of cases of **foodborne illness** in the United States every year, with symptoms ranging from brief periods of minor nausea to severe gastrointestinal cramping, vomiting, diarrhea, and fever, and outcomes ranging from momentary inconvenience to death. This range of symptoms and outcomes reflects the wide variety of sources and types of foodborne illness that occur, as well as variations in the ages and health conditions of stricken individuals. Infants, the elderly, and people suffering from chronic illness are the most vulnerable members of the population.

Because foodborne illness is potentially life threatening, sanitation and safety are very serious responsibilities for all foodservice managers and employees. A manager could lose her job for not following proper sanitation procedures, but that would be the least of her problems if someone were to die because she allowed unsafe food to be prepared or served, or if she allowed her employees to work in an unsafe environment.[1]

The Partnership for Food Safety Education (PFSE) outlines the following factors that make controlling foodborne **pathogens** challenging:

- Improper sanitation practices on the part of both customers and foodservice employees who do not wash hands and utensils thoroughly or thaw meats and other foods properly

- The never-ending development of new pathogens requiring constant vigilance and new interventions

- The global nature of the food supply

- The growing preference for food that is prepared and eaten away from home

The good news about food safety and sanitation is that by following some very clear rules, we can ensure that the food served in all foodservice operations—restaurants, hospitals, workplaces—and the preparation of that food are safe for customers and employees alike.

What Is a Foodborne Illness?

A foodborne illness is commonly known as food poisoning. Simply put, the term refers to any illness caused by consuming food, but in reality it covers a wide variety of symptoms caused by a wide variety of pathogens (disease-causing organisms) such as bacteria, viruses, and toxins produced by certain organisms, as well as by contaminated water. Recently, for example, drug-resistant **microorganisms** and allergic reactions to food have been added to the list of causes of foodborne illness.

Food safety occupies the scientific discipline that studies the handling, preparation, and storage of food to prevent foodborne illness. Food safety is so important because many organisms occur in food naturally. Nearly all the food consumed by humans comes from either living plants or animals. Plants and animals (including us) host many bacteria, particularly in the gastrointestinal tract and bodily fluids. Thus, during the butchering process, for example, meat can be contaminated if not handled properly. Most vegetables grow in the ground, which contains many types of bacteria and other contaminants. Food must therefore be washed or cooked or stored in an environment that limits or controls the continued growth of bacteria and other pathogens. The whole purpose of proper food handling is, then, to control the growth of pathogens or, in the case of cooking, dramatically reduce the incidence of bacteria and other potentially dangerous pathogens. It is not surprising that, because human error is inevitably involved, the major forms of foodborne illness are caused by improper food handling. In this chapter, we cover food-handling processes that help prevent bacterial contamination, as well as less prevalent causes of foodborne illness such as chemical contamination and, more improbably, bioterrorism.

Among the challenges facing foodservice operations in their efforts to track and control foodborne illness is that it often goes unreported, and not merely because food handlers conceal dangerous practices. Consumers are in the best position to report foodborne illness but often do not, especially when their illnesses are perceived to be mild. A person may feel nauseated, for example, or suffer from diarrhea for a day or two, but not go to the doctor or visit a health clinic. When the symptoms pass, the individual might not even link it to the food he or she has consumed, or decide that such a mild case is not worth reporting, chalking it up to "24-hour flu."

This underreporting problem means that the total annual number of cases of foodborne illness must be estimated. According to one authority, perhaps 76 million cases of foodborne illness occur every year, with approximately 325,000 hospitalizations and 5,000 deaths.[2] Another report estimates that foodborne illnesses cost the United States between $6.5 billion and $34.9 billion per year in medical expenses and lost productivity, depending on how many cases go unreported.[3] Even without factoring in the unknown cases, nearly 13.8 million cases reported annually are caused by known agents—30 percent by bacteria, 67 percent by viruses, and 3 percent by parasites.

Figure 7.1 is a table from the USDA's website that displays the major forms of foodborne illness. It identifies where they are found, describes how they are transmitted, and lists the major symptoms.[4]

We commonly refer to the better known bacteria listed in this table by convenient, shortened forms of their full scientific names, such as *Listeria* and *E. coli*. As the table indicates, bacteria can occur in many forms—in the case of Salmonella, for example, there are over 2,300 species!

Although bacteria are one of the most common pathogens that cause foodborne illnesses, many cases are caused by either viruses or parasites. The most common viruses involved in food safety issues—Hepatitis A, norovirus, and rotovirus—are generally introduced into food products by infected foodservice workers. The most common parasites are Anisakis simplex, Cryptosporidium parvum, Cyclospora cayetamesis, Giardia duodenalis, and Trichinella spiralis.

Additional information on all the foodborne pathogens mentioned here, and many others as well, can be found in the FDA's *Bad Bug Book*.[5]

The pathogens that cause foodborne illnesses are microscopic organisms, so it is virtually impossible to observe or experience evidence of contamination when it is first introduced. Once introduced even in small quantities, they continue to grow undetected and can cause illness. They can also continue to grow after they are ingested. By the time perceptible symptoms have set in, the tiny contaminants have multiplied and perhaps spread through various bodily systems or organs. The key to prevention is therefore to understand the conditions under which bacteria, viruses, or parasites thrive and multiply and to modify the foodservice preparation environment to eliminate those conditions. Foodservice managers should make it a matter of policy to become familiar with these conditions, which are often referred to as FAT TOM—food, acidity, time, temperature, oxygen, and moisture:

- *Food*: The nutrients in some foods are sources for pathogenic bacteria and therefore such food items must be handled accordingly.

- *Acid*: The acidity of a substance is measured by it pH, which ranges from 0 to 14. Foods below 7.0 are acidic; foods above 7.0 are alkaline. Bacteria thrive at a pH level of 4.6 to 7.5 while most bacteria will not grow below pH 4.6.

Bacteria	Found	Transmission	Symptoms
Campylobacter jejuni	Intestinal tracts of animals and birds, raw milk, untreated water, and sewage sludge.	Contaminated water, raw milk, and raw or undercooked meat, poultry, or shellfish.	Fever, headache, and muscle pain followed by diarrhea (sometimes bloody), abdominal pain, and nausea that appear 2 to 5 days after eating; may last 7 to 10 days.
Clostridium Botulinum	Widely distributed in nature; soil, water, on plants, and intestinal tracts of animals and fish. Grows only in little or no oxygen.	Bacteria produce a toxin that causes illness. Improperly canned foods, garlic in oil, vacuum-packed and tightly wrapped food.	Toxin affects the nervous system. Symptoms usually appear 18 to 36 hours, but can sometimes appear as few as 4 hours or as many as 8 days after eating; double vision, droopy eyelids, trouble speaking and swallowing, and difficulty breathing. Fatal in 3 to 10 days if not treated.
Clostridium perfringens	Soil, dust, sewage, and intestinal tracts of animals and humans. Grows only in little or no oxygen.	Called "the cafeteria germ" because many outbreaks result from food left for long periods in steam tables or at room temperature. Bacteria destroyed by cooking, but some toxin-producing spores may survive.	Diarrhea and gas pains may appear 8 to 24 hours after eating; usually last about 1 day, but less severe symptoms may persist for 1 to 2 weeks.
Escherichia coli O157:H7	Intestinal tracts of some mammals, raw milk, unchlorinated water; one of several strains of *E. coli* that can cause human illness.	Contaminated water, raw milk, raw or rare ground beef, unpasteurized apple juice or cider, uncooked fruits and vegetables; person-to-person.	Diarrhea or bloody diarrhea, abdominal cramps, nausea, and malaise; can begin 2 to 5 days after food is eaten, lasting about 8 days. Some, especially the very young, have developed hemolytic-uremic syndrome (HUS) that causes acute kidney failure.
Listeria monocytogenes	Intestinal tracts of humans and animals, milk, soil, leaf vegetables; can grow slowly at refrigerator temperatures.	Ready-to-eat foods such as hot dogs, luncheon meats, cold cuts, fermented or dry sausage, and other deli-style meat and poultry, soft cheeses and unpasteurized milk.	Fever, chills, headache, backache, sometimes upset stomach, abdominal pain and diarrhea; may take up to 3 weeks to become ill; may later develop more serious illness in at-risk patients (pregnant women and newborns, older adults, and people with weakened immune systems).
Salmonella (over 2300 types)	Intestinal tracts and feces of animals; *Salmonella* Enteritidis in eggs.	Raw or undercooked eggs, poultry, and meat; raw milk and dairy products; seafood, and food handlers.	Stomach pain, diarrhea, nausea, chills, fever, and headache usually appear 8 to 72 hours after eating; may last 1 to 2 days.
Shigella (over 30 types)	Human intestinal tract; rarely found in other animals.	Person-to-person by fecal-oral route; fecal contamination of food and water. Most outbreaks result from food, especially salads, prepared and handled by workers using poor personal hygiene.	Disease referred to as "shigellosis" or bacillary dysentery. Diarrhea containing blood and mucus, fever, abdominal cramps, chills, and vomiting; 12 to 50 hours from ingestion of bacteria; can last a few days to 2 weeks.
Staphylococcus aureus	On humans (skin, infected cuts, pimples, noses, and throats).	Person-to-person through food from improper food handling. Multiply rapidly at room temperature to produce a toxin that causes illness.	Severe nausea, abdominal cramps, vomiting, and diarrhea occur 1 to 6 hours after eating; recovery within 2 to 3 days—longer if severe dehydration occurs.

Figure 7.1   Bacteria that cause foodborne illness.

- *Time* (*also known as the four-hour rule*): Food should not be in the **temperature danger zone** (see the next bullet) for more than four hours *total*.[6]

- *Temperature*: Foodborne pathogens thrive in temperatures between 41°F and 135°F, referred to as the temperature danger zone. (See Figure 7.2.)[7]

- *Oxygen*: Almost all foodborne pathogens require oxygen to grow.

- *Moisture*: All microorganisms require water to grow.

US Government Programs

Considering the social costs of foodborne illness, it is not surprising that the federal government addresses this problem through several agencies and programs. For example, Food Net is a joint project of the federal government's Centers for Disease Control and Prevention (**CDC**), the USDA Food Safety and Inspection Service, the Food and Drug Administration (FDA), and ten **FoodNet** sites in several states.[8] The project has four goals:

1. Determine the burden of foodborne illness in the United States.

2. Monitor trends in occurrences over time.

3. Identify specific foods and settings that contribute to specific outbreaks of foodborne illness.

4. Develop and assess intervention measures to prevent future occurrences.

The CDC has several other joint groups that conduct and publish scientific investigations of outbreaks to determine causes and prescribe remedies. The FDA, USDA, and CDC websites, among many others, offer detailed information on foodborne illness. An excellent and detailed review of the subject can also be found in the Academy of Nutrition and Dietetics' position paper on food and water safety.[9] These and many other organizations provide considerable resources to be used in training foodservice workers, which will be reviewed later in this chapter.

135°F

Temperature Danger Zone

41°F

Figure 7.2   The temperature danger zone.

We have noted that many people do not report foodborne illness because they do not realize that their sickness came from food. However, when a foodservice operation becomes aware of suspected cases, it has an obligation to report this to an appropriate authority—a local health department, a state health department, etc. According to the USDA, the following guidelines should be followed by individual consumers if they suspect they have contracted a foodborne illness:

1. *Preserve the evidence*: If a portion of the suspected food is available, wrap it securely, mark it "DANGER," and freeze it. Save all packaging materials, such as cans or cartons. Write down the food type, the date, any other identifying information, the time the food was consumed, and the time at which symptoms began. Save any other unopened packages of the same food items.

2. *Seek treatment as necessary*: If a victim is in an "at-risk" group (very young, very old, or ill), seek medical care immediately. Also, if symptoms persist or become severe (such as bloody diarrhea, excessive nausea and vomiting, or high fever), contact a physician.

3. *Call the local health department*: If the suspect food was served at a large gathering, a restaurant, an onsite foodservice venue, or is a commercial product, it must be reported.

4. *Call the USDA Meat and Poultry Hotline*: If the suspected food is a USDA-inspected meat product and you have saved the packaging, this agency will test it in order to identify the source of the illness.

BIOLOGICAL, CHEMICAL, AND PHYSICAL HAZARDS IN FOOD

Figure 7.1 lists the major bacterial food contaminants. These are usually in food or the immediate preparation environment, but food can also be contaminated by external sources—that is, by agents that are carried into that environment. As mentioned earlier, **viruses** are another common biological contaminant. The most common viral agent involved in foodborne illness is the **norovirus**, including Norwalk-type viruses, which are a common group of contaminants that cause gastroenteritis or "stomach flu." Viral contaminants are introduced to food by people, mostly food handlers, but sometimes infected customers as well (for example, at a salad bar). Think of a simple sandwich—two slices of bread, several slices of meat and cheese, and perhaps mayonnaise, lettuce, and tomato. Now consider how many hands had to be in contact with these components in some way before they became a sandwich. And suppose that sandwich was one of 50 made for a three-hour lunch period—time, as we have noted, is among the factors favorable to contamination—by the end of the lunch period those sandwiches could deliver quite a dose of viruses if contaminated.

Not surprisingly, the most common source of biological contamination is the restroom or, more specifically, people who use the restroom without washing their hands. A pathogen such as the norovirus can travel easily from one contaminated hand to another, as well as to foods. Since the restroom is such a common source of contamination, it is also the chief source of another common viral contaminant, Hepatitis A. This virus is transmitted mostly by contaminated water or by improper hand washing after using the toilet. Most outbreaks have been associated with a single individual or source in a restaurant or childcare center. Raw seafood is another common carrier of Hepatitis A. The rotovirus is similar to the norovirus in its route of transmission.

All these viral contaminants cause gastrointestinal symptoms including cramping, diarrhea, nausea, and vomiting.

Parasites are the other main source of biological contamination. Although parasites do not represent a major cause of foodborne illness, the two most common are Cryptosporidium, which is a protozoon, and Cyclospora, which is also a single-celled parasite. Both are spread through water or food that has been contaminated with feces.

Biological contamination originates in yet another source, **toxins** that are produced by organisms found naturally in certain foods. In this case the toxin produced by the organism, not the organism itself, causes the illness. Some major examples:

- Shellfish toxins—several kinds cause neurological symptoms

- Systemic fish toxins

- Plant toxins—"poison" mushrooms, rhubarb leaves, jimsonweed, hemlock, apricot pits

- Toxins related to molds

Chemical contaminants represent yet another category of agents involved in foodborne illness. Most chemical contaminants found in food are thought to result from pesticides or other agricultural chemicals. For example, food scientists are concerned about the hormones used to encourage growth in food animals, which could be reaching consumers and causing long-term effects. In addition, the antibiotics that are routinely fed to food animals have been implicated in the development of drug-resistant bacterial strains that have evolved in recent years. The CDC, the FDA, the EPA and the USDA have been monitoring these issues, and have already moved to eliminate the use of some of these agents. In the case of pesticide-contaminated fruits and vegetables, there has been an increasing partnership of growers and users of produce dedicated to addressing the issue. Sustainability programs emphasize buying meat and produce locally, which enables better communication regarding the content of products purchased. Relating to the discussion of food miles in Chapter 3, "farm to food" or "farm to fork" programs are also improving food supply safety and acknowledging that food additives and agricultural inputs can have long-term consequences.

Another other major chemical contaminant is mercury in the environment. Nearly all fish and seafood contain traces of mercury, but some fish from specific sources (certain rivers, for example) contain more than others do, depending in some cases on how a particular fish metabolizes food and reacts with the water in which it lives. Of course, the density of mercury contamination in a particular body of water also makes a difference. Mercury is a heavy metal that can be harmful to humans as it builds up over time. High levels of mercury poisoning can cause nerve, brain, and kidney damage. Some wonder whether diseases such as autism can be traced to mercury poisoning, but no clear links have been established. Nevertheless, the federal government has issued guidelines and recommendations for consumption of fish that carry mercury, sometimes with specific warnings against consuming more than a specified amount of particular species of fish, especially for consumers such as children and pregnant women who are believed to be at greater risk of mercury poisoning. For example, pregnant women should limit their intake of red snapper and mahi mahi to once a month. Yet, in its brochure "What You Need to Know about Mercury in Fish and Shellfish," the FDA concludes that for most people there should be little concern about eating fish and shellfish in moderate amounts. "Fish and shellfish are an important part of a healthy diet. Fish and shellfish contain high-quality protein and other essential nutrients, are low in saturated fat, and contain omega-3 fatty acids. A well-balanced diet that includes a variety of fish and shellfish can contribute to heart health and children's proper growth and development. So, women and young children in particular should include fish or shellfish in their diets due to the many nutritional benefits."[10]

Physical hazards in food are typically identified as foreign objects such as glass or metal fragments, although cases involving dead mice, insects, and other unpalatable objects have occurred. Physical hazard contamination can cause choking or harm to the digestive system. Most physical hazards are the result of accidents in the kitchen, such as a broken plate or glass from which a stray shard accidentally ends up in food. The wrapping or packaging in which food comes into the kitchen is another potential danger. When a wrapper is not fully removed, bits of it may remain in the food and find its way to the table. Also, hazards are often introduced to the food chain in large-scale food production facilities such as canning factories, where pieces of machinery can break off and fall into food products or packaging.

There is yet one more source of food contamination that merits discussion. Except for the rather rare disgruntled employee who may knowingly contaminate a customer's food, most incidents of food contamination involving the sources we have described are accidental. **Bioterrorism** is the purposeful adulteration or poisoning of food in order to cause widespread illness or death, presumably in service of a political or social cause.[11] Insight into this potential danger is found in a review of a presentation by James Snyder of the University of Louisville School of Medicine, discussing the possible vulnerability of the US food and water supply. According to Snyder, "Contamination of food has been a target by groups either for political reasons or as an attack of terrorism in the past. However . . . few chemical agents . . . are used directly on food . . . [It is not likely that] water would be a target since biological agents are not effective in a municipal water supply due to the treatment of the water by chlorine, and onsite purification by distilling."[12] Those who plan such acts are, however, continually refining and adjusting their methods, so constant vigilance is necessary. To the extent possible, such attacks can be prevented only by careful planning and preparation involving well-trained employees who know how to look for and calmly react to such situations. The US established the Bioterrorism Act of 2002 to delineate potential targets and to examine our degree of preparedness. The FDA website has information on the implementation of this act.[13]

FOODBORNE ILLNESS PREVENTION

It is possible to prevent or minimize the occurrence of foodborne illness only by implementing a prevention program based on effective training and monitoring at every stage in the foodservice process, from receiving to storage to preparation to presentation. Foodservice managers now have at their disposal many resources with which to address foodborne illness. Any foodservice manager must commit to ensuring the safety of the food his organization serves. When a manager truly realizes the importance of monitoring and training and does it well, employees will follow his lead. In this regard, the manager has four primary duties:

1. Identify and use the correct training program.

2. Implement that program with passion, enthusiasm, and determination.

3. Communicate with and listen to employees so that obstacles to correct procedures are removed or corrected.

4. Monitor to reward appropriate behavior and correct unsafe food-handling practices.

General Prevention

This may sound like a complex approach, but many foodborne illnesses could be prevented by the simplest of practices: washing one's hands. Hand washing is so basic to every aspect of food preparation and service that whole companies and training classes are devoted to it. Hand washing involves five seemingly obvious steps, but apparently they are not so obvious, as improper washing of hands is responsible for many outbreaks of foodborne illness. The steps can be summarized as follows:

1. Wet hands.

2. Apply soap.

3. Scrub soapy hands.

4. Rinse.

5. Dry.

All states mandate that every restroom contain at least a sign instructing employees to wash their hands before returning to work, and most require that specific instructions for hand washing be included. Hand-washing signs may be provided by local health authorities or purchased from a variety of training websites. A detailed set of instructions (on its website) is provided by "The Hand Washing for Life Institute," which is dedicated to helping foodservice operators set and achieve safe hand hygiene standards.

This website extends the basic process mentioned above with additional information:[14]

1. Pre-rinse hands with a solid flow of warm water.

2. Dispense enough liquid or foam hand soap to match the level of soil on hands.

3. Lather by rubbing hands vigorously, palm-to-palm, palm-to-back, tips-to-palms. Pay particular attention to finger tips and nails, side of thumb and index finger, wrists, and forearms.

Many local regulations extend this level of detail even further, including specifications of water temperature and the use of brushes, in addition to the amount of time involved (such as lathering for at least 20 seconds), particularly at the scrubbing step. This is not excessive attention to detail because the human hand is full of possible receptacles for contamination—fingernails, cuticles, cracks in the skin, and all those spaces between fingers are obvious examples. Employees are often directed to use paper towels to turn off the water as well, so as not to contaminate their freshly cleaned hands.

Employees who smoke cannot do so in any kitchen or in most foodservice operations at all, but when they do smoke in a "designated smoking area" they must wash their hands when they return to work. The act of smoking brings the hands into contact with saliva on the cigarette, an obvious source of contamination.

Hand-washing sinks that are easily accessible and well equipped with effective supplies must be appropriately located in all foodservice organizations. Regulations prohibit hand washing in food preparation sinks—there must be a separate hand-washing area. Local and state regulations may, and usually do, dictate how many such areas must be provided in an operation, depending on its size as well as where hand-washing instructions must be posted in relation to these sinks. If an inspector finds an empty soap dispenser or empty paper towel rack at a hand-washing sink, the foodservice operation will be cited.

Fight Bac! is another excellent reference for information pertaining to food safety and prevention of foodborne illnesses. It is the program developed by The Partnership for Food Safety Education, a not-for-profit organization that unites industry associations, professional societies in food science, nutrition and health, consumer groups, and the US government to educate the public about safe food handling.[15] This website has many free materials regarding food safety. Their four simple steps for Safe Food Handling are particularly helpful:

1. Clean hands and surfaces often.

2. Separate, don't cross-contaminate.

3. Cook—to proper temperatures.

4. Chill—refrigerate promptly.

In addition to the hand-washing information already reviewed, we add that the surfaces on which food is prepared must be constantly cleaned and sanitized, with a correctly mixed and monitored sanitizing solution. Again, regulations will specify how often such a sanitizer must be used to be effective. Cleaning suppliers should provide directions for proper use of such chemicals as well as testing kits to determine effective concentrations. (See Figure 7.3 for an example of such a test kit.) Such procedures are usually covered by local regulations. The FDA Food Code for 2010 provides the following definition:[16]

Figure 7.3 Sample sanitizer strips.

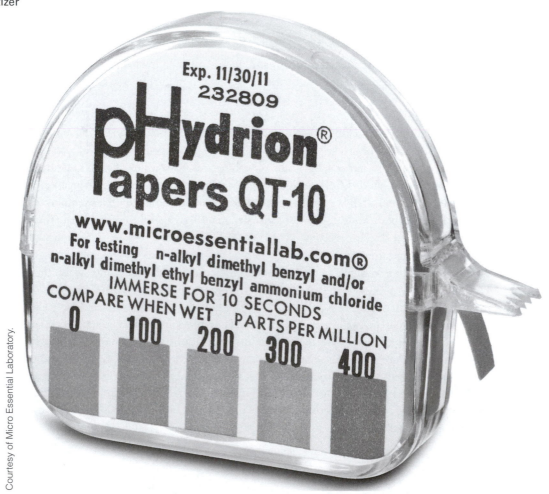

Courtesy of Micro Essential Laboratory.

"**Sanitation** means using heat or chemicals to clean food-contact surfaces, that, when tested shows a reduction of 99.99% reduction of disease microorganisms of public health importance."

Food contact surfaces can be sanitized as follows:

- Immersion in a sanitizing solution—this method is recommended for pots, pans, and utensils. There must be a three-compartment sink large enough to accommodate the pans and utensils used by a particular foodservice operation.

- Hot water and a detergent-based washing agent must be used in dishwashers for dishes, eating utensils, glasses, cups, etc.

- Surface spraying with chemical sanitizing agents is suggested for tables and similar food contact preparation areas because they coat the surface with sanitizing agents, giving more uniform coverage and therefore greater effectiveness. Spray bottles must be properly labeled and agents must be mixed according to the manufacturer's directions. All spray bottles must be emptied at the end of the day and mixed freshly each day. When sprayed, surfaces should be wiped dry with paper towels.

- Specially identified (usually red) buckets must be used for storing cloths that are used for wiping surfaces. One of the mixes listed for sanitizing must be used, tested with test strips, and cloths must be replaced with some frequency (usually every two hours or if they are visibly dirty).

More information about the correct use of chemicals is included at the end of this chapter in the discussion of workplace safety.

Cooked and raw products must never be mixed on the same cutting surface, and there should be separate cutting boards for cooked and raw products. In addition, in storage areas, raw products (such as raw beef) should always be stored below cooked products, to ensure that no contamination accidentally drips onto the cooked products. **Cross-contamination** can occur in many situations but particularly whenever a cooked product and a raw product come in contact with each other in any way, including when the same utensil is used for both products. This is also true for serving utensils with cooked products: A separate utensil should always be used for each product.

Cooking to proper temperature means following guidelines for specific internal doneness temperatures for various types of food. Subscribing to Fight Bac! for free "e-cards" enables a foodservice operation to receive e-mail cards such as the one shown in Figure 7.4, which indicates correct cooking temperatures.

Since bacteria multiply rapidly when in the temperature danger zone, cold food should be stored below 41°F and hot food should be cooked and served at the temperatures listed above. This is why the last of the four Fight Bac! food-handling tips is to "refrigerate promptly" (see Figure 7.4). Hot food inevitably passes through the temperature danger zone on its way to becoming safely chilled, but as long as this happens in the refrigerator or freezer it does not allow enough time to encourage bacterial growth. It should be noted here, however, that hot food that is being refrigerated should be chilled before it is covered. Placing hot food in the refrigerator with a cover allows the food to retain heat longer and therefore it could enter the temperature danger zone. There have been many outbreaks of foodborne illness caused by placing hot food in a deep pan (food should be stored to a depth of only two inches) and then covered while still hot. Such a practice keeps the heat in the container long enough for bacteria to grow, even though the food has been cooked.

Using any major search engine, one can enter the key words "food safety" or "food sanitation and safety" to reveal an incredible number of training programs covering every aspect of the issue. It is important that a manager select a program that is certified by and acceptable to

Figure 7.4   Fight Bac! e-card with proper cooking temperatures.

whatever authority regulates a given type of operation, most commonly a state or local health department. It is such an agency that must inspect all foodservice operations that provide or sell food to the public. One of the most widely used training programs for all foodservice personnel is ServSafe®. This program is developed and administered by the National Restaurant Association Solutions, LLC. Another leading program is administered by the National Environmental Health Association (NEHA) (see Figure 7.5). Both organizations offer high-quality training options for foodservice managers. Materials can be used in the classroom or online and in several languages. It is also important to pass a certification exam by an ANSI/CFP (American National Standards Institute/Conference for Food Protection) accredited program. Currently, there are only three programs that hold the ANSI/CFP accreditation: ServSafe, Prometric, and The National Registry of Food Safety Professionals. The associated certifications are nationally recognized.[17]

The websites for the following organizations also provide resources, both free and for a fee, for food safety training for managers and employees. A local or state regulatory agency

Courtesy of the National Environmental Health Association.

Figure 7.5   NEHA logo.

will often require at least one onsite Certified Food Safety Manager, or, for larger facilities, one or more per shift.

- Hand Washing for Life

- US Department of Agriculture

- The US Food and Drug Administration

- Fight Bac!

- Partnership for Food Safety Education

- NSF International: The Public Health and Safety Company

HACCP

It stands to reason that training is essential to foodborne illness prevention, but an HACCP system—as we explained in Chapter 4, the letters stand for Hazard Analysis Critical Control Point—offers a framework within which to implement both effective training programs and procedures that ensure that everyone in a foodservice operation is practicing what they learned in training. As alluded to earlier, it is a preventative, systematic approach to safety assurance. HACCP monitors chemical, biological, and physical food hazards from purchase to service. Introduced in the 1960s, the HACCP system, which was originally thought to be more useful in food processing plants than in foodservice operations, was considered too cumbersome and "impractical" to work in a foodservice setting. By the late 1990s, however, large-scale outbreaks of foodborne illness fueled the drive to establish responsibility for and prevention of such occurrences. This shifting orientation moved HACCP into the spotlight.

The HACCP system begins with food producers and processors, all of whom are expected to identify and manage the **critical control points** in that process. The application is similar to how we used it in menu development, but here is even more robust. Consider the following example: Spinach leaves might touch soil that has been contaminated by animal urine or feces or by improperly applied pesticides. This example underscores two critical control points that must be monitored for proper execution: the stage at which agricultural workers apply pesticides or fertilizers and the stage at which spinach is washed prior to processing. The foodservice manager who buys the spinach from a produce vendor expects the spinach to have been handled properly throughout processing and trusts that the vendor has kept it safely refrigerated (proper refrigerated storage from production through transport is the vendor's critical control point). Having procured the spinach, the foodservice manager's first critical control point within the foodservice facility is refrigerated storage, the second is the wash station, and the third is final preparation. At these stages, it is the manager's responsibility to ensure the safety of the spinach for the sake of the consumer. This example oversimplifies a typical HACCP program to some extent, but it illustrates the concept of a critical control point. In essence, a critical control point is found at any step during which food could become dirty, be stored improperly, or be handled improperly during final preparation for the table, thereby encouraging bacterial growth.

Successful implementation of an HACCP program depends on having a training routine in place regarding safe handling and preparation of food and proper sanitation procedures. Such an HACCP program then makes it possible to monitor the critical control points. State and local regulations are now largely based on HACCP principles, even though few actually mandate their use in food preparation areas. However, large operations such as major hospitals and large campus feeding areas will all have HACCP plans in place. As of 2006, HACCP-based regulations are mandatory for school foodservice operations funded by the USDA. The basic HACCPs are detailed as follows:

- Conduct a hazard analysis that includes the development, documentation, and implementation of standard operating procedures (e.g., proper hand washing).

- Determine critical control points—menu items should be reviewed to understand the risks and proper handling (note the recipe in Chapter 4, Figure 4.1, which, because it involves both the preparation and chilling of hot foods, must comply with HACCP regulations).

- Establish critical limits (define what will cause the product to be kept or discarded).

- Establish monitoring procedures (to track cooking temperatures, storage temperatures, and thawing procedures and temperatures).

- Establish corrective actions (e.g., new training topics, changes in the frequency of monitoring, replacing a missing thermometer).

- Establish verification procedures (to verify that the corrective actions have worked).

- Establish record-keeping and documentation procedures (e.g., determine who should monitor temperatures and when, who should record them, and where are they kept and for how long).

To illustrate HACCP principles, consider which of the following foodstuffs require a thorough HACCP analysis and plan—a sealed individual-serving bag of potato chips or a prepared spinach salad. Obviously, a foodservice operator must be confident that the potato chips come from a reliable source with an HACCP plan in place for the processing, frying, and packaging of the chips. But the foodservice operator is not responsible for opening and handling the contents of a sealed individual item. In the case of spinach salad, however, the foodservice operator is responsible for ensuring that all HACCP steps have been followed from the time the spinach is received until it is served.

HACCP plans take considerable time to develop, so it is recommended that foodservice operators apply them first to the most vulnerable products. Meats, for example, may pass in and out of the temperature danger zone several times during storage, preparation, and service. Therefore, most operations would begin with meat-handling HACCP procedures rather than with bread-handling HACCP procedures.

The following are excellent resources of information on HACCP principles and training procedures (search words: <HACCP> or <HACCP training>):

1. www.fda.gov and www.USDA.gov: Both provide a variety of links to HACCP resources and include basic HACCP information.

2. This website of the United Nations' Food and Agriculture Organization includes an excellent training manual and can be accessed via a link on the USDA site.[18] This manual is highly detailed, but the section on "Principles and Methods of Training" and the section on "HACCP Principles" are excellent.

3. www.cfsan.fda.gov/dms/hret2toc.html: Center for Food Safety and Applied Nutrition, US Department of Health and Human Services, FDA. Managing food safety. A manual for the voluntary use of HACCP principles for operators of foodservice and retail establishments.

4. Conference for Food Protection website.

Outbreaks of E. coli can help to clearly illustrate how to identify critical control points. As noted in Figure 7.1, there are hundreds of species of E. coli found in the gastrointestinal tracts of humans and animals. The symptoms of the foodborne illness caused by E. coli are severe and can cause bloody diarrhea, blood problems, kidney failure, and even death. Since only a small amount of the bacteria can cause illness, one must examine the entire lifecycle of a food product, from field to slaughterhouse to foodservice operation to dining table, to identify the critical control points. These points have been outlined as follows:[19]

- Contaminated water—If water is polluted with sewage or runs through fields where animals have defecated, it can be a source of E. coli contamination for vegetables irrigated with this water.

- Handling during harvest—During transportation or storage prior to processing, harvested vegetables could be exposed to animal or human waste.

- Processing prior to packaging—Contamination can occur at any time during the washing, pretreatment, or packaging of the product.

- Contaminated meats—Since E. coli occurs in the intestinal tract, it can contaminate meat at any time during the slaughtering and processing of meat, particularly if processing equipment is not carefully washed and sanitized. Grinding meat exposes more surface area to contamination.

- Cross-contamination—If the same cutting board or surface area is used for raw and cooked product or the same knives or other utensils are used, the cooked product can be contaminated.

- Person-to-person contact—If hands are not properly washed, particularly after using the bathroom, this can begin the process of transmission to food. When an individual is infected, the pathogen can remain in the feces for several weeks even after symptoms are gone.

Of course, rigorously following the food safety principles discussed earlier in this chapter should prevent E. coli contamination, but in the final analysis the foodservice manager is responsible for ensuring that all safety procedures have been followed throughout the process. Complaints on the part of employees or customers regarding food handling or symptoms of foodborne illness must be regarded seriously and addressed promptly.

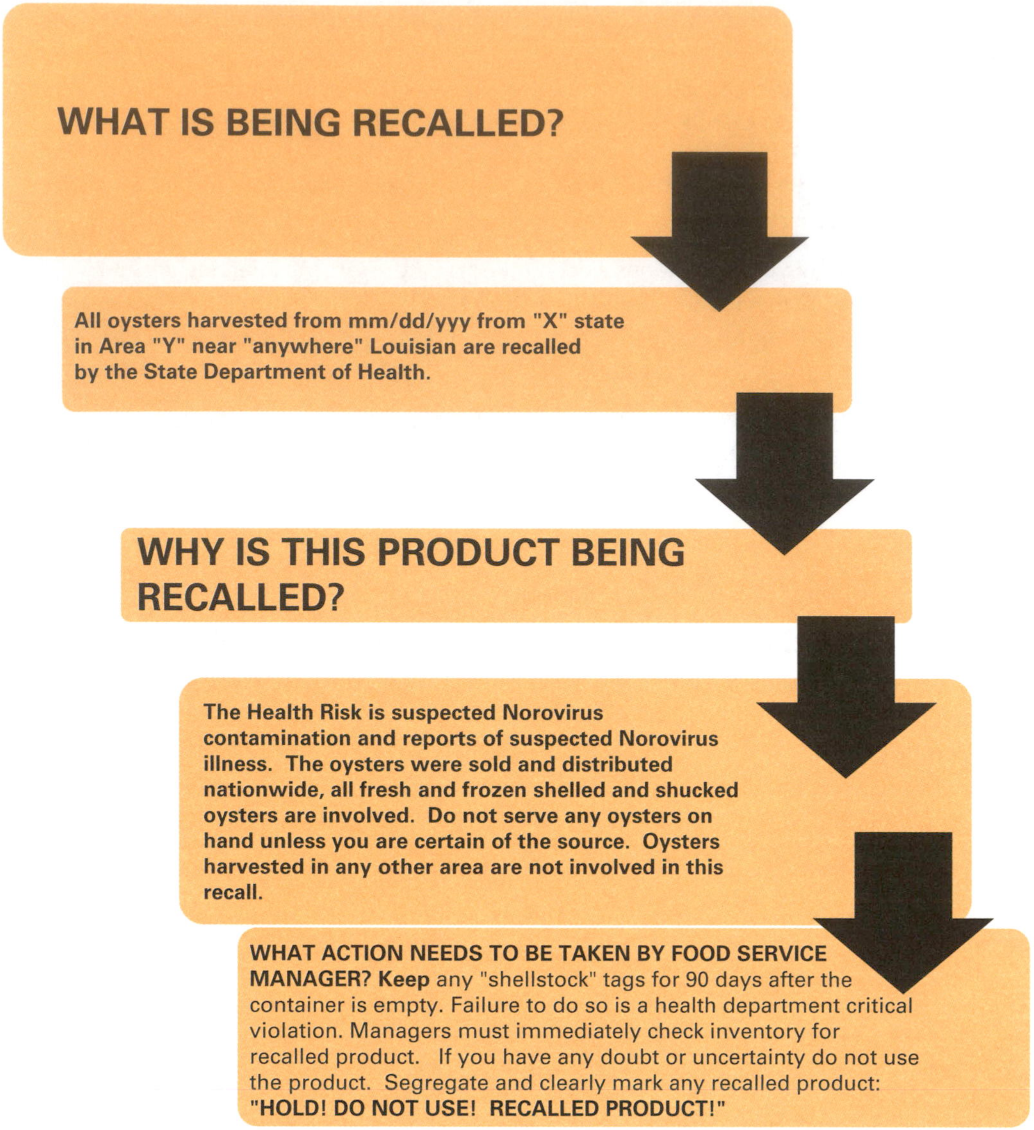

WHAT IS BEING RECALLED?

All oysters harvested from mm/dd/yyy from "X" state in Area "Y" near "anywhere" Louisian are recalled by the State Department of Health.

WHY IS THIS PRODUCT BEING RECALLED?

The Health Risk is suspected Norovirus contamination and reports of suspected Norovirus illness. The oysters were sold and distributed nationwide, all fresh and frozen shelled and shucked oysters are involved. Do not serve any oysters on hand unless you are certain of the source. Oysters harvested in any other area are not involved in this recall.

WHAT ACTION NEEDS TO BE TAKEN BY FOOD SERVICE MANAGER? Keep any "shellstock" tags for 90 days after the container is empty. Failure to do so is a health department critical violation. Managers must immediately check inventory for recalled product. If you have any doubt or uncertainty do not use the product. Segregate and clearly mark any recalled product: **"HOLD! DO NOT USE! RECALLED PRODUCT!"**

Figure 7.6 Sample recall notice.

Recalls: When the system fails in some way, there is one last resort to protect consumers and foodservice managers alike. The recall process is based on a "trace-back" system and is typically implemented when a grower or processing plant has identified an error or possible source of contamination. During a recall, all foodservice organizations that have purchased the suspect product should return it for credit to their suppliers. Food recalls are becoming more frequent as more incidents of foodborne illness are recognized, reported, and traced back to specific foods. Both the FDA and the USDA have websites with up-to-date recall information. Foodservice organizations can subscribe to receive such updates automatically.

Figure 7.6 offers a generic sample of a recall notice showing the kind of information that is typically included. Every recall should include the producer's name, lot numbers or locations of infected animals, as well as information about what should be done with the product and the nature of the problem. A recall notice might include additional information if there have been actual documented cases of illness; for example, such a notice might note that 15 cases of norovirus were reported by consumers on a specific date after eating oysters from a contaminated area. Foodservice managers must remember to check all inventory areas for any such product. It is important to remember that recalls are issued to insure safety, not to cause panic. Every kind of foodservice organization should have a written policy specifying who within the organization receives recall notices, who is responsible for checking all inventory areas, and where the notices are to be posted in the facility.

Other resources for information about recalls are:

Consumers and operators can sign up for food recall notices at www.recalls.gov.

The FDA and the USDA both maintain websites (Ref) to which foodservice organizations can subscribe for recall information:

www.fda.gov/Safety/Recalls/default.htm

www.fsis.usda.gov/Fsis_Recalls/index.asp

www.foodsafety.gov also has a recall news widget that can be downloaded at www.foodsafety.gov/widgets/index.html

The USDA Meat and Poultry hotline can be reached at 1-888-674-6854 or 1-888-MPHOTLINE.

For other products the FDA hotline number is 1-888-723-3366 or 1-888-SAFEFOOD.

Both hotlines are open from 10 A.M. to 4 P.M. ET.

The Partnership for Food Safety Education also operates Recall Basics website. This site is intended for consumers, but is instructive for foodservice managers as well.

WORKPLACE SAFETY

Maintaining a safe work environment in today's complex workplace, even in a ten-table restaurant, is a major management responsibility. All foodservice managers must consider employee workspaces, equipment, and workplace tasks. *A foodservice operation is a dangerous place!* Any foodservice operation includes many potential safety issues:

- There are heavy objects to lift, perhaps when a worker is alone and in a hurry.
- There are very sharp knives to use (often in a hurry), perhaps kept in a pile in a drawer.
- There are many very hot surfaces surrounding the workspaces.
- Floors may be wet or slippery.
- Strong chemicals must be handled and used to keep the various equipment and surfaces clean.

Perhaps surprisingly, falls are the most common cause of foodservice injury, and they can be very serious—sometimes resulting in long-term absence or disability. The loss of any experienced employee to injury may be costly to an operation in terms of healthcare and health insurance costs and as well as the cost of replacing the missing worker. Workplace safety is the right of every employee, but it is also good business for managers of any type of foodservice operation.

Foodservice workplace safety also includes fire and emergency preparedness. All employees in any foodservice operation must understand basic fire safety procedures—how to use fire extinguishers, when to service them, and where they are kept. Workers also need to know what to do if a fire starts and how to extinguish it. Local fire departments regularly assist businesses with fire safety.

When Things Go Wrong Outside the Foodservice Operation

Not all foodservice safety issues arise within the workplace. Every year hurricanes, earthquakes, and floods have devastated areas surrounding foodservice operations. A restaurant located in an area devastated by a hurricane or flood may be forced to close, perhaps permanently. When such an operation is able to re-open, it typically needs to be issued a new permit following a thorough safety inspection. All onsite foodservice organizations operate within larger facilities, some of which—such as hospitals and residences—strive to remain open under challenging circumstances following a disaster. When this happens, the operation must ensure workplace safety in spite of the challenges. Onsite operations are also often responsible for feeding rescue workers or other volunteers, including search-and-rescue dogs. The following steps should be part of any disaster preparation plan, and every onsite feeding operation must have one:

- Post emergency phone numbers for all managers and employees.

- Post emergency call numbers for vendors.

- Maintain an emergency food and supplies inventory.

- Ensure compliance with the larger organization's disaster plan.

Separate plans and menus are needed for:

- Water supply failure

- Employee strike/labor shortage/increased or unexpected surplus of patients/residents

- Gas supply outage

- Electrical outage

- Elevator failure

- Undeliverable food and supplies

- Refrigeration/freezer failure

- Sewage back-up or other unsafe conditions in food preparation area

Every state and most communities feature emergency management agencies that issue detailed guidelines to assist organizations in developing disaster plans. As noted, any legitimate onsite organization will have a plan covering emergency procedures for the entire facility, and the foodservice operation will play an important role in implementing that plan.

Restaurants might also be asked to provide food preparation assistance in a disaster area. In such cases, in addition to maintaining workplace safety, safe food-handling procedures must also be followed, since emergency workers cannot work effectively while suffering from foodborne illnesses. Moreover, foodservice operations must strive not to add foodborne illness to the other afflictions suffered by disaster victims.

Governments strive to achieve or improve workplace safety by enacting laws to enforce the principles we have reviewed in this chapter. Violating such laws results in serious legal difficulties and, in extreme cases, foodservice operations can be closed. The US Department of Labor (DOL) has the overall responsibility for the administration and enforcement of laws enacted to protect the safety and health of workers:

- As introduced in the previous chapter, the Occupational Safety and Health Act (OSHA) is administered by the DOL's Occupational Safety and Health Administration. OSHA applies to almost all industries, including foodservice. In addition to their responsibility for complying with OSHA regulations, employers are responsible for keeping work activities and the workplace free of serious hazards.

- The Fair Labor Standards Act (FLSA) is administered by the DOL's Wage and Hour Division (WHD) with the intent of protecting children. It covers employees under the age of 18 (of whom there are many in the foodservice industry), regulating the times of day and hours they can work and the jobs they may perform.

- The Office of Workers' Compensation Programs administers major disability programs that provide wage replacement benefits, medical treatment, vocational rehabilitation, and other benefits to workers who are injured on the job or develop an occupational disease.

There are several other agencies that administer workplace safety, but those listed here are the ones that are most often encountered by foodservice organizations. An employee who feels she has been injured due to a safety violation may file a complaint with OSHA, which will likely visit onsite to evaluate the situation.

MATERIAL SAFETY DATA SHEETS (MSDS)

We have discussed the importance of workplace sanitation. Today's sanitizing agents are very effective, but only if the manufacturer's directions are followed exactly. The product containers provide instructions for dilution and usage, but such instructions can be difficult to read or understand. Every manufacturer must therefore provide a separate sheet of information about such a product, known as the Material Safety Data Sheet, or **MSDS**. In most situations, a foodservice operation is required to keep a book containing all the MSDSs for every chemical agent used in the facility. Such a book must be clearly marked and easily accessible to all employees. The requisite information is illustrated in Figure 7.7.

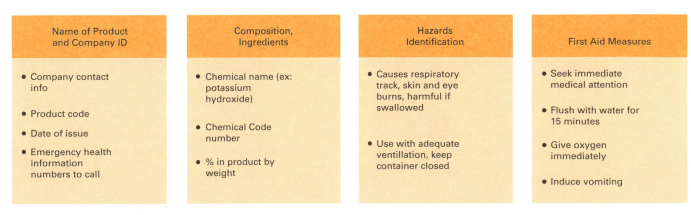

Name of Product and Company ID	Composition, Ingredients	Hazards Identification	First Aid Measures
• Company contact info • Product code • Date of issue • Emergency health information numbers to call	• Chemical name (ex: potassium hydroxide) • Chemical Code number • % in product by weight	• Causes respiratory track, skin and eye burns, harmful if swallowed • Use with adequate ventilation, keep container closed	• Seek immediate medical attention • Flush with water for 15 minutes • Give oxygen immediately • Induce vomiting

Figure 7.7   Types of MSDS information.

The MSDS information is also critical since chemicals must be used under the proper circumstances (floor products on floors, stainless steel products on stainless steel, etc.) and mixed in the proper dilution. Many such chemicals can react dangerously if mixed together. For example, many people believe that bleach can be mixed with other cleaning agents to boost their cleaning power, but doing so can lead to serious accidents, usually involving the inhaling of caustic fumes.

The first page of any MSDS book typically lists emergency numbers that are available 24 hours a day for each company's products. The book should also provide a complete listing of every sanitizing and cleaning agent used by the foodservice operation, constituting a comprehensive chemical inventory:

- Manufacturer

- Product brand name

- Hazardous chemicals

- Severity of potential hazards (usually indicated by a rating number—e.g., a hand sanitizer would have a 1 rating indicating minimal danger while a phosphoric acid–based cleaner might have a 3 rating indicating much more serious danger)

- Reactivity indicator, also given in a numeric code

- Container size

- General usage (sanitizer, degreaser, etc.)

- Recommended treatments for exposure, spills, etc.

Disposal of such chemicals must also be approached cautiously, as they cannot be simply poured down a drain in large quantities without exposing people and animals outside of the workplace to similar hazards.

MANAGERIAL IMPLICATIONS

Sanitation and safety are two key concerns for today's foodservice manager, which is highly appropriate insofar as foodborne illness is potentially life threatening. Controlling pathogens that can lead to foodborne illness requires a foodservice operation to deploy a range of complex processes, beginning with basic practices that ensure that food and workplace conditions are safe for customers and employees.

A foodborne illness is any illness caused by consuming food, but to understand foodborne illnesses adequately requires identifying a wide variety of symptoms caused by a wide variety of pathogens (disease-causing organisms) such as bacteria, viruses, and toxins. Correspondingly, food safety occupies the scientific discipline that studies the handling, preparation, and storage of food to prevent foodborne illness. The key to prevention is therefore understanding the conditions under which bacteria, viruses, or parasites thrive and multiply and modifying the foodservice preparation environment to eliminate those conditions. The conditions that are fundamental to causing foodborne illness apply to food, acidity, time, temperature, oxygen, and moisture.

The government includes numerous agencies and programs that address food safety. Some are intended to prevent foodborne illness by providing information and training; others are designed to research and track related causes and effects. Still other programs are available to provide training for foodservice employees, including ServSafe, a program developed and administered by the National Restaurant Association Educational Foundation.

The hazards associated with food safety can be categorized as biological, chemical, and physical. Biological hazards generally include bacteria and viruses; the most common way for these pathogens to make their way into food is improper sanitation on the part of food handlers who fail to wash their hands thoroughly, particularly after using the restroom. Parasites are another biological contaminant and are typically spread through water or food that has been contaminated with feces. Toxins such as those found naturally in certain foods are yet another biological hazard. Most chemical contaminants found in food are the result of pesticides or other agricultural chemicals; another is mercury, which is ubiquitous in the environment—especially in water—and is typically ingested when eating some forms of seafood. Finally, physical hazards are foreign objects in food that typically find their way into food products accidentally during food preparation. Bioterrorism, on the other hand, is the purposeful adulteration or poisoning of food in order to cause widespread illness or death.

The simple process of hand washing is one of the best ways to prevent foodborne illness. All states mandate that every restroom contain at least a sign instructing employees to wash their hands before returning to work, and most require that specific instructions for hand washing be included. Many local regulations extend this level of detail even further.

Other seemingly commonsense practices lead to improved food safety. For example, cross-contamination can occur in many instances but particularly whenever a cooked product and a raw product come in contact with each other, including the use of the same utensil for both products. Another example is keeping food out of the temperature danger zone (41°F–135°F).

A standardized approach to preventing foodborne illness is provided by the HACCP system, which offers a framework for training and procedures for safely handling food. Central to the HACCP system is the identification of critical control points, which are points, steps, or procedures at which controls can be applied and a food safety hazard can be prevented. Every foodservice manager should be familiar with the major steps included in the HACCP process.

The final major managerial issue is workplace safety, which includes employee workspaces, equipment, and workplace tasks. Foodservice workplace safety also includes fire and emergency preparedness. Furthermore, dangers in the workplace can be external, such as natural disasters, so foodservice managers must have disaster preparation plans in place for any foreseeable situation.

A related issue is the handling of sanitizing agents and other chemicals commonly used in foodservice. In most situations, a foodservice operation is required to keep a book containing all the MSDSs for every chemical agent used in the facility, which aids in using the right chemical in the proper concentration for the intended use. Such an MSDS is also important in cases where an employee is exposed to a dangerous chemical or if such a chemical is spilled.

Microban International

W.L. Morrison, a MIT-trained entrepreneur, noticed the telephone receiver in his hand, thought of the potential for contamination when using a public pay phone, and wondered how it might be controlled. This one question led to the development of the first antimicrobial polymeric products for both medical and consumer applications.

In 1994, Microban was founded by three biomedical engineers who refined Morrison's original work and transitioned his ideas from the laboratory to the real world. Through proprietary processes, they developed a way of engineering antimicrobial ingredients into solid products. The result was the development of antimicrobial solutions that give consumer, industrial, and medical products an added level of protection against damaging microbes such as bacteria, mold, and mildew that can cause stains, odors, and product deterioration.

And, in 1996, the company began marketing the benefits of antimicrobial product protection under the Microban® brand, modeling the success of other early ingredient brands such as NutraSweet®, Lycra®, and Teflon®. Today, Microban International, Ltd. is the global leader in built-in antimicrobial product protection, engineering durable antimicrobial solutions for consumer,

Courtesy of Microban International, LTD.

Figure 7.8 Cutting boards with Microban.

industrial, and medical products around the world. Microban uses a broad range of antimicrobial technologies that can be engineered into a similarly broad range of materials including polymers, textiles, coatings, paper, and adhesives. Microban licenses the use of the Microban trademark to more than 250 companies around the world and Microban technology is built into over 1,000 products during the manufacturing process (see Figure 7.9 for an example), including kitchen and bath products, apparel and home textiles, appliances, building materials, foodservice products, medical products, and others.

Microban antimicrobial product protection inhibits the growth of microbes, such as bacteria, mold, and mildew that can cause stains, odors, and deterioration of a product (see Figure 7.9).

It is important to understand that Microban advises consumers that its technology is not intended to replace or obviate standard cleaning practices and does not purport to protect consumers from foodborne illnesses in the absence of such practices. It promises only to reduce microbial populations on product surfaces, keeping products cleaner between cleanings.

Figure 7.9 Time lapse photos using a confocal microscope of cooking surfaces after 24 hours without (left) and with Microban. Note the substantial amount of microbial growth on the surface without Microban technology.

Courtesy of Microban International, LTD.

KEY TERMS

foodborne Illness 134
pathogens 134
microorganisms 134
temperature danger zone 137
CDC 137

FoodNet 137
virus 138
norovirus 138
toxins 139
bioterrorism 140

sanitation 143
cross-contamination 143
critical control point 145
MSDS 151

Food Safety at the Nursing Home

Jonathan was known to be an excellent foodservice manager at a large nursing home in a small town in the Midwest. He had run the operation for years and was respected by his employees and his boss. He was active in the community as the coach of a local baseball team. Jonathan succeeded because he made the rules clear. His employees always said: "Jonathan is tough, but you always know what to do. And he'd better not catch you not doing it!" Yes, Jonathan had a tough reputation, and while it meant that no one questioned him, it also meant that the organization had been running smoothly for years. It was almost running itself, he used to say.

A new unit opened in Jonathan's nursing home last year. It was designed to house individuals recovering from serious head and jaw surgery. Often, the reconstructive surgery was complicated and the recovery long, and patients needed care that could not be provided at home. They couldn't eat regular food, so at first they had to sip liquid food. As they recovered the ability to chew, their food could be ground up. The kitchen had to prepare 10 or 15 servings of ground food. Jonathan's team usually ground the meat after it was cooked and then kept it warm and served it. One day during flu season, several cooks had become ill, and a new cook decided to get some work done for the next day. He ground raw turkey, carefully fried it, and, just as Jonathan had told him to do, he placed it in a nice, deep pan and covered it tightly. He was preparing it for the next day and placed it in the refrigerator.

It was served as a ground turkey salad with jellied cranberry sauce garnish the next day for lunch. Starting about 7 P.M. that evening, after the kitchen had closed, patients began to feel nausea and then some experienced diarrhea. By 10 P.M., seven people had become ill, and the nurse called Jonathan at home. His first reaction was, "It's not possible—patients can't have gotten sick in my operation!" By the next day, however, they had isolated the offending organism in the turkey salad and in some biological fluid samples taken from patients.

1. What happened?

2. Explain how this outbreak of foodborne illness happened.

3. What could Jonathan have done to prevent it?

4. What should he add to his training program in the future?

REVIEW AND DISCUSSION QUESTIONS

1. Are there any groups for whom foodborne illness can be particularly serious?

2. Why might occurrences or outbreaks of foodborne illness seem more frequent today?

3. Define foodborne illness and food safety.

4. List the major types of pathogens that can cause foodborne illness and the specific conditions that help them to grow and multiply.

5. What steps should you take if you suspect you have become the victim of food poisoning?

6. In addition to bacteria, what other type of biological contaminant can be passed on in food? Discuss the most common way this contaminant is passed to food. What is the major way to prevent this?

7. Identify the major preventive system for preventing foodborne illness; in your answer, list its major components.

8. How does a foodservice worker know how much sanitizing solution to use in water? Describe the procedure.

9. What is "Fight Bac!" and what does it do?

10. Go to the National Restaurant Association's website. From the information provided, list three best practices regarding food safety.

11. Describe the responsibilities of any foodservice operation if an emergency or disaster happens.

12. What does MSDS stand for, and what is the purpose of an MSDS?

13. Go back to the story of Jonathan toward the end of this chapter. What might the manager might have done to prevent what happened?

14. Look at the pictures in the Industry Exemplar section at the end of this chapter. Why are there cutting boards of contrasting colors?

ENDNOTES

1. Partnership for Food Safety Education. www.fightbac.org. Accessed October 2012.

2. "Foodborne Illness." www.foodborneillness.com, sponsored by Marler Clark. Accessed October 2012.

3. Mead, P.S., et al. "Food-related illness and death in the United States." Emerg. Infect. Dis. 1999:5, 607–625. Centers for Disease Control www.cdc.gov. Accessed October 2012.

4. USDA Food Safety and Inspection Service www.fsis.usda.gov/Fact_Sheets/Foodborne_Illness.gov. Accessed October 2012.

5. Food and Drug Administration Center for Food Safety and Applied Nutrition. *Bad Bug Book: Foodborne Pathogenic Microorganisms and Natural Toxins Handbook.* McClean, VA: International Medical Publishing, 2004.

6. As noted at the ServSafe website, the FDA recommends cooling food in two stages—from 135°F to 70°F in two hours, then from 70°F to 41°F or lower in an additional four hours, for a total cooling time of six hours. However, this does not mean you have six hours straight through. It is important to realize that if the food does not reach 70°F in two hours, you cannot continue to cool the food; the food must be reheated to 165°F for 15 seconds within two hours before another attempt at cooling can be made.

7. According to the ServSafe website, the FDA lowered the holding temperature for hot potentially hazardous food from 140°F to 135°F based on input from the Conference for Food Protection. At the 2002 CFP, it was determined that enough scientific information existed to warrant this temperature change. Technical studies of key foodborne pathogens show that the upper limits of their growth range are well below 140°F (e.g., Bacillus cereus 122°F; Clostridium perfringens 127.5°F; Clostridium botulinum 118°F; Staphylococcus aureus 122°F). The temperature change was incorporated into the 2003 supplement to the 2001 FDA Food Code. Moreover, the National Restaurant Association reported recently that stemming from partnerships developed between the industry, academia, and regulatory agencies, and to help promote uniformity between industry and regulatory standards, the ServSafe materials will use 41°F (4°C) as the lower limit of the temperature danger zone.

8. Centers for Disease Control www.cdc.gov/FoodNet.

9. Position of the Academy of Nutrition and Dietetics: "Food and Water Safety." *Journal of the Academy of Nutrition and Dietetics* 109 (August 2009): 1449–1460.

10. Food and Drug Administration. "What You Need to Know About Mercury in Fish and Shellfish." www.fda.gov/Food/Resources for you/Consumers/ucm110591. Accessed October 2012.

11. Edelstein, Sari. "Protecting the U.S. Food Supply." *Today's Dietitian* (December 2009).

12. Puckett, R. "A Summary of Dr. James Snyder's presentation from ADA's Food & Nutrition Conference & Exhibition." *Market-Link*, the newsletter of the Management of Food & Nutrition Systems Practice Group (Winter 2003).

13. Food and Drug Administration. www.fda.gov/Food/FoodDefense/Bioterrorism/ucm080817. Accessed October 2012.

14. Hand Washing for Life Institute. www.handwashingforlife.com. Accessed October 2012.

15. Partnership for Food Safety Education, Fight Bac!. www.fightbac.org. Accessed October 2012.

16. Food and Drug Administration. www.fda.gov/food/. Accessed October 2012.

17. ServSafe. www.servsafe.com/foodsafety. Accessed October 2012.

18. Food and Agriculture Organization of the United Nations. *Food Quality and Safety Systems—A Training Manual on Food Hygiene and the Hazard Analysis and Critical Control Point (HACCP) System.* Rome: Publishing Management Group, FAO Information Division, 1998.

19. Khan, M.A. "Education, Diligence Can Prevent Spread of E.Coli." *Nation's Restaurant News* (April 28, 2008).

CHAPTER 8

SUPPLY CHAIN MANAGEMENT

LEARNING OBJECTIVES:

After becoming familiar with this chapter, you should be able to:

1. Describe the activities related to the purchasing process and the role of the purchasing manager.

2. Understand how distribution channels function.

3. Determine how to select suppliers.

4. Explain the importance of ethics, particularly related to purchasing.

5. Identify the various methods and related issues pertaining to buying food and beverage products.

6. Appreciate the importance of accurate forecasting.

7. Calculate quantities of food items in various product categories using the most suitable method.

In its broadest sense, supply chain management involves coordinating interconnected businesses that result in a product or service for an end user. It encompasses the planning and management of all activities involved in sourcing, procurement, conversion, and logistics coordination. In the foodservice industry, the supply chain might begin with a farmer but most commonly begins with a vendor; this might be a national vendor of food products or a local producer of vegetables. As you might expect, such a chain of businesses is critical to a foodservice operation because without the necessary ingredients delivered in a timely manner, an operator cannot produce menu items of the highest quality and with the desired consistency.

We should note that previous generations of foodservice managers viewed this process more simplistically under the rubric *purchasing*. However, this view must be expanded today, in part because of globalization. Moreover, as diners' tastes have expanded to include a variety of cuisines, so has the need to source ingredients more broadly. Also, with the common goal of sourcing ingredients locally, the entire purchasing process has grown more complex. Today we understand that obtaining everything a manager needs to successfully operate a foodservice outlet requires a holistic understanding of the supply chain.

Thus, in this chapter we explore the various aspects of supply chain management, including purchasing, distribution channels, selecting suppliers, and several methods of buying products for the foodservice outlet. We conclude with a discussion of forecasting, as this is fundamental to managing a supply chain. The following chapter addresses the end of the supply chain, which involves managing the products once they arrive at the foodservice operation's back door.

PURCHASING

We have already discussed menu design as well as the importance of delivering value. These issues are directly shaped by the items purchased to create menu items. And while improperly executed preparation techniques or poor service can negatively affect a guest's perceived value, the initial issue is the quality of each of the ingredients in a dish. After all, even the best chef cannot create a savory meal without good food products.

Interestingly, purchasing was historically given little attention in management training. This is understandable for small operations, since the manager of such an operation—a person for whom the phrase "chief cook and bottle washer" was invented—had little time to compare vendors by price or service quality given the other requirements of her job. In large operations, however, **economies of scale**—reductions in costs due to efficiencies (e.g., bulk pricing) gained as sales volume increases (as when the number of restaurants in a chain increases)—have made the purchasing function a leading factor in driving profit. Today, managers at both large and small foodservice operations understand that time spent on the purchasing process yields economic and operational benefits that cannot be ignored.

Purchasing Activities

In its most basic sense, purchasing—also referred to as **procurement**—entails buying an item not unlike how the average person buys food at the grocery store. In the foodservice industry, however, purchasing involves an array of management functions. The first of these, determining **product specifications**, is linked to the previously described process of menu development. For example, if an entrepreneur in designing his seafood restaurant wants to feature live Maine lobsters grilled to order, then the specifications would dictate the size of the Maine lobsters. Similarly, if a foodservice operator includes branded items on the menu (e.g., a sandwich made with Grey Poupon mustard), then the brand must be listed under the product specifications. Product specifications become increasingly important when a manager wants to negotiate prices with competing vendors; the specifications allow for an apples-to-apples comparison.

It should be noted that writing product specifications can be time consuming and labor intensive in that it requires a team approach. In a large medical center, for example, such a team might include the foodservice manager, the kitchen manager, a dietitian, a cook, and the person responsible for placing orders with vendors. Nonetheless, clear product specifications are critical in standardizing purchasing, food production, and quality.

What should be included in a product specification? The following is a general guideline for effective purchase specifications:

- Product name

- Intended use of the product (such as for specific recipes)

- General description of the product such as the size of the container or count per container and brand

- Detailed description that, depending on the item, might include:

  □ Geographic origin

  □ Product size

  □ Product type

  □ How it's packaged

  □ Fresh or frozen

  □ Grade

  □ Edible yield

- Test procedures such that when the product is received the employee can objectively assess it for quality, quantity, density, etc.

- Special instructions or requirements, which might include how a product must be handled

Finally, note that the product quantity listed on the purchasing specification serves multiple purposes. For example, tuna can be ordered in various-sized cans. In a large operation, buying a case of size 5 cans—the size most widely used for commercial foodservice operations that hold 56 ounces by weight—makes sense. However, in a small healthcare setting where tuna is rarely used, the product packaging should be smaller. Obviously, an operator needs to purchase an adequate amount of a given product, but certainly doesn't want to have an excess of perishable food items that if not used in a timely manner will result in financial loss. (We talk more about the associated task of forecasting later in the chapter.)

The next purchasing activity that takes place concurrently with the previous two is determining whether products should be purchased ready to use or prepared at the foodservice operation, which is sometimes referred to as a **make-or-buy analysis**. For example, say a college cafe plans on serving stuffed chicken breasts as part of the cycle menu and also features chicken soup. The operator must decide if whole chickens should be purchased, in which case the breast meat could be removed and used for the entrée while the remaining parts could be used for soup and other dishes, or purchase prepackaged chicken breasts. This is both an operational and a financial decision. Purchasing prepackaged chicken breasts is more expensive but requires less labor to prepare the menu item. Buying whole chickens would save money in food cost but requires skilled labor (and therefore increased labor cost) to properly prepare the chicken for its various uses.

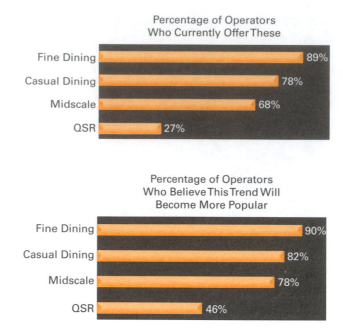

Figure 8.1 Statistics on locally sourced or locally manufactured foods.

A related decision is whether to use locally sourced and locally manufactured foods, which undeniably shapes how the supply chain is approached. Foodservice operators frequently cite local products' superior freshness as a key advantage related to using local products. Other advantages include the reduction in food miles (introduced in Chapter 3), along with reducing the associated carbon footprint. As shown in Figure 8.1, the trend is moving in this direction.

The remaining purchasing-related activities, such as understanding distribution channels, selecting suppliers, identifying optimal buying methods, and forecasting are addressed individually later in the chapter.

Purchasing Managers

Given the sizable purchasing decisions required, the role of the purchasing manager has grown as the foodservice industry has evolved. In fact, in large onsite foodservice companies such as ARAMARK, the purchasing function is executed by an entire department that has specialized purchasing managers delineated by product category. In large, multicampus medical centers, too, the food purchasing may be facilitated by at least one dedicated purchasing manager along with support staff.

In addition to the obvious operational issues that accompany the determination of product specifications and product quantity, the other vital issue mentioned earlier is financial impact. Economies of scale lead to better pricing, but today food manufacturers and distributors also want to guarantee their sales volume. This is typically done through **rebates**—money paid to the foodservice organization when certain volume thresholds are reached. For example, say a regional onsite foodservice company expects to use 500,000 pounds of ground beef during the year. They will negotiate a price with the supplier given that volume, say $1.80 per pound. In order to ensure that the company will purchase that amount, the supplier might provide a rebate of $.05 per pound if the foodservice company exceeds the purchase of 500,000 pounds. This would mean an end-of-year rebate to the foodservice company of $25,000.

This use of rebates is becoming more commonplace in a variety of industries as huge companies wield ever-increasing purchasing power and manufacturers seek guarantees for the sale of their products. Not surprisingly, this trend has transformed purchasing departments in large foodservice companies from support functions to actual profit generators. It has also created new opportunities for managers looking for jobs that are related to but function outside of the foodservice operation.

DISTRIBUTION CHANNELS

Building on the purchasing function as part of the entire supply chain management process, we next address **distribution channels**. By definition, a distribution channel is the path or pipeline through which goods flow from a vendor to the consumer while payment flows in the opposite direction. Distribution channels are a central component of the overall concept of distribution networks, which are the real, tangible systems of interconnected sources and destinations through which products pass on their way to final consumers. Foodservice operators use multiple channels of distribution, but the management and profit opportunities are the same.

Product Management

One of the best ways to understand distribution channels is to explore how products move from the source to the guest—and how these transactions must be managed (see Figure 8.2). The source—farm, ranch, fish hatchery, and so on—is the first critical piece of the channel. The source is important first because it has to be capable of providing a consistent level of products to the market. This is not always easy. For example, the availability of wild, line-caught fresh fish is determined by what fishermen catch, which cannot always be guaranteed. Similarly, growers are subject to weather conditions (as well as other uncontrollable issues).

Another key aspect of the source, one that has become very important today, is that of the business practices and processes that the company employs. This is seen frequently in the coffee industry where **fair trade coffee**—coffee that when traded bypasses the coffee trader and therefore increases the producer's (and buyer's) profits—is often touted. Many foodservice companies also prefer to buy agricultural products that are grown or raised with sustainability in mind. This concern for environmental health, economic profitability, and social and economic equity—the underlying principles of sustainability that we have mentioned repeatedly throughout this book—is vital.

The next stage in the distribution channel that must be managed (remember that the foodservice operator may build relationships with each party in the supply chain) pertains to the manufacturer or processor. Almost all food and beverage ingredients require some sort of

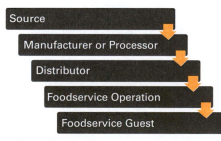

Figure 8.2 Key distribution channel stages.

processing: Grain is milled and converted to flour, cattle is slaughtered and fabricated into wholesale and retail cuts, grapes are fermented into wine, and sugarcane byproducts are distilled into rum. Thus, the manufacturer or processor adds value to the sourced products for which they charge the purchaser.

Such manufacturing processes often entail multiple steps. For example, a manufacturer may buy meat from a processor who has slaughtered beef to make frozen entrees or canned soup. A manufacturer that produces baked products would similarly purchase flour and related products from a processor rather than purchasing wheat from the source.

The distributor, the next participant in the distribution channel, has the most direct contact with the foodservice operation owing to their proximity in the supply chain. Distributors, also referred to as purveyors, suppliers, wholesalers, or vendors, serve as the intermediaries between manufacturers and the foodservice operation. By purchasing products from manufacturers located around the globe and warehousing and delivering to the foodservice outlet as needed, distributors add value for the foodservice operator (and charge prices that reflect this).

In the foodservice industry, distributors do much more than just deliver food and beverage products. Many provide free assistance with menu development (ensuring that the operator builds on products from that distributor). Some also provide money-saving alternative food products. Many, too, furnish promotional material, nutritional information, and ingredient information. Finally, large distributors frequently host open houses in which foodservice operators can tour the warehouse and learn about new products.

In concluding our discussion of distributors, we should comment on the role of **brokers**. Brokers are intermediaries who represent processors or manufacturers and deal with assisting purchasing managers. While they represent processors and manufacturers, they are not employees but, rather, work as independent contractors. Their role is also distinct from that of the distributor's sales representatives, as brokers typically work with many manufacturers (although they do not generally work with manufacturers of similar products). Today's brokerage firms, which employ large numbers of food brokers, provide assistance to foodservice operators not only in locating food and beverage products but also in promotion and marketing

Intracompany Distribution Channels

Another area of supply chain management that has not existed until recently is **intracompany distribution channels**. In large foodservice organizations, distribution of some food products is facilitated through company-owned warehouses and distribution trucks. This allows the foodservice operator to shorten the supply chain and even take on some of the roles traditionally served by manufacturers and processors. For example, a large QSR chain might purchase lettuce from a regional grower and then slice and package it at its company-owned warehouse, delivered in standardized package sizes to each unit. This aids in quality control and reduces labor requirements at individual restaurants; it also reduces cost by eliminating steps in the distribution channel.

An additional form of intracompany distribution channel, again used by larger, multiunit foodservice companies, is a modification of the distribution channel described earlier. Under this model the foodservice company contracts directly with the processors and manufacturers. The goods then are delivered through existing distribution systems, which are either used exclusively by the foodservice company or shared with similar companies such as grocery stores and other restaurants.

Precursors to intracompany distribution channels are corporate-developed purchasing agreements with manufacturers. Utilized in many onsite foodservice companies and restaurant chains, this approach ensures standardization and allows for the benefits of the aforementioned economies of scale. Simply stated, a firm's management identifies products and determines their costs with the manufacturer, processor, or broker. A large distributor is then employed almost as an exclusive delivery agent for all the chain's units. Each location is required to use only those products and each pays the same cost.

Profit Maximization

Food and beverage products are generally distributed to foodservice operators in one of six ways:

1. By large national or regional distributors with broad product lines

2. By large national or regional distributors with very specialized product lines

3. By distribution companies owned by or contracted with the foodservice company

4. Through commissary systems, in which food is prepared or portioned prior to distribution to local units

5. By local independent full-line distributors

6. By local distributors specializing in regional, limited-availability products

Deciding which of these to use, or whether to use a combination of them, has direct ramifications for the bottom line. Unless the parent corporation specifies how the distribution channel is used, then, foodservice managers must assess which method best suits the specific operation's situation. In doing so, several factors must be considered. First, local distributors are rapidly being absorbed into national chains, and those that aren't may not be able to compete on price. They may, however, provide a level of service that includes more frequent deliveries, which can reduce waste and ensure freshness.

Even if an operator has selected a national full-line distributor, it is unlikely that such a distributor will have every product needed by the foodservice establishment. However, some distributors prefer exclusivity agreements that limit the foodservice manager from using competing suppliers. Then there are prices. No single distributor offers the lowest prices on everything. Some may sell lettuce at a better price than the competing distributor but the potatoes may be more expensive. Thus, in comparing one distributor with another, the operator must take a **shopping bag approach** in which a wide variety of items are compared. This can be accomplished by preparing for a week's operations and then asking each distributor to provide prices for the items at the quantities listed. This provides a more accurate picture of the pricing available from each distributor.

The last consideration that affects profit directly is that of terms of payment. Some distributors require payment within a limited number of days. Depending on the foodservice operation's cash flow, then, it might be better to select a distributor that requires payment over longer periods, such as 30 days.

■□ SUPPLIER SELECTION

These decisions, which should be aimed at maximizing profit by effectively managing the supply chain, cannot be made in a vacuum or on the basis of price alone. Much as service is critical in a restaurant, service from the distributor is important. Consider the distributor that arrives at noon at the onset of the lunch rush, or the distributor that is a day late in delivering food to the hospital foodservice operation; the hospital kitchen certainly can't close early because it runs out of food.

Supplier as Partner

An emerging practice in supply chain management views the foodservice operation-distributor relationship not simply as a business arrangement but as a partnership. With this new view, the needs of both parties are recognized and the entities work together for their mutual benefit. Indeed, such a strategic relationship between the parties is based on compatible goals, the pursuit of mutual gain, but with a high level of mutual independence.[1]

Such a partnership, like any relationship, is influenced by a variety of factors. First, what is the purchasing volume? Obviously a high-volume restaurant with limited storage requires a distributor with the capability of delivering frequently. On a related note, how many types of items are needed? And are fresh, direct-from-the-processor, items required? A restaurant in a mall that features hot dogs with a wide choice of toppings will likely not use the same vendor as a large, upscale restaurant chain.

Location is also a factor. The service requirements of a restaurant in the lesser-populated part of Maine will differ markedly from those required by Les Halles in New York City. Also, the number of units and their locations make a difference. A multinational restaurant company that wants to contract with a single distributor would be a valued client for that distributor. And this notion of partnership is perfectly exemplified here: The supplier can help the restaurant company immensely with product consistency, as they can manage inventory back through the supply chain.

The next concern that pertains to maintaining a relationship is the variety of foodservice operations involved. For example, a large, onsite foodservice company might have operations in medical centers, stadiums, prisons, colleges, and automotive-assembly plants. With such a diverse set of operations, the number of distinct food products as well as the spread of the geography will require a distributor that can meet the client's needs in terms of both products and delivery availability.

The final consideration in working with a distributor as a partner is expertise. Some foodservice operators may be excellent marketers but less adept in selecting substitute food items when a requested item is unavailable. Distributors exhibit varying levels of expertise and amounts of support that they provide to their foodservice clients. An operator that wants a supplier with advanced ordering capabilities, automatic substitutions, or policies that ensure no substitutions must select distributors accordingly. In addition, many healthcare foodservice operations either elect to use or must develop an agreement with their major suppliers for water and emergency food supplies in the event of a disaster such as severe storms. Thus, distributors must have the ability to comply with such needs. (See Chapter 7 for more on disaster planning.)

Suppliers and Ethics

The research on foodservice operators and distributors partnering in business clearly shows that mutual trust is key. While these types of partnerships provide a sustainable competitive advantage for both parties, establishing trust is the critical factor. As foodservice operators share information with their suppliers that they would not willingly share with their competitors, the suppliers can better service the foodservice operators. This trust can also lead to collaborative activities and a better alignment of business goals. At the same time, partners with a strong relationship make better decisions as greater trust permits a greater variety of options to be explored. The development of trust-based partnerships in supply-chain relationships is likely to become one of the most powerful purchasing strategies in the decades ahead.

These benefits of mutual trust are plain. Indeed, with mutual trust and clear, effective communication in place, both parties can excel in their respective business ventures. However, the reality of the foodservice industry is that in the past it has been plagued by unethical practices on the part of both distributors and foodservice operators. Some ethical breaches do little harm while others provide an unfair competitive advantage. Consider the following two scenarios:

Scenario One: The Gift

Jan, the general manager of a successful casual-theme restaurant, is very proud of the wine list that she developed in partnership with her wine distributor. She has spent countless hours training her staff in the art of recommending wines to guests. She has also recently added wine-pairing recommendations to the menu adjacent to every entree description. Beginning last summer, she started competitions among the foodservers, challenging them to see who would sell the most wine in a given period; the winner is rewarded with a cash bonus at the end of each month.

As a result of this concentrated effort, Jan is one of the wine distributor's best customers. In fact, she sells more wine than any other single restaurant operator that the distributor services. Thus, the distributor ensures that Jan is made aware of any specials or discounts. The distributor also sends a thank-you gift to Jan's home, along with a Season's Greetings card every December. In past years, the thank-you gift was a bottle or two of wine. This year, Jan mentioned that she is having a large holiday party and would like to serve more of the fine wine that the distributor usually sends as a gift. She hints that a case or two would probably be enough. The distributor's salesperson who has worked with Jan for years gladly accommodates her and sends two cases of wine to her home just before the party. He writes in the greeting card: "With our compliments to our favorite customer. Have a great party and holiday season."

The gift didn't cost the restaurant anything since the distributor simply wrote off the expense as "marketing." Is this a breach of ethics?

Scenario Two: The Roof

Ed has been the general manager of the family-owned Italian restaurant for years. He started working there as a busboy in college and assumed a management position after graduation. He has been there ever since—almost 18 years. The family, which has little involvement with day-to-day operations, considers him an adopted son.

In the course of the usual upkeep, Ed has noticed that the restaurant needs a new roof. He budgeted for the sizable expense this year and has decided that, with the summer months approaching, now is the time to have the new roof installed.

Recalling conversations he's had with his primary distributor, Ed calls a salesperson to see if the distributor can recommend a contractor. Ed remembers the distributor talking about routinely working with contractors for warehouse and corporate office maintenance. In their conversation, Ed tells the salesperson what he needs and notes that the owners have already approved his budget of $50,000 for the new roof.

The salesperson gives Ed the names of three persons to contact for bids on the job. The first two provide similar estimates of around $32,000. The third estimate is $49,999. Ed asks for a meeting with the third contractor to explore why the estimate is so high. Don, the contractor, explains to Ed that, while his quote may seem a bit high, he can deliver more value, especially to Ed himself. Don goes on to explain that he knows the distributor's salesperson quite well; they play golf together almost every weekend. Don also tells Ed that the salesperson commented that it's not just the restaurant that needs a new roof; Ed's house could use a new roof, too. Don suggests to Ed that for $49,999 he will do a great job in replacing the restaurant's roof—and he will put a new roof on Ed's house at no charge.

If Ed hires Don and accepts the deal, is it a breach of ethics?

These scenarios are anything but unusual. In general, the transactions that pose these ethical dilemmas within foodservice management fall into three categories. The first concerns information. As distributors work with many foodservice entities in a given geography, they are often privy to inside information. It violates professional standards when a distributor shares proprietary information or a manager asks for it.

The second category of ethical dilemma, which is related to both of the scenarios included here, involves the manager's personal gain. Here, the implications are not as clear-cut as one might imagine. For example, if a distributor holds an open house for its clients and serves free food and beverages, is this personal gain? What if the new salesperson for the distributor invites the restaurant manager out for dinner so they can discuss the restaurant's needs; is it unethical for the manager to accept a free meal? Many organizations place a dollar-amount restriction on gifts that its managers can accept in an attempt to make the associated challenges easier to solve. But even this practice does not ensure that ethical violations do not occur. For example, if the company policy is that a manager cannot accept a gift from a distributor valued at more than $50, but the salesperson brings a $40 bottle of liquor as a gift every month to ensure he keeps the manager's business (with both knowing that a competing supplier is cheaper), then the policy has failed to conform to ethical standards.

The third category of ethical dilemma does not involve gifts or gain but rather, the ethical treatment of distributors. Relating back to our discussion of trust, the distributor must be able to trust that the foodservice manager will abide by the terms of whatever agreement is in place and not exploit the distributor. Such ethical violations might include a manager who reports a delivery as damaged ("the lettuce is spoiled, therefore I can't use it and I refuse to pay the invoice") when it is not, or sharing pricing information from a distributor with a competing supplier. Similarly, the supplier must be ethical in making claims regarding its products such as designations (e.g., "organically raised" vegetables or "free-range" chickens).

The best approach for any foodservice manager to ensure proper ethical behavior is to place the interest of the foodservice operation first and accept nothing that could be viewed as a personal benefit. Of course, this doesn't apply only to working with distributors. The need for ethical and professional standards is vital in every management function. A good reference source for ethics is the Academy of Nutrition and Dietetics' *Code of Ethics for the Profession of Dietetics and Process for Consideration of Ethics Issues.*[2]

METHODS OF BUYING

Foodservice operators typically weigh several options for purchasing food and beverage items. Some are dictated by an agreement with a given distributor. (Most distributors require some sort of contractual relationship in order to protect all involved. Such contracts include delivery schedules, order requirements in terms of quantities, and credit terms.) Others are subject to the unique needs of a particular foodservice operation.

As mentioned earlier, large onsite foodservice companies and large restaurant chains may engage in what is called **centralized purchasing**, under which purchasing responsibility and execution is assigned to a department or location that covers multiple foodservice outlets. For example, a school district could place food orders using centralized purchasing; the food is then delivered to the individual schools. A related approach to centralized purchasing is **group purchasing**. Group purchasing involves a cooperative agreement among unrelated foodservice operations that achieves shared economies of scale because of the collective volume and allows each individual operator to purchase food items at a lower price. Today, many **group purchasing organizations** (GPOs) have evolved to allow businesses to obtain discounts from vendors interested in leveraging the collective buying power of the GPO members.

Alternatively, **decentralized purchasing** may be used. Here, each unit makes purchases independently. The chef of an independent restaurant, for example, might place food orders while the bar manager orders beverage-related products. This is fairly typical in independent restaurants.

Whether orders are consolidated or not, there are still more approaches to consider. When a **prime supplier**—a large distributor with many product lines—is used, the order can be placed on the distributor's website. The foodservice manager can easily check prices and availability. As orders are placed, an automated system removes the items from inventory, which helps to prevent **stockouts**—items that are ordered but not delivered because the distributor could not fill all of the orders. Such systems also make recommendations on alternate items that either are cheaper or are necessary if the requested item is unavailable.

In terms of pricing, some foodservice managers contract with distributors for a specified time with price guarantees. Others use a **cost-plus** contract in which the foodservice operation agrees to pay prices that reflect a specified rate over the supplier's cost. In this case, it is best to use independent price sources (such as invoices provided by the processor) rather than relying on the distributor to provide the information.

Yet another option is referred to as **buy and inventory**. As storage in many foodservice operations is limited, this approach allows the foodservice manager to buy a large amount of a nonperishable item and enjoy the pricing afforded by the quantity. For example, a hospital might have 12 months of menus printed and pay for the entire year's worth at the beginning of the year. Then, the distributor would deliver only a portion of these every month. Similarly, a restaurant might buy and inventory a large amount of condiments or other items with long shelf lives.

Regardless of the ordering methodology or pricing, the last piece of the purchasing process that must be managed carefully is the **invoice**. When food items are ordered from a distributor, a buyer typically uses a **purchase order**. The purchase order includes the quantity, unit size, and description (which should align with the product specifications discussed earlier), as well as the unit cost and total order cost. When the items are delivered (we will talk extensively about receiving in the following chapter), the invoice should be checked against the purchase order to ensure parity.

FORECASTING

The final component in managing the supply chain is determining how much to order and when to order. **Forecasting** consists of predicting which food items will be needed for a specific daypart, day, or week. The basis for such forecasting can be represented by the following formula:

$$\text{Purchase quantity} = \text{Quantity needed} - \text{Quantity on hand}$$

Of course, one uses this formula on the assumption that if the items are ordered today they will arrive before they are needed tomorrow, which is usually not the case. The question it raises that directly relates to forecasting, however, is: What is the needed quantity?

Forecasting Models

Typically, forecasting sales—which translates directly into a forecast of what is needed—uses historical data such as the number of menu items sold per daypart during the same period last year. In healthcare, another part of the calculation would be items sold relative to a patient census. Similarly, in a correction facility, the number of food items used during a specific period should be considered in concert with the prison population numbers. Other information that is relevant includes changes in the competition, seasonality, increases or decreases in brand worth (for each brand represented in the operation), and changes in operational costs, such as dramatic swings in price of specific food products, or, in terms of labor, changes in the labor market that might translate into lower retention (and increased labor costs).

Forecasting models are numerous and range from relatively simple approaches to methods involving compound calculations. Determining which method to use depends on the desired level of accuracy, the availability of data, and the sophistication of the foodservice operator. Here we review a handful of the most commonly used methods, ranging from simple to complex, including simple averages, moving averages, weighted averages, modified moving averages, exponential smoothing, and causal forecasting.

Simple averages track trends over a selected length of time. This approach assumes that all the data are equally important no matter what other operation-specific factors have changed. An example would be taking the sales of a meatloaf entree for every daypart during which it is offered and calculating the mean number sold per daypart. This can be done for each day of the week (e.g., using data from past Mondays to forecast sales for next Monday) or it can be calculated in even more general terms such as number of items sold for a month or a quarter and then calculating the amount needed, on average, per day.

The **moving average** approach uses specific time-series data. Groups of data—say, sales of chicken cacciatore for every Wednesday lunch going back eight weeks—is averaged to produce a forecast for the following Wednesday (using the simple-average approach). The next forecast is calculated by adding the most recent number and dropping the oldest sales figure.

A **weighted average** also depends on historical data but allows the operator to apply distinct weights to data points that are deemed more relevant to the current period. For example, say a specialty fried shrimp platter, featuring large shrimp and offered only on Fridays, sold well in month 1 with a total of 318 sold. In month 2, however, a scarcity of large shrimp forced the manager to raise the price of the dish to offset the higher cost of the raw product; as a result, only 121 orders were sold. In month 3, the manager lowered the price because there was an abundance of shrimp at a good price from a new distributor; as a result, shrimp platter sales skyrocketed to 396 orders sold. In month 4, prices stabilized and the operator featured the item at the same price as in month 1. Sales leveled off to 262 orders, partially because customers disliked the increase in price over the previous period.

The operator then forecasts for month 5, during which she plans to lower prices slightly—somewhere between the price featured in months 3 and 4—hoping that sales will be better than in month 1. The weights, then, using the operator's experience as a guide, might be assigned as 20 percent for month 1 since this is a baseline for sales, 30 percent for month 2, 30 percent for month 3, and 20 percent for month 4. The resulting equation and forecast for month 5 would be:

Month 1		Month 2		Month 3		Month 4		Month 5
(317 × 0.20)	+	(128 × 0.30)	+	(396 × 0.30)	+	(262 × 0.20)	=	273 orders

The **modified moving average** approach averages historical data, weighting the most recent data more heavily. For example, an operator might use the last four periods to project sales for this upcoming period but would add more weight to the two most recent periods. Such a weighting is particularly appropriate when attempting to compensate for such factors as seasonality.

Exponential smoothing uses a smoothing constant as well as recent actual data and the forecast for the past period to estimate future sales for an item. This is appealing because it allows the operator to gauge the accuracy achieved in forecasting the previous period and facilitates the integration of a correction factor into the equation. (This factor might also reflect promotion strategies.) The smoothing constant is a number between 0 and 1—it should be closer to 0 if sales have been relatively stable in the past and closer to 1 if the menu item is experiencing continued growth or if promotion of the item has been increased.

Using the shrimp dish example and operating under the principle supporting this approach—that the forecasts will improve with each period—we take the forecast for month 5 of 273 orders and assume that the actual number sold was 283. The general formula is:

$$\text{New forecast} = \text{Past forecast} + [\text{Smoothing constant} \times (\text{Actual demand} - \text{Past forecast})]$$

Assuming that the operator plans to promote the dish for the next period relatively heavily, the forecast calculation might look like:

$$\text{Month 6 forecast} = 273 + 0.9(283 - 273) = 282$$

Finally, **causal forecasting** approaches are the most accurate and also the most complex of the approaches considered here. These approaches use multivariate statistical models, integrating regression analysis to predict outcomes based on a number of input variables. They make it possible for the operator to control for certain variables. In particular, causal forecasting allows an operator to integrate past sales data for each menu item to determine the forecast for a specific menu item, thereby accounting for the influence of one item on another. Since the presence of one menu item often influences the sales of another (as discussed in Chapter 4), this is advantageous. In addition, causal forecasting allows the operator to integrate advertising data—both past and present—as well as pricing strategies associated with the various menu items in the model. For example, factors that might be included in forecasting sales of a pasta entree might include:

- Number sold over the last several periods
- Number of other pasta entrees sold during the same periods
- Promotion dollars spent on the item
- Temperature change from the prior period (a possible surrogate for seasonality)
- Number of days in each period

Owing to its complexity, the casual approach is not often used by smaller foodservice operators but is used in some form or another by many larger chains. In order to deal with the associated nuances, not surprisingly, dedicated statistical software is generally warranted. As foodservice managers become more computer savvy and general computer applications become more robust, however, this method will likely gain acceptance throughout the foodservice industry.

Calculating Quantities

Calculating order quantities is relatively straightforward, assuming forecasts are accurate and production schedules are prepared accordingly. The more problematic factor is product delivery to the operation. If all items are delivered daily and in specific quantities, the process is simple. Usually, however, distributors deliver two or three times per week and deviations from standard quantities carry extra charges. Unfortunately, this has led to a practice common in foodservice management known as the *just-in-case approach*—extra inventory is kept on hand just in case vendors are late in making deliveries, mistakes are made in the ordering process, items disappear from inventory, and so on.

As we noted earlier, many large vendors have simplified ordering through automated systems that allow operators to place orders and receive information on product availability in real time. Thus, there is no longer a question about whether shrimp ordered on Monday will arrive as planned on Wednesday. Still others provide the hardware and software necessary for placing orders. Some vendors even offer guarantees regarding the availability of certain items, making the foodservice manager's job easier.

Nonetheless, the chief objective in ordering is to maintain a minimum amount of inventory on hand at all times. More is said about this in the following chapter; however, it is sufficient to say here that this is a generally accepted principle of quality foodservice operations. Exceptions include staples or regularly stocked items that afford the operator a benefit when ordered in larger quantities or when the cost of placing an order is sufficient to persuade the operator to order less frequently.

In many operations where specific items are used routinely, a **par system** is used to trigger orders. Here, a "par" or average amount of the item that is used is calculated. For example, a dessert kitchen might have a par of 50 pounds of flour. When the amount on hand drops below the par, the manager knows to reorder flour. Pars are established with both usage and delivery information included.

Pars are not practical, however, for high-cost items or items that are highly perishable. For these types of items, managers often employ a **just-in-time (JIT)** approach—a quality initiative designed to minimize unnecessary steps in production, labor, and costs achieved when all ingredients necessary for a menu item arrive "just in time" for the production process. When supply schedules are dependable and forecasts accurate, this approach can be extremely cost effective.

Much like the par system, however, JIT ordering does not work for all items used. For other items, a common approach to calculating optimal order quantities and order timing is a process known as **economic order quantity (EOQ)**, referred to as early as the 1930s as minimum cost quantity. EOQ is essentially an accounting formula that determines the point at which the combination of order costs and inventory carrying costs is lowest. Originating in the manufacturing sector, it is beneficial to almost every foodservice operation.

A good example illustrating an ideal application of EOQ would be the clamshell containers that a QSR routinely uses to package hamburgers. These are usually purchased in bulk, as they are used often. To determine the most cost-effective quantity of hamburger clamshells (and the associated order time), the EOQ formula is

$$EOQ = \sqrt{\frac{2UFx}{Hc}}$$

where

- U = Annual usage

- Fx = Fixed cost associated with placing an order

- Hc = Annual holding cost per unit

Using the example of disposable containers, assume the QSR uses 360 cases (approximately 30 cases a month; each case holds 1,000 units) of disposable containers per year and the cost of placing an order with the vendor is $21.25. Furthermore, assume that the cost of carrying inventory, which entails insurance, storage costs (particularly if the item needs refrigeration), and typical loss due to damage, runs around $17. The EOQ calculation is:

$$\sqrt{\frac{2 \times 360 \times \$21.25}{17}} = 30$$

Thus, the optimal ordering amount is 30 cases. The manager now knows that he needs to order 30 cases every month (this is, coincidentally, the number used in a month) for optimal, cost-effective ordering.

It is important to note that EOQ considers only the holding and order cost. It is based on even (and therefore known) demand, and the cost of goods is fixed at any order level. Finally, there is the explicit trade-off between the cost of carrying excess inventory and the cost of placing additional orders. While there are challenges associated with these assumptions, the value of EOQ is considerable. The key is to routinely recalculate the EOQ and reevaluate ordering quantities accordingly.

Unexpected Impacts

We conclude here by acknowledging that forecasting and purchasing quantities also brings challenges that did not exist prior to the proliferation of huge chain operations. The perfect example is a mega chain such as McDonald's. When McDonald's launched its Apple Dippers—around ten crisp apple slices packaged with a caramel dipping sauce—it soon became the largest purchaser of apples among restaurant chains in the country. In fact, the year after the new product launched, the chain bought some 54 million apples. This, in turn, shaped how major growers planted new trees in anticipation of future industry demand, effectively changing this area of the agricultural world. Thus, in the current era of foodservice management, quantity determination entails knowing how many items are needed *and* whether there is an adequate supply—not just with a single supplier, but across an entire industry.[3]

MANAGERIAL IMPLICATIONS

Effective management in the foodservice industry today requires a thorough understanding of the entire supply chain. Purchasing and the associated economies of scale that can be achieved through related activities are central to this understanding. Moreover, effective management in this area yields both economic and operational benefits.

Product specifications, while time consuming and labor intensive to create, are vital. They allow for effective purchasing practices, including negotiating with distributors and accurately comparing vendors while also aiding in standardizing food production and quality. Related to these decisions are determinations regarding the level of processing that purchased items require. The example used involved chicken breasts—should they be purchased separately or cut from a whole chicken with the remaining parts used for other dishes? This is a trade-off between food cost and labor cost, as prepared items cost more but items closer to their original state require more labor to process. Similarly, managers today must decide whether to focus on locally sourced and manufactured items. The current trend suggests that this practice will become much more widespread in the future.

Purchasing managers are able to contribute to the financial success of a foodservice operation in a number of ways, such as rebates. Indeed, this area of foodservice management is becoming much more specialized.

Sysco

Building customer relationships requires time, effort, and sincerity.

For Sysco, it began with a promise to assist foodservice operators in providing consumers with solutions for meals consumed away from home. Since the initial public offering in 1970, when sales were $115 million, Sysco has grown into a corporation that achieved $37 billion in sales for fiscal year 2009 with net earnings of $1.1 billion. Today, it is the largest foodservice distributor in North America.

Many solid customer relationships have been nurtured along the way, countless dining trends and meal alternatives have evolved, and today the decision to consume meals prepared away from home is as much a matter of necessity as of choice. In 1977, Sysco surpassed its competitors to become the leading supplier to "meals-prepared-away-from-home" operations in North America. Since then, the industry it serves has expanded from $35 billion to more than $200 billion.

Today, Sysco has sales and service relationships with approximately 400,000 customers and remains committed to helping them succeed in the foodservice industry and satisfy consumer appetites. Operating from 170-plus locations throughout the contiguous United States and

Foodservice operators use multiple channels of distribution. Understanding product flow from the source to the end user (the guest) and maintaining relationships with the various intermediaries (including manufacturers and distributors) is key. Also, using products that are raised in a sustainable manner and buying from companies that support sustainable business practices is becoming more commonplace.

The existence of intracompany distribution channels was not witnessed by earlier generations of foodservice managers. Today, large restaurant chains may shorten the supply chain and serve as their own processors and distributors. Foodservice companies may also align themselves with distributors for exclusive delivery routes for their units.

While the distribution methods for food and beverage products form a relatively small set, they can be combined and on that basis effectively managed to maximize profits. It is important to focus on more than the price of a single item, considering a variety of items to determine which vendors one should employ. Payment options and terms also provide opportunities to enhance the bottom line.

Increasingly, foodservice buyers view distributors as business partners. Such partnerships—when based on compatible goals, pursuit of mutual gain, and a high level of mutual independence—can result in optimal outcomes for all involved. Even if a distributor is not embraced as a partner, the ethical pitfalls related to purchasing in the foodservice industry are many. Such violations of ethics and responsible business practices may include improper use of a competitor's proprietary information, personal gain at the expense of the foodservice organization, or improper treatment of the vendor by the foodservice manager.

Today's foodservice manager can choose from a variety of purchasing methods, including centralized and decentralized purchasing as well as group purchasing. Many foodservice operations choose to use prime suppliers in order to minimize the number of distributors, reduce the number of stock outs, and obtain the distributor's assistance in related areas.

Finally, we have reviewed several forecasting models from which the manager can choose depending on available data and the operator's managerial acumen. Similarly, calculating order quantities can be approached from the most basic just-in-case approach, under which extra inventory is kept on hand despite the added expense, to accounting-based techniques such as the economic order quantity approach. Industry leaders need to understand all these approaches, including par systems and just-in-time ordering, in order to optimize the purchasing process.

portions of Alaska, Hawaii, and Canada, Sysco's product lines are as diverse as the 50,000 employees who support its daily operations. They include not only the ingredients needed to prepare meals but also numerous ancillary preparation and serving items. As a result, Sysco can make a difference in its customers' lives as well as in the success of their businesses.

Sysco is the global leader in selling, marketing, and distributing food products to restaurants, healthcare and educational facilities, lodging establishments, and other customers who prepare meals away from home. Its family of products also includes equipment and supplies for the foodservice and hospitality industries.

Copyright © Sysco Corporation 2010.

KEY TERMS

Purchasing in University Dining Services

Carly has just begun working in her new position as the purchasing manager for a large public university's dining services. The university has some 40,000 students spread across its 720-acre campus. In addition to the dining halls in the freshmen dorms, the campus features cafes, coffee kiosks, and convenience stores. Previously, the dining services department did not have a purchasing manager, but the general manager hopes that, by instituting this new role, she can save money. In reviewing last year's financial information, Carly notes that last year the university spent some $16 million on food-related products.

Having worked previously with a large restaurant chain, Carly is well aware of the economies of scale that can be achieved in purchasing. She's spent her first week at the new job meeting with distributors' representatives and acquainting herself with the campus. She's a little overwhelmed by the number of vendors, but she knows that she can achieve her boss's main objective, which is to reduce spending on food products without sacrificing quality.

Today, Carly met with the four executive chefs. In essence, the foodservice operation is divided into four quadrants, with each including one of the four dining halls and an associated kitchen. Each chef is responsible for food preparation for the respective dining hall and surrounding eateries. Food preparation is completed at each of the kitchens. The chefs have been with the university for many years and work together well. That being said, they operate rather autonomously. The menu at each dining hall is created independently. The belief is that students enjoy the variety of menus and food-preparation styles. Indeed, surveys indicate that the students generally like the food, and the dining services management rarely receives complaints.

Toward the end of the meeting, Carly explores the topic of purchasing. She wants to know why the university uses two national distributors and several local distributors. The chefs explain that they each place orders and that they are satisfied with their distributors, even if they can't agree on using the same vendors.

As she returns to her office, Carly is dismayed that, on any given day, four vendors are on campus delivering the same category of item but each one to a different kitchen. She reviews the invoices from last year, and finds that prices for the same food item vary considerably across vendors while the specifications for the items are the same. She also learns that since each chef uses a small amount of the various products (as compared with the amount used if purchased as a single order) they are not receiving any volume discounts.

What are some changes Carly might consider?

REVIEW AND DISCUSSION QUESTIONS

1. What is a supply chain, and why is it important that we understand it in terms of managing the purchasing process?

2. Provide an example that illustrates how a restaurant chain might benefit from economies of scale.

3. Pick a meat product that you like to prepare and develop product specifications for it using the general guidelines described in the chapter.

4. You've been hired to manage a cafe in a small regional hospital. Kitchen space is limited and your staff has only basic culinary skills. On average, you sell 50 chicken breast entrees (all require five-ounce boneless, skinless chicken breasts prepared in a variety of ways including grilled, baked, and fried).
Should you purchase whole chickens or boneless breasts? Explain your answer.

5. What are rebates?

6. Why is it beneficial to buy agricultural products that are grown or raised with sustainability in mind?

7. Provide an example (differing from the ones provided) of a hypothetical restaurant chain's intracompany distribution channel.

8. Why is trust important in a foodservice company–distributor relationship? How might this trust be violated?

9. You are the general manager of a large restaurant and bar. Your bar manager is responsible for booking

bands for weekend nights. The bar is very profitable, and the extra business that the live music generates more that justifies the considerable sums you pay the various bands. You've just learned that one of the bands that the manager routinely selects is also playing at his daughter's wedding—at no charge. Is this an ethical violation?

10. Name two benefits of centralized purchasing.

11. Search the Web for healthcare GPOs (examples include MedAssets, Health Trust, and MediGroup). What is a common theme in terms of the benefits they provide to clients?

12. Go to FoodSupplier website. What is the firm's primary role? Who would use such a site?

13. Sales data from a nearby restaurant indicate that sales of its pesto shrimp with linguini include the following: March: 1,425 orders sold; April: 1,398 orders sold; May: 1,241 orders sold; June: 1,367 orders sold. Use two forecasting models to forecast July's sales for the item.

14. Explain the par system, then provide an example of a food item for which this approach is appropriate and one for which it is not.

ENDNOTES

1. For research on this, see Brownell, J., and Reynolds, D. "Strengthening the Food and Beverage Purchaser-Supplier Partnership: Behaviors That Make a Difference." *Cornell Hotel and Restaurant Administration Quarterly* 43(6) (2002): 49–61.

2. www.eatright.org/healthprofessionals/content.aspx?id=6868.

3. In his critique of the fast-food industry, Eric Schlosser, author of *Fast Food Nation*, notes that purchasing such volumes of uniform products likely influences the entire agriculture industry.

FOOD MANAGEMENT

LEARNING OBJECTIVES:

After becoming familiar with this chapter, you should be able to:

1. Understand what is essential to the receiving function, including invoice processing.

2. Identify the requirements for proper storage of the full range of food types in various states of preparation.

3. Explain the inventory management function.

4. Determine how to valuate inventory items, depending on type of foodservice operation.

5. Apply inventory-turnover analysis.

6. Appreciate the importance of a range of issues pertaining to food production and food quality management.

Having covered supply chain management, culminating in proper food ordering processes that meet the requirements for optimal foodservice operation, we now move on to cover the phase of food management that begins with its delivery at the back door. While this perspective on food management involves the ordering process, we have separated food ordering from the subsequent steps to focus in this chapter on the processes involved in a sequence that runs from receiving food to preparing it for delivery to the guest.

We begin our introduction to food management processes by considering how to execute efficient and accurate receiving and storage of food and beverage products. Next, we address inventory management—a process with potentially substantial financial implications. We then address food production and its many intricacies, addressing both quality and quantity issues.

RECEIVING

The basic **receiving** function has not changed very much since the early days of foodservice management. First, the receiver compares the delivered product with the purchase order and the invoice to ensure that they match, and then verifies that the quality, size, and characteristics meet the products' specifications. (Product specifications were detailed in the previous chapter.) He then ensures that the price is the same as was quoted when the order was placed. He notifies the kitchen manager or chef about any shortages or missing items and documents any variations between order and delivery. Finally, he begins processing the invoice and delivering the products to their respective storage locations.

New technology makes the receiving job easier than ever today. Most products delivered by large distributors are packaged with **barcodes**. This allows the receiver to enter data automatically into the inventory database by quickly scanning a package's barcode. Of course, visual inspection remains a necessary step in ensuring that the package contains what the barcode reports.

Thanks to continually declining prices, some larger foodservice operations and distributors are also employing **RFID** (radio frequency identification) tags. RFID uses radio waves for communication between a tag (a data carrier or RF transponder) and a reading device. An RFID tag is a tiny microchip with an aerial that can contain a range of digital information about a particular item. Such tags are encapsulated in plastic, paper, or similar material, and are fixed to the product or its packaging, to a pallet or container, or even to a van or delivery truck.

RFID tags result in fewer readability issues than barcodes do and can be read remotely, often at a distance of several yards. Several tags can be read at once, enabling an entire pallet-load of products to be checked simultaneously. Certain types of tag can also be overwritten, enabling information about items to be updated. Again, of course, visual inspection remains necessary to ensure that products are not damaged and that they meet product specifications.

Do not be fooled by the apparent simplicity of the receiving task or the advent of technological conveniences into believing that receiving is anything but a critical function for a foodservice operation. A mistake such as failing to report missing items can result in inadequate quantities of ingredients, which, in turn, means that some menu items will be unavailable or limited in quantity. On the other hand, accepting food that was not ordered but is charged to an operation can result in lost profits. The mistakes made in the receiving process are so numerous and the results so dramatic that great care must be taken throughout it.

Receiving Essentials

What is arguably the most important function in receiving is carried out by the person charged with completing the task. The receiver must know enough about food products that she can discern whether the products coming into her operation meet the specifications by reference to which they were ordered. As noted earlier, even small deviations from product specifica-tions can have far-reaching ramifications. The receiver must also be trustworthy. As we discuss at length in the chapter on internal control, receiving is one of the areas in which theft can be difficult to detect.

It would be easy to assign the task of receiving to the executive chef, the sous chef, or even a manager. Indeed, these individuals would know food products and could quickly assess the quality of delivered items. However, these individuals are generally too busy performing their primary duties to incorporate the series of steps involved in receiving into their job descrip-tions. Moreover, it is unadvisable for the receiver to be the person who places the orders, due to internal control issues. And, realistically, the person who is assigned the receiving duties usually draws a lower salary than, for example, the chef. Still, in spite of the vital importance of receiv-ing, the job of moving sizable orders to their respective storage locations is somewhat menial.

The receiver's most important tool is a scale (see Figure 9.1). The most exacting foodser-vice managers recommend that *every* item be weighed, without exception. In practice, how-ever, the only items that are sure to be weighed are those that have a weight associated with them on the product specification sheet. This includes full cases, as well as individual portions within those cases. It should be noted here that weighing items is time consuming, and most delivery personnel will not want to wait while this is accomplished. Nonetheless, weighing items must be completed before formally accepting delivery. (Note: Most scales today in large operations are digital and can handle a wide range of weights and items.)

Ideally, the receiving area should consist of or be located adjacent to a dedicated dock that is clean, secure, and convenient for accepting and storing items and transporting them to the kitchen. It should be large enough to accommodate the largest deliveries a given foodservice operation needs. (A small deli might need little space whereas a central production facility for a large school district might need a space large enough to accommodate a forklift.) In reality, how-ever, many receiving areas double as employee entrances or refuse disposal areas. Unfortunately, many also serve as smoking areas for employees; this practice should be avoided.

Receiving Procedures

Before we address specific steps in the receiving process, it is important to note that deliver-ies should be accepted only during designated times. This allows foodservice management to ensure that a receiver will be available. This also permits management to supervise as needed. If an operation's receiving area serves other functions, a regular delivery schedule can ensure that employees are not arriving just as the receiver is checking in deliveries. It also facilitates regular cleaning and maintenance of the receiving area so that deliveries arrive under appropriately sani-tary conditions.

Step One: Confirm that the delivery matches the purchase order.
Using a printout of a purchase order generated during the purchasing process, the receiver compares the actual delivery with the information listed on the purchase order. Smaller vendors running nonautomated operations produce their purchase orders manually. Purchase order summaries—historically referred to as *receiving clerks' daily reports*—generated by integrated software packages such as CBORD (this chapter's Industry Exemplar) make this process even more efficient as multiple deliveries can be checked against a single purchase order summary sheet (see Figure 9.2).

During delivery confirmation, food items are weighed and inspected for quality based on product specifications, which, again, it is the receiver's responsibility to know. If the product standard for the foodservice operation for ground beef is ground chuck that

Figure 9.1 Kitchen scale.

Courtesy of Julia Reynolds.

Main Kitchen Production Unit

61 Brown Road
PO# 4436
Ithaca, Ny 14850
Phone:607-257.2410
Account #: 123456

Purchase Order

PO Number: **MKP000012365**
PO Date/Time: 12/14/20XX 08:52:04
Delivery Date: 12/15/20XX
Confirmation:

Vendor
Prime Vendor - Acme Foods
123 State St
PO Box 883
Lansing, NY 14882
Attn: Margie McMillan / Matt Foster

Ship To
Main Kitchen Production Unit
61 Brown Road
Building 2
Ithaca, NY 14886
Attn: Fred Johnson

Vendor Phone:607-555-2376 Vendor Fax:607-555-2379

Description	Purchase Unit	Item ID	Quantity	Price	Total
PIE SHELL RTB 9IN A/V	20 9 OZ	1972876	2	23.45	46.90
BEEF FOR STEW DICED IQF	2/10 LB	1178942	8	36.32	290.56
BEEF GROUND PATTY 80/20	40/4 OZ	6478221	15	14.52	217.80
BEEF ROAST CH INSIDE TOP	2/8#	2217823	2	71.04	142.08
VEAL PATTY BRD CKD	64/3OZ	2325597	6	25.45	152.70
CEREAL RAISIN BRAN BULK	4/54 OZ	1459190	2	31.95	63.90
PINEAPPLE TIDBIT JCE	6 #10	4156253	1	26.46	26.46
TOMATO WH PLD IN JCE	6 #10	4113767	4	16.88	67.52
CRACKER SALTINE	500 2 PK	4008561	11	10.22	112.42
JUICE ORANGE CONC 3X1 CTN	12 32 OZ	1165018	3	13.55	40.65
MANICOTTI CHEESE 4 IN IQF	60 2.75OZ	1042878	2	26.68	53.36
PIZZA CHEESE RND 5IN BULK	54/5 OZ	8673324	4	35.10	140.40
CAULIFLOWER IQF	12 2 LB	2419380	2	27.20	54.40
PEA GREEN GR A P	12 2.5 LB	1259530	2	21.35	42.70
POTATO FF STR 3/8" A GRD	6 5 LB	6306765	7	12.85	89.95
HAM BUFFET BNLS SMOKED FANC	1/11#AVG	1234232	3	31.79	95.37
SAUSAGE PORK PATTY	80/2OZ	3495334	1	16.78	16.78
TURKEY PULLED	1/10#	8166436	2	24.56	49.12
SPICE PEPPER GRIND TABLE	1 LB	5935739k	4	4.95	19.80
SALT SEASONED	5 LB	4043378k	1	13.25	13.25
OIL CANOLA	6 1 GAL	4119061	5	25.68	128.40
JELLY ASST #2 90GP/60MF/80CH	200 .5 OZ	5055058	5	9.96	49.80
KETCHUP PACKET (GLD/HNZ)	1000 9 GM	4029500	7	21.95	153.65
MUSTARD PACKET	500 1/5 OZ	4006649	3	7.76	23.28
SUGAR PACKET	2000 1/10OZ	4563003	4	8.86	35.44
Totals:			106		$2,126.69

Authorized by _____ Receiver _____ Date _____ Time _____

Tuesday, December 14, 20XX 08:55:13   Facility   The CBORD Group, Inc.   Page 1 of 1

Figure 9.2 Purchase order.

is 90 percent lean, for example, then the receiver must ensure that any delivered ground beef be classified as 90 percent lean. Even though it is labor intensive, the receiver must open every case and ensure that all products are acceptable. It is common for produce on the top of a case to appear fresh and of good quality, while items near the bottom are bruised and rotted. Meat items, particularly seafood, are sometimes packed in ice. In such circumstances, it is important to remove food items from their packaging to weigh them without the ice to ensure that the cost to the operation represents only the meat or seafood items' prices. Finally, the receiver must check that perishable items have been kept at proper temperatures while in storage and transport.

Some delivery personnel will offer to bring items into the kitchen for inspection. While this might seem like a gracious gesture, one likely not malicious in intent, such a practice is not acceptable. Only the foodservice operation's employees should be in the kitchen or storage areas. Similarly, only the receiver should count items for official purposes, even if it is tempting to allow the delivery person to count them. This protects the operation against mistakes made by suppliers—what matters above all else is that the delivered goods match the purchase order. It does the operation no good for suppliers' paperwork to be in order if what is delivered does not meet order specifications.

Some foodservice managers prefer **blind receiving** to labor-intensive confirmation steps. Here, the receiver compares what is delivered with the invoice or with a purchase order that does not contain quantities (forcing the receiver to add the quantity of each item to the purchase order). This practice ensures that the operation is charged only for what was delivered. Yet blind receiving brings its own challenges. The receiver can too easily accept items inadvertently that were not ordered or needed or arrive in incorrect amounts relative to what was ordered; he may unintentionally accept items that do not meet product specifications. These potential problems call this approach into question.

Step Two: Confirm that the invoice matches the purchase order.

Having confirmed that the delivery aligns with what was ordered (we explain what to do when items are missing, incorrect, or unacceptable below), the next step is to compare the purchase order with the invoice. As the invoice is in essence a bill, its accuracy is important. In addition, prices should be thoroughly checked during this step to ensure accuracy.

Step Three: Make accept-or-reject decisions.

If everything meets the appropriate criteria and the purchase order and invoice reflect the same information, the receiver will acknowledge delivery with a signature and the invoice will be retained and processed. If this is not the case, if any items fail to match across the documentation trail or fall below quality standards, such items should be declined at the point of delivery. One other consideration must be made at this step: The receiver must consider recall notices that may pertain to any item received and ensure that these are not accepted.

Step Four: Complete the paperwork.

In a highly automated operation, the receiver will indicate that ordered items have been received via a computer interface (commonly accessed on a handheld device) and the items will automatically be placed in the inventory records. In smaller operations, she will record the delivery confirmation by hand. Some operations use **invoice stamps** for this purpose; such a rubber stamp creates a form on the invoice or purchase order where the receiver can indicate the date and other relevant information. Yet, as technology continues to spread across the foodservice industry, manual recording will be gradually phased out, even in small operations.

As part of the process, the receiver will also record the locations within the operation's storage areas where the respective items are to be stored. For example, some items will go directly to the kitchen for immediate use while others will go into storage. This step facilitates inventory management (discussed later in this chapter).

In the event that something listed on an invoice was not received—because it either wasn't included in the delivery or was rejected—or the price is overstated on the invoice due to an error, the delivery person will issue a **credit memorandum**. This serves as a credit against the invoiced amount for the undelivered items. The credit memorandum is then attached to the invoice so they can be processed at the same time.

A final note on receiving: The use of barcodes and RFID tags facilitates the automation of the receiving process (as well as of the overall inventory-management process), which reduces errors and labor costs associated with managing food in an operation. Still, we cannot entirely replace the vital role of the receiver, who is responsible for ensuring freshness and quality. Ultimately, only an experienced foodservice working can make such judgments based on visual and olfactory inspection. The receiver will therefore remain an indispensable part of food management well into the future.

Invoice Processing

Managing an operation's cash flow (discussed in greater detail in Chapter 10) includes careful handling of invoices. This is achieved in part through an **invoice payment schedule**. Such a schedule reflects the terms of an agreement with an operation's distributors. The payment schedule also includes information about discounts associated with early payment. For example, some invoices include terms such as "2/10 net 30." Such a notation indicates that if a payment is received within 10 days of delivery, a 2 percent discount can be taken by the foodservice operation. Otherwise, the full amount is due within 30 days. Net 30 payment terms typically apply an interest penalty for noncompliance that begins accruing on the 31st day after the delivery is made.

Not surprisingly, such discounts can result in substantial savings for large operations. Similarly, costs associated with penalties for late payments needlessly increase expenses. Fortunately, many if not most of the steps involved in invoice processing can be completed electronically. This allows savvy foodservice operators to optimize financial management by maximizing the use of discounts while not paying unnecessarily early (leaving operating capital available for a longer time).

▪▫ STORAGE MANAGEMENT

Stored items must be managed properly to maintain quality, prevent pilferage, and provide for proper use. Most foodservice professionals agree that there is never enough storage space, which also means that storage processing and management are critical. Storage area design should maximize convenience and accessibility. However, security is also a vital issue, sometimes overshadowing all others. While we reserve much of the discussion on internal control and theft for a later chapter, we note here that we cannot overstate the importance of safeguarding a foodservice operation's assets.

In small operations, the storage areas typically are located immediately adjacent to the kitchen. In massive operations, some storage areas may be close to the kitchen while others may be located on separate floors or even in separate buildings. In spite of these differences, however, the processes involved in managing these areas are similar. Since most operations, regardless of industry segment, differentiate among dry storage, refrigerated storage, and frozen storage, we address issues pertaining to each category in its own section.

Dry Storage

Dry storerooms, as the name implies, are designed to keep dry goods that do not require refrigeration. They should be kept within a temperature range of between 50°F and 70°F. Humidity should be maintained within a range of between 50 percent and 60 percent, with adequate ventilation. Because some dry goods are susceptible to sunlight damage, no direct sunlight should enter a dry storage area. Furthermore, such areas should be safeguarded against rodents, insects, and other pests.

In some industry settings—and depending on local regulations—items cannot be stored directly on the floor, and often must be stored at a specified minimum distance from the floor surface. (With nothing stored on the floor and adequate room under the bottom shelf, the floor can be cleaned more easily without worrying about getting food items wet with mop water.) Shelving should allow for ventilation through the shelves, and there should be room behind the shelves to allow air to flow. Shelves should also be labeled clearly with product and product category names.

Access to storage areas should be strictly limited to personnel whose job responsibilities require it. For larger operations where the cost is justified, electronic monitoring systems should also be employed. Again, food is an asset and must be treated as such.

Dry storage areas should be segregated from cleaning goods; no cleaning chemicals should ever be stored in food areas. Moreover, items should be arranged to employ a first-in, first-out (**FIFO**) approach. Practicing FIFO aids in rotating inventory efficiently and using the oldest items first. The adoption of FIFO works best when all products regardless of storage area are dated at the time of purchase. Many seasoned foodservice operators advocate dating every single item as it is received. Without question, this is vital for perishable items, even those with extended shelf lives. In some huge operations where turnover of certain nonperishable items is very high, dating may be impractical. In such cases, new items should be stored behind previously purchased items to ensure compliance with the FIFO principle.

Refrigerated Storage

Refrigerated storage is required for fresh meats, vegetables, fruits, dairy products, and some beverages (such as juices). Items in refrigerated storage are usually kept at a temperature of between 32°F and 37°F. Refrigerated storage involves two categories of equipment: **walk-in** refrigerators (see Figure 9.3) and **reach-in** refrigerators (see Figure 9.4) that are usually located in or near cooking areas for easy access to items prepped for service. Where available, refrigerators may be designated for select product categories that optimally call for slightly different temperatures. For example, fresh fruits and some vegetables are ideally kept at between 40°F and 45°F; other vegetables are better stored at between 32°F and 37°F. Alternatively, some walk-in refrigerators have temperature- and humidity-controlled zones for specific food groups.

Temperatures in refrigerated and frozen areas should be closely monitored. To this end, a monitoring system (preferably automated) should be in place as well as a visual temperature display outside of the refrigerator or freezer. Systems that in addition to monitoring temperatures can alert a manager via cell phone if temperatures become dangerously high provide yet another safeguard. Depending on the setting, such systems are highly desirable, can reduce costs associated with food that must be replaced due to unsafe storage, and can prevent foodborne illness resulting from using improperly held food products.

Courtesy of Julia Reynolds.

Figure 9.3 Walk-in refrigerator.

Courtesy of Julia Reynolds.

Figure 9.4 Reach-in refrigerator.

Frozen Storage

Frozen food storage should be maintained at temperatures of between −10°F and 0°F. While many products freeze at temperatures just below 32°F, dangerous microorganisms continue growing under such conditions. Furthermore, storing frozen food at a temperature of 10°F can cut its storage life by nearly 50 percent. Some vegetables stored at 10°F will discolor within two months but can last up to a year if stored at the recommended temperature.

The humidity in a freezer unit should be high to prevent or reduce moisture loss. Moisture loss is tantamount to freshness loss, so all food items should be thoroughly wrapped and sealed in airtight bags or containers. This also helps to prevent **freezer burn**, which manifests as light-colored spots on or discoloration in frozen foods caused by surface evaporation, which is quickly followed by internal moisture loss.

Frozen foods, once thawed, should never be refrozen, and, finally, they should be thawed for use only under normal refrigeration temperatures. Never thaw food by leaving it exposed to room temperature.

INVENTORY MANAGEMENT

Inventory management, which in its broadest sense includes receiving and storage, is yet another critical function in foodservice management. Proper inventory management can reduce costs, increase operational efficiency, and ultimately lead to greater guest and employee satisfaction. Conversely, improper inventory management can quickly lead to a foodservice operation's untimely demise.

We should begin by asking a simple question: What is *inventory*? In accounting terms, it is a list of assets owned by the firm. In the foodservice industry, inventory refers to all food and beverage products on hand. It is important to note that as these products sit on shelves or in the reach-in refrigerator in the kitchen prep area, they are also considered **nonperforming assets**—items that produce no revenue until they are sold. This underscores the importance of inventory management. The food items shown in Figure 9.5 have been purchased by the restaurant, school cafeteria, or medical center cafe, but they bring value to the foodservice operator only when they are sold.

Issuing

In smaller operations such as a family-owned pizza restaurant, the cook would simply go into the dry storage area or walk-in refrigerator to gather items needed to prepare a pizza. Most likely, this same person would place the orders so he knows what is on hand. In such a setting, the number of items in the inventory is limited, the likelihood of waste is minimal, and theft is relatively unlikely, especially when only family members work at the restaurant.

In a large operation, however, it is undesirable to have several members of the kitchen staff simply take things from storage without some keeping a record of such actions. **Issuing**, then, is the process used to requisition items from storage for kitchen areas or units in an onsite foodservice operation. This is also the case for food and beverage outlets in a hotel; there may be three bars in a hotel, but the liquor is usually stored in a central location. Here, bartenders for each of the bars would requisition what is needed for their shifts (preferably the night before). The order is then filled—the items are issued—to the respective bars.

Carrying out this seemingly tedious task is the only way in which large operations can effectively manage inventory. It also places the responsibility on the cook, bartender, or server (who might requisition condiments for the tables) and allows for accurate tracking (see Figure 9.6). Fortunately, large operations use automated inventory management systems to facilitate the process of entering data efficiently.

Perpetual Inventory

So how is information pertaining to the issuing process used? One important inventory management tool for using such information is a **perpetual inventory** system. A perpetual inventory is a running record of which products are on hand; the inventory is updated in real time through integration with point-of-sale terminals, requisition orders, and invoices. In the event that minimum and maximum quantities of each inventory item are established, a complete perpetual inventory system will flag items that need ordering or that are overstocked.

Perpetual inventory systems were once considered too labor-intensive for large foodservice operations. That perception, thankfully, is changing. Through sophisticated software packages (see Figure 9.7), the implementation and maintenance of perpetual inventories offer a myriad of advantages.

Figure 9.5 Food items are nonperforming assets until they are sold.

Commissary

Transfer Requisition

Date: 12/7/20XX	**Reason:** Production Request	**Meal:** Dinner	
From Unit: Commissary	**Prep Area:** Cold Food		
Reference: KPR120710	**Approved by:** JBL	**Attn:** KAM	
Account: 1320000023	**To Unit:** Main Kitchen Production Unit	**Ship to:** Main Kitchen Production Unit	
Number: 8 **Type:** Transfer	**Status:** In Progress	**Approval Code:** Committed	

Key Name	Item Name	Quantity	Unit	Price	Extended Price
Applecious	Apples Red Delicious	2	125/CS	44.75	89.50
AvocaFresh	Avocado Fresh	1.00	18 Ct/Cs	15.00	15.00
BananColor	Banana Green Tip Color	3	40 lb case	37.25	111.75
Broccettes	Broccoli Fresh	3	10 lb case	18.25	54.75
Cabbaedium	Cabbage Green Medium	6	Head	0.75	4.50
CabbageRed	Cabbage Red	2	Head	4.25	8.50
CarooPack	Carrots Bulk	5	25 lb case	14.50	72.50
Celery	Celery	7	Head	1.25	8.75
CilanBunch	Cilantro Bunch	12	Bunch	2.25	27.00
Cucumbers	Cucumbers	2	5 lb case	5.50	11.00
Eggplfresh	Eggplant Fresh	22	Eggplant	0.25	5.50
Garlifresh	Garlic Cloves Fresh	5	5 lb bag	25.75	128.75

Number of Items: 12   **Total Cost:**   537.50

Notes: 1. _____
2. _____
3. _____
4. _____

Issued by_____	Date_____	Time_____	Initials_____
Received by_____	Date_____	Time_____	Initials_____

Figure 9.6 Sample requisition sheet.

≣ The CBORD Group, Inc.

Net Handheld Inventory Management System

NetHIMS Benefits

- Reduce the time you spend managing inventory and resolving errors

- Wireless connection eliminates the need to download data

- Improve data integrity with up-to-the-minute inventory tracking

- Manage your business away from your desk

For Colleges and Universities

Track Product from Ordering to Sales

Track products at the loading dock, in the kitchen, in the freezer, or out in the retail case! Using CBORD's software on a mobile, wireless handheld device, you are free to work anywhere in your organization, wherever the product or inventory is. Whether you need to eliminate manual entry, paper count sheets, reduce errors, Net Hand Held Inventory Management System (NetHIMS™) provides you with the tools you need to simplify your inventory management process and track product as it moves through your entire operation.

Automate Tracking with Barcode Scanning

A component of Foodservice Suite® (FSS) and NetMenu®, this powerful software allows you to scan UPC barcodes on inventory or menu items. The system supports scanning of multiple barcode formats, including UPC-A and UPC-E. Using a wireless, handheld computer, you can remotely update the inventory management system. Inventory may be recorded and organized based on unit, storage location, bin, and date. New inventories can be created from scratch on the handheld, making it easy to update inventory on the fly. In addition, system administrators may link UPC codes to general items in FSS and NetMenu right on the handheld.

Windows® Mobile Operating System

NetHIMS is built on Windows® Mobile Operating System using .Net technology. Communication is done over a wireless network. NetHIMS updates FSS and NetMenu via a wireless connection, ensuring real-time data integrity. The user interface is clean, simple, and easy to use. The system works with a variety of handheld devices using Windows Mobile Operating System, including ruggedized models

The Core Product

Inventory Management: Track physical inventory by storage locations.
Barcode Scanning: Scan more than 18 of the most popular UPC barcode formats.
Linking UPC Barcodes to Items: Associate UPC barcodes to general items and vendor items for multiple pack and case sizes.

Comprehensive Solutions. Innovative Products. Dedicated Service.

The CBORD Group, Inc.
61 Brown Road, Ithoca, NY 14850
607.257.2410 • FAX: 607.257.1902
www.cbord.com

Figure 9.7 CBORD's handheld inventory management inventory system for healthcare foodservice.

☰ **The CBORD Group, Inc.**

Add-On Modules

Transfers: The NetHIMS Transfer module allows you to bring up actual transfers on the handheld device while selecting orders. You can also verify a product is correct by simply scanning the UPC. Any adjustments to an order can be made immediately on the handheld with the Transfer module so that there is no delay in updating these corrections into FSS, ensuring efficiency and accuracy.

Issuing: The NetHIMS Issuing module allows you to keep track of products that need to be thrown out due to being "Out of Date," "Damaged," or "Sampled" in a retail product case. Simply use the Issuing module to scan each of the products being thrown away and to record in an issue requisition on the handheld device, the quantity, and reason the product is being removed from the case. Product wasted is recorded immediately on the handheld so that there is no delay in updating these corrections to perpetual inventory into the FSS application.

Service Actuals: The NetHIMS Service Actual module allows you to scroll through a Service Menu, items, or scan product labels on the cafeteria line for each of the products served. This gives you the ability to accurately record either the amount of product actually served or leftover, which can assist in forecasting production needs for future cycle menus. The information is immediately updated into the FSS service menu for future forecasting and post service cost analysis.

Compatible with
Foodservice Suite®
NetMenu®

Comprehensive Solutions

CBORD provides campus card systems, integrated security solutions, housing management, food and nutrition management, catering solutions, and off-campus programs to more than 6,000 organizations. Our focus is on comprehensive solutions that increase revenue, reduce costs, enhance campus safety, improve student satisfaction, and integrate systems seamlessly.

Innovative Products

Our innovation is customer driven. Working in partnership with users, we listen to the industry's evolving needs and develop solutions to keep you a step ahead.

Dedicated Service

The quality of our products is made greater by the caliber of our employees. Through open dialogue with you, our customers, CBORD strives to not only meet, but exceed your expectations; we are committed to providing superior service in all aspects of our customer relationships. You can reach us twenty-four hours a day, seven days a week, and know you have a team dedicated to your satisfaction and success.

Comprehensive Solutions. Innovative Products. Dedicated Service.

The CBORD Group, Inc.
61 Brown Road, Ithaca, NY 14850
607.257.2410 • FAX: 607.257.1902
www.cbord.com

Figure 9.7 *(continued)*

Physical Inventory

Even with a perpetual inventory system in place, a physical count of items in all areas of an operation is critical to maintaining accurate records. A **physical inventory** is taken weekly, biweekly, or monthly, depending on the nature of the foodservice operation. Again, this process can be simplified by any of the many inventory management software packages that are available. It is also made even easier with the use of barcodes or RFID readers (discussed at the beginning of the chapter).

In manual applications, two members of an operation's management team begin with a list of all items used (typically separated and ordered to align with specific storage areas). One person then takes a physical count of each item on the list while the other records the information. Once the data are gathered, the value of the inventory on hand is calculated by extending the purchase price of each item by the number of items on hand. (We address inventory valuation more fully in the next section.)

The resulting dollar amount is then used to calculate the cost of food used during the period. The formula for this is:

Beginning inventory + Food purchased − Ending inventory = Food costs

As you can surmise, the beginning inventory dollar amount is simply the ending inventory from the previous month. The food purchased is the amount spent as recorded on any invoices received during the period. Obviously, it is critical to have an accurate measure of the beginning inventory, the amount of food purchased, and the ending inventory.

It is difficult or impossible to maintain accurate financial records without an accurate physical inventory process. Physical inventory is also fraught with opportunities for mistakes and, potentially, for dishonest employees to hide past or planned thefts (a problem that we address at length in a later chapter). In this regard, the **inventory audit** is a valuable tool that can minimize or eliminate potential problems in the physical inventory process. An inventory audit is a recount of randomly selected items that is undertaken immediately following the physical inventory process. Members of a management team usually perform such audits, typically of expensive or universally popular (meaning most likely to be stolen) items such as meats and alcoholic beverages. Inventory audits can also be conducted on a spot basis between scheduled physical inventory dates in cases where specific items have been subject to mysterious disappearances.

Inventory Valuation

As noted earlier, the value of each item in an inventory must be calculated in order to determine the cost of goods used during a given period. The challenge in conducting **inventory valuation** is that not all purchases are made at the same price for a particular item. It is not uncommon for an item's price to change once or even several times during a month. So which price do we use?

Here we introduce five ways in which to assign values to inventory items: the actual purchase price method, the FIFO method, the weighted average price method, the latest purchase price method, and the last-in-first-out (LIFO) method. Each of these methods produces a different valuation amount. For our purposes, let us use a single item to illustrate how these approaches are applied. Table 9.1 includes data for a high-volume martini bar that uses premium stuffed olives, which are available only in cases that contain six seven-ounce jars each. The price of these olives tends to fluctuate due to the small amount manufactured by the producer in Spain.

TABLE 9.1   Prices Paid for Premium Stuffed Olives—Zebra Bar

Date	Number of Cases	Price	Extension
Opening Inventory, July 1, 20XX	10	$58.75	$587.50
Purchased on July 10, 20XX	25	$58.95	$1473.75
Purchased on July 18, 20XX	25	$62.00	$1,550.00
Purchased on July 26, 20XX	14	$61.50	$861.00

A physical inventory conducted at the close of business on July 31 showed that there were five cases remaining in stock. The number of cases used in July can be calculated as follows:

Opening Inventory:	10	$587.50
Plus Cases Purchased:	64	$3,884.75
Minus Ending Inventory:	5	$?
Cases Used:	69	$?

Thus, the valuation of the 69 cases used as well as of the five remaining cases must be determined.

Actual Purchase Price Method: The most logical approach would seem to involve calculating the value of items used by simply recording the amount paid for each item. In situations in which the price is marked on each case, such a determination is easy to make. If the information is not recorded and there is no record of what was used first, then this approach is impossible to use. For our purposes, let's assume that the cases were marked. The value of the five cases is:

$$1 @ \$58.75 = \$58.75$$
$$2 @ \$62.00 = \$124.00$$
$$2 @ \$61.50 = \$123.00$$
$$5 = \$305.75$$

Since the beginning inventory and purchases totaled $4,472.25, we can determine, using the actual purchase price method, that the valuation of olives used in July totaled $4,166.50 ($4,472.25 − $305.75).

FIFO Price Method: An alternative procedure that is consistent with our earlier recommendation to always observe the FIFO principle is to use the value associated with the last or most recent purchase of a particular item. In other words, the "first in" items are gone so we need to valuate the remaining items, which were the ones most recently purchased. Since the last order was for 14 cases and at the end of the month there were five remaining, we can calculate the ending inventory as:

$$5 @ \$61.50 = \$307.50$$

The food cost using the FIFO price method would then be $4,164.75 ($4,472.25 − $307.50). If the cases are dated, then such an approach is accurate. If cases were taken out of inventory or the stock was not properly rotated, however, then this valuation method is susceptible to error.

Weighted Average Purchase Price Method: If there is no assurance that stock was effectively rotated following the FIFO principle, particularly where a large volume of the same items are involved, the weighted average purchase price method may be appropriate. Here, we multiply the number of units in the opening inventory and in each purchase by their respective purchase prices and add these values together; next, we divide by the number of units involved. In our case, we add the extensions in Table 9.1, which total $4,472.25, and divide by the number of cases, which is 74, yielding a per-case price of $60.44.

The ending inventory using this technique is:

$$5 \text{ @ } \$60.44 = \$302.20$$

The food cost of olives for July using this method would then be $4,170.05 ($4,472.25 − $302.20). While the approach is mathematically logical, it would be far too laborious to make the associated calculations for hundreds of items in a noncomputerized system. Still, it is worth understanding how this approach is designed to work.

Latest Purchase Price Method: A widely used approach, owing to its simplicity and justifiability, is simply to use the latest price paid for an item regardless of the number used or the number on hand. The main justification for using this approach is that when an operator has to replace items, the most recent price paid is most likely to be the closest to its price on the date of replacement. Using this approach yields the same outcome as the FIFO method. (This would not be the case if the number on hand at the end of the period exceeded the quantity of the most recent order.) Thus, the ending inventory is:

$$5 \text{ @ } \$61.50 = \$307.50$$

The food cost is $4,164.75 ($4,472.25 − $307.50).

Last-In, First-Out Method: In certain unique situations, management may choose to calculate values based on the prices of the oldest units on hand, known as the last-in, first-out (**LIFO**) approach (In other words, the newest items are used first. Hence the value of the products remaining is associated with the older costs.) This practice is rarely advisable as it can distort food costs for a given period and can lead to apparent (but nonexistent) fluctuations in month-to-month comparisons. Still, we mention this approach to illustrate how results vary by method.

Using the LIFO method, we would calculate the ending inventory as:

$$5 \text{ @ } \$58.75 = \$293.75$$

The food cost for olives used in July, then, is $4,178.50 ($4,472.25 − $293.75).

Obviously, these methods vary in both utility and valuation results. Ultimately, management should adopt an approach that fits its operation, carries reasonable labor costs, and results in the most accurate calculations for a given situation.

Inventory-Turnover Analysis

One of the best tools for monitoring the overall inventory management process is **inventory-turnover analysis**. Inventory turnover can be calculated as:

$$\frac{\textit{Food cost for the period}}{\textit{Average inventory value for the period}} = \textit{Inventory turnover for the period}$$

For example, assume that a large cafe in a company's headquarters has monthly retail sales of $200,000 with an associated food cost of $70,000. For the targeted month, the beginning inventory was $18,000 and the ending inventory $17,000, producing an average inventory value for the month of $17,500. The inventory-turnover statistic for the period is:

$$\frac{\$70,000}{\$17,500} = 4 \; turns \; per \; month$$

Of course, a single period's turnover statistic is not a valid benchmark for assessing overall inventory-management success. A more useful measure would be to calculate the inventory-turnover statistic over a multi-month period. Such a calculation is easily applied to categories of food and beverages and even to individual food items in cases where problems with the inventory-management process are severe (serving much the same purpose as an inventory audit). Such analyses are especially helpful in identifying unexplained spikes in item-specific usage, particularly for high-priced items.

The utility of the inventory-turnover statistic is perhaps most obvious when comparing a single operation over time with a number of very similar operations—as in a chain environment or in a large onsite foodservice company. Yet even if an operator regularly achieves levels of turnover similar to those of his peers, anomalies may indicate cause for concern.

Figure 9.8, for example, illustrates the average monthly inventory-turnover statistic for a hypothetical medical center.[1] In healthcare operations, the target range for the statistic is from 2.5 to 4.0 for healthcare foodservice operations. (This range is also applicable to educational and correctional operations; in B&I, the range is 3.5 to 4.5; and in restaurants across segments it is 4.0.)

In this example, the operator appears to have managed inventory well for the first half of the fiscal year, surpassing the unit's targeted turnover measure. Over the next several months, however, a disturbing pattern has emerged. The downward trend is undesirable; the turnover statistics for the last three months signal a serious problem.

Such a pattern of inconsistency signifies erratic inventory management, which is undesirable under any circumstances. Moreover, the decline's midyear beginning may indicate an unexpected change in sales or reflect other operational problems; in either case, the information warrants immediate investigation. Finally, the decline in turnover may be the result of employee theft or collusion in the inventory-valuation process. No matter what the cause of the decline, such a

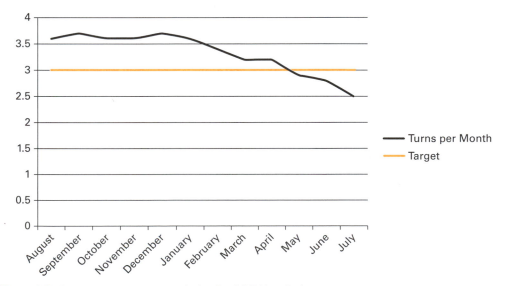

Figure 9.8   Inventory turnover statistics for ABC Hospital.

periodic analysis is a bellwether that indicates management should investigate other operating statistics to identify and remedy the problem. Granted, the cause may be innocuous, such as a change in vendor accompanied by a new delivery pattern. The point is to know when something out of the ordinary is happening, and to be prepared to do something about it.

Inventory turnover analysis is also helpful in identifying undesirable trends in inventory valuation. For example, if a management team rotates physical inventory duties and notable increases or decreases appear when a certain manager or pair of managers takes responsibility, then an investigation is necessary. It may be that the employees are making consistent errors or are attempting to hide fraudulent activity.

In summary, such analytical approaches to inventory management (we discuss several others in subsequent chapters) can also be critical in identifying situations normally thought of as highly unlikely (such as a favored employee's stealing food). Without question, the growing complexity of today's foodservice operations calls for innovative tools and approaches. This one deserves to be in every manager's toolkit.

PRODUCTION MANAGEMENT

Suppose an operation's food has been ordered to the desired specifications and in quantities corresponding to painstaking forecasting, received using the proper methodology, stored and issued to the proper parts of the operation, and valuated accordingly. The last step in food management prior to delivery to the guest is actually preparing the food to be served.

While production methods vary by type of foodservice operation and industry segment, some food-management practices are universal. In this section, then, we discuss production procedures, managing food quality, and quantity food production.

Production Procedures

The first step in food production is forecasting production needs. This is completed largely during the purchasing phase (discussed in the previous chapter). Again, the importance of forecasting cannot be overemphasized. Poorly executed forecasting can result in either of two outcomes. The first is **overproduction**. In this case, there will be an overabundance of food compared with what is sold to customers, resulting in needless waste. **Underproduction** also brings undesirable consequences: Guests will be displeased when items are not available, and offering alternative items may result in unnecessarily higher food costs.

Production procedures work best with the generation of a **production sheet** (sometimes referred to as a production schedule). Production sheet formats vary by type of foodservice operation, but all share a number of common elements (see Figure 9.9 for an example). These include the following:

- Name of outlet (in operations where multiple outlets are available)
- Day of the week
- Date
- Daypart
- Total volume forecast
- Forecast for each individual item
- Portion sizes
- Production methods

Main Kitchen Production Unit

Production Worksheet

Preparation Area:	**Bakery**		For Production On: Tuesday 12/7/20XX	
Item	Yield		Portion	Service Pan

1 *Breakfast*

Item	Yield		Portion		Service Pan
Brownie Chewy Chocolate	4.84	*Sheet Pan*	225.01	*Brownie*	
Brownie Espresso	8.07	*Sheet Pan*	374.99	*Brownie*	
Brownie Peanut Butter	18.75	*Sheet Pan*	675	*Brownie*	
Cake Chocolate with Frosting	1	*Baking Pan*	47.83	*2 x 3 sq*	12" x 18" x 2" Baking Pan
Cake Lemon Poppy Seed	1	*Baking Pan*	48	*2 x 3 sq*	12" x 18" x 2" Baking Pan
Cake White with Frosting	1	*Baking Pan*	48	*2 x 3 sq*	12" x 18" x 2" Baking Pan

3 *Lunch*

Item	Yield		Portion		Service Pan
Cookie Chewy Chocolate Chip	225	*Cookie*	225	*Cookie*	
Cookie Milk Chocolate Pecan	563	*Cookie*	563	*Cookie*	
Cookie Oatmeal Chocolate Chip	338	*Cookie*	338	*Cookie*	
Cookie Peanut Butter Chunk	383	*Cookie*	383	*Cookie*	

5 *Dinner*

Item	Yield		Portion		Service Pan
Cake Carrot with Cream Cheese Frosting	28	*Baking Pan*	1,344	*2 x 3 sq*	12" x 18" x 2" Baking Pan

Figure 9.9 Production sheet.

The production sheet's complexity and level of detail will vary not only by type of foodservice operation but also by the kitchen staff's culinary expertise and the degree of standardization characterizing an operation. However, the purpose of every production sheet is the same: To establish production goals and standards and to serve as a control tool for management.

At the end of a given service period (either a daypart or an entire day), a production sheet is used as a record of what was sold, what sold out, and what, if any, items remain. Thus, it becomes part of the forecasting mechanism for subsequent days. It also immediately provides management with important information regarding sales and potential unforeseen costs due to overproduction in the event of inaccurate forecasts.

With production sheets in hand, most managers will then conduct a **production meeting**, which provides an opportunity for management and staff to review what has transpired recently and to discuss the day's upcoming issues. Typically, cooks review production sheets during such meetings so that questions can be addressed as a group. In addition to building camaraderie, these meetings also provide an excellent venue for management to hear what is on the minds of the kitchen staff.

Managing Food Quality

Several of the measures that we have already addressed should go a long way to ensuring that an operation serves high-quality food. These include standardized recipes that provide consistency and uniformity. Product specifications lead to a consistent level of quality in raw ingredients. The inventory management processes described earlier provide that only the freshest ingredients are on hand and that there is minimal waste due to ordering, receiving, or issuing errors. Finally, food production sheets present the necessary instructions on the basis of which the staff prepares menu items.

Still, as anyone who has eaten in a restaurant knows, food preparation is not foolproof. So another first step that management can take to ensure quality is to establish **quality standards**. Quality standards represent minimum levels that must be met before items are presented to guests. Such measures include temperature, taste, and appearance. These standards may include pictures of plated items (often included on a standardized recipe) to ensure that every plate including the specific item leaves the kitchen looking the same day after day. Such standards are necessary regardless of the setting.

In a college dining hall where hundreds of students are served breakfast, for example, such standards dictate the temperature at which the scrambled eggs are held, the appearance of individually plated pastries, and the time for which coffee is held. In a healthcare setting, there are quality standards for both patient food and for items served in the cafe. In QSR, where items are cooked prior to being ordered (consider a busy QSR with a double drive-through that must make items before they are ordered in anticipation of demand during peak periods), the time for which items are held before they must be discarded if not sold are dictated by quality standards. Finally, in fine dining there may be standards that dictate how much time can pass between when food is plated and when it is served.

Employee training is also vital to ensuring quality foodservice. While we address this more fully in the chapter on human resource management, the importance of training cannot be overemphasized. A cook who is not trained to meet a specific operation's standards cannot be held accountable for maintaining them.

The last ingredient in managing food quality is the equipment that is used for food production. As we noted at the beginning of this textbook, everything starts with the menu. Selecting the equipment in the kitchen also begins with the menu. For example, if the menu includes a number of fried items, then a fryer that is capable of producing these is necessary. It may even be necessary to have more than one fryer if temperature requirements vary for several menu items. While it is beyond the scope of our discussion to discuss kitchen equipment in detail, it suffices to say that employees cannot meet production standards if they lack the necessary tools.

Quantity Food Production

Quantity, the most fundamental aspect of which is **portion control**, must be accounted for when managing food quality. Portion control in food production ensures that serving sizes are uniform. Think of a lemon meringue pie. Depending on the portion size, the pie might be sliced into six, eight, or even ten slices. Portion control dictates exactly how big a slice should be, as well as how many slices a pie should produce.

The steps required for effective portion control are as follows: First, a foodservice manager must determine what size per portion is desired. This decision depends on the menu, the type of foodservice operation in question, and the value proposition (think back to Chapter 2). Next, the chosen portion sizes must be communicated clearly to all relevant staff as a component of the operation's quality standards. The third step is to measure items, which could require a portion scale or measuring utensils. (This is why commercial ladles are available in a range of sizes, each with a distinct handle color, to help employees measure servings in the desired portions.) Finally, portion control must be monitored. A bartender hoping for a better tip may be inclined to add more alcohol to a drink, exceeding the portion specification. Similarly, a cook wanting to please customers may add an extra shrimp to a dish. In both cases, this notion of portion control is violated and costs are needlessly increased.

Portion control is affected by almost every step in the food management process. For example, if the recipe for a menu item includes a five-ounce lobster tail, then this must be considered in developing the product specification, the ordering, and the production. If sandwiches are served using sliced meats, then slicing the meats must allow for portions that correspond to the standardized recipe's portion amounts. (Think of the operational challenges of making sandwiches with three ounces of meat with meat that is processed into four-ounce slices.)

Another aspect of portion controls was introduced in Chapter 5: yields. Again, a food yield is an equivalent measure of a specific food. Consider a chicken breast with bone and skin still attached. The yield of chicken meat after cooking is 66 percent of the original weight. An even more dramatic example is found in a live Maine lobster. After cooking, the yield of actual lobster meat is only 25 percent of the original weight!

MANAGERIAL IMPLICATIONS

In this chapter, we have described several vital steps that any foodservice manager must master. Once food has been ordered, the food management process continues with properly receiving items from suppliers. In some settings, the use of barcodes or RFID tag readers expedites the process. Still, the human element involved in checking items through visual and other means of inspection to ensure that they are of the proper type, weight, and quality cannot be replaced. Furthermore, all steps in the receiving procedure must be followed properly, including confirming that a delivery matches the corresponding purchase order, confirming that the invoice matches the purchase order, making accept-or-reject decisions, completing the paperwork, and processing the invoice correctly.

Storing food is the next order of business. Apart from obvious food safety issues, convenience, accessibility, and security are the main concerns related to storage. Access to stored food should be limited and storage areas must be kept clean and free of pests. Furthermore, if possible an operation should apply the FIFO approach, which works best if items are dated when they are received. Finally, while temperature and humidity parameters are specific to a given storage area, monitoring temperatures constantly is critical, particularly for refrigerated and frozen storage areas.

Managing inventory, which involves nonperforming assets, is facilitated first by proper issuance of food to the operation's respective areas or departments. Data used in the issuing process also help to maintain a perpetual inventory system. The application and preponderance of such systems is increasing due to advances in technology.

A physical inventory is necessary to confirm the accuracy of perpetual inventory (when used) and to calculate food costs. Tools used to protect the integrity of the process include inventory audits and inventory-turnover analysis, with the latter allowing for internal and intrachain comparative analyses.

The manner in which inventory valuation is calculated is also vital to accurately managing a foodservice operation's financial performance. Here we reviewed five ways in which values can be assigned to inventory items, with each producing a different valuation amount. Managers must understand how and when to use the various approaches.

Finally, production management is the last step in managing food from purchase to preparation. Procedures should be in place to prevent overproduction and underproduction, as both have negative consequences, including production sheets, which are typically discussed with kitchen staff during a production meeting. Quality standards, portion control, and understanding yields are the remaining issues to be considered.

INDUSTRY EXEMPLAR

CBORD

The CBORD Group, founded in 1975, is the world's leading provider of campus and cashless card systems, food and nutrition service management software, nationwide student discount and off-campus commerce programs, housing and judicial process management software, and integrated security solutions. CBORD prides itself on being the only provider that can offer such a broad portfolio of solutions designed to improve its clients' daily operations and help them provide their customers with greater convenience and satisfaction. It is regarded as the largest application provider in the foodservice industry.

CBORD serves colleges and universities, K-12 schools, healthcare facilities, chain restaurants, supermarkets, continuing care facilities, corporations, and a host of other market segments. CBORD products and services are used by more than 6,000 organizations in the United States, Canada, Europe, South Africa, New Zealand, the Middle East, and Australia. Today it employs more than 450 professionals throughout North America and in Australia.

The CBORD Group, Inc. operates as a unit of Roper Industries, Inc. (NYSE: ROP). Roper Industries is a market-driven, diversified growth company and is a constituent of the Fortune 1000, the Russell 1000, and the S&P 500 indices. Roper provides engineered products and solutions for global niche markets, including water, energy, radio frequency, and research/medical applications.

The CBORD Group is perhaps best known for the quality of its client services and support. Its development programs for both products and services have been driven by formal collaboration with its User Group since the company's inception. CBORD is headquartered in Ithaca, New York, where the company has been a member of the business community for more than 30 years. According to President Tim Tighe, CBORD is changing the foodservice world by introducing integrated foodservice management systems to common business practice.[2]

KEY TERMS

receiving   180

barcodes   180

RFID   180

blind receiving   184

invoice stamps   184

credit memorandum   185

invoice payment schedule   185

FIFO   186

walk-in   186

reach-in   186

freezer burn   188

nonperforming assets   189

issuing   189

perpetual inventory   189

physical inventory   194

inventory audit   194

inventory valuation   194

LIFO   196

inventory-turnover analysis   196

overproduction   198

underproduction   198

production sheet   198

production meeting   200

quality standards   200

portion control   201

■■■■■■■ Case in Point ■■■

The Automotive Plant

Recently, Chen joined the management team that operates the foodservice operation at an auto-manufacturing plant in the southeastern United States (see Figure 9.10). The foodservice is available 24 hours per day, seven days per week. (The plant runs three eight-hour shifts per day.) On average, they serve about 4,500 meals per day. As the general manager, Chen oversees a team of seven managers and 57 employees.

Figure 9.10   Car manufacturing plant.

Case in Point *(continued)*

During the hiring process, the plant's administration made it clear to Chen that their business is assembling cars—not foodservice management. Still, they assured him that they want to provide quality food to their employees; they just prefer not to be bothered with operating what they consider a support service. That's why he'd be hired. Moreover, they don't want to lose money—they can't afford to subsidize the foodservice operation even as a benefit to employees. Thus, their directions to Chen were simple: Manage the foodservice such that high-quality hot food is available 24 hours a day—and don't lose money doing it!

Chen's first order of business, then, was to wrap his arms around the financials. He knew the labor cost would be higher than in some operations owing to the 24-hour-a-day operation. He also knew that, given the volume of food served, inventory management would be an important element in his success.

Chen was immediately struck by the incredible amount of food stacked and piled up in the various storage areas. It was not very orderly. The meat refrigerator, for example, had three areas in which hamburger meat was stored. He also noted that nothing was dated.

He met with the production manager, John, to discuss inventory issues. John explained to Chen that receiving staff were just too busy to date items when they arrived. He added that, since the volume of foodservice was so high, it would be almost impossible for food to go bad. As for the abundance of food, John said that he'd been managing the kitchen for 15 years and until now no one had complained about inventory levels.

Not particularly pleased with John's responses, Chen decided first to check the accuracy of the operation's inventory valuations. In this way, he could perhaps better help John to improve the situation. He performed an inventory audit of the major meat items and found that the amounts listed on the inventory sheets far exceeded the amounts that were on hand. He also learned that the prices listed for items had not been updated, which artificially lessened the resulting food cost determinations.

Chen sat at his desk wondering about his next steps. Obviously, someone was inaccurately recording the amount of food on hand. In addition, why weren't the prices updated?

What steps should Chen take next?

REVIEW AND DISCUSSION QUESTIONS

1. What technologies are streamlining the receiving process?

2. Why must the human element remain, at least to some extent, integral to the receiving process?

3. Describe the perfect receiving area. Be sure to include a description of any equipment that should be included.

4. What are the disadvantages of blind receiving?

5. Name three reasons why a food item might be refused.

6. You just received an invoice that reads "3/10 net 20." What does that mean?

7. List the temperatures that should be maintained for dry storage, refrigerated storage, and frozen storage.

8. Why is the food in a foodservice operation's inventory described as a nonperforming asset?

9. You just completed the inventory at your cafe, resulting in an ending inventory of $28,090. The beginning inventory was $25,000. If the food used during the period totaled $92,910, how much food did you purchase?

10. Using the numbers from the previous question, what is the inventory turnover for the period?

11. Using the criteria listed in this chapter, create a production sheet for your favorite entrée.

12. Go to the CBORD website and peruse the site. List the various foodservice segments they serve.

13. Identify three areas of quality standards and describe how you could measure each one.

14. Name five types of measurement that might be used in controlling portions.

ENDNOTES

1. This example is adapted from Reynolds, D. "Inventory-turnover Analysis: Its Importance for On-site Food Service." *Cornell Hotel and Restaurant Administration Quarterly* 40(2) (1999): 54–59. The article also provides other information about inventory turnover analysis that is beyond the scope of this discussion.

2. Personal communication, August 13, 2010.

PART 4

GENERAL MANAGEMENT

Having concluded the foodservice product cycle discussion of the previous chapters, we now provide a more holistic perspective on general management. We begin with financial management (considered by many foodservice veterans to be the keystone to everything else), followed by customer service, marketing, human resources, and, finally, leadership.

FINANCIAL MANAGEMENT

LEARNING OBJECTIVES:

After becoming familiar with this chapter, you should be able to:

1. Describe what generates foodservice sales and understand why we need to apply accounting principles.

2. Understand the components of income statements, balance sheets, and cash flow statements.

3. Apply analytic tools to the various financial statements.

4. Explain the various cost concepts as they apply to foodservice operations.

5. Appreciate the importance and nuances involved in creating a budget and describe what is involved in budgeting for capital improvements.

Throughout the first three parts of this book we have considered the foodservice business from a variety of perspectives and with a keen focus on operational issues. Now we take up financial management, a thread that has run through the entire fabric of this introduction to foodservice management fundamentals. Whether you are managing a restaurant within a five-star resort or a cafe in a corporate headquarters or a foodservice unit in a medical center, the one measure that is universal is this: Is your operation making money (or meeting the budget in the case of a non-profit)? The following discussion will give you the tools you need to answer this question.

ACCOUNTING OVERVIEW

Managing its financial resources effectively is paramount to any foodservice operation's success. While we have already discussed many issues that play into financial management, including menu planning, menu pricing, recipe costing, supply chain management, and food management, managing finances is the ultimate test for management. If an operation is profitable, it can increase wages and salaries, enhance the physical aspects of the dining area, invest in more efficient kitchen equipment, and engage in aggressive marketing efforts—all of which fuel continued success. However, a foodservice establishment that is not profitable (or, again, in the case of a nonprofit that is not meeting the budget) will inevitably go out of business.

Restaurant Industry Dollars

In Chapter 2 we discussed how generating revenues in the various industry segments shapes the foodservice business. We have also considered how **sales generators**—those categories that lead to total revenue—affect average revenue per foodservice operation (although we referred to the sales generators as simply food and beverages). The National Restaurant Association's latest operations report, as shown in Figure 10.1, illustrates the breakdown for full-service restaurants.[1] Not surprisingly, the contribution from beverages is smaller in restaurants with a lower check average, likely because the majority of these are QSR or fast-casual restaurants. (Recall from the previous chapter that *beverage* pertains only to beer, wine, and spirits; sodas, coffee, and tea are considered food for financial reporting.)

How were the expenses associated with these sales distributed by check-size category? Figure 10.2 provides an answer.

These comparisons are useful not only because they portray financial differences across segments but also because they identify the considerable expenses associated with operating any foodservice operation. They also show that, regardless of segment, two categories represent the bulk of the expenses: food and beverage, and labor.

Unique Industry Aspects

In spite of the factors that differentiate the various foodservice industry segments, such as onsite operations and traditional restaurants, several financial variables are common to all foodservice operations, and each of these potentially affects an operation's finances. One of these is the lag effect on sales related to the overall economy. For example, when the global economic crisis began in early 2008, restaurant sales were not immediately affected. However, within six months of the crisis's onset, foodservice operations in all segments began to feel the financial impact.

Among the several principal explanations of this phenomenon are consumer behavior and the interrelationship between hospitality and general business practices. In terms of consumer behavior, humans are typically slow to change. Even if a person's salary is reduced, she will continue for a while, for example, to eat at a familiar cafe every day for lunch. Over time, however, such a person may be forced by newly limited financial resources to save money by packing lunch for work. As these behavioral changes take effect, they cause the lag effect noted earlier, in part perhaps it takes a while for the bills to stress one's personal resources. The other issue concerns the effects of economic downturns on the hospitality industry. When businesses face financial challenges, they eliminate or reduce expenses that are the least crucial to immediate profitability, such as corporate travel. Thus, executives may be asked to cancel travel plans and use alternative ways

Average Check per Person Under $15

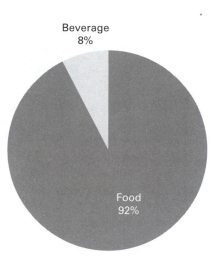

Average Check per Person $15–$24.99

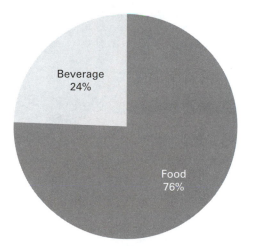

Average Check per Person $25 and Over

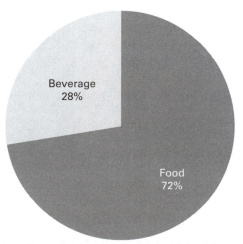

Figure 10.1   Average foodservice sales generators in the United States.

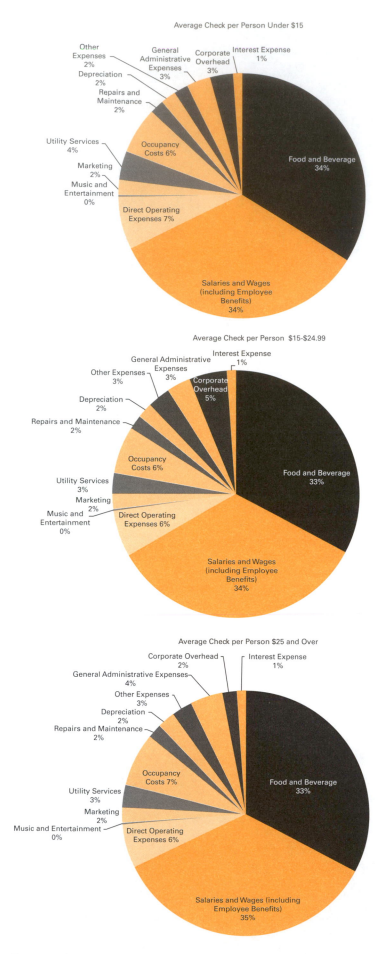

Figure 10.2 Expenses by category.

to hold meetings such as video conferencing. Because instituting such changes takes some time, hospitality businesses do not feel the effects immediately. Inevitably, however, such reductions in business travel will reduce demand for hotel rooms and out-of-town meals, thereby reaching the hospitality industry.

Another unique aspect of foodservice finances pertains to our discussion in Chapter 8 of supply chain management. In foodservice operations, it takes a relatively short time to order, receive, produce, and sell a menu item. In other words, stockpiling and advanced production requirements are minimal (consider, for example, the time it takes to build and sell a house or assemble, deliver, and install a CT scanner in a hospital). This is a competitive advantage for foodservice operators. In addition, foodservice operations typically have less than 5 percent of their total assets invested in food.

Yet another unique aspect is the labor intensiveness of foodservice operations. While many manufacturing sectors and even some in hospitality have replaced **human capital** with technology and automation, even highly automated restaurants (for example, the curiously named 's Baggers, featured in Chapter 1, was referred to recently by ABC News as the world's first "robotic restaurant"), need prep cooks and managers.[2] This matters greatly in financial management, because whereas food cost was traditionally the largest expense for foodservice operators, today most agree that labor cost as a percentage of sales is the highest cost category for many operations (see Figure 10.2). This puts the onus on management, then, to manage this cost category very carefully (Figure 10.3 underscores the labor component of the foodservice industry). We will address the "how" part of managing the cost of labor in subsequent chapters.

© Sodexo.

Figure 10.3 The people part of the foodservice business.

Accounting Principles

In the foodservice business, as in many business sectors, we have a **uniform system of accounts**.[3] This standard accounting classification system for foodservice operators makes apple-to-apple comparisons possible. The system allows operators to classify expenses accordingly (for example, matchbooks—often given away at hostess stands to market restaurants—are classified as direct operating expenses under a subcategory of "guest supplies," while professional development seminars for managerial staff are classified as general and administrative expenses under the subcategory of training). The uniform system of accounts also eliminates the undesirable practice of lumping various unique expenses into the "miscellaneous" category, which makes both auditing and unit-to-unit comparison problematic.

This uniform system of accounts and the associated accounting methods are based on established accounting principles. Among these principles that are critical for understanding this chapter's later discussions, consider first the **cost principle**, which dictates that when an item is purchased, it is the price paid that is used for accounting purposes. For example, suppose a foodservice operator purchases a 500-gallon aquarium for the dining room (see Figure 10.4 for a great

Figure 10.4 Downtown Aquarium, Houston, Texas.

example of a restaurant with an aquarium). The firm selling the aquarium also provides services to maintain the fish tank, such as routine cleaning. Hoping to win the contract for maintaining the aquarium, the company sells it to the foodservice operator for $4,000—less than half the retail price. The cost principle requires that the value of the aquarium be recorded as $4,000, not the true retail value, which is much higher.

The next principle is referred to as the **business entity**. This is mainly a matter of common sense, but it is nonetheless important to state. This principle requires that each business maintain its own set of accounts, separately from those of the owner(s). We discussed this in Chapter 8 as in part a question of ethics. Suppose a restaurant owner takes home a case of steaks for the weekend. This asset belongs to the restaurant. Even though the owner is the one consuming the steaks and they're being consumed at home, the cost of the steaks has already been recorded in the restaurant's accounting system, when the invoice was received. This principle requires, then, that the cost of the steaks be charged to the owner's account, removing the expense from the restaurant's food cost calculation.

The last principle that we address is **consistency**. Several accounting methods apply to the various foodservice functions. For example, when we discussed inventory valuation in Chapter 9, we saw that the prices paid for the total inventory of a given item might vary, depending on when and from which vendors they were purchased. We illustrated a variety of methods for valuating such items, each resulting in a slightly different value. The consistency principle requires that management select the proper method and then continue using it. This allows for realistic comparisons over time. In the event that changing circumstances recommend an alternative valuation method, management must disclose the change and make appropriate adjustments to the related financial statements.

■□ FINANCIAL STATEMENTS

This discussion of accounting principles serves as an ideal segue to the next topic: financial statements. Thus, in this section, we address income statements, balance sheets, and cash flow statements.

Income Statement

Also referred to as the statement of income and retained earnings, the **income statement** is probably the most important financial statement for foodservice operators. It provides a summary of the operation's profit (or loss) for a given period, which is typically calculated on a weekly or monthly basis. It also supports trend analysis for both revenue and expenses by category over time.

The income statement may vary slightly from segment to segment. For example, a large chain restaurant may need to include a greater number of categories than a small, privately owned pizzeria would. Consider a chain restaurant that sells merchandise, such as the Hard Rock Cafe (see Figure 10.5). Such an operation would require separate sales categories beyond food and beverage and would need corresponding expense categories. Alternatively, such an operation might treat merchandise sales completely separately. Even smaller restaurants that sell specialty items such as embossed chopsticks would need separate categories. Other differences might be found in onsite foodservice between operations that are self-operated and those that are run by managed foodservice companies. For the latter, there will typically be an expense category such as "corporate overhead" that would not be necessary in the self-operated unit's income statement.

Figure 10.5 Retail sales in the Hard Rock Cafe, Penang, Malaysia.

Acknowledging that there might be some slight variations, we now discuss the standard income statement for the foodservice industry. For convenience, we will use a hypothetical income statement for a fictional restaurant (see Figure 10.6), followed by a brief explanation of each element.

Notice that the first information presented is the name of the financial statement and the company name, followed by the period to which the statement applies. We cannot overemphasize the importance of this information. Consider a stack of income statements without dates; the information they contain would have very little value.

Sales. This category is the basic element that all foodservice operations share. As we noted earlier, some operations might have "other" sales. Because we want to establish a consistent basis for comparison and food and beverage are the primary revenue generators, "other" sales are included, perhaps not very intuitively, under expenses, as a negative expense.

Cost of Sales. Cost of sales, referred to in other industries as cost of goods sold, is the cost of the raw goods (as calculated in Chapter 9). It is important to note here that the percentages pertain to the cost of food divided by food sales and the cost of beverages divided by beverage sales. A common error is dividing the individual category costs by total sales.

Gross Profit. This is the profit shown after the cost of goods is subtracted from the sales. Again, the associated percentages are calculated for the respective categories separately.

Riverside Grill and Bar Month 1, 20XX	Amounts	Percentages
Sales		
Food	$241,564	76.0%
Beverage	$76,099	24.0%
Total Sales	$317,663	100.0%
Cost of Sales		
Food	$81,322	33.7%
Beverage	$14,588	19.2%
Total Cost of Sales	$95,910	30.2%
Gross Profit		
Food	$160,242	66.3%
Beverage	$61,511	80.8%
Total Gross Profit	$221,753	69.8%
Operating Expenses		
Salaries and Wages	$105,685	33.3%
Employee Benefits	$7,453	2.3%
Direct Operating Expenses	$18,697	5.9%
Music and Entertainment	$2,400	0.8%
Marketing	$5,405	1.7%
Utility Services	$9,444	3.0%
Occupancy Costs	$17,890	5.6%
Repairs and Maintenance	$5,428	1.7%
Depreciation	$5,856	1.8%
General and Administrative Expenses	$8,733	2.7%
Other Expense/(Income)	$0	0.0%
Total Operating Expenses	$186,991	58.9%
Operating Income	$34,762	10.9%
Interest	$2,280	0.7%
Income before Income Taxes	$32,482	10.2%

Figure 10.6 Income statements (numbers are for illustrative purposes only.

Operating Expenses. These items comprise expenses other than the basic food and beverage expenses already addressed. In the example given, all of the foodservice operation's expenses can be grouped. Although a small operator might be inclined to combine categories, keeping them separate allows for better control and analysis.

Let us pause to mention some important aspects of operation expenses. First, note that employee benefits are separate from salaries and wages. While in our example they represent only 2.3 percent of sales, they equate to over 7 percent of salaries and wages. Depending on the type of benefits offered, this number could run substantially higher. Moreover, when management salaries are separated from hourly payroll, the benefit percentage for management can be as high as 40 percent of salaries. Also, keep in mind that employee benefits involve more than just healthcare and retirement benefits. If employee meals are included, that food expense should be included here (and subtracted from the food expense under cost of sales).

Direct operating expenses, as the name implies, include items that are directly linked to providing food and service. These can include uniforms, menus, china, and glassware. Music and entertainment expenses may be nominal for some operations but substantial in a foodservice operation that features nightly live entertainment. Marketing pertains to the costs associated with promoting the foodservice operation. (As we discuss in Chapter 13, advertising is just one aspect of marketing.) In chain operations in which the franchisee pays a marketing fee, the cost of such a fee is usually listed separately.

Utility services include the cost of expenses such as water, gas, and electricity. Where utilities are provided as part of a lease agreement, these expenses are paid by the landlord and are part of the lease expense to the operator. In such a case, the expense in the category is zero but is appropriately reflected in the following category, occupancy costs. Occupancy costs include rent, property taxes, and property insurance.

Repairs and maintenance expenses can include routine maintenance to the **heating, ventilation, and air conditioning (HVAC)** systems, and emergency repairs that include fixing a plumbing leak and addressing the breakdown of a single HVAC component. Other examples are repairs to computer systems, grounds maintenance and landscaping, and snow removal.

Depreciation is the operational expense that results from the gradual conversion of the cost of a tangible capital asset or fixed asset (excluding land because it has unlimited life). For example, say a small cafe operator buys a new computer for generating financial statements and monitoring expenses. The purchase price is $1,500 and the expected life of the asset is three years. While a variety of depreciation methods are available, she uses the straight-line method:

$$\frac{\text{Cost of asset} - \text{Salvage value}}{\text{Years of useful life}} = \text{Annual depreciation amount}$$

In this case, the annual depreciation is

$$\frac{\$1,500 - \$0}{3 \text{ years}} = \$500$$

Some assets decline in value faster during the early years (technology being a perfect example). In such cases, it is appropriate to use accelerated depreciation schedules that correspond to asset type.

General and administrative expenses are overhead expenses not directly related to providing food and service to guests. Examples include telephone service, postage, office supplies, payroll services, and legal fees. If members of the management team are provided with cell phones for business use, the associated expense would fall into in this category.

A category for other expense/(income) was mentioned earlier. In the event that an expense is incurred and is not included in the uniform system of accounts for restaurants, it should go here. As we noted, however, this should not be used as a catchall category for expenses that the manager does not know how to classify.

Finally, interest is the cost of borrowed capital. Interest expenses can vary depending on loan type. Nonetheless, interest on all debt-related obligations, short- or long-term, is included in this category.

Balance Sheet

The **balance sheet**, also referred to as a statement of financial position, presents a summary of a foodservice operation's financial condition at a given point in time. It is so named because it reflects a balance between the operation's assets and the combination of liabilities and shareholder's equity. As is true with the income statement, the balance sheet allows the operator to make important business decisions by providing an accurate picture of the operation's financial well-being. For the following discussion, Figure 10.7 illustrates the statement in question.

Assets. On the balance sheet, **assets** are current, fixed, or other. Current assets include cash or assets that will be converted to cash shortly, such as food inventory items. Fixed assets include

Balance Sheet
Applewood Smokehouse
June 30, 20XX

ASSETS			LIABILITIES AND SHAREHOLDERS'S EQUITY	
Current Assets			**Current Liabilities**	
Cash on Hand	$27,000		Accounts Payable	$2,489,400
Cash in Banks	$1,278,000		Current Portion of Long-term Debt	$54,000
	$1,305,000		Wages Payable	$95,400
Accounts Receivable:			Total Current Liabilities	$2,638,800
Customers	$48,600		**Long-term Liabilities**	
	$48,600		Long term Debt(less Current Portion)	$73,800
Inventories:			Other Non-current Liabilities	$14,400
Food	$900,000		Total long-term Liabilities	$88,200
Beverage	$327,600		**Shareholder's Equity**	
Supplies	$14,400		Capital Stock	$225,000
	$1,242,000		Retained Earnings	$253,800
Total Current Assets	$2,595,600		Total Shareholder's Equity	$478,800
Fixed Assets			**TOTAL LIABILITIES AND SHAREHOLDER'S EQUITY**	**$3,205,800**
Land	$108,000			
Buildings	$468,000			
Leasehold and Leasehold Improvements	$99,000			
Furniture, Fixtures and Equipment	$21,600			
Uniforms, Linens, China and Silver	$16,200			
Less Depreciation	($225,000)			
Total Fixed Assets	$487,800			
Other Assets				
Liquor License	$72,000			
Rental Deposits	$50,400			
	$122,400			
TOTAL ASSETS	**$3,205,800**			

Figure 10.7 Balance sheet (numbers are for illustrative purposes only).

items used by the foodservice operation that are relatively permanent, such as land, the cafe, furniture, and so on. Finally, other assets include the purchase price of a liquor license or a deposit on utility services such as gas or electricity.

Liabilities. At the top of the right side of the balance sheet, opposite assets, is the first category that serves to balance with the assets: **liabilities**. These are separated into current and long-term liabilities. Current liabilities are those that must be paid within one year and can include invoices to vendors yet to be paid, wages for hours worked but that haven't yet been paid, and the current mortgage payment yet to be paid. Long-term liabilities include any debt associated with loans extending beyond one year of the balance sheet date. Other noncurrent liabilities may include certain pension or employee-benefit plans.

Shareholders' Equity. The other portion that balances with the assets is **shareholders' equity**. When a foodservice operation is owned by an individual proprietor or partnership rather than by a corporation, this is referred to as **owner's equity** and may sometimes fall under the category of net worth. For corporations (as in the example shown in Figure 10.7), this might include capital stock and retained earnings. For a proprietorship, it would include the amount in the owner's account.

Statement of Cash Flows

An income statement neatly depicts the aggregate revenue and expenses for a given period. The balance sheet effectively reports a foodservice operation's financial position as of a certain point in time. What is missing, however, is a financial statement that shows how cash generated from the operation (and from other sources such as investments) was used during the period to create the position depicted by the balance sheet. The **statement of cash flows**, the last financial statement we will discuss, does just that. It is also particularly useful in determining the short-term viability of a foodservice operation, particularly with respect to its ability to pay bills and remain solvent.

The cash flow statement is separated into three activities. The first is cash flow resulting from operating activities. For the foodservice industry, this primarily involves buying raw food and beverage items (cash outflows) and sales of the resulting food and beverages (cash inflows). Other cash outflows in the category include wages and salaries paid to foodservice employees and managers. Another inflow would be refunds from vendors.

The second activity category is investment. These include the purchase or sale of such assets as land, buildings, and equipment. Another example would be loans made to suppliers. Payments related to acquisitions would also fall into this grouping.

The third category for cash flow statements is financing activities. These include cash inflows from investors, including banks and shareholders. Cash outflows in the category include dividends that a restaurant or managed-service company might pay as the company generates income.

Cash flow statements can be prepared using either of two methods: the **direct method** or the **indirect method**. The direct method begins with its principal components, operating cash flow from customers and cash paid to suppliers and employees, the sum of which is net cash flow from the foodservice operation's primary operating activities. The indirect method starts with net income and adjusts it for revenue and expense items that do not result from foodservice operations, such as depreciation and the deferred portion of income tax expense. Both methods are acceptable from an accounting perspective. For foodservice operators, the direct method is arguably better because it provides additional information on cash inflows and outflows, but it is also more difficult to prepare. While we need not address each line of the statement, as each is self-explanatory, Figure 10.8 provides an example of the direct method, and Figure 10.9 shows the result of the indirect method.

Statement of Cash Flows
Midstate Medical Center Food Court
Fiscal Year Ending June 30, 20XX

CASH FLOWS FROM OPERATING ACTIVITIES:	
Cash Received from Customers	$ 1,620,000
Cash Paid to Suppliers and Employees	(1,516,770)
Interest Paid (Net of Amount Capitalized)	(3,600)
Income Taxes Paid	(1,800)
Net Cash Provided by Operating Activities	$ 97,830
CASH FLOWS FROM INVESTING ACTIVITIES:	
Proceeds from Sale of Equipment	$ 1,800
Cash Payments for Leasehold Improvements	(18,000)
Down Payment on Equipment Purchase	(5,400)
Net Cash Used in Investing Activities	$ (21,600)
CASH FLOWS FROM FINANCING ACTIVITIES:	
Net Borrowings under Line-of-credit Agreement	$ 27,000
Proceeds from Issuance of Long-term Debt	18,000
Dividends Paid	(9,000)
Net Cash Provided by Financing Activities	$ 36,000
Net Increase (Decrease) in Cash and Cash Equivalents	$ 112,230
Cash and Cash Equivalents, Beginning of Period	$ 1,192,770
Cash and Cash Equivalents, End of Period	$ 1,305,000
Reconciliation of Net Income to Net Cash Provided by Operating Activities	
NET INCOME	$ 47,430
ADJUSTMENTS TO RECONCILE NET INCOME TO NET CASH PROVIDED BY OPERATING ACTIVITIES:	
Depreciation and Amortization	$ 32,400
Provision for Doubtful Accounts	900
Loss on Sale of Equipment	900
Change in Assets and Liabilities:	
Decrease in Accounts Receivable	$ 27,000
Increase in Inventory	(18,000)
Increase in Prepaid Expenses	(1,800)
Increase in Accounts Payable and Accrued Expenses	9,000
Increase in Interest and Income Taxes Payable	3,600
Decrease in Other Liabilities	(3,600)
Total Adjustments	$ 50,400
NET CASH PROVIDED BY (USED IN) OPERATING ACTIVITIES	**$ 97,830**

Supplemental Schedule of Noncash Investing and Financing Activities:

The Company issued xxx additional shares of common stock in exchange for the conversion of $xx,xxx of long-term debt.

Disclosure of Accounting Policy (for Footnotes):

For purposes of the statements of cash flows, the Company considers all highly liquid debt instruments purchased with a maturity of three months or less to be cash equivalents.

Figure 10.8 Statement of cash flows—direct method (numbers are for illustrative purposes only).

Statement of Cash Flows
Midstate Medical Center Food Court
Fiscal Year Ending June 30, 20XX

CASH FLOWS FROM OPERATING ACTIVITIES:

Net Income	$ 47,430
Adjustments to Reconcile Net Income to Net Cash Provided by Operating Activities:	
Depreciation and Amortization	$ 32,400
Provision for Doubtful Accounts	900
Loss on Sale of Equipment	900
Change in Assets and Liabilities:	
Decrease in Accounts Receivable	$ 27,000
Increase in Inventory	(18,000)
Increase in Prepaid Expenses	(1,800)
Increase in Accounts Payable and Accrued Expenses	9,000
Increase in Interest and Income Taxes Payable	3,600
Decrease in Other Liabilities	(3,600)
Total Adjustments	$ 50,400
Net Cash Provided by Operating Activities	**$ 97,830**
CASH FLOWS FROM INVESTING ACTIVITIES:	
Proceeds from Sale of Equipment	$ 1,800
Cash Payments for Leasehold Improvements	(18,000)
Down Payment on Equipment Purchase	(5,400)
Net Cash Used in Investing Activities	**($21,600)**
CASH FLOWS FROM FINANCING ACTIVITIES:	
Net Borrowings under Line-of-credit Agreement	$ 27,000
Proceeds from Issuance of Long-term Debt	18,000
Dividends Paid	(9,000)
Net Cash Provided by Financing Activities	**$ 36,000**
Net Increase (Decrease) in Cash and Cash Equivalents	**$ 112,230**
CASH AND CASH EQUIVALENTS, BEGINNING OF PERIOD	**$1,192,770**
CASH AND CASH EQUIVALENTS, END OF PERIOD	**$1,305,000**
Supplemental Disclosures of Cash Flow Information (for indirect method only):	
Cash Paid During the Year for:	
Interest (Net of Amount Capitalized)	$2,000
Income Taxes	$ 1,000

Supplemental Schedule of Noncash Investing and Financing Activities:

The Company issued xxx additional shares of common stock in exchange for the conversion of $xx,xxx of long-term debt.

Figure 10.9 Statement of cash flows—indirect method (numbers are for illustrative purposes only).

ANALYZING FINANCIAL STATEMENTS

As you can see, these financial statements carry a wealth of information. Making sense of and applying this information can be tricky. The first step, of course, is compiling them and ensuring their accuracy. The next step involves using the information to identify problem areas, make operating decisions, and plan for the future. In this section, we discuss several approaches. Note that even more advanced analytic techniques are presented in Chapter 17.

Income Statement Analysis

Looking back at Figure 10.6, we see that the income statement is divided into three basic sections: sales, cost of goods, and operating expenses. The most basic approach, then, to analyzing this statement is to consider each of these categories separately. In each, the first step is comparing actual with budgeted figures (we discuss the procedure used in developing a budget later in the chapter), which is called **variance analysis**. For sales, we need to assess whether food and beverage sales exceed, match, or are less than the budget. If such sales come in below budget, the operator must determine why this is occurring. We also want to understand the sales mix; are beverages selling at the percentage budgeted? Again, variances from the budget indicate cause for further investigation.

Keep in mind that, regardless of the sales or expense category, negative variances are undesirable while positive ones are generally welcome. Note also that calculating such variances differs for sales and expenses. For sales dollars, the calculation is this: actual-less-budget. The percentage is calculated by dividing the result of actual-less-budget by the budgeted sales dollars. For expense categories, the calculation is this: budget-less-actual. The percentage is calculated by dividing the result of budget-less-actual by the budgeted expense dollars.

Consider the variance report presented in Figure 10.10. While beverage sales are up, food sales are 4.8 percent below budget. Are sales being recorded? Another question: Why is the percentage of beverage sales higher than expected? The related issue is food and beverage expenses. If beverage sales are above the budgeted amount, we expect expenses also to be higher than budgeted. However, the variance report illustrates another cause for concern. Although beverage sales are 6.3 percent higher than budgeted, beverage expenses are 10.7 percent higher than budgeted! Similarly, food sales are down by 4.3 percent but food cost is only 1.4 percent lower than the budgeted amount. These findings raise concerns about internal control and production management and point managers charged with correcting problems in the right direction.

This same variance analysis should then be performed for all direct operating expenses.

With food sales coming in lower than desired, we expect that salaries and wages should also be below budget. After all, if there are fewer customers, the operator should use fewer foodservers and could possibly operate with fewer people in the kitchen. The example provided, however, shows that the opposite is true; labor expenses are 8.3 percent higher than expected. (Again, note the negative numbers in the variance columns indicating unsatisfactory financial performance.) It is curious that employee benefits are below budget.

Further analysis of the variance report indicates several other operational issues that deserve immediate attention. As with labor, direct operating expenses should be lower than budgeted since sales are down. Instead, they are 13.5 percent above budget. The negative variance in repairs and maintenance may be explained by problems with a dish machine that required massive repairs this period—or it could indicate that expenses are being charged to the foodservice operation that are not related to the business. (Remember our example of the

Variance Report
BBQ Pit Grill and Tavern
Month 1, 20XX

	Actual—YTD		Budget—YTD		Variance	
	Amounts	Percentages	Amounts	Percentages	Amounts	Percentages
Sales						
Food	$241,564	76.0%	$253,773	78.0%	($12,209)	−4.8%
Beverage	$76,099	24.0%	$71,577	22.0%	$4,522	6.3%
Total Sales	$317,663	100.00%	$325,350	100.0%	($7,687)	−2.4%
Cost of Sales						
Food	$88,011	36.4%	$86,790	34.2%	($1,221)	−1.4%
Beverage	$23,681	31.1%	$21,400	29.9%	($2,281)	−10.7%
Total Cost of Sales	$111,692	35.2%	$108,190	33.3%	($3,502)	−3.2%
Gross Profit						
Food	$153,553	63.6%	$166,983	65.8%	($13,430)	−8.0%
Beverage	$52,418	68.9%	$50,177	70.1%	$2,241	4.5%
Total Gross Profit	$205,971	64.8%	$217,160	66.7%	($11,189)	−5.2%
Operating Expenses						
Salaries and Wages	$105,685	33.3%	$97,605	30.0%	($8,080)	−8.3%
Employee Benefits	$7,453	2.3%	$9,110	2.8%	$1,657	18.2%
Direct Operating Expenses	$21,055	6.6%	$18,545	5.7%	($2,510)	−13.5%
Music and Entertainment	$2,400	0.8%	$1,952	0.6%	($448)	−23.0%
Marketing	$7,500	2.4%	$6,500	2.0%	($1,000)	−15.4%
Utility Services	$9,444	3.0%	$9,435	2.9%	($9)	−0.1%
Occupancy Costs	$17,890	5.6%	$17,894	5.5%	$4	0.0%
Repairs and Maintenance	$8,597	2.7%	$4,810	1.5%	($3,787)	−78.7%
Depreciation	$5,856	1.8%	$5,856	1.8%	$0	0.0%
General and Administrative Expenses	$18,971	6.0%	$15,617	4.8%	($3,354)	−21.5%
Other Expense/(Income)	$2,018	0.6%	$325	0.1%	($1,693)	−520.9%
Total Operating Expenses	$206,869	65.1%	$187,649	57.7%	($19,220)	−10.2%
Operating Income	−$898	−0.3%	$29,511.00	9.1%	($30,409)	−103.0%
Interest	$2,280	0.7%	$2,280.00	0.7%	$0	0.0%
Income before Income Taxes	−$3,178	−1.0%	$27,231.00	8.4%	($30,409)	−111.7%

Figure 10.10 Variance report.

manager who could have had his roof replaced at the foodservice operation's owner's expense in Chapter 8.)

The other red flag that the variance report raises for management is the negative variance for other expenses. As was noted earlier, very few items should go into this category. Thus, either a mistake was made when compiling the data or items are being charged to the operation that may not be related to it. (Consider the unethical manager who sends his wife flowers and then charges them to the restaurant, filing the expense under "other expense.")

Finally, income is the biggest issue in this example. While total sales are down only 2.4 percent, income before income taxes is down 111.7 percent. Obviously, this operation has some serious problems. With these negative variances, management must take serious corrective action or the business will soon fail. Of course, in such a situation, the owners would likely replace one or all members of the management team (typically starting with the general manager or foodservice director).

Operating Ratio Analysis

In addition to using variance analysis, foodservice managers also may analyze a variety of financial ratios in order to determine what is going well and what needs closer attention. One of the most basic of these is **average check**, which is calculated as:

$$\frac{\text{Sales}}{\text{Number of customers}} = \text{Average check}$$

The average check may indicate that customers are not ordering as many appetizers or desserts as expected or are ordering appetizers in place of entrees. Corrective action may include having foodservers promote appetizers and desserts or launching a drink special.

The next two ratios also pertain to sales. The first, **seat turnover**, indicates how many times you are turning the dining room—in other words, how many guests per daypart use a given seat. Low seat turnover may suggest that more marketing is needed while high turnover may warrant installing new seating areas such as outdoor dining. (Note that the desired seat turnover depends on the segment and unique characteristics of a foodservice operation.) Seat turnover is calculated for a given daypart as:

$$\frac{\text{Number of customers}}{\text{Number of seats}} = \text{Seat turnover}$$

The related ratio is **sales per seat**. Here, the foodservice operator can assess whether sales for the period, whether a week or a month, are sufficient for profitable operation. In fine dining settings, the seat turnover may be low but the sales per seat should be strong. Monitoring seat turnover and sales per seat can also provide extremely useful information to onsite foodservice operators. The ratio is calculated as:

$$\frac{\text{Sales for the period}}{\text{Seats}} = \text{Sales per seat}$$

The next set of ratios focus on expenses. The first two, **food cost** and **beverage cost**, were introduced earlier but deserve mention again. Food cost is calculated as

$$\frac{\text{Cost of food sold}}{\text{Food sales}} = \text{Food cost percentage}$$

Beverage cost is calculated as:

$$\frac{\text{Cost of beverages sold}}{\text{Beverage sales}} = \text{Beverage cost percentage}$$

An associated ratio is the **cost of goods sold**. Here we look at food and beverage expenses as a function of total sales. The cost of goods sold is calculated as:

$$\frac{\text{Cost of food and beverages sold}}{\text{Total sales}} = \text{Cost of goods sold}$$

Along with these three ratios, most operators closely monitor labor expenses. An easy measure is the **labor cost** percentage, which includes the cost of salaries, wages, *and* employee benefits, and is calculated as:

$$\frac{\text{Total cost of labor}}{\text{Total sales}} = \text{Labor cost}$$

The last ratio we introduce here, which like food cost and beverage cost is reported as a percentage, is the **prime cost**. Prime costs include food and beverage sales and total sales. This is a useful ratio for quickly assessing how well the major cost categories in any foodservice operation are being managed. It is calculated as:

$$\frac{\text{Cost of food, beverage, and total labor}}{\text{Total sales}} = \text{Prime cost}$$

A caveat must be offered in concluding our discussion of ratio analysis. That is, while ratios are useful for analysis and as barometers of a foodservice operation's success, other measures are more important. As every seasoned foodservice manager understands, profit in terms of cash at the end of the period is the best measure of the operation's performance, which explains the old adage: *You can't take percentages to the bank.* This chapter's Case in Point demonstrates this vividly.

Balance Sheet Analysis

While the previous section used data from the income statement and statement of cash flows to calculate operating ratios, we now examine information provided on the balance sheet to aid in analyzing a foodservice operation's overall financial health. The ratios discussed here can be grouped in common ratio categories that include liquidity, solvency, asset management, and profitability.

Liquidity ratios are generally used to assess a foodservice operation's ability to meet its short-term financial obligations. The most common of these is the **current ratio**, which is calculated as:

$$\frac{\text{Current assets}}{\text{Current liabilities}} = \text{Current ratio}$$

Suppose that the current ratio for a given midscale restaurant is 1.5. This means that for every $1 the restaurant has in current liabilities, it has $1.50 in current assets. Is this good? The answer depends on your perspective. To creditors, higher is better because a higher current ratio means that the operation is in a better position to pay off its debts. Owners usually prefer a low current ratio, however, because they prefer investments in noncurrent assets over investments in current assets, as noncurrent assets are usually more productive.

A very high current ratio may also indicate that accounts receivable are too high, possibly owing to slow collections (which could be the case for a caterer). Thus, a high current ratio will likely lead an operator to assess the **accounts receivable turnover**. The first step in such an analysis is to calculate the average accounts receivable for the year. The accounts receivable turnover is then calculated as:

$$\frac{\text{Total revenue}}{\text{Average accounts receivable}} = \text{Accounts receivable turnover}$$

Obviously, a high accounts receivable turnover is more desirable because it indicates prompt payment of outstanding invoices.

The last liquidity ratio we consider is the **acid-test ratio**, which is a more stringent test of liquidity than the current ratio because it accounts for cash and other assets that can be quickly converted to cash. In this case, creditors again prefer a high ratio while owners prefer a low one. The acid-test ratio is calculated as:

$$\frac{\text{Cash, marketable securities, notes, and accounts receivable}}{\text{Current liabilities}} = \text{Acid-test ratio}$$

The next ratio category to consider pertains to solvency. Solvency ratios measure the extent of debt financing that a foodservice operation has assumed and serve as partial indicators of the operation's ability to meet these long-term obligations. The most basic of these is simply called the **solvency ratio**, which is calculated as:

$$\frac{\text{Total assets}}{\text{Total liabilities}} = \text{Solvency ratio}$$

Any foodservice operator wants her assets to exceed her liabilities. However, owners often prefer to use debt to finance assets to maximize their return on investments. Creditors prefer a thicker cushion in the operation's financial position and therefore prefer a higher solvency ratio.

The other measure of solvency, and one that is commonly calculated, is the **debt-equity ratio**. As the name implies, this ratio compares an operation's debt to its net worth (owners' equity), and is calculated as:

$$\frac{\text{Total liabilities}}{\text{Total owners' equity}} = \text{Debt} - \text{Equity ratio}$$

The various interested parties have the same perspective on the debt-equity ratio is they do on the solvency ratio.

Next, we consider two asset management ratios. The first is **fixed asset turnover**. This ratio measures a foodservice operation's ability to generate sales from fixed-asset investments—namely, the foodservice operation itself along with the furniture, fixtures, and equipment it contains. A high rate of turnover, which is desired by all concerned, indicates that the foodservice operation is using its fixed assets effectively to generate sales. It is calculated as:

$$\frac{\text{Total revenue}}{\text{Average fixed assets}} = \text{Fixed asset turnover}$$

A related measure is the **asset turnover ratio**. It is calculated as:

$$\frac{\text{Total revenue}}{\text{Average total assets}} = \text{Asset turnover ratio}$$

This ratio measures how efficiently assets are being used. Again, all parties prefer a high asset turnover ratio.

The ratio category that attracts the most attention and is considered the capstone of financial ratios comprises profitability ratios. These ratios integrate all aspects of a foodservice operation, with some drawing only from the balance sheet and others drawing also from the income statement and statement of cash flows. We consider three here that offer the greatest utility when applied to a broad range of foodservice operations.

Profit margin is a key ratio because it paints a very clear picture of management's ability to generate sales, control expenses, and produce a profit. It is calculated as:

$$\frac{\text{Net income}}{\text{Total revenue}} = \text{Profit margin}$$

An arguably better profitability ratio is the **operating efficiency ratio**. It is considered a better indicator of management performance because it excludes those uncontrollable expenses. (We define controllable expenses in the next section.) It is calculated as:

$$\frac{\text{Income before fixed changes}}{\text{Total revenue}} = \text{Operating efficiency ratio}$$

The final profitability ratio we address is **return on assets (ROA)**, which is an indicator of a foodservice operation's profitability relative to its total assets. This measure indicates how efficiently management is using its assets to generate earnings. The ROA figure also gives investors an idea of how effectively the foodservice operation is converting the money it has to invest into net income. The higher the ROA, the better, because a high ROA indicates that a restaurant or onsite foodservice operation is earning more money based on less investment. The ROA calculation draws on two ratios that we have already discussed: profit margin and asset turnover. It is calculated as:

$$\text{Profit margin} \times \text{Asset turnover} = \text{ROA}$$

■□ COST CONCEPTS
□■

To interpret financial statements and the associated ratios accurately, we must understand the types of expenses that foodservice managers must manage. For example, we mentioned earlier in the discussion of the variance report that if food sales are below expectations, the food costs should be proportionately lower. Why is that? The following discussion of cost concepts should enhance your understanding of the larger issue of financial management.

Fixed versus Variable Costs

It is possible to consider the various expenses by viewing them in terms of how they change based on business volume. For example, **fixed costs** such as monthly rent or management salaries do not change whether a foodservice operation is very busy or very slow; the amount paid is the same. Fortunately for the foodservice industry, there are relatively few fixed costs (compared with, say, the fixed costs involving in operating a hotel). Conversely, **variable costs** change in direct proportion to sales. Referring back to our earlier discussion of food cost, for example, we can see that the cost of selling 10 steaks is exactly 10 percent of selling 100 steaks. Thus, each item sold has an associated cost that varies directly with the volume of sales.

It is easy to understand that property insurance is fixed and beverage expenses are variable. Some costs are, however, partly fixed and partly variable, and are commonly referred to as **semi-fixed** or **semivariable**. For example, consider a midscale restaurant. When the restaurant opens for dinner, it needs to have a minimum number of foodservers. Whether 2 people come to dine in the first hour or 25 people show up, you need to have the employees ready. Then, more servers are scheduled to arrive later corresponding to the forecasted increase in guests. At the end of the daypart, servers may be sent home or asked to stay longer, depending on how busy the restaurant is. Thus, the associated wages paid to the servers are semivariable.

Two other examples help to clarify this unique cost category. The first is shown on the income statement as "repairs and maintenance." Some of the associated expenses are fixed. For example, routine monthly maintenance is performed on the dishwasher; this cost doesn't change. If, however, owing to a huge increase in business the dishwasher breaks, it must be repaired immediately, and this is not a fixed expense. So, again, this is considered semifixed.

Consider, by analogy, a cell phone contract. Many contracts offer a fixed number of calling minutes for a fixed price. However, if the user uses more minutes than those specified, he pays an incremental amount more for every minute used. Thus, this personal expense is partly fixed and partly variable.

Controllable Costs

In our earlier discussion of operating efficiency ratio, we mentioned fixed costs. We removed these from the equation because management cannot directly change them. For example, a restaurant manager cannot change the amount he pays for rent; this is typically arranged by the owner. However, other expenses are considered **controllable costs**. That is, management can directly control them. For example, a chef or kitchen manager specifies the cut of meat needed for a certain menu item and then finds a vendor who offers it at the best price. She then controls the receiving and storing processes to ensure the item is not lost, stolen, or damaged. Finally, she takes the necessary precautions to minimize waste during the preparation of the meat. Similarly, the cafe manager who writes the employee schedule for the week controls who works and when.

This notion of controllable costs is also important insofar as owners and executive-level managers must understand that, while a foodservice manager manages all controllable expenses, operating losses might stem from cost categories that he cannot control. It is for this reason that some income statements prepared at the unit level have a line for profit before uncontrollable expenses. Such a calculation is sometimes the best indicator of a manager's skills.

Overhead

A prime example of an uncontrollable cost is **overhead**. To consider an apt example of an overhead cost, let's look at an onsite operation that is operated by a managed services company. Supporting the unit-level management team is a corporate office that may include human resource professionals, marketing directors, and even a corporate chef. These positions do not directly generate revenue, but they provide services to the unit locations. Thus, the costs of operating the corporate office, including rent, salaries, insurance, and so on, must be allocated to the various units. This overhead cannot be controlled by the unit-level manager yet is a very real expense.

So how is overhead allocated? Let's assume that a managed services company provides food-service management to 100 retirement communities. One approach would be to calculate the total overhead required to sustain the company's administration and allocate 1 percent of the total expense to each unit. However, it is unrealistic to expect a small retirement community to be able to absorb such an expense. Thus, overhead allocation calculations are often made based on unit-level revenues. The rationale for this is that a larger retirement community would require more corporate support than a smaller one would. While this might not be proportionate to sales levels, it nevertheless provides an objective calculation.

▪▫ BUDGETING

The final piece in the financial management puzzle returns us, in some ways, back to the beginning. We have in previous chapters discussed menu planning, market identification, and forecasting. All of these concepts contribute to the formulation of a budget. A budget, in essence, is a financial plan for an operating period, a plan that integrates all aspects of a foodservice operation. It is a roadmap that includes expectations, except that this map is stated in dollars. A more formal definition of budgeting is:

> An organized plan of operation for a specified period of time that forecasts sales activity and corresponding income, determines and includes all itemized expenses, and concludes with an estimate of an overall financial position (profit or loss) at the end of the pre-determined period with the specificity dictated by the type of foodservice operation.

There are many advantages to crafting a budget. A budget serves as a goal with quantified objectives. It serves as a benchmark of operating performance. It assigns responsibility appropriately. And it can help an operation cope with foreseeable adverse situations.

Although calculating a budget is absolutely necessary in every foodservice operation, doing so has some disadvantages. First, creating a budget, especially for a new restaurant or onsite foodservice operation, requires a considerable investment in time. Next, it is based on forecasts, which may not be accurate. In a chain or managed-services setting, a budget is effective only if it is supported by the overarching organization. Similarly, a budget that is created in a corporate headquarters and simply given to a particular unit without consideration of the operation's particular situation, market, or location may be wildly inaccurate. Finally, budgeting requires full disclosure about all areas of an operation (this relates to our earlier discussion of "other expenses").

There are many types of budgets. For our purposes, we will address two: the operations budget and the capital budget.

Operations Budget

The **operations budget**, sometimes referred to as the revenue and expense budget, is the most common in foodservice management. The time frame is typically a year (calendar or fiscal), and is formatted using the sales and cost categories, as shown earlier in Figure 10.6. It may reflect a monthly breakdown (which is important when business fluctuates from month to month). Finally, it includes percentages (again as shown in Figure 10.6).

There are four major elements in the budget preparation process, and each involves several requirements. The first element is the organization's financial objectives. Perhaps surprisingly, not all financial objectives reduce to profit maximization. Consider, for example, a healthcare setting in which the overarching goal is patient, employee, and guest satisfaction and the foodservice operation is considered a support center rather than a profit center. Here, the budget is most likely written with the objective of revenue meeting rather than exceeding expenses (this chapter's industry exemplar illustrates just such an operation). Conversely, a cafe in a large corporate headquarters or an outsourced restaurant in a hotel may have a clear, overarching goal of maximizing the bottom line.

The other elements in creating an operations budget align directly with the key budget categories, which are revenue, expenses, and net income. These areas can be approached in two ways. The most traditional is **incremental budgeting**. Here, managers use historical information and make incremental changes to reflect differences that the upcoming year might bring. Such differences might reflect competition or a changing economy. The other approach is called **zero-based budgeting**. Here, a manager does not rely on historical data at all but forecasts, calculates, and justifies every revenue and expense item. The advantage to this approach is that it drives managers to rethink all aspects of a foodservice operation and challenge previous modes of operation. It also serves to identify and eliminate wasteful or obsolete practices. However, zero-based budgeting can be very time consuming and its accuracy is based wholly on a manager's expertise and knowledge of her operation. It also ignores trends that would be readily evident by looking at multiple years of operating statistics.

Suppose the incremental approach is used. The manager has sales data for the past five years. He can then use any of the forecasting methods that we presented in Chapter 8 to calculate the expected sales for the year. (The sophistication of forecast methods used would depend on the type and size of foodservice operation and the manager's expertise in applying forecasting models.) Expenses, then, can be forecasted or calculated as a percentage of sales, again using data from earlier periods.

The final element is net profit. If the foodservice owner has mandated a specific target or, in the case of a nonprofit, has simply matched revenue with expenses, then this number must be used and sales and expenses adjusted accordingly. However, a budget must be a *realistic* plan. Thus, manipulating sales and expenses with no rationale other than simply producing a specific profit percentage is a waste of time.

Capital Budget

While certain expenses are built into an operations budget, such as pots and pans, china, and utensils, there are other items that affect an operation for a period that extends well beyond the operations budget's time frame. For example, consider a foodservice operation that is contemplating adding a variety of pizzas to its menu. When pizzas were offered as dinner specials, the sales were overwhelming. However, in terms of cooking enough pizzas to meet the expected demand, the operator will need to purchase a dedicated pizza oven, such as the one shown in Figure 10.11.

Such a huge purchase requires a **capital budget**. Capital expenses are usually rank ordered from those that are critical such as equipment that is mandated by law to those that while not urgent would benefit the foodservice operation. Other considerations include equipment that is in constant need of repair and will therefore cost more over time to repair than to replace.

As foodservice companies have multiple capital expense needs (imagine a large, multichain restaurant company comprising several contrasting concepts), they need to apply formal methods to make capital budgeting decisions. Here we discuss the two most appropriate capital budgeting methods for the foodservice industry: net present value and internal rate of return.

The **net present value (NPV)** is the present value of cash flows minus the investment that makes those cash flows possible. The decision is a simple one: If the net present value is positive, you make the investment. Of course, it also requires estimating those cash flows accurately and using a realistic discount rate.

Determining a realistic discount rate depends on accurately calculating the **time value of money**. The time value of money is the value of money figuring into a given amount of interest earned over a given amount of time. For example, $100 today if invested for one year and earning 7 percent will be worth $107 after one year. Thus, $100 today is the same as $107 paid exactly one year from now. This applies to our net present value calculation because we have to know the value today of sales that take place in the future.

Photo courtesy of the author.

Figure 10.11   An example of a conveyor pizza oven.

Year	Cash Flow	Present Value Factor (7%)	Present Value of Cash Flow
0	($50,000)	1.0000	($50,000)
1	$8,000	0.9346	$7,477
2	$9,200	0.8734	$8,035
3	$10,000	0.8163	$8,163
4	$12,000	0.7629	$9,155
5	$14,500	0.7130	$10,339

Net Present Value: $1,922

Internal Rate of Return: 15%

Figure 10.12 NPV and IRR example—do we purchase the pizza oven?

Using our pizza-oven example, let's assume that the oven costs $50,000 and has a useful life of five years. Our comprehensive forecasting calculations suggest that profit from pizza sales are as listed in Figure 10.12.

The present value can easily be calculated with a financial calculator, but we have included the present value discount factors to fully illustrate the resulting calculations. As we see, the NPV is positive, which indicates that the investment should be made. Again, however, the decision is based entirely on the sales forecasts and discount factor used.

The other capital budgeting approach, which also considers cash flow and the time value of money, is the **internal rate of return (IRR)** model. The IRR on an investment or project is the annualized effective compounded return rate or discount rate that makes the NPV of all cash flows (both positive and negative) from a particular investment equal to zero. A capital investment made by a foodservice operation is considered acceptable if its IRR is greater than an established minimum acceptable rate of return or cost of capital, which is called a **hurdle rate**. The formula is:

$$0 = \frac{CF_1}{(1 + r)} + \frac{CF_2}{(1 + r)^2} + \frac{CF_n}{(1 + r)^n} - PC$$

where:

CF = Cash flow

r = Actual internal rate of return

PC = Project cost

Returning to our pizza oven example, let's assume the parent company will support capital expenditures that are greater than 10 percent. Again, using the five years of cash flows shown in Figure 10.12, we can calculate the actual rate of return, which is 15 percent (this calculation is found much more quickly using a financial calculator or the IRR function in Excel®).

While seemingly complex at first glance, capital budgeting models simplify the capital budgeting process immensely. When used in concert with carefully prepared operating budgets, they also facilitate sound financial management. The result? Profitable, successful foodservice operations.

MANAGERIAL IMPLICATIONS

Financial management lies at the core of any foodservice operation's success. This includes understanding how sales generators as well as the mix of food and beverages contribute to the bottom line. Similarly, it is useful to understand how the foodservice industry is affected by changes in consumer behavior and the global economy.

Driving sales and controlling expenses is more easily achieved with consistent accounting practices, including the application of a uniform system of accounts that facilitates the proper categorization of all expenses into the correct categories and at the correct cost. In addition, creating and monitoring financial statements can aid management immensely and can serve as a compass to direct management's attention to problem areas. This requires a thorough understanding of each component. Furthermore, a strong foodservice manager must be able to analyze financial statements. To produce an income statement, the most important approach is variance analysis. Other analytic techniques, regardless of the financial statement, are also important to understand and apply. Of course, this requires a comprehensive understanding of how costs function.

The final aspect of financial management is budgeting. The budget serves as a plan for the following year and, while creating one consumes considerable time, it provides a goal and a benchmark with which to measure performance. The most common budget used in foodservice management is the operations budget, which integrates the organization's financial objectives and a forecast of sales, expenses, and net profit.

A capital budget is used when considering the purchase of items that affect the foodservice operation beyond a one-year horizon. Whether or not it makes sense to use the expenses expressed in a capital budget depends on net present value and internal rate of return, both of which require an understanding of the time value of money.

INDUSTRY EXEMPLAR

Pullman Regional Hospital

The small college town seems like an unlikely place to find a leading hospital, one that is ranked number one in overall patient satisfaction in the state of Washington (HCAHPS 2008-2009), one that has a CEO awarded "Outstanding Healthcare Executive—Non-Metro Region" by *Seattle Business* magazine (2009), one ranked number 17 in the "100 best places to work in healthcare" by *Modern Healthcare* magazine (2008), and one that was named one of the top 25 "Most Wired Small & Rural Area Hospitals" (*Hospitals & Health Networks* magazine) for three consecutive years. Yet here in the heart of the Palouse, a vast geographic area spanning northern Idaho and southeastern Washington, Pullman Regional overlooks the campus of Washington State University, and provides healthcare services to the Palouse community of more than 30,000 students and residents.

The hospital provides an array of medical treatment and preventive services, along with a medical staff of more than 60 physicians representing primary care to specialty medicine. Services and features of the hospital include:

- 24-hour emergency, intensive, and urgent care
- Full-time staff of board-certified emergency physicians
- Fully digital imaging center

- Sleep center and cardiac rehabilitation clinic

- Occupational, speech, and physical therapy

- BirthPlace with labor, delivery, recovery, and postpartum birthing suites

- State-of-the-art surgical suites and same-day surgical center

Pullman Regional Hospital also has a reputation for sound fiscal management. Since its opening in 2004, it has been profitable despite a challenging economy and ever-increasing reductions in insurance reimbursement rates. The fiscal responsibility is also seen in the hospital's foodservice operation.

One may think that a restaurant-style menu, which allows patients to order anything appropriate to their medical condition from the menu from 7 A.M. until 7 P.M., would create financial challenges. One might also see the prices in the Red Sage Cafe, which are below those found in surrounding restaurants, and assume they might result in financial losses. However, thanks to strong leadership both in administration and in the foodservice operation, this is not the case. While the foodservice department is not viewed as a profit center, the hospital is committed to providing affordable, quality food to patients, guests, and employees, so the foodservice operation plays an essential role in overall satisfaction.

Photo courtesy of Pullman Regional Hospital.

KEY TERMS

■■□ Case in Point ■■■

You Can't Take Percentages to the Bank

Carl had worked hard in his several years of food-service management. He lacked a college degree, but he had prevailed in the competitive industry by using common sense and an appreciation of how people, namely one's employees, can make the difference between success and failure. He also took the time to read industry trade magazines.

So, when he got the call from Mutual Insurance's corporate headquarters to run its sizable cafe, he knew he was ready. The first few days on the job were spent getting to know the employees, the facility, and the customers. He was excited and confident that he was in the right position at the right time. Following this brief orientation, he was scheduled for a meeting that would set the parameters of his mission.

When he met with his new boss, the vice president of human resources, he immediately noted that the tone was very different from the upbeat, cheerful attitude that Carl had encountered during his interviews. Today, Candace Sherman was all business. Candace started by explaining to Carl that his predecessor was asked to leave Mutual Insurance because of the losses the cafe had incurred. The food was excellent, the foodservice staff was relatively happy, and the customers were generally pleased with the food, but the man Carl had replaced had not managed the costs well. Candace added, "Your predecessor was a very nice person, but for the six months he worked here he ignored my requests for a financial report. He kept telling me that he had all the numbers in his head and that the operation was profitable so there was no need for concern. He said that food cost and labor cost were each under 40 percent, so he knew he was profitable. When we were audited last month, we learned that he was losing about $10,000 a month. This is why he was fired. We can't afford to lose money anymore. That is why we hired you, owing to your many years in the business."

Carl wasn't sure what to say. On the one hand, it sounded like he was receiving a compliment, but on the other it sounded like a warning. Until today, he had no idea what had happened to the previous manager.

After an unpleasantly long silence, Candace leaned forward over her desk and looked Carl straight in the eye.

"By Friday, I expect a comprehensive budget for the food-service operation. I will hold you to the budget, and while I don't expect the cafe to make a ton of money, I expect the realistic profit shown on your budget to be achieved."

With that, the meeting was over. Carl went back to his small office and found that the drawers were empty. There were no financial records of any kind. There wasn't even a calculator. It was then that Carl began to panic. He had never created a budget, and while he knew that controlling expenses was important, he'd never been asked to consider the financial side of the business.

If you worked for Carl, how would you help him?

REVIEW AND DISCUSSION QUESTIONS

1. In a full-service restaurant, why is it typically preferable to have strong beverage sales relative to food sales?

2. Explain the business entity principle. Provide an example other than the one in the chapter that illustrates how this principle might be violated, either intentionally or unintentionally.

3. How might a hospital foodservice income statement differ from that of a fine dining restaurant?

4. Assume you have an asset that should be depreciated over six years and it is appropriate to use the straight-line method. The cost of the item is $4,662. What is the annual depreciation amount?

5. Provide an example of an asset, a liability, and shareholders' equity that you might find on a foodservice operation's balance sheet.

6. Why is the statement of cash flow's direct method more difficult to use than the indirect method?

7. On the cafe's monthly variance report, you notice that budgeted sales are $100,000 but actual sales totaled $110,000. Would you expect the actual cost of food to be higher than the budgeted amount? If so, what percentage increase (negative variance) is acceptable?

8. As a foodservice manager, would you prefer increased sales per seat or increased seat turnover?

9. Is a high current ratio a good thing? How about a high asset turnover ratio—is that good or bad?

10. Find a foodservice company's annual report either online or at the library. Using the balance sheet, calculate three of the ratios described in the chapter.

11. Describe a situation in which marketing expenses are fixed and another in which they are semifixed.

12. Is overhead a controllable expense? Explain your answer fully.

13. In this chapter's Case in Point, should Carl use an incremental approach or zero-based budgeting to create the budget for Candace?

14. Using the IRR example in the chapter, assume the hurdle rate in 18 percent. Should you make the purchase?

15. Your front-of-the-house manager wants to redesign the dining area of the cafe, including new furniture, lighting, and artwork. The project cost is $500,000. He has forecasted that the changes will produce $135,000 of increased profit in each of the subsequent 5 years (the time over which the equipment will be depreciated). Taking your advice, he is using a discount factor of 7 percent. You have also told him that the hurdle rate in calculating the IRR is 10 percent. Calculate both the NPV and IRR. Should you go ahead with the project?

ENDNOTES

1. National Restaurant Association, & Deloitte LLP. *Restaurant Industry Operations Report—2010*. Washington, DC: National Restaurant Association, 2010.

2. Please see wn.com/ABC_News,_robotic_restaurant,_Nuremberg_Germany.

3. For more information, see National Restaurant Association. *Uniform System of Accounts for Restaurants*. Washington, DC: National Restaurant Association, 1996.

CUSTOMER SERVICE

LEARNING OBJECTIVES:

After becoming familiar with this chapter, you should be able to:

1. Identify several examples of customer service philosophy and explain what they mean to a foodservice organization.

2. Identify factors that should be measured to identify service problems and successes.

3. Review quality control and quality maintenance issues and understand how to set standards of quality performance.

4. Identify service failures and apply service recovery techniques.

"The customer is always right."

"The customer may not always be right, but he is always the customer."

"You only have one chance to DO IT RIGHT."

"We go the extra mile."

"The customer is number one."

"Treat others as you would like to be treated."

"Go out there and knock their socks off."

"Perception is reality."

Listed here are but a few of the hundreds of customer service slogans that are routinely drilled into foodservice workers. They impart commonsense principles that serve us well in our interactions with others. In the foodservice industry, however, they take on added significance because they may well affect the bottom line. It would seem that well-trained foodservice workers would always take them to heart and apply them in their daily tasks. There is only one small problem—evidence indicates that many people do not take them seriously. Everyone can tell horror stories of their worst customer service experiences, from being ignored by a service person to being spoken to brusquely or insultingly. We are all experts in what makes for good customer service, particularly when we need it and do not get it.

The foodservice industry has one additional problem in this area: Everyone eats. Thus, every customer, patron, resident, patient, or client knows two things: She knows food and she knows how she expects to be treated. Of course, the server also feels that he knows food because he is in the foodservice business, so he thinks that he knows customer needs because he is a professional. Unfortunately, all too often the customer's service expectations are not matched by the server's performance, resulting in a very unhappy customer and a frustrated server.

■■□ STYLE AND PHILOSOPHY
□■

Somewhere in the past there seems to have been a perfect world. People commonly complain that, "when they were young," people knew how to treat customers. Somehow this wonderful era in customer service seems always to have existed at least a generation back in time. However mythical this rosy past might be, it is undeniable that heavy workloads and pressure to be efficient above all else can produce a workforce that does not value the needs of customers. In many industries, the department called "customer service" was in place to stifle complaints and fight off angry customers. This lack of customer focus began to attract scholarly and managerial attention two or three decades ago, resulting in many "gurus" of customer service who developed a series of ideas and philosophies to help everyone "relearn" how to treat customers. In 1991, for example, Anderson and Zemke wrote that, for some time, the "customer service industry" seemed to prefer people who woke up every day saying: "I'm going to go to work and tick off the first 217 people I see." They note that this was not a very positive image and that, beginning in the mid-1980s, businesses began to note that companies that emphasized service were seeing better results.[1] Researchers began to document and confirm a causal relationship between improved customer service and business success. The race was on for all organizations to learn to develop a **customer service mentality**.

There really are not multiple styles and philosophies of customer service. There is only one, but there are many excellent explanations to help businesses "get it right." As Anderson and Zemke point out. ". . . what it really comes down to is: You. What you do is important. What you do is work—hard work: Answering questions . . . solving problems . . . untangling corporate logjams . . . fixing what's broken and finding what's lost . . . soothing the irate and reassuring the timid . . ." This is a perfect description of any foodservice operation:

- The work is important.

- The work is hard.

- Thousands of questions are answered, from "What's for dinner?" to "What's in the Lobster Salad?" or "Where is my waiter?"

- Solve problems—we do that thousands of times a day. How do we get the beef stew to taste like momma used to make, when everyone's momma made it differently?

- Corporate logjams? You don't have to run a big corporation to subject your customers to inconvenience. You can run a 100-bed hospital where lunch isn't delivered on time because the elevators are jammed between 11:30 A.M. and 1 P.M. Or a little 25-table restaurant with a "no substitutions" sign.

- Fix what's broken. What does a restaurant do when the credit card machine doesn't work?

- Soothe the irate and reassure the timid. The steak is overdone—no excuses, fix it immediately. The timid? Yes, everyone fears the customer whose steak is overdone and never complains—he just never comes back and tells ten of his friends why they shouldn't eat at your restaurant.

Oh yes, the foodservice industry provides the perfect model for all customer service successes and failures. Consider the following true story, in which only the names have been changed.

She never went back . . .

Phyllis stopped in for a quick snack at a nationally franchised QSR. Friendly staff took her order. As she was getting her drink and condiments, she saw a roach on the condiment stand. Phyllis politely whispered this information to one of the employees behind the counter. The employee replied that it had been very busy, went out and removed the roach, and whispered to Phyllis as she returned, "Oh, don't worry, it was dead." Phyllis was a bit discouraged, but had already ordered her meal. When she got her meal, the bread was moldy. She was furious, but after the reaction to the roach, she simply finished her side dish and drink and left. She has never returned to that QSR—or any other outlets in that chain!

As the customer service movement began to catch on decades ago, another apt phrase came into usage. Eric Harvey founded the Walk the Talk® Company in 1977. The company name employs a famous phrase that means that you have to do more than simply "talk a good game"; your actions have to show that you practice what you preach. Since then, the company has produced many publications, seminars, and training materials all dedicated to helping companies develop and maintain organizational practices that are consistent with their company's values and strategic objectives. Now it is obvious that, in Phyllis's case, the strategic objectives of that national chain did not involve showcasing dead roaches or serving moldy bread. The employees did not seem to understand the impact of their attitudes and failure to check for dead roaches and moldy bread. One of the best summaries of the customer service orientation was offered by Harvey. Here is Harvey's "Crash Course on Customer Service: The most important phrases you can say." [2]

- **The 10 most important words:** "I apologize for our mistake. Let me make it right."

- **The 9 most important words:** "Thank you for your business. Please come back again."

- **The 8 most important words:** "I'm not sure, but I will find out."

- **The 7 most important words:** "What else can I do for you?"

- **The 6 most important words:** "What is most convenient for you?"

- **The 5 most important words:** "How may I serve you?"

- **The 4 most important words:** "How did we do?"

- **The 3 most important words:** "Glad you're here."

- **The 2 most important words:** "Thank you."

- **The most important word:** "Yes!"

In the early 1960s, Robert Farrell founded and ran Farrell's Ice Cream Parlor and Restaurant (see Figure 11.1), and it became known for the juicy dill pickles that were served with the

Figure 11.1 The Newest Farrell's location in Mission Viejo, California, along with the menu.

Figure 11.1 (continued)

meals. One time, a customer asked for an extra pickle, and the server told him that it would cost 45 cents. The customer was furious, and wrote to Farrell, complaining. It was obvious that the employee was doing as she was instructed, but this was certainly not the intended consequence of the action. Farrell's instruction to all of his employees after that incident was, "Just give 'em the pickle!"

Inspired by this incident, Farrell gave employees motivational talks, wrote several books, and his website offers a vast array of "pickle training" aids and pickle products as well.[3] The moral of the story is that, when customers need something, we should get it for them because we are here to serve them, not just to "make a buck." If your eye is only on the bottom line and your employees live in fear that they will suffer for every small cost associated with doing the little things for your customers, your business will end up "nickel and dime-ing" the customers—and your business—to death. Farrell advises foodservice operations not to make it hard for customers to enjoy themselves.

Customer Service Experience

Pamela Parseghian wrote about one of her best customer service experiences.[4] She was having a bad week, and went into a busy fast-casual restaurant in New York's Penn Station during rush hour. She saw that the cooks were very busy, but an unusual breakfast item drew her eye and she asked the manager to describe the smoked salmon-wasabi sandwich. He not only explained it to her, he suggested she try it and said, "If you like it you can buy it. If you don't, don't pay for it." She was amazed, tasted it, liked it, and paid for it, but she was even more impressed that this busy manager took the time to explain this item to her and give her individualized attention. She became a loyal customer.

Ask anyone what the gold standard is for customer service, and two companies will usually be mentioned: Disney and Southwest Airlines. This is particularly interesting since both operate in markets that almost make this seem impossible. Disney's resorts, restaurants, hotels, theme parks, and other offerings probably serve more customers than any other entertainment enterprise, and Disney's goal is to make everyone have a "magical time" (see Figure 11.2). Southwest Airlines is part of an industry that has become emblematic of poor customer service and yet it has remained profitable and known for their service as other airlines have slipped into bankruptcy. At the beginning of this chapter, we talked about how difficult it is to make foodservice customers happy because everyone is an expert on food. It is for this reason that Disney and Southwest are such great models for foodservice organizations to study.

The Disney organization has developed many techniques and programs for customer service training. At Disney, every customer interaction is known as a Magic Moment. There is a lot of meaning in that simple phrase. If every employee in every foodservice organization truly understood the meaning of "Magic Moment," there would be no need for this chapter or for any training on the concept of customer service.

The Disney Institute publicized its style in 2001 in a small book called *Be Our Guest: Perfecting the Art of Customer Service*.[5] The only words on the first page? "Always remember, the Magic begins with you." From the company's very beginnings, Walt Disney believed in this philosophy. The company's performance record has consistently been recognized as one of the **benchmarks** of excellence in customer service. It still never ceases to amaze everyone that Walt Disney selected 47 square miles of simmeringly hot and humid Florida scrubland, devoid of any remarkable characteristics except for the heat and humidity, to become "the happiest place in the world, Walt Disney World (WDW)." (See Figure 11.3.) WDW employs 55,000 people and is a city in itself. Yet, even the smallest restaurant can use the simple philosophy that is essential to the Disney experience.

Figure 11.2 Disney's Founder, Walt Disney.

Figure 11.3 Guests dining and Cinderella's royal table.

Guestology is Disney's term for market and customer research—learn who the guests are and understand what they expect when they come to visit. Customers are constantly invited to complete face-to-face surveys in the parks. "Listening posts" are created at specific locations to answer questions, solve problems, and collect information. Comment cards are everywhere, and cast members throughout the parks collect the opinions and observations of guests as part of their jobs.

And Disney measures more than just enjoyment. The company collects information about when people ride which rides, occupancy rates at their resorts, how many people ride the monorails and when—everything is measured and evaluated. Guestology uses another interesting concept. Once they learn who guests are, where they come from, how far they have traveled, and so on, they also learn who guests are NOT. This allows them to develop strategies that help them attract those who are not coming. This is all part of customer service.

Exceeding Expectations

Still other researchers have written about going beyond your good service to exceed the customer's expectations and offered the following five dimensions in quality customer care:[6]

- *Reliability*: Do what you say you are going to do, when you say you are going to do it, and do it right the first time.

- *Responsiveness*: Be absolutely tuned in to the needs of your customers; no one should enter your operation without someone's greeting him and helping him know what to do. Nothing is worse than standing in an establishment for several minutes waiting for something, anything, to happen.

- *Feeling of being valued*: Nothing makes a customer feel valued more than a smile, eye contact, and listening; other imperfections may be overlooked if the customer is made to feel welcome.

- *Empathy*: Everyone has a bad day now and then, and anyone who cares can see this in a person's eyes, hear it in her voice, and see it on her face. **Empathy** can be the most important dimension of quality customer service, and often the most lacking.

- *Competency*: This is really the nuts and bolts of customer service. If you are a coffeehouse, do you have the best coffee? Why else would people pay $3.00 a cup? If you are a bagel shop, do you have the best bagels? People could get their "average" bagels at the supermarket. Why bother to offer less than the best?

At the beginning of this chapter, we discussed the idea that good customer service is good business, regardless of industry or type of foodservice organization. We focus here on an individual who has had a particularly strong influence on the healthcare industry. While he targets all aspects of healthcare—not just foodservice—his impact on quality care and customer service has extended to healthcare and residential care foodservice as well. Quint Studer was originally a hospital administrative officer and CEO who worked in particularly challenging healthcare locations. He assumed control of two hospitals whose patients rated them exceptionally poorly, but by implementing customer service and quality service strategies the patient ratings of these hospitals rose to the top level within several years. Today he is a consultant who works with many hospitals to accomplish similar results. He uses the concept of **hardwiring**—the integration of purpose, worthwhile work, and the ability to make a difference—to explain how to make customer service part of the fabric of an organization in which it has often been thought to be an impossible task.

Employee valuing and goal setting will be discussed in later chapters, but it is worth noting here that Studer's most valuable observation was that the healthcare industry, and consequently healthcare foodservice, was happy with middling or even terrible customer service rankings.[7] There was no sense of urgency—there were only excuses: "We are short staffed; we've had budget cuts; patients are sick so no wonder they don't like the food." There was no sense of being involved in competition. But patients began voting with their feet by choosing other hospitals. Studer observed that such an "excuse-based" mentality can be overcome only with passion and self-motivation. One may associate passion for service with nurses, but it is not at all unusual for healthcare foodservice workers to say that they chose to work at a hospital because they wanted to take care of people. The problem is that the desire to care for people can be lost when people work within a culture of excuses. "I'm going to avoid room 227 today—he is constantly complaining." (Now why would that be?) Studer's approach is based on strengthening the passion and motivation to change the healthcare environment, and it yields principles that apply across the foodservice industry.

One of the first principles Studer espoused was "rounding for results." Rounding means making the rounds of a facility, which in healthcare meant that, as the CEO of the hospital, he physically went to every department on every shift, visiting staff and patients and asking staff what they needed to do their jobs better. In this way he discovered the many obstacles that were keeping patients from having an excellent experience. If the nursing unit was short on "over-the-bed" tables, how could patients eat their meals comfortably? If a tray had to sit in the corner while someone searched for a table, the food was cold and there was a dissatisfied patient.

The concept of rounding applies to every foodservice operation, not just those in healthcare. When the waiter comes back to ask how your meal is, that is step one, but the chef or the manager should stop by as well. Such direct customer contact is invaluable for identifying problems. Obviously, the best rounding technique is not simply to rush past a table and say, "How was the food?" The chef should approach the table, make eye contact, introduce himself, and say, "Good evening. I'm Jamie, the executive chef here at Pandora Grill. May I ask how you are enjoying your meal? Is there anything we could do to make it more enjoyable?" Note that, by asking open-ended questions, Chef Jamie can elicit specific feedback from customers. The same is true in a hospital or anywhere else. It is so important for a foodservice manager to find out what has gone wrong while it can still be fixed.

Finally, consider Fred Lee, who has taken the Disney philosophy and applied it to healthcare as well.[8] In his book, *If Disney Ran Your Hospital*, he describes the most significant themes for teaching patient-focused care:

- *Sense* people's needs before they ask (Example: The foodservice worker notices that, on the morning pancakes are served, everyone always complains that there is not enough syrup—he automatically begins to ask people if one packet is enough).

- *Help* each other out (Example: Tom finished delivery of his patient trays 15 minutes early today, so he went down to the next floor and helped Angela finish delivering hers).

- *Acknowledge* people's feelings (Example: Angela enters a patient's room and the patient is crying—should Angela "get involved" or put the tray down quickly and leave, avoiding any patient contact?).

- *Respect* the dignity and privacy of everyone (Example: Courtesy is not so common today, but Tom carefully knocks and identifies himself before he enters a room since some patients may be using a bed pan, or be involved in treatment).

- *Explain* what's happening (Example: Angela always lets patients on liquid diets know that their doctor has ordered this for a specific reason and that she hopes they will be able to eat solid food soon—Angela will never forget the time a patient told her he thought it was odd that hospitals served only liquids to their patients, not knowing this was because he was having a test the next day).

Many other organizations, such as the Pike Place Fish Market and the above mentioned Southwest Airlines, are known for legendary customer service. These two companies excel at applying employee development policies and programs to enhance their ability to cultivate satisfied and loyal customers.

MEASUREMENT

Our discussion has thus far centered on various approaches to customer service as it applies to foodservice organizations. We have pointed out that if providing good service were natural to everyone, no one would have to be taught how to do it. We all think we know when we experience poor service, and we all think we know what constitutes good service. This raises the question: Is there an objective measurement of good service? As it turns out, yes. Measuring customer satisfaction is very important, and has become a useful tool for foodservice operations.

By far the most sought-after measurement of customer opinion is immediate feedback from customers themselves. Yet how do operators elicit that feedback? Obtaining information that is scientifically accurate and objective is difficult. If she uses improper methods or measures, a restaurant manager can spend a lot of time trying to figure out why her customers are unhappy without learning anything useful.

We have seen that listening is an important aspect of customer service. So, listening to customers should provide useful information, right? It's not that easy. For example, a manager might ask customers about the food, but not about the service . . . and the service may be his problem. Or, he might ask every customer a different question, which means he cannot compare their answers. Managers usually need help to gather such data, and today's managers have many choices. Among these choices, the manager can contract with an outside company to design a survey or develop a computer program or even conduct such a survey.

Research from the Center for Hospitality Research at Cornell University suggests that many disgruntled patrons are saving their complaints for later, making it hard for an operator to correct real or perceived wrongs.[9] The study addresses a real problem for managers: Some guests will immediately confront a manager with a problem, but many will wait until later, maybe by sending a letter. Such letters can be all too easy to ignore because they may be poorly written or the complaint may seem unfixable, but such after-the-fact complaints should be addressed formally. And management must recognize that complaints made in this way were never remedied during the dining experience.

Problem Identification

Most complaints involve situations or products that do not meet guest expectations, so if unhappy guests receive no response to their complaints, no matter when or how they are given, they will most likely not return. On the other hand, identifying problems can be as easy as noticing frowns or sullen silence when a guest is leaving. Servers should also be trained to follow up with a customer if an item is barely touched. Preparing servers to hear the worst is the rule here, so that they will be comfortable listening to whatever a given problem is. Many larger chains or companies monitor Internet sites where customers review restaurants, just to look for issues in their own restaurants.

Traditionally, restaurants and onsite foodservice operators have relied to a considerable extent on comment cards or other such feedback channels. These feedback channels may bring useful criticism or praise directly from the customer, but the information they provide has no systematic basis. When a customer has no pen or is in a hurry or her story is too long to tell, a restaurant never finds out about the lapse in service or quality that motivated her to fill out the card. Some restaurants use "secret shopper" or "mystery shopper" services, by paying auditing companies to send "shoppers" to patronize their facilities unannounced and provide the operators with feedback on quality and customer service satisfaction. The feedback such services provide is, however, delayed and in some cases costly. (We discuss mystery shoppers at length in Chapter 15 regarding their role in maintaining internal control.) Today, fortunately, technology provides many opportunities for customers to provide immediate, live feedback, including the following:[10]

- *Recorded customer phone calls.* Prompted by reminders with phone numbers listed on cash register receipts, pizza boxes, menus, websites or, yes, comment cards, phone calls from customers provide raw feedback about the customer experience that can be played back immediately for crew members. Call recordings can be delivered rapidly to employees via e-mail or downloaded in a digital audio format onto other electronic devices. When listening to such calls it is possible to hear the emotion in a customer's voice, which is an effective motivational tool when played to employees.

■ *Self-administered guest surveys*. There are hardware and software products that support guest surveys. Some operations make small, hand-held devices available at the table, where the survey results can be fed back to employees or management before the customer leaves. Some systems on which such surveys are conducted allow guests to close out their tabs and swipe their own credit cards. These systems also offer promotions and other feedback opportunities, with the added benefit of moving guests out of the restaurant more quickly—a favorite of guests. Such self-survey systems can also provide games and other entertainment for guests as they wait for service. Some operators note that the results of these touch screen, self-done surveys are collected in real time, providing immediate information about trends or training opportunities.

■ *Second-generation Web services*. Recent developments in interactive Internet services make it possible for customers to log on to Web pages to provide live comments to operators. One restaurant noted more than 6,000 customer exchanges in a year.

■ *Online dining reservation websites*. Through these websites it is possible to book reservations online at restaurants and other hospitality venues. Such sites typically apply to a specific city or region but some book reservations nationally and some book group reservations. Many of these sites provide diner feedback tools that can generate hundreds of thousands of responses monthly.

In the onsite foodservice healthcare segment, operators need another kind of scientifically tested feedback to access performance. Hospitalized patients do not like being sick or lying in the hospital for extended periods, and they are often afraid to complain about the food or other service for fear of offending staff. They are also "trapped" in the hospital for three meals a day until they can go home. It should be added that most patients have heard stories about bad hospital food, which lowers their expectations considerably. That is little comfort, however, when those low expectations are met. Hospital foodservice directors and other management staff routinely make rounds to solicit feedback, but patients may be too sick, or in the midst of receiving treatment, or have visitors at the time of rounds, and staff members receive no feedback from those patients at those times. Also, a hospital seeks feedback on all of its services, not only on food, because the hospital's overall performance score is made public for all potential patients to see.

Hospital patients can now ask their doctors to send them a specific hospital based on customer satisfaction scores. It is true that a patient would not elect to have his brain surgery at a mediocre hospital because it had very good food, but a patient might opt for elective treatment at a hospital whose overall satisfaction ratings were higher. In today's competitive hospital environment, hospitals must pursue every possible customer.

Like restaurants, hospitals conduct their own customer satisfaction surveys or contract "patient satisfaction companies" to provide this information. Since a hospital stores patient contact information following discharge, these companies can call or send a survey document to a patient's home to be returned after completion. Such surveys can easily pose 50 or more questions about all aspects of care, with several pertaining to the food and service. Survey companies work on a contract basis and are experts at statistical analysis and survey development.

Surveys are often available in multiple languages, and telephone surveys will have translators available.

Questions relating to foodservice might look something like these hypothetical examples:

- On a scale of 1 to 5, with 5 being the best, how would you rank the foodservice at Hospital Z during your recent stay?

- How would you rank the food service employees who brought you your meals during your recent hospital stay?

    ☐ Excellent

    ☐ Very good

    ☐ Fair

    ☐ Poor

- Was the food you received served at the proper temperature? Yes_____ No_____

- The quality of food I received during my stay was very good.

    ☐ Strongly agree

    ☐ Agree

    ☐ Disagree

    ☐ Strongly disagree

NOTE: These sample questions show several possible question formats.

To make sure the data collected from such a survey are reliable, questionnaires should be distributed only to a scientifically chosen, random sample of discharged patients by an independent third party. Data **reliability** depends on using a survey tool that produces consistent results, which means that if you used it again under the same circumstances, the scores would be the same. In that case, the hospital can feel comfortable basing management decisions on the trends shown by such data. And while reliability is the consistency of the measurement, the **validity** is the strength of the conclusions or inferences; both are critical. Among the many companies that conduct patient satisfaction surveys through contracts with individual hospitals are Press Ganey, PRC, and Gallup. All survey companies use statistical tools, survey development techniques, and analytical tests that are similar to those used in public opinion surveys we hear about on the evening news.

Hospitals also compare themselves with other hospitals, and so there is a considerable body of comparative data available on all of the hospitals surveyed by each company. If a company is contracted to survey the patients of 10,000 hospitals and Hospital B is one of them, then Hospital B will receive its own scores along with the mean scores of the other 9,999 hospitals. They may get their results compared with other hospitals of their same size, or for the previous month, quarter, or year. Some survey companies also provide rankings that indicate whether a given hospital is in the top 10 percent or the bottom 90 percent of all surveyed hospitals.

Each individual department receives a similar score and analysis, so a foodservice unit will have its scores compared with those of other hospital foodservice units. It is very important for a new manager to know what company her hospital uses and what the scores are when she takes responsibility for a foodservice department. Jobs are lost based on these scores so a manager wants to know how customers felt before she took over, and, if scores improve, she knows that some of her efforts have been successful.

Data Management

Suppose that a healthcare foodservice manager receives survey feedback indicating that the hospital's food is often served cold and that patients often are not served what they ordered. Even if the manager has been rounding and has heard this directly, having objective feedback is important. Now she can meet with her managers and develop a detailed plan to "get the food hot." The plan has a clear goal: Food temperature scores will increase by five points at the end of the second quarter. The manager reviews the plan with her boss, who is glad to know that she is on the case. As new survey data come in, she can determine whether the plan is working or needs to be strengthened. In addition, her boss now has objective information from the survey and from her—she is in charge and taking action.

There is an old statistical saying:

What gets measured gets done!

The meaning is clear. It is easy to ignore something that is not right before your eyes, screaming "YOU'RE STILL SERVING COLD FOOD!"

Consider the list of phrases near the beginning of this chapter that expressed customer relations truisms. The last one was "perception is reality." If a customer is served a meal and the soup is cold, even if everything else is warm he will remember that the food was cold. Maybe the baked chicken, vegetable, potato, and coffee were all perfectly hot . . . but the cold soup has altered the customer's perception and has become reality. The food was cold. In the foodservice business, all that matters is customer **perception**. That is why measurement tools need not be extremely specific. They do not need to determine when the food was cold or which foods were cold or how "cold" was defined by the customer. Customer satisfaction measurement tools therefore need to determine only if the customer *believed* the food was cold. It is then up to the manager to figure how to make it hot enough for most people in order to keep patients or customers happy and coming back.

Even without the time and expense involved in conducting surveys, managers, chefs, and dietitians can ask customers: "What can we do to make it better?" That in itself makes most customers feel better and provides managers and their team with good information. The days are gone when managers can write off most complaints by saying, "Oh, some people are just too picky," or, "You just can't please everyone." That attitude will never achieve excellence, and who wants to introduce himself like this: "My name is Charles, and I work at a mediocre restaurant on 5th Street"?

Customer satisfaction measurements tell a manager how his foodservice operation is performing, but measuring performance does little good without accurate, well-organized record keeping and documentation. A manager who has found a method with which to measure the customer's relationship with a foodservice organization must maintain an accurate record of this relationship. Good records identify recurring problems that an operation must address eventually or lose its competitive advantage—and revenue. It is important to keep track of who was involved in an incident or complaint, where and when it happened, and how it happened. When possible, it is also important to determine the cost of the problem, including the occupation of managers' time and other company resources, and develop a plan of action to prevent recurrences.

Before we discuss quality and standards in the next section, we close this one with a caveat about the use of customer feedback. It is very important for managers to remember that a customer's opinion might well identify a problem, but it will not necessarily reveal the cause of the problem. For example, we can imagine a customer reporting that servers were ignoring her, suggesting they were just talking in the kitchen, but upon checking discover that they were actually meeting with the chef to review menu items. The problem was less that they were inattentive to the customer and more that they should have met at a different time. Thus, good management of customer relationships requires careful investigation of customer complaints. Jumping to conclusions does not solve problems.

QUALITY AND STANDARDS

Earlier in the chapter, we discussed Disney's customer service philosophy and its Magic Moments concept. Its catchphrase "the Magic of Service" expresses its guest-centered orientation, in accordance with which it is the job of each cast member to understand the needs, wants, perceptions, and emotions of its guests. As noted, this is what Disney calls guestology, as it ceaselessly collects information on its guests, fine-tuning its offerings while improving performance continually. Adopting such a **service theme** that can be propagated throughout its workforce and drive strategic decision making is essential to every organization, but especially so in foodservice and other hospitality industries. Disney's service theme, "*To create happiness for people of all ages everywhere,*" has given it a distinct competitive advantage, but the same is possible for any small restaurant in any local market that adopts as its service theme anything that induces its staff "to serve great food and make our customers happy." If the three or four employees of such a restaurant were to buy into that philosophy completely, there would never be bad food or bad service.

To accomplish this service theme, Disney established four criteria of action or **service standards** of behavior to empower its employees (cast members) when making decisions (Figure 11.4).

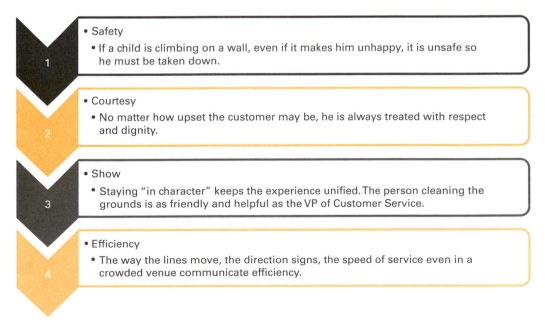

Figure 11.4   Disney service standards.

Source: *Adapted from the Disney Institute.* Be Our Guest: Perfecting the Art of Customer Service. *New York: Disney Editions, 2001.*

It is worth considering how to translate these standards into any foodservice operation:

- *Safety*: Any condition or incident that jeopardizes safety must be corrected immediately. If there is a spill on the floor, for example, it should be wiped up immediately and the wet area marked or segregated. It is not enough simply to loudly warn guests to "Watch out for the spill" just because your restaurant is busy. Each year more than 3 million foodservice employees and over 1 million guests are injured in restaurant slips and falls, costing over $2 billion.[11]

- *Courtesy*: Respond quickly and politely to any customer suggestion or complaint without second-guessing. If a customer says his burger is too rare, it is too rare. It makes no difference that it was cooked to a temperature that usually counts as medium. Replace it without any negative employee comment, glance, or "body language," and compensate the customer in some way for his inconvenience.

- *Show*: Welcome customers conspicuously as soon as they enter an establishment and let them know how much you hope they will enjoy their experience. If "Papa Joe" is the only person in his deli, and he is behind the counter, he should look toward the door and say, "Welcome to Papa Joe's! Come in. Our menu is over the counter. Start thinking about which one of our great sandwiches you'd like!" (With a greeting like this, who could resist eating at Papa Joe's, even if it takes a bit longer?) Remember that at Disney all employees are "cast members" in costume to play the role of entertaining the guest, so a restaurant can drive business by reminding its customers that everyone working there is part of "the show."

- *Efficiency*: Even Papa Joe will benefit from setting up his counter properly with all the supplies he will need within easy reach, displayed at the appropriate temperature, in a clean showcase. He will remove his gloves before handling money, and then put on a clean pair. He will have a separate utensil for every item in the deli case. Papa knows that clean and safe is efficient.

Irwin Press is one of the cofounders of Press Ganey, a survey company used by many healthcare facilities, which we mentioned earlier. Press argues that patient (or customer) satisfaction is the summation of all a person's experiences in a hospital (or restaurant).[12] To improve customer satisfaction, management and staff must change the experience of care or the experience of service. Press gives an excellent rank ordering of a customer's reaction to an experience, shown in Figure 11.5.

Figure 11.5 Rank orders of customer priorities.

Source: Adapted from Press, I. Patient Satisfaction: Defining, Measuring, and Improving the Experience of Care. Chicago: Health Administration Press, 2002.

We see in Figure 11.5 another set of behavioral standards. They should ensure that any hospital that abides by them serves good food delivered by friendly staff members who communicate information about the menu, the diet, and other issues in a caring manner that demonstrates their understanding that the patient is afraid, angry, in pain, and so on.

Again, we present these standards, whether emerging from the broader hospitality industry or from the healthcare foodservice segment, as examples that can be modified to be as specific as any foodservice operation needs them to be:

- The good food standard can include serving temperatures, the quality of serviceware, the menu setup, etc.

- The friendliness standard will include eye contact, smiling, courtesy, etc.

- Communication may even include sample scripts so that employees learn how to introduce themselves, explain the menu, cater to customer diets, etc.

- Empathy must come from the heart, and employees need to know how to show their (appropriate) emotions and how to communicate their empathy to patients. "I know it is hard to be in the hospital, but we are here just to serve you . . . what can I offer you that might sound good today?"

Of course, the whole purpose of standards is to ensure that the quality experience a foodservice operation communicates is actually experienced by the customer. When that happens, so does customer satisfaction. Standards, once measured, can produce an overall satisfaction score, which, as noted earlier, can be compared with those of similar organizations using the same standards.

Not every organization cares more about how they stack up against others than about how they do in their own right. They want to set their own goals, known as **performance benchmarks**. To understand performance benchmarks, consider speed of service in a QSR. For drive-through service, this is measured as the time interval spanning order placement through delivery at the service window. So, a foodservice manager might identify 90 seconds as the performance benchmark. This provides a goal and expectation for employees.

Suppose that a manager has learned to meet a performance standard, say an 80 percent customer satisfaction rating, which he achieves through hard work and conscientiously doing what that standard requires. If nearby competitors begin to achieve 85 percent customer service ratings, his boss is likely to raise the bar on him and set a new benchmark accordingly. It might be tough to achieve, but that is how using standards raises performance.

Success

The question now arises: If a foodservice operation achieves outstanding performance benchmarks, how does that translate into success as a business? How does it build a customer base of people who return, again and again, to the same restaurant or facility? What ensures that return? *Loyalty* is the answer. Loyal customers will encourage others to buy from you. Disney identifies what people expect and then goes beyond that—that is the magic that brings loyal vacationers back to the same theme park for their next vacation, creating lasting, memorable impressions.

This notion of success leads us to another crucial aspect of customer service, commonly referred to as **moments of truth**. A moment of truth is when the customer experiences something that leads to a change in his opinion or impression. In foodservice, there are many, many opportunities for a moment of truth. And keep in mind that the change in attitude can be good or bad. Imagine a customer who goes to a steakhouse for dinner because he's heard that the beef served there is exceptional. The waiter talks him into an appetizer to savor before the steak—and the customer finds the appetizer to be the best thing he's ever eaten. The moment of truth, however, is when he eats the steak. On the one hand, if it does not meet or exceed his expectation, the perception he forms will be negative. On the other hand, if the steak is as good as the appetizer, the moment of truth will result in a positive perception.

SERVICE FAILURE AND RECOVERY

A foodservice operation is a complicated business. Décor is important, location is important, employees are important, the product is delicate and subjective, and many things can go wrong. Indeed, it is inevitable—some things *will* go wrong in the best of places. Yet every failure is a valuable opportunity, so it is important to have a plan in place for managing a wide range of service failures. Activity undertaken to address mistakes, failures, and misfortunes is called **service recovery**.

Service Recovery Strategies

Whether a foodservice operation is in a large medical center with a team devoted to developing a service recovery plan, or such a plan exists only in the mind of the owner/chef for when she needs it, every operation needs a formal plan laying out a sequence of specific steps to take for every type of problem. Most operations want to reduce complaints, sometimes specifying a certain number per quarter by which to reduce their overall total. In addition to establishing a plan, an operation needs a service recovery theme, because when a guest is angry or upset about a mistake, employees become uncomfortable. That is human nature. A little help remembering how to handle difficult situations is important. Here are some suggestions with easy-to-remember acronyms:[13]

- ACT:
  - ☐ Acknowledge and apologize with no excuses.
  - ☐ Correct the issue/make it right.
  - ☐ Take action or take it forward.

- GIFT:
  - ☐ Give a sincere apology
  - ☐ Inform the customer.
  - ☐ Fix the problem.
  - ☐ Thank the customer.

- RELATE:
  - ☐ Recognize the problem.
  - ☐ Empathize with the customer.
  - ☐ Listen closely and pay attention.
  - ☐ Apologize.
  - ☐ Take action to correct the problem.
  - ☐ Explain.

■ The "A" Team:

- □ Awareness of the problem.

- □ Acknowledge the mistake.

- □ Apologize. Actively listen.

- □ Act to amend.

Applying these principles no doubt requires some training and finesse. Note that several of these examples call for careful listening. It is important to understand exactly the basis of a customer complaint, but it can be tricky to elicit a clear description from an irate customer. It requires civility and politeness. Rather than asking a customer to repeat what he's trying to say in anger, respond with, "Let me see if I have this right . . . So your wife's dinner arrived and the waiter set it down and went back to the kitchen without saying anything about yours?" Such an approach is likely to calm the customer and provide a more accurate description of what went wrong.

Sticking with the same example, after initiating service recovery in this way, the rest of the exchange might go like this:

> I am so sorry [the apology] you had to wait 30 minutes for your dinner [acknowledge the problem]. There is no excuse for that [no blame] and I would also be upset in this situation [empathy]. I want you to know that there will be no charge for your meal [reassurance]. I was able to determine what had happened—your ticket had slipped from the preparation table—and we have already instituted a numbering system to make sure this doesn't happen again [problem fixed]. We are having a special wine tasting next week and would love you to be our guest—here is a ticket [hopeful the customer will return].

Making amends depends in part on the situation and the type of operation involved. Every organization must identify what kinds of situation merit something more than an apology. An empty creamer or a missing fork or napkin generally deserves no more than a sincere apology, but a ruined or wrong entree may require a "freebie" of some sort—a gift certificate for the next meal, a free dessert, free wine during your next visit, and so on. Healthcare foodservice operations can provide a gift certificate to a local store, free meals for family members in an onsite cafe, or flowers from an onsite gift shop. In fact, it is common for every department in a large organization to stock standard service recovery gifts. The use of such gifts can also serve as a performance measure. When a manager observes zero usage of such gifts, she may be encouraged but she should not necessarily relax—it might be that employees are regularly missing opportunities to correct mistakes. On the other hand, too much usage might indicate that corrective actions are not being implemented.

Results

Remember Phyllis? She was the customer who never returned to the QSR where she saw the dead roach. Her situation could have been corrected with a proper apology and perhaps a gift such as movie passes to the local movie theater at the time she reported seeing the roach. (In this case, free food would probably not serve as an enticement.) This did not happen, and the customer was lost. Employees must therefore be empowered to make decisions about how and when to make amends. They should not have to go back to the boss or seek her permission to offer a free dessert. Wait staff should feel comfortable making "peace offerings" to customers. However, an apology from a manager is always in order, because it tells the customer that there is an institutional response to a complaint.

Service recovery, the last step in any customer service strategy, is truly an opportunity to turn a lost customer into a loyal customer. It is amazing how many foodservice organizations do not have, or even understand what is involved in having, a service recovery plan.

Starbucks

Enter any Starbucks anywhere and you will find the same quality of product, the same well-trained employees (partners), and a comfortable environment. Go to the same store two or three times and they will remember you; go a few more times and they will remember your name and your usual order. They have perfected the art of making customers feel important and welcome. The company's website tells the story but we excerpt some of it here for your enlightenment.

Our mission: to inspire and nurture the human spirit—one person, one cup, and one neighborhood at a time.

Here are the principles of how we live that every day:

Our Coffee

It has always been, and will always be, about quality. We're passionate about ethically sourcing the finest coffee beans, roasting them with great care, and improving the lives of people who grow them. We care deeply about all of this; our work is never done.

Our Partners

We're called partners, because it's not just a job, it's our passion. Together, we embrace diversity to create a place where each of us can be ourselves. We always treat each other with respect and dignity. And we hold each other to that standard.

MANAGERIAL IMPLICATIONS

The foodservice industry is blessed with having the word SERVICE as an integral part of its name. There is no way to deny that when people eat outside of their own homes they expect both the food and service to be positive. No one chooses to eat where he will be ignored or made to feel uncomfortable. Customers will never choose being uncomfortable over being comfortable. There is a wealth of information on this topic available (we have referred you to several worthwhile sources), and there are many training manuals to assist managers in training employees to maximize customer satisfaction. We began this chapter with a list of phrases about customer service. We end it with this summary of customer service, which we allude to throughout the chapter:

- Service is more about perception than reality.
- Any moment that makes an impression is a moment of truth.
- It's the little things that make the biggest impressions.
- Customers want to know you care.
- Know—and then exceed—thy customer's expectations.

Customer Service Training Websites:

Walk the Talk®

Give 'Em the Pickle!™

Studer Group®

Disney Institute

Pike Place Fish Market™ (Fish! Philosophy)

Press Ganey®

Our Customers

When we are fully engaged, we connect with, laugh with, and uplift the lives of our customers—even if just for a few moments. Sure, it starts with the promise of a perfectly made beverage, but our work goes far beyond that. It's really about human connection.

Our Stores

When our customers feel this sense of belonging, our stores become a haven, a break from the worries outside, a place where you can meet with friends. It's about enjoyment at the speed of life—sometimes slow and savored, sometimes faster. Always full of humanity.

KEY TERMS

Case in Point

Pineapple or Pickle—Who's to Say?

Jake is a foodservice director at a 500-bed university hospital. He is a registered dietitian with a master's degree in business administration. He has 20 years of experience, having worked his way up from pot washer to waiter to chef's assistant. After college, he chose to work in the healthcare segment, and ultimately he landed his dream job, for which he is very well qualified. Jake deals with customer service issues every day. On this particular day, he is told by one of the foodservice workers that a patient in room 715 is irate and has already called administration to register a complaint. As Jake glances at his phone, he sees a text message from his boss regarding this incident. Jake is very busy today—there are five major catering events requiring his attention, an employee disciplinary panel to attend, the monthly budget analysis

is due, and he was hoping to leave early to catch his son's soccer match. The associate tells Jake that the patient would not really tell her what the problem was—she just kept mumbling something about rotten food.

Jake immediately tells his catering manager to proceed with the first event without him and heads up to the seventh floor, dreading the confrontation he knows is coming. He checks in with the nurse who is responsible for this patient. She tells him the patient is very ill and very upset about her illness. He knocks on the door of Room 715, asks if he can come in, and, upon entering, introduces himself as the foodservice director. He sees a middle-aged woman, very pale and thin, with several IV lines in both arms—Mrs. Martin. She does not look at him, but says, "How on earth can you serve rotten food to sick people in a hospital?" Jake pauses a moment, and then says how sorry he is that something was wrong with her food. He adds that he will just need a bit more information to be sure he can correct the problem. He also quickly adds that any error in this hospital's foodservice delivery is unacceptable to him because he knows how difficult it is to be sick and in the hospital. "Rest assured," he notes, "I will personally guarantee your future meals are problem-free. Now, can you tell me what happened?"

Mrs. Martin frowns, but finally makes eye contact with Jake, who has moved to a point by her bed where she can easily see him. She says that she loves pineapple, but when she took a big bite of this morning's pineapple it was rotten. (Now Jake knows that the pineapple came in fresh yesterday and he himself had some for breakfast in the hospital cafe. There have been no other complaints.)

How does Jake handle the rest of this situation, and what is your prediction about the outcome?

REVIEW AND DISCUSSION QUESTIONS

1. Using your choice of search engine, find three customer service slogans appropriate to the foodservice industry that are not cited in the chapter.

2. Search the Farrell's Ice Cream Parlour website. List three approaches or practices that pertain to customer service.

3. Again using a search engine, find a story about Southwest Airlines regarding its customer service and summarize it. (Be sure to include the link.)

4. List and expand on the five dimensions of quality customer care.

5. What approach did Studer use to enhance customer service? Explain how this could be applied to a specific operation in any segment of foodservice.

6. Which is better: Learning of the customer's dissatisfaction during the dining experience or learning

of it through a survey after the experience is over? Explain your answer.

7. List five ways in which customers might provide feedback regarding a dining experience to a foodservice operator.

8. What is the purpose of service standards?

9. Think of a job you've had in the foodservice industry (or any service-related job). What were three service standards that you observed?

10. What is *service recovery,* and why is it important?

11. List six key points of a service recovery exchange in which you, the manager, converse with a disgruntled guest.

12. What is meant by the following phrase: "Service is more about perception than reality"?

ENDNOTES

1. Anderson, K., and Zemke, R. *Delivering Knock Your Socks Off Service.* New York: American Management Association, 1991.

2. Harvey, E. *180 Ways to Walk the Customer Service Talk.* Dallas: Performance Publishing Company, 1999.

3. Farrell, R. Give *'Em the Pickle and They'll be Back.* Greensboro, NC: Legacy Communications, 1998.

4. Parseghian, P. "Hospitality Beyond the Call of Duty Can Lift Customers' Spirits and Spur Them to Return." *Nation's Restaurant News* (April 14, 2008).

5. Disney Institute. *Be Our Guest: Perfecting the Art of Customer Service*. New York: Disney Editions, 2001.

6. Ford, L., McNair, D., and Perry, B. *Exceptional Customer Service*. Avon, MA: Adams Media Corporation, 2001.

7. Studer, Q. *Hardwiring for Excellence*. Gulf Breeze, FL: Fire Starter Press, 2003.

8. Lee, F. *If Disney Ran Your Hospital*. Bozeman, MT: Second River Healthcare Press, 2004.

9. Prewitt, Milford. "Cornell Study: Fix Guests' Complaints Before They Walk Out." *Nation's Restaurant News* (May 12, 2008).

10. Liddle, A. J. "Guests Get Their Say Quickly and Easily with Electronic Aids." *Nation's Restaurant News* (July 14, 2008).

11. National Floor Safety Institute. Website: www.nfsi.org

12. Press, I. *Patient Satisfaction: Defining, Measuring, and Improving the Experience of Care*. Chicago: Health Administration Press, 2002.

13. Clark, P. A., and Malone, M. *Making It Right*. Marblehead, MA: HCPro, Inc., 2005.

MARKETING

LEARNING OBJECTIVES:

After becoming familiar with this chapter, you should be able to:

1. Define marketing, understand that there is a scientific basis for marketing, and discuss some of the major approaches.

2. Discuss the implications associated with social marketing.

3. List the concepts involved in and understand the value of strategic marketing to foodservice operations in all sectors.

4. Appreciate the nuances involved in service marketing.

5. Understand how marketing works within an organization and across key segments of the foodservice industry.

6. Explain the use and application of branding.

According to the American Marketing Association,[1] marketing comprises the activities, institutions, and processes employed in creating, communicating, delivering, and exchanging offerings that have value for customers, clients, partners, and society. Marketing identifies an operation's customers and helps retain those customers by shaping their demand for products. The customer is the focus of its activities.

This characterization of marketing, with its focus on the customer, makes it obvious why this chapter follows the one on customer service. Marketing and customer service must be coordinated to give the customer what he wants. In the competitive foodservice industry today, marketing is a way of life. There are so many opportunities to dine out that every foodservice manager must either become a marketer herself or know how to find one. Satchel Paige, the great baseball pitcher who made the leap from the Negro Leagues to the Majors in the 1940s and was known for his colorful way with words, once said: "Don't look back. Something might be gaining on you."[2] What a perfect metaphor for foodservice marketing. Successful operations, whether franchised or individually owned, must be fresh and innovative every day if they are to stay on top. No matter how well things are going for you now, without constant vigilance and self-reinvention, something *will* be gaining on you.

▪▫ THE SCIENCE OF MARKETING

Marketing was not always thought of as a science but, as the process has evolved, a considerable body of research has accumulated, providing empirical support for today's emphasis in marketing on creating and maintaining relationships with customers and building customer loyalty. The science of marketing, as practiced by market analysts and marketing scholars, employs an array of sophisticated statistical tools to identify customers and measure customer demand, and to determine how production units and processes can deliver what customers want.

Writing in the introduction to the February 2010 issue of the trade journal *Food Management*, editor John Lawn underscores this and notes that "the customer base is far more diverse today and not just ethnically."[3] To achieve high participation rates and customer satisfaction foodservice operations must feature "characteristics that appeal to a broad mix of demographic, cultural, and age groups." Throughout the foodservice industry, dining must appeal to those in a hurry, those who want to relax, those who want to work over lunch, those who want to forget about work, and many more. Lastly, Lawn reminds us that "the food is also important . . . variety and convenience remain important as does the right marketing and promotional mix, front-of-the-house dining experience, and retail product mix."

In this same issue of *Food Management*, there is a review of consumer research concluding that consumers "define value differently in different meal contexts."[4] The article quotes Bonnie Riggs of the NPD Group, who did the research: "We found clearly that in the context of perceived value, 'price of a meal' doesn't necessarily mean cheapest. It means an affordable price that is seen as reasonable given how the food's quality and other attributes of value are perceived." (Note that this aligns with the discussion in Chapter 2.) What does this say to the foodservice manager? It says very clearly that he needs to rely on the science of marketing to help him position his operation precisely where his customers want him to be.

Any endeavor that defines itself as a science must have individuals who practice scientific methods to build a knowledge base upon which to base judgments and plan strategies. Marketing involves two types of research: primary and secondary. The research mentioned above pertaining to the perceptions of foodservice customers found the typical customer base to be quite complex. The research involved is primary research, conducted in the field by gathering data from actual restaurant customers or personnel. In primary research, a problem or question is identified, a study is designed and conducted, and data are compiled and analyzed. Secondary research involves gathering data from existing sources (government databases, trade organization databases, etc.) to characterize the status of the current market or competition. For example, a chef wanting to open a new vegetarian restaurant might want to determine in which part of town a greater concentration of vegetarians lives based on available demographic data. Thus, the science of marketing lays the foundation for strategic decision making.

SOCIAL MARKETING

Today, marketing experts also emphasize the social benefits of products and services. One growing trend in foodservice that reflects this **social marketing** orientation finds foodservice operations advertising their contributions to environmental and health issues. Following today's successful marketing approaches, foodservice operations can:

- Reduce the amount of, or the impact of, their waste byproducts on the environment.

- Stress their healthy, nutritious food, thus appealing to the current health-conscious customer.

- Offer locally or organically produced foods.

- Build energy efficiency into their production areas, dining areas, etc.

Whether these trends pay off in increased revenues is no longer a matter of speculation but, rather, of marketing science, as we noted in the previous section. If being socially responsible or more environmentally friendly makes for good marketing, analysts should be able to confirm corresponding hypotheses through statistical analysis of empirical data. The trend toward "green" foodservice operations demonstrates, however, that social marketing across the foodservice industry, even if it advances with one eye squarely on the bottom line, may benefit an operation's customers and many others as well.

Another trend in social marketing reflects the diversity of foodservice customers, personnel, and offerings. The foodservice industry is replete with individuals who start at the entry level and work their way up. This means that the diversity of the foodservice workforce, as well as the diversity of its ethnically specialized dining opportunities, must be involved in the marketing process. Consequently, menus and product mixes increasingly reflect the changing demographics of the larger society, as operators seek to expand their customer bases even as they broaden the taste preferences of the public.

STRATEGIC MARKETING

"In a world where eating out is not a particularly unique practice, it becomes ever more important that operators work smarter so that they can attract that savvy customer—through understanding what is important to service, menu and experience" (Jim Sukenik, discussing the "smart kitchen" and smart operator).[5] This statement is an excellent way to look at foodservice marketing.

In a previous section, we mentioned a study finding that consumers do not necessarily perceive that the cheapest meal is the best value. Quality often drives customer preferences or judgments of product value more directly than cost alone. It is interesting that marketing strategy has shown that low cost is unsustainable over time—it is *best* cost that customers seek. In other words, customers look for food whose quality justifies its cost. The Hot Dog Palace might run a 99-cent hot dog promotion on the first Saturday in May, but suppose that, to offer this deal, the "HDP" had to buy exceptionally cheap hot dogs and smaller buns. A consumer who is happy to stop by for a "freebie" promotion might choose never to eat at Hot Dog Palace again because of the poor quality of the hot dogs. (Later in this chapter, we consider more carefully how such a promotion might work.) This is a good example of an unsuccessful strategy. The promotion no doubt increased traffic on the day it was run, but it did not showcase the customary quality of Hot Dog Palace food and therefore failed to attract new customers. The best approach to formulating strategy begins with a clear objective or end goal. As the goal of Hot Dog Palace was almost certainly to grow its customer base, its strategy of giving away inferior-quality hot dogs likely backfired, especially if it not only attracted few new customers but weakened the customer loyalty of some of it regulars.

Strategic marketing helps an organization do the following things:[6]

- Position itself against its rivals

- Anticipate changes in demand and technology and adjust accordingly

- Influence the nature of the competition by changing the market

Consider, for example, a restaurant that features "fresh, healthy food" and provides far more nutritional analysis information than is required by law or common practice. If the restaurant becomes successful, other operations will undoubtedly follow suit. It is imaginable that once this practice becomes a trend, it will permeate other segments and may become a ubiquitous practice.

Competitive Forces

Michael Porter has been a leading thinker in strategic marketing for over 40 years. In 2008, he published an updated version of his well-known paper introducing the "five forces" of strategic marketing.[7] As Figure 12.1 portrays, he notes that these **competitive forces** apply to all business areas, although their relative weights vary by industry.

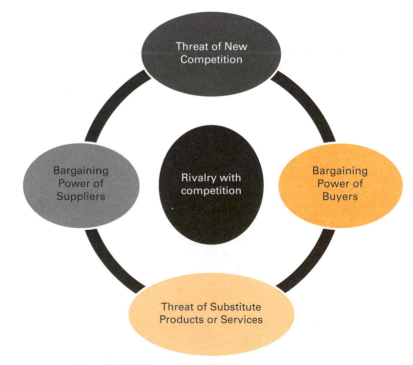

Figure 12.1   Michael Porter's five forces.

Source: *Adapted from Porter, M.E. "The 5 Competitive Forces That Shape Strategy."* Harvard Business Review *(January 2008).*

Charlie's Italian Bistro Faces the Five Forces of Porter	What Is Charlie to Do? He Needs a Marketing Strategy, Right?
Threat of New Entrants: Competition from new market entries constantly threatens established businesses. In the restaurant business, however, it is so much a fact of life that it has to be expected. Let's assume that our imaginary restaurateur, Charlie, completed all the planning, obtained funding, selected a location, and began construction of Charlie's Italian Bistro. He looked out the window about three weeks before opening and noticed a big "Coming Soon" sign for a national chain family-style Italian restaurant about one-half mile down the street!	Charlie may not be able to cut costs and compete with the chain on price, but he can offer an unusual homestyle atmosphere, serve recipes from his momma, and build customer loyalty based on familiarity with his neighbors. By focusing on his core strengths, he can become a barrier himself to the "big guys."
Bargaining Power of Buyers: Charlie will need to become familiar with the pricing of his competition, assuming that other local eateries, and not the chain restaurant, pose the greatest threat. He already knows his neighborhood well. He chose it because he grew up there and he knows there are many families worried about cost. It's a neighborhood of smaller, starter homes and smaller, practical cars.	Charlie knows his neighbors and knows they don't have a lot of buying power. They may want some Chianti, but nothing expensive. He knows that many of these families don't have time to cook, but will require a menu featuring inexpensive pasta dishes if they are to eat out more often.
Threat of Substitute Products or Service: A more affluent neighborhood begins about eight or ten blocks away from Charlie's place. There aren't many "storefronts" left for small restaurants in that area. This is why the "chain restaurants" are opening a bit farther out.	Charlie can craft his menu to avoid competition from substitute products. He knows their menus, but they do not know his, so he can create **differentiation** for his restaurant. The more clearly he can set his Italian Bistro apart from other local operations, the more his customers will become attached to those differentiating characteristics.
Bargaining Power of Suppliers: The cost of food from major vendors is negotiable to some extent, but there is a low margin of profit. The power of suppliers comes from their ability to offer volume discounts to large buyers. This is a worry for Charlie—he's not a big chain.	Charlie has many contacts with members of the local chef's association, and several others with the specialty import grocers he needs to make his products ethnically distinct. He decides to feature several varieties of fresh mozzarella cheese and make his own ricotta. He can overcome some of the large-volume buying power of the "big guys" by featuring quality and well-executed homestyle menu items.
Rivalry among Existing Competitors: The classic "mom and pop" restaurants have been struggling in Charlie's area, and several owners have retired. Charlie was planning to be the first of the new "mom and pop" restaurants so he faces very little "unfriendly rivalry." However, the potential for rivalry with the new, larger chain restaurants might well become an issue.	Charlie should focus on meeting the needs of his customers to build loyalty to his brand. By positioning himself to provide fresh, homestyle offerings rather than the common chain fare, he can be an aggressive rival to his competition. Charlie can also go green and local, using his chef friends as resources to locate reliable local suppliers of fresh products.

Figure 12.2 Charlie's Bistro and the five forces.

The job of a strategist is to understand and cope with competition, and market analysis informed by these forces provides a clear picture of what must be done to improve a company's strategic position. Let's now see what happens if we apply this framework to the foodservice industry (see Figure 12.2).

Marketing strategy does not guarantee that Charlie's Italian Bistro will be a brilliant success, but it should help him analyze his market and make specific decisions about products, costs, menus, and recipes that might have been different had he not considered the market forces that could operate against him.

Mark Beauchamp, cofounder of a small but rapidly growing chain called Café Yumm!, wrote about his business for *Nations Restaurant News*.[8] Originally located in Eugene, Oregon (see Figure 12.3), it is an environmentally friendly fast-casual restaurant that touts the fresh,

Figure 12.3 Café Yumm!'s original location.

healthy quality of its food. The owner notes, "People are hungry for the information that someone is trying to do something. They want to find someone who has a shared vision, a shared philosophy. They enjoy that sort of added value to their experience." The chain uses biodegradable utensils, 60 to 70 percent of its food is certified organic, and it emphasizes value with very competitive pricing.

If this sounds a lot like Charlie's marketing strategy, it is. And since Café Yumm! is now a growing chain, it looks like Charlie's chances of success are good, as long as he sticks to his vision and strategy. That brings up another point about a marketing strategy and plan—while Charlie needs to "stick to it," he may have to adjust it from time to time. An old strategy may no longer fit as times and competitive forces change.

Such a change is everywhere today in the form of Internet-based marketing and Internet operations. It seems like the whole business world has become "i-everything" and "e-everything."

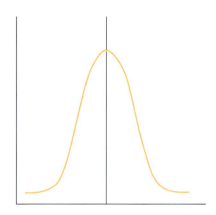

Figure 12.4   The Normal Curve.

Chris Anderson is editor-in-chief of *Wired* magazine. Anderson's "new economics of culture and commerce" is based on "**the long tail**." He argues that the unlimited choices in today's market-place are driving business in a completely new direction. He developed this idea in his 2006 book, *The Long Tail*.[9]

Figure 12.4 illustrates the **normal curve** or "bell-shaped" curve. The center line marks the mean while the rest of the curve displays an even distribution around the mean, trailing off into two short tails. Due primarily to the Internet and the technology that surrounds it, the following things have happened:

- Everyone has immediate access to almost everything.

- Anyone can write a book and attract readers and fans without printing a single page.

- Anyone can get a band together and write songs and record them and make them available for online purchase.

- Satellite radio offers hundreds of channels broadcasting old, alternative, hip-hop, classical, and every other type of music imaginable.

- Food of all kinds is available in all but the most remote areas.

This last entry on the list reflects growing trends toward ethnic diversity, comfort foods, burgers and fries, specialty desserts and breads, and gourmet coffee, offerings that are not only cropping up all over the place but are also available from online stores. The effect of all of this is that no single factor or group of factors can dictate what is a "hit," what is "in," or what is "big." Customer satisfaction is no longer clustered around a narrow range of offerings but is distributed more thinly along a broader range. This forms the long tail.

What Anderson is describing with the figure of the long tail (see Figure 12.5) is that, while the darker part of the curve represents a large number of people and there are still a lot of "hits" there, the lighter tail portion is devoted to small numbers of people making many individual choices. Taken together, this diversity of choice has a big impact on marketing, sell-ing, and reaching customers. Consider Charlie's Italian Bistro again. Charlie may never have a thousand bistros distributed all over the country, but he could develop a page on a social net-working site or develop his own simple website and sell his very special tomato sauce directly to consumers rather than exclusively on the pasta he serves in the restaurant. This could pro-vide him with a small but loyal following out there in the long tail. To his fans, Charlie could become the guru of tomato sauce. This would illustrate Anderson's remark that "the future of business is selling less of more."

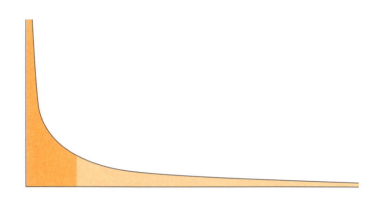

Figure 12.5 A graph with a long tail.

Another approach to understanding strategic marketing is to consider why some ideas "stick" and others do not. For example, some Internet stories or urban legends can be heard once and most people will remember every detail, while marketers, government officials, and teachers, for example, try to communicate information that simply does not "stick." A **sticky idea**, then, has the following characteristics: [10]

- It is simple.
- It is unexpected.
- It is concrete.
- It is credible.
- It is emotional.
- There is at least one story that ties all of these properties together.

Going back yet again to Charlie's Italian Bistro, we see that his concept is *simple*—Italian home cooking for today's young families. It is likely *unexpected* that someone would open an independent restaurant in a neighborhood that has lost all of its "mom and pop" places. It is *concrete*—the proof of the pudding is in the eating, and Charlie's customers will judge his success by the quality of the food he serves. Charlie is *credible* because he is Italian, he grew up in the neighborhood, and he wants to be there. It has *emotional* appeal because it takes people back to a simpler time. And Charlie has a great *story*, a narrative that begins with learning all of his mom's recipes, his first trip to Italy to meet his grandmother, the special recipes she shared with him, and so on.

Again, we should not forget that, if Charlie loses his passion for his little bistro, his idea could lose its *stickiness*. Nevertheless, he seems to be on his way.

Marketing Mix

Throughout our discussion on strategic marketing, we have assumed that the foodservice operator has clearly defined her target market (and we have alluded to this several times in previous chapters as well). This is indeed the primary step in any strategic marketing approach. The second and equally important step applies to creating the appropriate **marketing mix**, which is the combination of elements that a foodservice manager manipulates to maximize business. A marketing mix consists of specific configuration of product, price, place, and promotion (often referred to as the four P's of marketing):

- *Product.* As we've mentioned, the product in any foodservice operation is not just the food or the service; it is the entire dining experience. This is true whether a guest is in a coffee shop, an employee cafe in a manufacturing plant, or is buying a hot dog from a street vendor. It is always more than just the food. (The related notion of service marketing is addressed later in this chapter.)

- *Price.* We have considered price in terms of an operation's value proposition (see Chapter 2), and, similarly, price in the marketing mix means charging the right amount given all the factors involved with the dining experience, particularly the other elements in the mix.

- *Place.* Long before William Dillard coined the phrase "location, location, location" and Ellsworth Statler applied it to hotels, foodservice operators understood the importance of where the foodservice entity is located. And this is central to a marketing strategy. This notion of place also explains why colleges and universities often have eateries located both in the center of campus and near the dormitories and why healthcare centers place coffee kiosks in places of high foot traffic.

- *Promotion.* Promotion involves activities and practices that influence purchasing behaviors that draw new customers and retain existing customers. Sales promotion can be designed explicitly to increase sales volume, such as a promotional menu geared around a holiday, or to generate good will, such as partnering with a local shelter to feed the less fortunate.

The integration of product, place, price, and promotion leads then to developing a **marketing plan**, which is an outline of how the marketing will take place. Much like the other planning activities discussed in previous chapters, planning related to the marketing effort must integrate all major operational considerations. We have already discussed the first, the target market. Next, the marketing plan must align with the foodservice operation's core values and operating objectives. Finally, the plan must consider the operation's short- and long-term goals. (As a side note, we acknowledge that some marketing-textbook authors have increased the number of P's, adding such words as "people," "process," and even "packaging"; however, we prefer to focus on the four listed here as they represent the foundation of a marketing plan.)

SERVICE MARKETING

Marketing a service is very different from, say, marketing a product. The tangible nature of a product makes it easy to convey its attributes to a potential customer. For example, a car manufacturer can easily point out attractive features about a new car such as comfort and styling. Another sort of strategy is needed to market the car dealer's customer service offering. Such a strategy belongs to **service marketing**.

Service marketing is based on relationships and value. For a foodservice operator, such a relationship involves building a customer's affinity for a restaurant and instilling a belief that dining at this restaurant represents a good value. This is often done in subtle ways and in many cases is based on a customer's related experience. A customer may, for example, consider the service at a downtown bistro to be excellent simply because he's had bad experiences with the service at nearby restaurants.

The intangible aspects of the foodservice business are also important to consider in the context of service marketing. When the guest first enters a restaurant, what is his first impression? Imagine walking into an Italian cafe and your mouth begins to water immediately due to the garlic and butter aroma. On the other hand, what is your first impression if you walk into a restaurant and find the hostess stand unattended with dirty dishes on it—what is your first impression of the restaurant?

Another issue related to service marketing is the perishability of service. If a table is empty during dinner, the loss in sales cannot be recouped later. The same is true with service delivery; if the waiter does not deliver the food in time, he cannot reverse time and remedy the poor service. A related concept is the **customer-service gap**, which is the difference between the service customers expect and the service they actually receive. For example, customers may expect to wait only 15 minutes to be seated for dinner; when they are not seated for 30 minutes, they have experienced a customer-service gap. The size of the customer-service gap corresponds to the degree of dissatisfaction.

The final point is that the foodservice business, owing to the many variables involved, changes every day. No two servers are exactly alike. Similarly, guests have differing expectations. One person might like that the waiter is very friendly and talkative while the next might find the overt familiarity offensive. Thus, those engaging in service marketing must try to anticipate customer preferences along with potential customer peculiarities.

MARKETING AND UNIT-LEVEL OPERATIONS

"If you can't be first in a category, set up a new category in which you can be first." This is Law #2 of the "22 Immutable Laws of Marketing."[11] In fact, it's unit-level marketing in a nutshell. The fast-casual segment is sub-segmenting into ethnic fast-casual, healthy fast-casual, and even gourmet fast-casual. No doubt, other permutations will evolve. Generic fast-casual was very impressive in itself, but soon people said, "I can do that but I'll be best at Asian fast-casual."

In onsite dining, hospital foodservice moved lockstep for years with patients and foodservice managers alike, accepting the idea that "institutional food" was the best they could do. One day, someone said, "I'm going to treat my patients more like they would be treated in a restaurant. I'm going to give them a choice or two." Today patients in many hospitals can select meal choices from a restaurant-style menu. Fewer patients and hospitals tolerate "boring hospital food." In onsite operations, marketing within your own company, healthcare facility, or school system becomes your major focus. Your customers may be under the same roof, or nearby roofs, but they won't *choose* to eat in your nice little cafe unless you give them a reason to come and keep on coming.

The same is true in traditional restaurants. Customers have more choices than ever regarding where and what to eat. Against this background, we now consider some ideas that nicely illustrate successful unit-level marketing in foodservice.

Text Your Papa

We begin with an example of the use of new technology in marketing. The Papa John's pizza chain has about 2,700 stores in the United States. There are more than 100 million cell phone users in the country, and most of them have text messaging capability. Writing in *National Restaurant News*, Julie Ritzer Ross notes that Papa John's officials say that a text-messaging ordering system they launched in 2007 increased sales.[12] Papa John's mission is to be as convenient a source of meals as possible and text messaging fit this goal. It made good competitive sense. The Papa John's application allows the customer to create an account on the chain's website and select four favorites that can be ordered as FAV 1, FAV 2, and so on. The system routes orders to the nearest Papa John's outlet for delivery.

The use of text messaging and other electronic means of communication has migrated to onsite dining, too. Many onsite operations accept text messages or e-mails for preordering of menu items from their dining facilities. This eases the burden on staff during peak business hours and shortens the wait time for staff who choose to dine on site. It also attracts an affluent, young crowd that now associates the operation with the latest in technology.

The Test of Taste

Chain operations have recently pushed taste tests in their marketing campaigns. One writer noted that, in a study conducted by a national research firm in ten major cities over two months that compared Dunkin' Donuts coffee with Starbucks coffee, 54.2 percent said they favored Dunkin' Donuts coffee.[13] This played into a major Dunkin' Donuts ad campaign. Similarly, Domino's Pizza introduced four new oven-baked sandwiches that it marketed in direct competition with Subway. A local TV station conducted a taste test, and 64 of 75 people said they preferred Domino's sandwiches. In terms of Porter's Five Forces, these chains are demonstrating the force of rivalry, blanketing the media almost instantly with ads regarding the outcomes of these tests. Taking this approach to rivalry is not without risk. A taste test must be valid and completely above criticism or the competition will win a huge victory at no cost. Moreover, such a campaign, by design, will at best bring a customer into one's facility once. After that, if the product does not meet customer expectations, the campaign will have failed.

Onsite Foodservice Marketing

Dining services on any large university campus comprise a mix of restaurants and other facilities, all competing for students' business. Such units should not be content to sit back and assume that their captive audience will come. Today's mobile students often work and live off campus, so they can easily find alternatives to campus dining. The campus dining market is further complicated in that individual campus feeding units may find themselves competing with each other, not just with independent restaurants located on or close to campus. The diversity of the student population adds yet another factor that must be considered by any on-campus dining unit. Yet despite the unique characteristics of the campus market, the same marketing forces are at work. Moreover, today's students will expect to be more technologically in touch with campus dining. The influence of the long tail is strong here. Students who crave Asian today will want healthy tomorrow and steak on the weekend. They may very well hope to text their orders into campus outlets, especially if they can do so at nearby local restaurants.

Healthcare facilities do not always run multiple foodservice units, but in many cases their dining operations must be available for 24 hours a day, seven days a week. Here unit-level marketing, as noted, often must contend first with brown bagging. A healthcare foodservice operation must develop a very careful strategy to combat brown bagging—anything smacking of coercion or self-serving persuasion is likely to alienate the potential customers. In this case, unit-level marketing strategy must be driven by what customers want. Unfortunately, this all too often ends up being the proverbial "free lunch" which, of course, does not exist. In addition, any marketing strategy is likely to be informed by the organization's view of health, weight control, sustainability, and so on. This can provide an opportunity to connect emotionally with customers, who while under care or while visiting someone who is under care are likely to feel a heightened sensitivity to health-related issues.

Healthcare foodservice marketing lately emphasizes both grab-and-go eating as well as a take-home concept. Nursing personnel find it particularly difficult to leave their work areas so, for them, brown bagging is a time saver. However, if they could pick up something from the on-site facility and eat while in or near their work areas, they could be persuaded to be customers. In addition, busy people who work long days will often want to pick up food on the way home, and if the healthcare facility's food is attractive and conveniently packaged, there is no more convenient way to get dinner than from one's own workplace.

As we noted at length in Chapter 11, patients at healthcare facilities are customers, too. Their diversity will match that of the community in which they live, but they will, on average, be older, and likely feeling poorly (at least at the beginning of a hospital stay). The same marketing forces apply to their wants and needs, however, but within the context of the caring or treatment for which they are present. Healthcare customers need that extra step of concern, in part perhaps because they often have little appetite for food. Simply handing them a menu with many tasty chef-designed choices will not do. They might not even have the energy to read it. What becomes important to them is that someone takes the time to talk with them and offer them tea and toast or ice cream or something to brighten their day.

What about children, especially young children? How can a generation raised with the Internet accept any limits on their choices? And, with all that TV marketing selling them hamburgers, fries, and a supersized drink, is there any hope for a school foodservice operation? Several school foodservice directors were interviewed for an *ADA Times* article, "Say Good-Bye to Mystery Meat."[14] In a clear statement of unit-level marketing awareness, one of the school foodservice directors noted, "We are one of many school foodservice operations working hard to change the perception of school food." These directors often operate as businesses within school districts, and if they are not successful in today's competitive environment, they will be replaced.

The marketing strategy here must acknowledge that the audience is captive but very pronounced in its likes and dislikes. School foodservice directors have to communicate effectively to students, parents, teachers, staff, and the community. One of the directors interviewed for this article noted, "Not only are our meals nutritionally sound and balanced, but I'm proud of the variety." She says you must listen to the children, conduct taste tests, and offer foods they want that are prepared to be as healthy as possible. When students in one district expressed a desire for Asian fare, the district started offering dishes with tofu, brown rice, and bok choy. In another district, students find sushi, calamari, frozen yogurt, and fresh grilled vegetables along with the chicken nuggets and pizza. Wellness and sustainability are also important.

BRANDING

In foodservice, **branding** is the inclusion of brand-name products or concepts into the menu or product mix. A branded product or concept is one that is easily recognized by customers who associate it with key features, flavors, or other attributes. Branding is about image; the goal for any brand is to communicate a sort of identity that customers will embrace.

Brand names originated with merchandise but quickly spread to the service industry. Once a tool that only marketers truly understood, branding of any sort is so pervasive in today's society that the lack of a name is at times more conspicuous. To maximize its utility, however, foodservice operators must understand the subtle as well as overt aspects of branding and learn to implement it effectively.

Branding Basics

In foodservice management, there are four types of brands, starting with **national concepts**. A national concept has nationwide, and sometimes global, name recognition. Leaders in the quick-service restaurant segment are good examples: McDonalds, Burger King, Pizza Hut, etc. **Regional concepts** enjoy substantial brand awareness but only at the regional level. Residents of Southern California are very familiar with In-N-Out Burgers, but would likely be unfamiliar with Legal Seafood, located throughout metropolitan Boston, or Pollo Campero, a chicken concept popular in Costa Rica.

Signature brands, or in-house brands, are those developed internally. For example, when Outback Steakhouse opened its first restaurant in 1988, it featured its signature "Bloomin' Onion," a dish consisting of one large onion that is cut to resemble a flower, breaded, and deep-fried. Similarly, managed-services companies in the onsite sector have a variety of signature brands, some of which generate considerable brand recognition.

The fourth type of brand is **manufacturers' brands**. Manufacturers' brands are most commonly used to accent a relatively standard menu item by giving it added market appeal. Examples are sandwiches featuring Grey Poupon mustard, burritos with Tabasco pepper sauce, ribs with Jack Daniel's barbeque sauce, and margaritas made with José Cuervo tequila.

Strong brands of all types must possess several key factors. First, a brand must deliver a clear message, quickly and succinctly. If the consumer is unclear about the type of product that is branded, or about the icon's link to the product, the brand will fail to generate positive identification for the user. A brand must also project credibility and quality. There are brands in the marketplace that have lost credibility; as a result, their value has severely diminished.

The leading brands educe an emotional response from consumers. If a brand of food or restaurant makes a customer's mouth water, the brand image is working. Such a Pavlovian response indicates that the customer links the brand with satisfaction in terms of a desired flavor, texture, or—at the optimal extreme—experience. These critical factors must converge to motivate action on the part of the consumer. For restaurants or food products, this action should take the form of initiating a purchase.

Keys to Successful Implementation

Strong brands usually equate to increased revenues. Foodservice operators have learned, however, that merely introducing a brand to an operation is not enough. The addition of one, two, or multiple branded concepts can create an elevated image of the entire operation. For instance, there is no reason why an operator cannot introduce a manufacturer's brand (such as the Grey Poupon example cited earlier). Yet this doesn't necessarily communicate much to the customers.

On the other hand, an artful combination of national, regional, signature, and manufacturers' brands can convey to customers that a particular eatery is dedicated to quality (communicated by the familiar brand names and imagery) and that the offerings are expansive (illustrated by the multiple-brand approach). Sometimes referred to as **umbrella branding**, this integration of diverse yet complementary branded concepts and products ultimately serves to create a branded image for the eatery itself. This, in turn, results in greater customer loyalty, higher traffic flow, and improved positioning in the marketplace.

MANAGERIAL IMPLICATIONS

This chapter has examined foodservice marketing science and strategy. We have seen that every foodservice manager in every industry segment must understand and use established marketing principles, both strategically and operationally. This includes social marketing, which is more important today than ever before.

Strategic marketing helps organizations harness the competitive forces. It also involves understanding and embracing how technology is changing the foodservice business. Following the proper identification of their target markets, foodservice managers can build their strategic marketing capabilities by considering the marketing mix, including how the key variables interrelate. Ultimately, this leads to a marketing plan, which serves as a guide for all of an operation's marketing efforts.

Service marketing is based on relationships and value rather than on physical product characteristics. The intangible aspects of the foodservice business make service marketing particularly important as a means of closing the customer-service gap.

Utilizing current technologies plays into a marketing strategy that attracts an affluent, sophisticated customer base. This is marketing for the future. In fact, marketing is both more exciting and more complex than ever because of the wide range of possibilities that exists. This is true in virtually every foodservice segment.

The final key marketing topic is branding, or the inclusion of brand-name products or concepts into the menu or product mix. A branded product or concept is one that is easily recognized by customers who associate it with key features, flavors, or other attributes. The goal for any brand is to communicate an identity that customers will embrace, generating greater sales.

INDUSTRY EXEMPLAR

Freshëns

Freshëns is focused on innovative, healthful products for consumers looking for convenient, portable, and great-tasting options. Freshens products are healthy while still being indulgent. Freshens proprietary yogurt and smoothies are all natural, with no high fructose corn syrup and no trans fats. Freshëns is also proud to be first in the industry to add Truvia, an all-natural, zero-calorie sweetener, to all the proprietary smoothie and yogurt base mixes. Freshëns also features handcrafted savory, dessert and breakfast crêpes, in addition to its signature frozen yogurt and smoothie platform.

The innovative organization is particularly appropriate for this chapter's exemplar because it is widely

recognized for its incredible marketing. For example, Freshëns advocates a culture of commitment to both the environment and the community, and communicates this effectively through its marketing efforts. And, refreshingly, this culture is not just for marketing purposes. The company treats its sustainability initiative seriously, constantly seeking to leave a smaller environmental footprint. Even the store design is part of this. Each unit includes Greenguard™ certified laminates, countertops composed of recycled materials, and signage manufactured from recycled aluminum and plastics, plus LED lighting.

Another example of Freshëns's effective marketing is the company's website. Here you will find information on everything from nutritional facts for all of its products to store design. Moreover, one of the main tabs on the home page is Marketing!

Courtesy of Freshëns.

KEY TERMS

Case in Point

The Entrepreneurial Baker

Carole has always loved carrot cake. Even as a teenager, she began to bake her own, always tweaking the recipe, making subtle changes to the ingredients. She became particularly interested in achieving not only the perfect taste but also the healthy properties of carrot cake. She carefully selected oil with more "omega-3's" and healthy sweeteners to augment the nutritional value of carrots. She often enlisted her friends to taste her experiments, and finally, in her last two years of high school, she actually began a small business—she was considered *the* source of birthday cakes for most students in her school. There was no doubt that Carole would become a pastry chef, and that she did.

After attaining her culinary school diploma, Carole's intent was to operate her own business. The catch was, there were many bakeries in the large city in which she lived, and a lot of them featured very well trained pastry chefs with high-profile reputations. They were turning out great cakes in all kinds of shapes and decorations. The competition was fierce. Carol found a very small storefront, which had housed a bakery that had gone out of business. It had most of the equipment she needed. She also had a friend who would be able to assist her in obtaining the smaller pieces of equipment she needed. What she did not have was a plan.

1. Help Carol develop a marketing plan by devising a slogan she can use to market her bakery.

2. What are the major issues Carole will have to consider in developing her marketing plan?

3. What should be the major focus of Carole's strategy?

4. Be creative—describe what you think Carole's shop might look like.

5. Carole has her carrot cake, but can she stay in business on carrot cake alone? Suggest some additional products Carole might add and explain why they fit her mission.

6. Suggest some names for Carole's store.

REVIEW AND DISCUSSION QUESTIONS

1. Why is marketing different today? Give three specific examples.

2. What is a growing trend in terms of foodservice social marketing?

3. Why should a foodservice operation engage in strategic marketing? What will it gain in doing so?

4. Consider your favorite restaurant, cafe, or coffeehouse. How does Porter's model fit its marketing strategy? (See Figure 12.2 for an example.)

5. Compare the websites of three foodservice operations. From a marketing perspective, find three common themes. Next, find something that, again from a marketing perspective, is unique to each.

6. In this chapter, we introduced Café Yumm! What marketing approach do you find on its website? How is the business described? Are you tempted to eat there?

7. Again with reference to Café Yumm!, how is it extending the long tail?

8. Based on either your experience or a search of food-service websites, identify a sticky idea that pertains to this industry.

9. Explore the Papa John's website. Before you can build your "favorites," what information must you enter? Why does it require that information?

10. Describe something that the foodservice operation at your college or university is doing that integrates technology into its marketing.

ENDNOTES

1. American Marketing Association. www.marketingpower.com Accessed October 2012.

2. Satchel Paige: The Official Website. www.satchelpaige.com/quote2.html. Accessed October 2012.

3. Lawn, John. "Participation: A Universal Imperative." *Food Management* (February 2010).

4. "Outlook 2010: Rebuilding the Model." *Food Management* (February 2010).

5. Sukenik, J. "Ten Elements of Any Smart Kitchen and Smart Operator Practices." *Foodservice Equipment and Supplies* (April 1, 2010).

6. Allen, C. "Strategic Marketing for Growing Companies." www.allen.com. Accessed October 2012.

7. Porter, M. E. "The 5 Competitive Forces That Shape Strategy." *Harvard Business Review* (January 2008). Accessed online at www.hbr.org/2008/01.

8. Elan, E. "Green Efforts Can Add Value to Customer Experience." *Nation's Restaurant News* (April 21, 2008).

9. Anderson, C. "The Long Tail." New York: Hyperion, 2006.

10. Heath, C., and Heath, D. *Made to Stick*. New York: Random House, 2007.

11. Ries, A., and Trout, J. *The 22 Immutable Laws of Marketing*. New York: Harper Business, 1993.

12. Ross, J. R. "Papa John's Boosts Sales with Text Message Ordering System." *Nation's Restaurant News* (June 9, 2008).

13. Cebrzynski, G. "Chains Tout Taste Test Victories in Competitive Marketing Campaigns." *Nation's Restaurant News* (November 17, 2008).

14. Mannion, A. "Say Good-bye to Mystery Meat: RDs Bring Nutrition to Students Through the Foods They Love." *ADA Times* (March/April, 2007).

CHAPTER 13

HUMAN RESOURCE MANAGEMENT

LEARNING OBJECTIVES:

After becoming familiar with this chapter, you should be able to:

1. Write and interpret a job analysis and job description.

2. Identify the basic techniques of employee recruitment, selection, and retention.

3. Understand the principles of and methods that apply to scheduling and staffing.

4. Appreciate the applicable laws and processes involved in determining compensation.

Human resource management (HRM) comprises the administrative policies and activities involved in managing an organization's most valued assets—the people working there who individually and collectively contribute to achieving its business objectives. HRM means hiring people, developing their capacities, utilizing their skills, and compensating them for their services in accordance with job and organizational requirements. Note that we identify an organization's personnel—the people who devise and implement its strategy, carry out its processes, and deliver its products to customers—as its most valued assets. This is such a powerful notion that one can often gauge the personality of a company by looking at its HRM philosophy and policies.

An organization is only as good as its people. In the case of foodservice organizations, there is an interesting human relations issue. Traditionally, the face of a foodservice operation, the person who engages the customer directly—a waitperson or perhaps a maître d'—works near the bottom of the organizational structure. Thus, is it not uncommon for a person who knows little about the operation's strategic plan or management philosophy to be responsible for delivering the final product, the operation's food and service, to customers. How effectively that food and service are delivered depends crucially on how well the operation performs HRM.

HRM can be frustrating—a person who loves food and wants to spend her time working with customers often feels that she spends most of her time dealing with "employee issues." Many managers feel unprepared for this and, in the worst cases, can be less effective because they *are* spending too much time on HRM. Consider absenteeism. Whether a manager runs an operation of 5 or 105 employees (with several managers to assist him), unscheduled absences—a chronic problem in service industries—make for long days.

The problems associated with HRM are also expensive. People might be an organization's most important asset, but they are also one of the greatest expenses, as we noted in Chapter 10. An organization must create job descriptions; complete job analyses; orchestrate the recruitment, selection, and retention functions; and manage the compensation strategically. To this end, this chapter reviews all of these aspects of HRM.

WHAT IS THE JOB?

HRM begins with hiring "the right person for the right job." The first step is to know what is involved in "the right job." If you don't know what you want a person to do, you will never be able to hire the right person. Therefore, before hiring, an organization must carefully analyze the duties or tasks involved in a particular position to ensure that it accomplishes what is necessary without duplicating work that is done by others within the organization.

HR managers in large organizations such as chain restaurants, large hospitals, schools, or university foodservice operations formulate generic job overviews based on the organization's strategic plans and organizational structure. At the other end of the industry spectrum, a small restaurant with a few employees might be able to improvise a job narrative to some extent, but will suffer the consequences of poorly written descriptions if new employees do not understand what is expected of them or how the food and service is positioned in the local market. At any organizational scale, the more concrete and detailed are an operation's job descriptions, the more successfully it will be able to deliver what customers demand and expect.

Job Analysis

Writing an accurate, effective job description begins with **job analysis** in the course of which an organization's HR team spells out in detail the particular duties and sequence of tasks involved in a given job, indicating where it is positioned in the chain of command and characterizing its importance to the organization's strategic goals. The organizational research and analysis involved should provide a clear picture of the tasks, responsibilities, and duties that any particular job should entail in the course of a work shift. Such a job analysis is often conducted with the assistance of a job analyst consultant. Job analysis typically involves conducting interviews, administering questionnaires, observing employees on the job, monitoring work logs, and so on.

In a small-scale operation, the operator may acquire all the information she needs by walking through a "day in the life" of a waitperson, developing a list of tasks that, when accomplished in the right order, provide the desired outcomes in terms of service and product delivery. The most important result of job analysis is likely to be a set of job descriptions that reflect the results of the analysis. In summary, job analysis can benefit an organization in the following areas:

- Writing job descriptions and otherwise developing selection and recruitment strategies
- Identifying training needs, evaluating training programs
- Determining compensation based on risk (hazards or skills), education, or responsibilities (supervision, budgetary responsibility)
- Conducting performance evaluations

Job Description

Whether or not an operation conducts job analysis, the next step in HRM is to write **job descriptions**, which specify the functions or roles involved in particular positions and lists the specific responsibilities or tasks to be performed. Typically, a job description also indicates the managerial level to which the position reports, specifies required qualifications or certifications, suggests salary ranges, and so on. The following outline lists everything one will need to include in a job description:

- Job title
- Salary grade/salary
- Division or department (if applicable)
- Chain of command: to whom the job holder reports
- Date the job description was last revised
- Brief summary of the job
- Primary responsibilities
- Additional responsibilities
- Knowledge and skill required, including training or certification
- Working conditions (hours, environment, clothing, activity, physical demands, etc.)

Society for Human Resource Management

The Society for Human Resource Management was founded in 1948 as a professional organization for those working in personnel management. Beginning with 28 members, it now can boast of having over 250,000 members throughout the world in 140 countries. This growth (as well as the existence of similar organizations) indicates the importance of HRM in today's world. The SHRM website lists as its mission the goal of being a

(continued)

SHRM
SOCIETY FOR HUMAN RESOURCE MANAGEMENT

globally recognized authority whose voice is heard on the most pressing personnel management issues of the day—now and in the future. Members can use the website to access a variety of resources, including a databank of existing job descriptions and HRM policies. Why does the SHRM compile job descriptions? Successful HRM begins with job descriptions, which not only specify the details involved in performing a job, but also convey to job applicants an organization's philosophy and strategic framework. Turning a fresh recruit into a real asset begins with the job description.

This very broad outline highlights the main elements of a job description. Individual employers may add details about specific organizational or job characteristics, such as:

- Whether the job is covered by the Fair Labor Standards Act (which regulates such employment conditions as eligibility for overtime pay)

- Whether the job is covered by Equal Employment Opportunity laws

- A job's specific internal code

- Performance standards or criteria for successful performance

In the sample job description shown in Figure 13.1, the "Knowledge, Skills, and Abilities" section serves as a **job specification**. A job specification describes the conditions, minimum skills needed, and educational or training qualifications associated with a job. Such a specification must define precisely the qualifications needed. It would be inappropriate to require more education than necessary, for example, but it could become a major issue if the specification allowed unqualified people to be hired because the operation might be liable for any injuries or other harms caused as a result of a worker's inadequate qualifications or training. However, an organization that considered only people who were overqualified for a given job would face possible action from within. There would be no legal basis for hiring only someone with a bachelor's degree for a job specified as requiring only "at least two years of college."

Other requirements may be included in job specifications. In the case of the sample health care job, certain accreditation information is required, such as indication of age-specific knowledge. The phrase at the end of the duties list, "Other duties as assigned," is very important. Employees must know that they may be required to fill in for absent co-workers or to perform unusual tasks in case of emergency. In addition, some job specifications include **performance standards**. When the standards for acceptable performance are included as part of the job specification, the new employee has no difficulty determining what is going to be expected of him. Performance standards will be discussed in greater detail in the following section.

Job Description

Job Title: Patient Foodservice Assistant   **Department:** Food and Nutrition Service
Job Code: 5430   **Salary Grade:** 7
Reports to: Foodservice Manager   **FLSA:** Non-exempt

Summary
The Patient Foodservice Assistant is responsible for patient food service on assigned unit involving patient and nursing communications as appropriate, assistance with menu selection, tray assembly, tray deliveries, and tray pickups. Prepares some items such as milkshakes. Generally plates and assembles all foods ordered by patients on a delivery tray. Takes inventory of items necessary for meal service in workstation area. Orders, receives, and correctly stores supplies and food. When meal service is completed, cleans workstation and sanitary standards; records and monitors refrigerator temperatures and temperatures of hot and cold food as directed. Provides between-meal food delivery and special requests as necessary.

Age of Patients to be Served
Neonate-Toddler (0–3)   ___
Pediatric (4–12)   ___
Adolescent (13–20)   x
Adult (21–64)   x
Geriatric (65+)   x
NA   ___

Job Duties and Responsibilities

1. Prepares all between-meal nourishments and snacks for patients (10:00 A.M., 3:00 P.M., and at bedtime). Labels each item with the patient's name, date of birth, room number, product, and date and time of feeding. Delivers and serves patient nourishment and assists with tray delivery when necessary.

2. Assists with early coffee service and tray delivery as needed.

3. Exhibits a friendly, caring attitude to patients when introducing the menu or servicing staff, families, and patients.

4. Sets up workstation and keeps station adequately stocked.

5. Answers nursing calls in absence of supervisor, enters information into computer for processing. Offers menu alternatives according to dietary prescriptions, food allergies, and cultural, ethnic, or religious preferences, as shown by computer.

6. Follows plating pictures and tray diagrams for placement of all items. Follows any clinically ordered modifications or patient-requested modifications as directed. Seeks clarification from dietitian and/or nurse to resolve questions about proper procedure.

7. Maintains accurate information on assigned unit for each patient, including two patient identifiers, e.g., birthdates, and name.

8. Interacts with nursing staff to ensure patient diet prescriptions are accurate, and patient food needs are met.

9. Orders, receives, and stores all deliveries of supplies and food to work station.

10. Picks up trays after meals and snacks as directed, properly stores temporarily in designated location, returns soiled permanent service ware to dishwashing area.

11. Cleans work area and other assigned areas. May assist in sanitation inspections. Follows all uniform and patient safety guidelines.

12. Observes safety rules promulgated by department and regulatory agencies.

Figure 13.1 Example of a job description.

13. Provides service appropriate to the patient's age; demonstrates knowledge and skills necessary to meet the patient's physical, psychosocial, educational, and safety needs.

14. Presents a courteous and helpful age-appropriate demeanor to all patients, visitors, other employees/medical staff members, or any other person an employee encounters while representing the hospital.

15. Maintains current knowledge related to applicable statutes, regulations, guidelines, and standards necessary to perform job duties in accordance with hospital policies. Complies with the requirements of the Code of Conduct and Compliance Policies and Procedures, including training requirements.

16. Performs ather duties as assigned.

Knowledge, Skills, and Abilities

Minimum Requirements:

1. High school diploma or GED for employees hired effective from May 1, 2013.

2. Current Food Handler's Card.

3. At least one year of experience in foodservice operation.

4. Ability to perform basic math operations.

5. Ability to direct others.

6. Ability to follow oral and written instructions.

7. Ability to lift 50 pounds, push/pull heavy carts, and carry objects.

8. Ability to perform motor skills such as bending, twisting, turning, kneeling, reaching out/up, wrist turning, grasping, and finger manipulation.

9. Ability to communicate orally to patients, customers, and co-workers.

10. Ability to operate telephone system and utilize computer as trained.

11. Ability to interact positively and empathetically with patients, customers, and co-workers.

Preferred Qualifications

1. Experience in customer service.

2. Healthcare foodservice or restaurant experience.

Primary Contacts

Primary contacts are with patients, their families, and other hospital employees.

Working Conditions (Check one or all depending on the working conditions of the position.)

Normal hospital working environment; requires good oral and written communication skills. Must be able to speak and read the English language.

Job involves standing, stooping, walking, bending, pushing, pulling and lifting up to a maximum of fifty (50) pounds without assistance.

The above statements are intended to describe the general nature and level of work being performed by employees in this position. They are not intended to be an exhaustive list of all duties, responsibilities, and qualifications of employees assigned to this job.

Figure 13.1 *(continued)*

FINDING, HIRING, AND KEEPING THE BEST PEOPLE

Imagine a CEO of a foodservice company addressing her management team as follows: "In order to become a world class service organization, we must first recognize and reward the exceptional service efforts of those people who will ultimately create the level of service that exceeds our customers' expectations."[1] This statement sums up the importance of recruitment, selection, and retention by emphasizing an often-overlooked part of this process—reward and recognition. Employees who feel they are contributing to an organization's success and who feel valued by that organization are much more likely to stay and perform well.

It sometimes seems as if, from one generation to the next, every employer complains, "You just can't find good people today." The question is: Who are these "good people"? In the hospitality industry, "good people" need to love their jobs and their customers, and embrace the unpredictability of a constantly changing work environment (new menus, new customers, new foods, new equipment, new regulations, etc.). According to the website WhatsNext4Me, the hospitality industry is projected to continue to grow, creating more than 1.6 million new jobs over the near term. There is concern that as people graduate from high school, "they are often unaware of the range of career opportunities available and potential for advancement in the industry."[2] The purpose of the website, which is sponsored by several organizations, including the Multicultural Foodservice and Hospitality Alliance, is to enhance the image of the hospitality industry and promote awareness of the wide range of opportunities available. The Multicultural Foodservice and Hospitality Alliance is a nonprofit group that supports diversity in the food and hospitality industry, focusing on leadership development as well as employment. The foodservice industry has long been a source of minority employment, but not necessarily of promotional opportunities. Today's foodservice organizations are looking for diversity in management as well, and realize that a diverse workforce can enrich an organization by providing new approaches to food, customers, and service.

Recruitment

Finding and hiring the right people for the right jobs in the foodservice industry is a never-ending challenge. Fresh ideas often come from other industries, and one of the recognized leaders in recruiting customer-focused workers is Southwest Airlines. Southwest calls its HRM department the "People Department" and, when a new CEO took over in 1978, he charged the department with the responsibility of hiring people with a sense of humor. Freiberg and Freiberg describe Southwest Airlines' crazy recipe for business and personal success in their book, *NUTS!*.[3] One of the major contributions to their success is the practice described as follows: "Hire for Attitude, Train for Skills." The company always makes it clear that it wants people to have fun, but that it will also be hard work. This has kept qualified applicants coming through the doors for years. Southwest's recruitment and retention program can be summarized as follows:

- Hire people with a sense of humor.

- Give yourself the freedom to be yourself.

- Train for skill, but hire for spirit, spunk, and enthusiasm.

- Be religious about hiring the right people. If you make the wrong hiring decision, within the first 90 days make the tough decision to say goodbye.

- Do not take employees for granted.

- Do whatever it takes: Remember, there is very little traffic in the extra mile.

- Define your own standard of professionalism.

- Treat everyone with kindness and equal respect—you never know to whom you are talking.

So where does a foodservice manager go to find "the right people"? Local colleges with hospitality training programs and local churches and community groups are good resources. Open houses, job fairs, and rewards to existing employees for referrals of other employees are also effective.

Danielle goes hunting . . .

Danielle is a foodservice manager at a nursing home. Before she took her job, her 50-employee department was often short by five or more people. This produced constant overtime costs, frustration, and turnover, all of which made every day miserable for her good employees. One day, Danielle was enjoying a meal at a restaurant near the nursing home and she received particularly good service from the waiter. On the spur of the moment, as she was leaving a tip, she also handed the waiter her business card and said, "If you are ever job hunting, give me a call." Today, he is one of her assistants. After that, anywhere Danielle received good service, whether in a gas station or in a hotel, she was recruiting. She had about a 10 percent response rate to this technique, and it resulted in three or four good hires every year. Ultimately, her entire department was transformed into having very little turnover, and the nursing home now has a reputation as a great place to work.

This story reinforces our advice that you can't hire the right people until you find the right people. And you can't find the right people if you don't know what you're looking for. In the foodservice industry, almost anyone can learn the basic skills needed in food preparation; almost anyone can learn the routines, policies, and procedures involved in serving food. What sets the exceptional employee apart is the desire to do things right and provide the kind of service that exceeds customer expectations. Traditionally, foodservice managers have looked for employees with prior experience in a specific industry segment—restaurants, hospitals, schools, and so on. Unfortunately, there is no guarantee that experienced applicants will share your mission and values.

The first step in recruiting the "right people" is designing an effective job application. Fortunately, it is possible to design and read job applications that increase the likelihood of finding those right people. One foodservice leader suggests the following points concerning job applications:[4]

- Use a job application designed specifically for your organization that accounts for applicable local restrictions.

- Look for warning signs:

  - Leaving blanks—be sure all questions are answered, such as, "Have you ever been convicted of a crime?"

  - Scratch-outs—this may mean the employee has written something he would rather the potential employer not see.

  - Multiple or short-term employment stints or gaps in employment (could mean job-hopping, jail time, or lack of commitment).

  - Reasons for leaving—whom does the applicant blame for leaving the last job? (He cautions to watch out for applicants with a "victim" mentality.)

Selection

Once an organization has an effective job application in place, interviewing is the next step. The following is a good framework for this process:[5]

- Analyze the job. Clarify the required tasks, traits, and style, and then create interview questions that will help you decide if a person meets these requirements.

- Create an interview guide with carefully crafted behavioral questions. The same questions should be used for all applicants, to ensure fairness. (More information on behavioral interviews follows.)

- Include others in the interview process. Examples: potential team members, direct reports, peers, or even individuals from other departments who understand your concept of customer service.

- Consider using personality and skill assessments—in a large organization, the HRM department can assist with this. Several tools can be used to assess customer focus.

The **behavioral interview** has proven itself over time to be an excellent method for asking questions that allow potential employers and employees to evaluate each other. Behavioral interview questions ask applicants to give specific examples of how they have performed in the face of a problem in the past. An example: "Tell me about the most difficult situation you have ever had with a guest. How did you handle the situation and what was the outcome?"

It is important that a behavioral interview *not* consist of a series of yes/no questions, such as:

- Did you like your last job?

- Have you worked in foodservice before?

- Do you like to work with people?

Note that all of these examples can be answered with a yes or no, yet neither response will tell the interviewer much about the personality or behavioral tendencies of an applicant. For example, it is unlikely that someone applying for a foodservice job will tell the interviewer that he doesn't like to work with people.

Quintessential Careers provides advice to both interviewers and potential applicants regarding behavioral interviews.[6] Here are more examples of behavioral interview questions:

- Describe a time when you were faced with a stressful employee situation and explain how you handled it.

- Describe a time when you set a goal and were able to achieve it.

- Describe a time when you had to comply with a policy with which you did not agree.

- Describe a time when you had too many things to do and explain how you prioritized your tasks.

Panel interviews can provide input from multiple organizational tiers. In the panel interview process, a variety of individuals interview candidates using standardized interview questions. The candidates who emerge successfully from those interviews are then interviewed by a panel consisting of, for example, a department head, a supervisor, or perhaps a representative of HRM. Final hiring recommendations are made by the panel, with final decisions to hire individuals made by the department head or restaurant manager.

Peer interviews involve another type of panel. For example, in a hospital foodservice operation, a peer interview may be done by a supervisor, a patient foodservice assistant, and a dietitian. In a restaurant, the team could include the chef, the headwaiter, and a member of the wait staff.

Research suggests that such a process reduces turnover by providing a better cultural fit with the organization and at least some degree of acceptance of the employee by his peers. It also empowers employees and increases employee satisfaction. While a department head or designated manager generally makes the final hiring decision, organizations usually follow the recommendations of peer interview teams. One organization reduced turnover from 35 to 14 percent over a five-year period using this technique.[7]

Retention

Suppose now that your organization has found the right person, who has been interviewed and hired. How does the organization keep this person on the job? Keeping employees is known as **retention**. Retention—or reducing turnover—is a seemingly endless challenge in the foodservice industry. A management consultant recounts a story about sitting in a fast-food restaurant in an airport and observing that the employees "looked miserable and were giving miserable service." He says it may be easy see a difficult job as miserable, but he asserts that "a well-managed job, even a difficult one, can be a better job than a 'sexy' job that is poorly managed." [8] It is obvious that you can find miserable people in any job—rock stars can be as miserable as pot washers, and pot washers can be as excited about their jobs as rock stars. Every manager has to value her employees and let them know it—a lot!

Rewarding and recognizing a "job well done" helps successful managers retain employees. A simple thank-you note on a "yellow sticky pad" can go a long way, as long as such notes are sincere and distributed equitably. The phrase, "Let's catch someone doing something right," is an essential part of the successful manager's toolbox. Overhearing an employee gently and correctly handling a small complaint or noticing that an employee pitched in and helped another employee who was struggling to complete a task—even the simplest "thank you" goes a long way. Many organizations, large and small, select an employee of the week, month, or year. Doing so must be based on published criteria, and nominations should come from members of the workforce themselves as well as managers. A mismanaged recognition program can lower morale, especially if criteria are not clear and favoritism is suspected. Some organizations have also subscribed to services that set up a point system that qualifies employees to select gifts from a catalog as performance rewards. The caveat about this type of automatic recognition is that it is sometimes too little, too late. Employees need personal, ongoing, sincere recognition to keep them coming to work every day.

Another effective retention tool is the **stay interview**. In such interviews an organization periodically invites employees to discuss what it would take to keep them, what might cause them to leave, what energizes them about their jobs, and what the employer could do differently. They note that if you never ask employees how they feel or what it would take to make them stay, you will always be guessing and could easily be wrong.

Most organizations suggest conducting 30-day and 90-day reviews for newly hired employees. Such reviews catch things that are going wrong early, thus giving the manager the opportunity to correct them before they have gone too far. Of course, employees occasionally use such reviews to opt out of a job, but if that is the case, at least it happens before too much time and money have been invested in an unhappy employee.

As introduced earlier, performance standards allow managers to evaluate job performance with a high degree of objectivity. The key here is that these standards must be measurable. Examples of such standards might be:

- Knock on the patient's door before entering and ask permission to enter the room.

- Greet customers as they enter with a smile and welcome them to Captain Joe's.

- Be sure to talk with students and greet them as they move through the cafeteria line—ask them if they would like to try a new dish.

■ Notify a manager immediately if a customer reports a very serious problem (food not cooked properly, unsanitary conditions, a rude waitperson, etc.).

■ Regard customer safety and employee safety as the first priority.

Every organization also identifies circumstances or behaviors that provide grounds for terminating an employee immediately: theft, unexcused absence (no call, no show), serious sanitary code violations, and so on. Some specific performance standards are listed in Figure 13.2.

Usually such a format for displaying performance standards would identify areas needing improvement and suggest remedial action or training programs for employees working in those areas. Here again a large organization will very likely have in place a highly developed organization-wide performance evaluation system. Yet even small businesses or organizations should follow the same principles in this and all other aspects of successful HRM practice that we have introduced.

One of the more recent methods for conducting performance assessment is known as **360-degree feedback**. In the 360-degree process, a worker receives feedback from several sources: supervisors, to be sure, but also peers, subordinates, customers, suppliers, or others who are able to observe the worker's performance on the job. With some 360-degree processes these observations are anonymous. Many industry observers believe that 360-degree feedback provides a balanced performance review with a good foundation for setting up a training program, pursuing promotional opportunities, and obtaining objective feedback. Of course, performance standards must be developed and an organization must select its own criteria for this process. The advantages of such a process include the sense on the part of the employee that her performance evaluation is not one-sided or biased by personal animus, but it can be time consuming and difficult to administer. Poorly implemented 360-degree evaluations cause resentment and distrust. Perhaps because it requires subtlety and finesse, many consulting companies, online service providers, and publications are devoted to assisting organizations with the implementation of this approach.

Earlier in this section, it was mentioned that it is sometimes wise to allow an employee to seek other opportunities rather than remain with his present organization. After an organization has invested in hiring an employee, trained him, and done everything possible to provide

Rating Scale: 3 = Very Good, 2 = Acceptable, 1 = Needs Improvement (Check appropriate score)

Job Standard	3	2	1
Duty 7: Maintains accurate and current information on assigned unit for each patient; maintains patient notes and comments as needed			
Duty 10: Interacts with nursing staff to ensure patient diet prescriptions are accurate and patient food needs are met			
Duty 13: Cleans work area and other assigned areas; may assist in sanitation inspections			
Duty 14: Follows all uniform guidelines as reviewed in handbook			
Duty 21: Maintains confidentiality of all patients			
Duty 22: Remains positive even though others may be upset; responds tactfully and appropriately in difficult situations			
Duty 25: Actively listens with an open mind when patients report problems			
Evaluator Comments:			

Figure 13.2 Partial set of performance standards for Patient Foodservice Assistant.

feedback and otherwise improve his performance, it is best for everyone if he leaves when no improvement results. It is much more important to invest your time in developing and training your successful employees, because keeping the "nonperformers" will only reduce standards and lower morale. Letting a badly fitting employee go makes room for good performers who will help the organization continue to improve.

One author summarizes some of these performance standards in an open letter from a restaurant owner to his crew.[9] His points are paraphrased here:

- Service has always been our invisible product. It makes a good meal taste better.
- I don't pay you, the customer does.
- Always tell the truth.
- Be on time, no excuses.
- Build repeat business. Give them something memorable every time.
- Save the drama for your mama—it's not about you, it's about the customer. Things that matter most should never suffer because of things that matter least.
- Continuous improvement: If you see, sense, or know a better way to improve our people or our procedures, please let us know. We will always listen.
- Have fun. If you see somebody without a smile, give them one of yours.

These commonsense principles may seem obvious, but we've all had many experiences in foodservice operations of all kinds in which employees behave differently. Your most valuable asset can always use help learning to do it right.

When good people leave an organization, it is possible to achieve some organizational benefit using **exit interviews** to determine whether there's a fixable cause of the turnover. Berta interviewed Christin Myers, from the consulting firm Creative Restaurant Solutions, who helps foodservice companies reduce turnover.[10] Myers cautions that it is common for exiting employees to say that they are leaving to take advantage of a better opportunity, but that begs the question as to what makes it a better opportunity. Were they offered more money to do the same job? If so, how much more? Why were they looking elsewhere in the first place? Why did they choose to leave now? "We find there was usually a conflict with a supervisor or upper management. Not feeling like there are opportunities for growth or advancement is another [reason to leave]." The problem is that it is difficult to elicit from an exiting employee the real reason for leaving unless she is asked the right specific questions. It is clear, however, that exit interviews provide to managers an opportunity to identify and correct trouble spots in an organization.

Training and Development

The final aspect of retention is **training**, which for managers is often termed **professional development**. After finding, interviewing, hiring, and conducting performance evaluation for an employee, an organization may need to invest in yet another employee-related practice, which is providing training. Consider the following three reasons for training a veteran employee:

1. Teaching the right way to do something
2. Correcting a behavior that needs improvement
3. Instituting a new standard or method of complying with a regulation

For new employees, training is necessary in all aspects of the job. Simple details such as work hours, clothing and safety rules, and specific job duties must all be introduced. Nevertheless, subsequent training will assist employees in improving or maintaining standards. Figure 13.3 provides

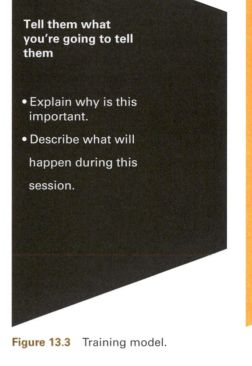

Tell them what you're going to tell them

- Explain why is this important.
- Describe what will happen during this session.

Tell them!

- Present clearly and simply.
- Listen and watch for understanding.
- Answer questions and check for feedback.
- Include practice if teaching a skill.

Tell them what you told them

- Clarify expectations for performance.
- Explain how they will get feedback on performance.
- Summarize all.
- Be sure any dates for completion are clearly understood.

Figure 13.3 Training model.

CHART: Council of Hotel and Restaurant Trainers

The Council of Hotel and Restaurant Trainers (CHART) is an active professional organization comprised of more than 500 upbeat and energetic members. Because of the lifelong relationships formed and the positive impact CHART has on members' careers, loyalty to and involvement in the organization is exceptional.

With members from more than 350 multiunit restaurant, onsite, and hotel companies, CHART represents a workforce of almost 5 million. CHART includes all aspects of hospitality training, learning, and performance assessment.

The organization's mission is to develop hospitality training professionals to advance industry training practices and improve operational results by providing access to education, tools, and resources.

Courtesy of the Council of Hotel and Restaurant Trainers.

CHART
Council of Hotel and Restaurant Trainers

an example of a general training model, but every organization's training program must be designed to meet its particular needs in terms of size, employee culture, organizational structure, and so on.

Effective training and correctly used feedback can be excellent motivation for employees. Foodservice managers should consider the value of employee **empowerment** in creating a committed work force with good morale. Empowered employees do not have to check with a supervisor at every little decision point. They have embraced the principles and goals of their organization and they understand that any decision they make that aligns with those goals is a good decision. Whenever you hear the words, "I'll have to ask my manager about that . . ." or, "I can't help you with that right now; my manager won't be in until 10 A.M.," you can be sure that the employee has not been empowered to make decisions.

To empower her employees, a foodservice manager should be sure that they understand and embrace the main goals of the organization. She can then tell the employees that wherever or whenever they observe something happening that is contrary to the goals, they should do whatever is necessary to correct the situation. They can send back a steak, fetch a patient a different salad, or provide a free dessert—whatever it takes. Some organizations will set some

Figure 13.4 Pike Place Fish Market.

priorities: Employees may be empowered to provide substitutes of the same value or up to a specific dollar amount, but beyond that they must check with the manager and inform the manager when a customer is seriously angry about something and the employee-initiated remedies have not worked (which are all part of the service recovery discussed in Chapter 11). Employee empowerment can provide considerable value to an organization, but only when it is the result of a well-executed system for selecting, hiring, retaining, and training employees: "Engaged employees generate 33 percent higher profits, operate at 50 percent higher productivity, and score 56 percent higher in customer loyalty."[11]

To offer an example of an organization that, like Southwest Airlines, features an excellent employee selection and retention record, we now profile Seattle's Pike Place Fish Market, which opened in 1930 but began a new life in 1965. See Figure 13.4. Pike Place Fish Market resides on the first floor.

> As a man in his mid-twenties, John Yokoyama viewed working for Pike Place Fish as just a job. But when he was offered the change to buy the small fish stand in 1965, all of that changed. His first order of business was to grow the operation, creating a new future for himself and his employees. His first goal was to become world famous—not just for the fresh fish but for the service they provided to customers. According to the website, this meant: ". . . going beyond just providing outstanding service to people. It means really being present with people and relating to them as human beings."
>
> In the decades since, he has ensured that his employees relate to each and every customer and making a commitment to remain focused on the people side of the business. The interesting part of this is that the customer service that one finds at Pike Place Fish depends on the individual customer. Some want information, some want the fun, exciting attitude that the employees exude. And for those who have experienced Pike Place Fish, it is clear that this fish market is definitely one of a kind.

This information about Pike Place Fish Market vividly illustrates how an organization can build employee empowerment into its business model. Employees at Pike Place Fish Market are famous for throwing fish to each other and to customers. It's their trademark for customer involvement. A foodservice operation in a hospital might not be able to throw fish at its patients, but it can certainly empower its employees to care for customers and meet their needs.

■■ STAFFING AND SCHEDULING

Staffing and scheduling are often planned together, but they are not the same process. Some include recruitment, hiring, and placement under staffing, but doing so oversimplifies the term. Staffing is based on job analysis and is conducted in order to determine how many people are necessary to perform the various tasks that must be accomplished in the course of a workday or shift. Once that number is determined, scheduling distributes the work time of those employees across a given range of hours and workdays.

Unfortunately, in almost all areas of the foodservice industry, a day lasts longer than eight hours, and many foodservice operations are active seven days a week and even 24 hours a day. Many restaurants take off one day a week, so most must schedule for 6-day weeks and 8- to 12-hour days. School foodservice units and some in-plant operations generally feature 8-hour shifts in 5-day weeks, but university, healthcare, and nursing home foodservice operations almost all run 24/7 facilities. This makes for a very complex pattern of both staffing and scheduling. To manage complex scheduling situations, many organizations employ the concept of **full-time equivalent**, or FTE employees. Simply put, if an operation uses 8 full-time employees who each work 40 hours per week and 4 part-time employees who each work 20 hours per week, the number of FTEs is 10. That is because the four part-timers are equivalent to two full-time employees. This may seem simple, and its simplicity is one reason that so many large organizations use it.

Any foodservice manager with more than a handful of employees under her supervision spends a great deal of time working on schedules, communicating about schedules, clearing up confusion about schedules, or delegating all that work to someone else. To illustrate the complexities of scheduling foodservice staff, we take as a simplified example of this process a cafeteria-style onsite feeding location in a large corporate facility. The company employs 800 people and is in operation Monday through Friday from 7:30 A.M. to 3:30 P.M. Its foodservice unit offers a simple grab-and-go breakfast period beginning at 7:30 A.M. featuring a take-out-only menu of preassembled dishes.

It is staffed by a full-time cashier and a part-time person who works 20 hours per week restocking the wrapped-to-go items, making coffee, and so on. This equates to a staff of 1.5 FTEs based on the functions described, with the cashier remaining in the area at all times. For regular service, the cafeteria line has three cashier stations, a hot food area, a grill-to-order area, a sandwich-to-order area, a salads-to-order area, an area displaying desserts, and a self-serve beverage area. The job analysis shows peak attendance from 11:45 A.M. through 1 P.M., with generally slow traffic before and after the peak. Each station must be stocked to fill customer orders; food is prepared and plated promptly with each order at each area, and immediately passed to the customer, who moves down the line towards the cash register. In order to do this, the operation must employ one person at each of the major food stations from 11:30 A.M. through 1:15 P.M. Only one person is needed to keep beverages and drinks as well as several refrigerated cabinets offering take-out items continually stocked. Thus the staffing component for the peak period is eight (five line staff plus three cashiers). The lunch period actually runs from 11 A.M. through 2 P.M., but at the beginning and end there are many fewer customers.

This information alone tells the onsite manager that he will need eight people on duty for that peak period, with his two breakfast people working to keep food moving from the kitchen to the serving area. He also knows he will need four production people, the chef, and three others. The company's housekeeping staff assists his department with heavy cleaning, usually providing most of that coverage in the two hours before closing. (Remember, there are other functions in the department, but this analysis concerns only the cafeteria function.) Now that the manager has some idea of how many people he needs to carry out the cafeteria function, he can also identify the skills needed to fill those positions. The cashiers, who because of their greater responsibility are likely to be higher-level employees, will probably be supervisors. The other workers will be preparation workers who can assist the chef before the meal and take care of storage, cleanup, and prep for the next day.

This simplified model illustrates some of the considerations that are involved in staffing. Staffing is rarely this simple, however, because it is one thing to know how many people are needed to staff a given shift or daypart, but it is quite another to calculate how many employees must be on permanent staff to cover absences due to illness, personal days, vacations, and so on—depending on the size and complexity of the operation. Our simple eight-hour, five-day schedule requires all the employees in the department to work every day, Monday through Friday, but how many would be needed during nonpeak hours? Moreover, the actual work needed to cover the company's daily foodservice needs would likely extend beyond the eight hours of actual service. For example, preparation work for the breakfast shift would perhaps begin at 6:30 A.M., and the manager would have to staff shifts properly for those who do both prep work and station work to ensure having enough food and enough staff at the food stations during peak time. Finally, one or more staff members would be needed after 3:30 P.M. for cleanup and storage.

Now suppose our hypothetical company falls on difficult financial times and the food-service manager has been asked to cut one FTE. He would then have to look at the functions revealed by the job analysis and either eliminate a functional unit (such as shutting down the sandwich station and offering only prewrapped, premade sandwiches) or combining the workload of two stations so that one person could cover both of them. This could eventually lead to menu changes (eliminating some offerings), procurement changes (purchasing more presliced or precooked items), and so on. The job of the manager is to analyze functions and distribute labor. That is staffing.

To manage the complexities of scheduling, foodservice managers can choose from a wide range of employee scheduling software. These applications automate the process of creating and maintaining a schedule, simultaneously tracking vacations, sick leave, and other variables that will be discussed in the next section. In the past, a small operation would simply tack up a handwritten daily schedule, but today even the smallest foodservice operation will benefit from a scheduling software package to keep abreast of ever-changing (and ever-tightening) labor laws and regulations. In addition, employees have the right (and the need) to know when they will be working at least a week ahead of time so that they can manage childcare issues, additional jobs, and otherwise pursue their lives. Flexibility on the part of management and employees is essential for today's workforce planning.

There are many easily accessible online software-scheduling programs. Such systems are often easy to learn and need not be installed and maintained onsite. Indeed, as soon as an operation grows to the point of needing employees to cover more than eight hours of work time or operation more than five days a week, scheduling software becomes a necessity. The most common format in which scheduling data are organized is the **timebar**. When a schedule is displayed on a timebar, it is clear to all exactly who is doing what job when. Figure 13.5 illustrates a timebar schedule. Notice that this schedule covers a seven-day week, and for this reason it begins on Friday so that weekend coverage and days off are clearly seen. Also, schedules like this one often cover a multi-week rotation. The schedule displayed shows one week in a four-week rotating schedule that will provide every other weekend off for each employee. We see also that the unit using this schedule is open 13 hours a day, so employees are covering early and late shifts. Scheduling software usually requires the user to plug in the number of employees, the weekend coverage pattern, and opening and closing hours, after which it develops a schedule like this one, which may present some coverage issues. Note that an extra assistant cook is needed for this rotation to provide full coverage of the operation's functional needs. That is often what a manager does—he can have a worker from another part of the organization fill a small gap in the schedule, avoiding adding an additional person when an FTE is not needed.

	Position	Hours	Friday	Saturday	Sunday	Monday	Tuesday	Wednesday	Thursday
AM	Steward	8	6:00–2:30	x	x	6:00–2:30	6:00–2:30	6:00–2:30	6:00–2:30
PM	Steward	8	11:30–8:00	11:30–8:00	11:30–8:00	x	x	11:30–8:00	11:30–8:00
Float	Steward	8	x	6:00–2:30	6:00–2:30	11:30–8:00	11:30–8:00	10:30–7:00	x
AM	Assistant	8	6:00–2:30	x	x	6:00–2:30	6:00–2:30	6:00–2:30	6:00–2:30
PM	Assistant	8	x	6:00–2:30	6:00–2:30	x2	11:30–8:00	11:30–8:00	11:30–8:00
Float	Assistant	8	10:30–7:00	x	x	10:30–7:00	10:30–7:00	10:30–7:00	10:30–7:00
	Cook Assistant			10:30–7:00	10:30–7:00				

Figure 13.5 Timebar schedule.

■□ COMPENSATION
□■

Suppose you have decided what you need your employees to do, and you have looked for the best candidates, interviewed them, and hired a competent, committed staff. You have set clear performance standards and you provide feedback on performance. You have empowered your staff to provide excellent service, boosting their morale. You have developed an effective work schedule. You also pay them, but figuring out how much was not as simple as it sounds. Why? Because providing compensation means more than just paying wages—compensation comprises wages (or salaries) plus fringe benefits (as we introduced in Chapter 10). Compensation is also highly regulated, with rules governing overtime pay, holidays, shift differentials, and other factors. Even a small restaurant has to manage some of these issues.

Compensation requires a system for managing everything you have agreed to give to your employees in exchange for their labor. The HR Guide provides the following expanded definition: "Compensation is the methods and practices of maintaining a balance between the interests of operating the company within the fiscal budget and attracting, developing, retaining and rewarding high-quality employees through wages and salaries which are competitive within the prevailing roles for similar employment in the labor market."[13] This may sound complicated, but a smart manager, even of a small restaurant, will know what neighboring restaurants similar to his offer their staffs. If he cannot match the market, he had better be able to offer something else, such as better conditions, future rewards, better hours, profit sharing, or other benefits.

Today's families will often trade some compensation value for convenient daycare services or proximity to home. Wages vary for many reasons, but every foodservice manager must know how much and under what terms the competition pays their staff or he will ultimately lose his carefully chosen workers. In addition, many federal laws are mirrored and even expanded on by state laws, so it is important that employers know all applicable state and local regulations. Although every workplace is unique, a compensation package, in addition to wages, can include healthcare, vision care, dental care, a retirement package, life insurance, disability insurance, and other benefits. In some foodservice operations, meals are calculated as part of compensation. Some of these benefits are partially funded by the employer and partially funded by the employee as a payroll deduction.

In addition to the subjective side of wage and benefit negotiations—whether the employee feels valued adequately by the offer—there are some very specific laws that govern compensation. As we have seen in earlier chapters, not every provision of such laws applies to very small foodservice operations, but even a "mom and pop" restaurant should know these laws, since they should comply with them voluntarily to avoid possible threats and lawsuits. Foodservice managers in large chain restaurants or onsite operations will have an HRM department that is well versed in these laws, but compliance remains the responsibility of the individual manager. Here are a few of the more important laws:

■ The Fair Labor Standards Act (FSLA) was discussed in Chapter 7 under Food Safety and Sanitation. It is the federal law commonly known for setting standards for the minimum wage, overtime pay, the use of child labor, and record keeping that apply to most private and public employees. This law gives the US Department of Labor the authority to assign civil and criminal penalties for violations of the law, and also includes provisions allowing individual employees to file private lawsuits. The 1989 amendments to the FLSA added a provision for civil monetary penalties for repeated or willful minimum wage or overtime violations. Such penalties have been in place since 1974 to punish child labor violations. In essence, this law regulates who is covered by the minimum wage standards, when overtime pay must be provided, what kinds of records need to be kept by employers, and other areas.

- The **McNamara-O'Hara Service Contract Act (SCA)** applies to workers on federal service contracts, while the **Walsh-Healy Public Contracts Act (PCA)** applies to federal supply contracts. These laws may seem inapplicable to foodservice operations, but they apply to foodservice managers who work for large organizations under contract with government facilities. Other foodservice managers work for contract management companies with extensive government contracts. If a manager finds himself in either situation, he should determine whether either of these laws applies to his operation.

- The Wage and Hour Division has certain responsibilities under the **Immigration and Nationality Act (INA)**, mostly involving enforcement of labor standards protections and inspection for compliance with employment eligibility verification and recordkeeping requirements.

- The **Family and Medical Leave Act (FMLA)** entitles eligible employees up to 12 weeks of unpaid, job-protected leave for certain family and medical reasons. At the employee's or employer's option, certain kinds of paid leave may be substituted for unpaid leave. Employees are eligible if they have worked for a covered employer for at least one year and 1,250 hours over the previous 12 months, and if there are at least 50 employees within 75 miles. The employee may be required to provide advance leave notice and medical certification. For the duration of FMLA leave, the employer must maintain the employee's health coverage under any group health plan. Upon return from FMLA leave, most employees must be restored to their original or equivalent positions with equivalent pay, benefits, and other employment terms.

- The wage garnishment provisions of the **Consumer Credit Protection Act (CCPA)** protect employees from being discharged by employers because their wages have been garnished over any single debt, and it limits the amount of an employee's earnings that may be garnished in any one week. This law applies to all employees who receive earnings for personal services but usually does not apply to tips.

- **Equal Employment Opportunity laws (EEO)** prohibit specific types of employment discrimination on the basis of race, color, religion, sex, age, national origin, or status as an individual with a disability or a protected veteran.

For detailed information on all of these laws, the US Department of Labor (DOL) website is a valuable reference.[14]

In the restaurant business, the cost of noncompliance with the FLSA and the wage-and-hour laws has become staggering. In fact, the number of lawsuits has increased dramatically. All of these laws have their roots in abusive practices that can be traced to the nineteenth century. Prior to the existence (and periodic strengthening) of the regulatory apparatus, employees were vulnerable to a host of exploitative practices and unannounced pay deductions. The minimum wage changes periodically, so employers must be prepared to adjust to such changes. The foodservice compensation landscape is further complicated by the considerable role of tips in making up the total compensation package for an hourly employee. For example, tips may not be pooled with management personnel or other staff who do not usually receive them. The penalties, damages, and legal fees even for a small restaurant can run into the hundreds of thousands of dollars. The most common areas of wage and hour violations in foodservice operations include:

- The failure to pay overtime for all hours worked.

- Improper application of the tip credit.

- Misclassification of individuals as exempt from overtime.

- The failure to maintain records chronicling either hours of work or application of the tip credit.

Foodservice managers who do not work for large organizations with HRM departments can often turn to a local restaurant association, their state department of labor, or the federal department of labor website listed above for information about applicable federal and state laws.

One other set of laws that apply to some organizations are those governing the bargaining rights of employees. A series of labor relations laws have been enacted since the 1930s, governing the employer's ability to interfere with employee rights to join a union or participate in union activities. The **Taft-Hartley Act** of 1947 specifies very clear rules regulating what employers can do, balancing the powers of labor and management. In 1974, this law was extended to healthcare facilities. Again, organizations large enough to attract the interest of applicable unions usually keep legal counsel on staff and provide HRM support to the foodservice manager. When it comes to the bewildering world of labor and compensation law, we strongly advise any aspiring foodservice manager not to guess whether a given legal provision applies to your operation. Obtain competent legal advice if you are uncertain about anything.

MANAGERIAL IMPLICATIONS

By far the most important lesson of this chapter for foodservice managers is to value and respect their employees. In *Good to Great*, Jim Collins writes that a person in charge of a company needs to be sure that everyone is on the "right bus" and in "the right seat on the bus."[15] In fact, the exact statement is: "The purpose of a compensation system should not be to get the right behaviors from the wrong people, but to get the right people on the bus in the first place and to keep them there. . . . It might take time to know for certain if someone is simply in the wrong seat or whether he needs to get off the bus altogether." A foodservice manager should intend to offer the best food and service possible for his customer base and menu. He cannot achieve this if he does not get the right people to do the right jobs. This is the major implication of all HRM processes. A wise manager will strive to adjust or train his workforce until his workers share the vision and goals of the foodservice operation. Only then will the majority of his employees work together to achieve that vision and those goals.

A manager has many tools at her disposal, but those tools need to be used correctly. She must keep job descriptions up to date and make sure her employees know them. A manager should always know the competition. She should look around at other departments or other restaurants in her area. If they can get good people then she should be able to do so as well. Yet managers need to admit when they need help with recruiting. It is so easy for a foodservice manager to look for a person with experience in foodservice but whose skills may not be the skills that are needed. One of the most difficult managerial skills is letting people know when they have done a good job. Knowing when to offer an immediate and sincere "thank you" is one of a manager's most important skills. Managers also need to remember that most employees leave their jobs because they do not feel valued. It is possible to make them feel valued not only through pay or rewards but also by training them right and empowering them to make decisions.

Finally, foodservice managers must be knowledgeable about the laws that govern various aspects of HRM. There is no excuse for breaking these laws, and the results can be costly. After all, creating the work environment is the manager's responsibility—work should always be fun enough to keep employees coming back every day. Every employee wants a good boss!

Morrison

Morrison is a member of the Compass Group, a UK-based company with its Compass-North America division in Charlotte, NC. On the Morrison website, the company publishes testimonials from current employees who have risen through the ranks to management positions, with an entire section devoted to associate engagement. The following excerpt from the "Keep Em" site summarizes the company's program for retaining and engaging valuable employees.

At Morrison we're committed to retaining our greatest assets—our team members. Through our exclusive agreement with Career Systems International, Morrison has developed programs to continually stay in tune with team member attitudes and satisfaction levels. From genuinely listening to each other, to regularly measuring employee satisfaction, Morrison maintains a one-to-one connection with people that results in a healthy, productive team environment. And it's working, as evidenced by two key measurements. For the first 5 years of the program, the number of associates who felt engaged in their jobs rose by 60%. And for the same period management turnover has decreased by 23 percent.

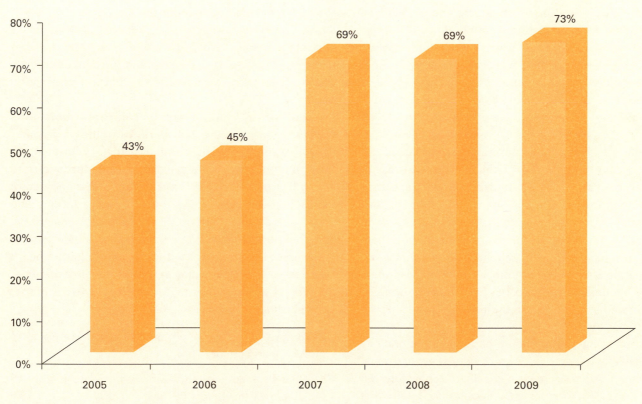

Associate Engagement

KEY TERMS

job analysis   282

job description   283

job specification   284

performance standards   284

behavioral interview   289

panel interview   289

peer interview   289

retention   290

stay interview   290

360-degree feedback   291

exit interviews   292

training   292

professional development   292

empowerment   294

full-time equivalent (FTE)   295

timebar   297

McNamara-O'Hara Service Contract Act (SCA)   299

Walsh-Healy Public Contracts Act (PCA)   299

Immigration and Nationality Act (INA)   299

Family and Medical Leave Act (FMLA)   299

Consumer Credit Protection Act (CCPA)   299

Equal Employment Opportunity laws (EEO)   299

Taft-Hartley Act   300

Case in Point

New Employees or New Motivational Techniques?

Johanna was furious. She has been the foodservice manager for a 500-student middle school for the past 15 years. She remembers how she felt when she was first hired as a cafeteria line person in a school in her hometown, 25 years ago. She was so excited to have the job, and she had always wanted to work with kids. Since she also loved food and wanted to go on to college, this would be a job she loved and one that could help her earn money for college. She loved her job. Or, as she often pointed out, she loved most of her job. The kids didn't always like the food, and they could sometimes be "difficult," but since Johanna was close to their age, she was often the one they came to with complaints. In the beginning, she would pass them on to her supervisor, who usually said there was no money, or the equipment was old, and nothing changed. Johanna eventually stopped passing these comments on and vowed she would run things differently. So why is she furious today?

She can't remember when it happened, but one day she noticed that her employees no longer seemed to care. The cafeteria line was messy, the lines repeatedly ran short on food, workers never smiled at kids, and, worst of all, they frequently called in sick. She hated Mondays because she was always having to work at least two jobs in addition to her own. She wished she had some way to catch these people out having fun when they had called

in sick. It happened again today and for her, it was the last straw. She went to see the school district's HRM director and told her story. "Why," she complained, "can't we get the right people these days? I would have loved to have one of these jobs. You have got to find me some good people . . ."

Leon, the HRM director, compared Johanna's departmental turnover numbers with those of other school departments and compared them with those of other middle schools in the district. Her turnover rate was much higher and complaints about the food were increasing. This made Johanna even more furious and she told Leon she might quit. Leon said that was not the solution. He said he could help her design a plan "to find her employees doing something *right*." Johanna heard that phrase, and something in it reminded her of something she learned in school. She calmed down and told Leon she wanted to try.

1. You are now Leon. List the things you are going to ask Johanna to do.

2. What skills do you think Johanna may have stopped using over the years?

3. What can she remember from her days as an employee to help her?

4. List some resources Johanna may want to use.

REVIEW AND DISCUSSION QUESTIONS

1. What is the difference between a job analysis and a job description?

2. Why is a job specification important? Give three examples of job specifications for a dishwasher

3. Most college graduates are encouraged to stay with their first post-graduation job for at least two years. In the context of HRM, and recruitment in particular, why is such advice important?

4. What is an advantage of peer interviews? What might be a disadvantage?

5. Think of a job you've had in the past (or have now). List four job standards.

6. If given the choice, would you prefer 360-degree feedback? Explain your answer fully.

7. Think of your recent experiences while eating in restaurants. Describe a situation where (a) you witnessed behavior suggesting the employees were empowered or (b) you discerned that the employees were not empowered.

8. Go to the HRSoftware website. Describe two offerings that you might use as a foodservice manager.

9. What is the difference between staffing and scheduling?

10. You manage 26 full-time employees, 4 employees who work 30 hours per week each, and 7 employees who each work 20 hours per week. How many FTEs is that?

11. List two of the governmental acts discussed in the chapter. How might they affect you as a foodservice manager?

12. Go to the WhatsNext4Me website and explore profiles of three people who work for companies that interest you. What is the common theme among these individuals?

ENDNOTES

1. Adapted from: Spectrum Health System. "Councils That Make a Difference." *Press Ganey Satisfaction Monitor* (March/April, 2008).

2. "Whats Next 4 Me." www.whatsnext4me.com. Accessed September 2012.

3. Freiberg, K., and Freiberg, J. *Nuts!* Austin, TX: Bard Press, 1996.

4. Jennings, L. "Professional Hiring Practices Can Go a Long Way Toward Weeding Out Lawsuit-happy Employees." *Nation's Restaurant News* (September 14, 2009).

5. Kaye, B., and Jordan-Evans, S. *Love 'Em or Lose 'Em.* San Francisco: Berrett-Koehler Publishers, Inc., 2008.

6. Quintessential Careers. Sample behavioral interview questions. www.quintcareers.com.

7. Studer Group, LLC. Selection and early retention. Presented as part of: Focusing Nine Principles on Food and Environmental Services. Las Vegas, 2005.

8. Berta, D. "Poorly Managed Jobs Can Lead to Indifferent Employees." *Nation's Restaurant News* (June 2, 2008).

9. Sullivan, J. "What You Get Paid For: An Open Letter from the Owner to the Crew." *Nation's Restaurant News* (December 14, 2009).

10. Berta, D. "Exit Interviews Reveal the Issues That Lead to Turnover." *Nation's Restaurant News* (June 23, 2008).

11. Career Systems International. *The Talent Edge: Daily Dose.* Career Systems International Training Materials ©2007.

12. Pike Place Fish Market. www.pikeplacefish.com.

13. HRGuide.com. www.HRGuide.com.

14. US Department of Labor. www.dol.gov.

15. Collins, J. *Good to Great.* New York: Harper Business, 2001.

CHAPTER 14

LEADERSHIP AND MANAGEMENT

LEARNING OBJECTIVES:

After becoming familiar with this chapter, you should be able to:

1. Describe how our conception of leadership has evolved over the last 100 years.

2. Understand the difference between leadership and management as well as the behaviors and functions each entails.

3. Identify the key principles that lead to effective supervision.

4. Appreciate the importance of ethics in foodservice management, and explain the ethical dimensions of customer and employee relations.

We conclude Part 3 with two elemental, indispensable aspects of foodservice operations. These aspects—leadership and management—may seem synonymous, but they are conceptually distinct and it is important to understand this distinction. Not every competent manager is a true leader. The task of organizing people and allocating resources has always been important, but in today's environment, with rapid globalization, accelerating innovation, and relentless competition transforming industry after industry, management through effective leadership makes the difference between success and failure in the foodservice industry. In this chapter we explore how leadership in the foodservice industry has evolved and, informed by this historical perspective, we compare leadership and management, and then distinguish these capacities from supervision. We discuss resource allocation and leadership development, the latter adding a new perspective to our discussion of training in Chapter 13. We conclude by examining key ethical issues with which managers and leaders must contend when managing their relations with both guests and employees.

▪▫ LEADERSHIP'S EVOLUTION
▫▪

Early philosophies of leadership focused exclusively on characteristics and competencies. The belief was that leaders were born with specific personality traits that made them successful in harnessing the will of others. These **trait theories** attempted to separate leaders from other members of an organization based on physical attributes, personality characteristics, and even appearance or age. The notion was that leaders naturally developed traits that made people follow them unconditionally. For instance, an early researcher defined leadership as "the ability to impress the will of the leader on those led and induce obedience, respect, loyalty, and cooperation."[1] Not surprisingly, this view of leadership has evolved. This evolution is most evident when we consider **behavioral theories** of leadership.

Before we address the leadership theories most relevant to foodservice management, we should note that all leadership theories in one way or another address the ways in which followers receive guidance and respond to leaders. This then shapes the effects of leadership on an organization. Foodservice managers who understand the differences among theories of leadership should be able to adapt their management styles most effectively, but because leadership theories have spawned such a voluminous body of literature, our goal here is to describe only those theories that are most likely to be useful to you in your foodservice career.

Leadership Theories

Behavioral theories of leadership emerged largely in response to the deficiencies of trait theories. After all, the erroneous notion that leaders are born and not made became more obvious as successful leaders adopted common strategies that led to success. Moreover, empirical research on leadership beginning in the 1940s showed that no single physical or personality trait distinguishes successful leaders from unsuccessful ones.

Three studies formed the foundation for the prevailing behavioral theories of leadership. The earliest research, conducted by Kurt Lewin, a German-American psychologist recognized as the founder of modern social psychology, identified three basic styles of leadership. The **Lewin studies** suggested that a leader's behavioral style does not change based on external factors such as situation or setting. The **autocratic style** is directive and controlling. The autocratic manager monitors and directs work closely with a low tolerance for ambiguity. Employees have little discretionary influence. The **democratic style**, on the other hand, is collaborative and inclusive. Everyone is welcome to make suggestions and the associated climate is inclusive with the intent of fostering creativity. Although the leader has the ultimate authority and responsibility, employees have a high degree of influence. The **laissez-faire style** is really nonleadership. Here, the leader abdicates responsibility, creating role ambiguity because of the failure to define work goals, responsibilities, and outcomes. Unless someone else steps in, the result is chaos and business failure. (We'll talk more about leadership styles later in the chapter.)

In the 1940s, the **Ohio State studies** provided a new way of looking at leader behavior. The intent was to describe a leader's behavior but not to evaluate or judge it. The results produced two underlying dimensions of leadership behavior. The first, coined **initiating structure**, is leader behavior aimed at identifying and organizing work processes and employee tasks and roles as well as establishing patterns for accomplishing the associated business outcomes. The second dimension was labeled **consideration**, which is leader behavior aimed at nurturing collaborative workplace relationships. The studies suggested that these are independent behavioral dimensions, and a leader could be rated as high or low in either or both of them.

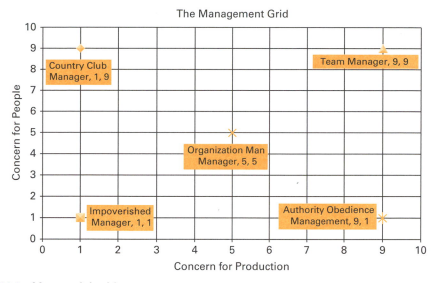

Figure 14.1 Managerial grid.

Adapted from "The Leadership Grid" figure from Blake, R. R., & McCanse, A. A. (1991). Leadership Dilemmas—Grid Solutions. *Houston, TX: Gulf Publishing Company, p. 29.*

The following decade, the **Michigan studies** adopted yet another approach to identifying leader behavior, assuming that a leader's behavior can be defined based on how she creates the emotional atmosphere of the workplace. The study found that successful leaders assume a more hands-off approach, directing firm policy at a higher level while leaving many details to be managed by subordinates. By contrast, unsuccessful leaders tend to micromanage, with the leader closely observing and controlling employees' work. Today, we consider leaders in the former category, those who achieve success by inspiring and exciting followers to high levels of performance—relying on personal attributes instead of their official position to manage employees—to be **transformational**. They contrast with **transactional** leaders, who focus almost exclusively on daily tasks and rely on a system of rewards and punishment to shape employees' behavior.

These, as well as many other studies, led psychology researchers Robert Blake and Jane Mouton to develop still another behavioral interpretation of leadership, which they called the **managerial grid**. Blake and Mouton divided a manager's attitudes and related behaviors along two dimensions. In this classification scheme, concern for production places the emphasis on output (such as menu items), cost effectiveness, and profit. Concern for people emphasizes promoting interpersonal relationships and employee satisfaction.

As Figure 14.1 shows, the Managerial Grid theory depicts five key styles of leadership based on how a manager rates with respect to the two attitudinal categories, concern for production and concern for people. The **country club manager** focuses almost exclusively on the needs of employees and interpersonal relationships within the workplace but focuses little time and energy on the quality or quantity of departmental output. In sharp contrast, the **authority-obedience manager** (similar to the transactional leader) emphasizes production and efficiency, in large part by minimizing the need for interpersonal contact. Behaviors associated with this leadership style are similar to those of the aforementioned autocratic manager. Characterized by behavior that is similar to that of the laissez-faire style of leadership, the **impoverished manager** largely abdicates responsibility for both employees and food-related products or service. The **organization-man manager** strives for adequate departmental performance with modest morale levels; this type of manager does little to affect the status quo and resists change. Finally, the **team manager** (similar to the transformational leader) emphasizes high levels of quality output while concurrently focusing on developing employees as well as fostering individuals' interconnectedness.

Categorizing leadership in this way underscores the strengths of some leadership styles, but it suffers from the weakness of presenting the associated traits as applicable regardless of the setting or situation. This is particularly problematic when applied to the diversity of business models that make up the foodservice industry, as the setting and situation are rarely the same from one operation to another, even within a given segment. To address this shortcoming of the foregoing theories we consider another theoretical approach based on **contingency theories**, which can be applied according to the unique situational variables present in a given setting.

Fiedler's contingency theory posits that the fit between a leader's preferred style and the favorableness of a situation dictates a foodservice operation's effectiveness and success. The theory separates leaders' styles into two types, one that is *task-oriented* and one that is *relationship-oriented*. It also separates the situations into three dimensions of favorableness: *task structure*, which refers to the quantity and clarity of rules, policies, and procedures; *position power*, gained through formal authority, which pertains to the leader's legitimacy in evaluating and rewarding performance and punishing noncompliance; and *leader-member relations*.

Situations are considered favorable when good leader–member relations exist, tasks are highly structured, and the leader is in a strong position of power. Conversely, an unfavorable leadership situation exists when relations are strained, little task structure exists, and the leader has little formal power. Between these two extremes, the leadership situation offers varying degrees of moderate favorableness.

Contingency theory also suggests that the task-oriented leader has a higher likelihood of success in both very favorable and highly unfavorable situations. The explanation for this hypothesis is that in highly favorable situations, the leader can easily move the operation toward the desired objective since the employees are trusting, the task is clearly delineated, and the leader's power is understood by everyone involved. In highly unfavorable situations, a task-oriented leader, as opposed to a relationship-oriented leader, is more likely to take charge and make decisions without soliciting input, whereas the latter will place greater emphasis on making people happy but will have greater difficulty accomplishing task objectives.

Path-goal theory sees the leader's primary role as that of clearing a path so that employees can reach a goal. As shown in Figure 14.2, according to this theory a leader should adopt the one of these four styles that is most suited to completing a given task. In doing so, the leader must consider both the foodservice setting and the types of employees who are charged with carrying out the task.

The *directive style* is used when a leader must give specific directions about how to accomplish work tasks, making the expectations clear. The *supportive style* is adopted when a leader needs to express concern for an employee's well-being, social status, or special situation. The *participative style* is appropriate when a leader must engage with employees' decision-making activities. The *achievement-oriented style* is appropriate when the leader sets challenging goals for employees, encouraging them and expressing confidence in their abilities.

Leader-member exchange (LMX) theory, initially called vertical dyad linkage, contends that leaders do not treat all subordinates alike. The differences are related to characteristics of subordinate-supervisor relationships that shape the behavior of both parties. For example, a subordinate, say a counterperson, who demonstrates commitment to an operation through such behaviors as good attendance, positive attitude, and general service orientation, will likely be rewarded with more of the leader's positional resources (such as confidence, concern, additional training, and possibly even more opportunities for advancement) than will others who do not display such behaviors.

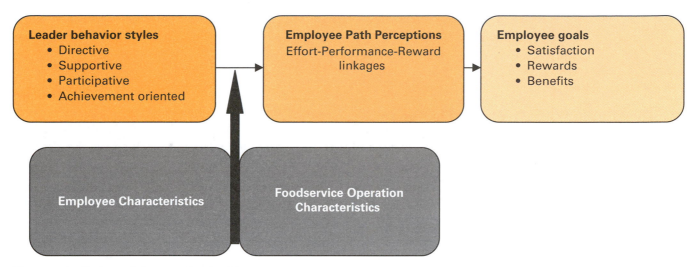

Figure 14.2 Path-goal theory of leadership.

As these relationships develop, a leader often acquires a propensity for attracting an "in-group" of subordinates, which consigns others to membership in an "out-group." The in-group consists of subordinates with established histories of positive exchanges with the leader and in whom the leader has greater confidence. As a result, these subordinates typically assume greater responsibility in the operation, contribute more effectively to its goals, and receive higher performance ratings than do those having low-quality relationships with the leader.

The final contingency leadership theory we consider here is depicted by the Situational Leadership® model. Developed by Paul Hersey and Kenneth Blanchard, this model focuses on the readiness of subordinates to respond as the primary condition of effective leadership. Like Fielder's theory, this model measures leader behavior along two dimensions: concern with tasks and concern with relationships. Based on these behavioral dimensions, this posits a range of leadership styles and measures their appropriateness with respect to four levels of subordinate maturity. Follower readiness is determined by employees' willingness and ability to accept responsibility for accomplishing operational tasks.

This model might strike a familiar note for students with foodservice management experience. According to the theoretical foundations of the model, a leader should adopt a *telling* style of leadership in response to immature followers—individuals who are unwilling and unable to accept responsibility for completing their work. Such a leadership style focuses almost exclusively on applying strong initiating structure behavior to the task and minimizes the influence of the superior-subordinate relationships. To work effectively with employees at the second level of maturity, leaders are advised to use a *selling* style, one in which their concern with both task and relationship is high. To work with able but unwilling employees, those at the third level on the maturity scale, the leader needs to use a *participating* style, which combines high concern with relationships with low concern with the task. Finally, the most mature followers require a *delegating* style of leadership. Mature employees accept responsibility, relieving the leader of concern for both the task and the relationship.

As these relationships develop, a leader often acquires a propensity for attracting an "in-group" of subordinates, which consigns others to membership in an "out-group." The in-group consists of subordinates with established histories of positive exchanges with the leader and in whom the leader has greater confidence. As a result, these subordinates typically assume greater responsibility in the operation, contribute more effectively to its goals, and receive higher performance ratings than do those having low-quality relationships with the leader.

The Leader of Tomorrow

In the final chapter of his seminal 1954 book *The Practice of Management*, Peter Drucker—considered the father of modern management—described the "manager of tomorrow." He wrote that the era of the "intuitive manager" had ended, bringing unprecedented demands on leaders to exhibit high levels of skill, knowledge, performance, responsibility, and integrity. He then listed seven new tasks that future leaders must embrace:

1. Manage by objectives.

2. Take more risks and for a longer period.

3. Make strategic decisions.

4. Build an integrated team wherein each member is capable of managing and measuring his own performance.

5. Communicate information quickly and clearly, motivating as he goes.

6. See the business as a whole, integrating its many parts.

7. Relate the businesses products or services to the total environment, including in his field of vision economic, political, and social developments in other markets on a global basis.

As history attests, Drucker's crystal ball provided a remarkably clear image. Although the terms would not appear in the literature for several decades, we see now that Drucker was describing a transformational manager with a global perspective.

Almost 50 years later, Drucker offered another set of predictions about the leader for the future. In his 1998 *Forbes* article, he noted that future leadership will not conform to any one style or theory of leadership.[2] "That one way or another people need to be managed remains the prevailing view, but it is wrong." He concluded that, in the near future, managers will not succeed by merely managing people, they must *lead*; but they must do so by capitalizing on the strengths and knowledge of their followers.

Many agree with Drucker. Even as early as the 1970s, some of the basic assumptions of leadership began to be questioned. Kerr and Jermier, for example, proposed that there might be substitutes for leadership that make leader behavior redundant.[3] As shown in Table 14.1, employee experience, ability, and training can substitute for or neutralize leadership. For example, when

TABLE 14.1 Substitutes of Neutralizers for Leadership

Subordinate Characteristics	Task Characteristics	Organizational Characteristics
Experience, ability, and training	Structured and routine task	Cohesive work groups
Professional orientation	Feedback within the task	Leader's low position of power
Indifference toward organizational rewards	Intrinsically satisfying task	Leader physically isolated from subordinates

a task is very satisfying to an employee and the associated feedback is positive, there is no need for leadership or any extrinsic motivation. Similarly—and this applies particularly to foodservice management—employees with direct customer contact (e.g., servers and bartenders) receive leadership from guests in the form of customer demands and rewards (either monetary or in the form of praise).

Our changing view of leadership brings us to the newest evolutionary stage in the theory, **servant leadership**. Here, the leader seeks to support and empower employees. In essence, leaders lead by serving others.

This new conception of leadership reimagines elements from earlier leadership theories and is aligned with Drucker's call for leaders to be flexible, adapting to the situations they face. Servant leaders are motivated by the desire to serve and empower; their primary focus is on developing employees as an end in itself. Notice how leaders who embody this concept differ from transformational leaders, who are, by definition, focused on the organization's needs and goals and achieve these through charisma.[4]

LEADERSHIP VERSUS MANAGEMENT

In the previous section, we focused on leadership. The theoretical approaches we introduced often treat leadership and management as equivalent concepts. Are these truly the same? Drucker, in differentiating the two, offers: "Management is doing things right; leadership is doing the right thing." Let's consider some of the similarities and differences, and then examine characteristic behaviors and functions that reflect that relationship.

Similarities and Differences

Here we regard leadership, in the most general terms, as the process of guiding and directing the behavior of foodservice employees to achieve an operation's benchmarks of success. (Notice that this is a traditional definition, not one embracing servant leadership.) More specifically, leadership brings about beneficial changes in a foodservice establishment, enhancing the experience for all concerned (customers, employees, vendors, managers, and owners). In a business and industry (B&I) setting, the guests are the employees of the organization so foodservice leadership might also contribute to achieving strategic goals set at a higher organizational level, such as a factory or corporate headquarters. In a healthcare setting, it might extend throughout all areas of a hospital.

Management, following the traditional model, involves (1) **planning**, (2) **organizing**, (3) **directing**, and (4) **controlling**. Consider this in the context of a foodservice manager. In preparing the upcoming year's budget, she is establishing a plan. In assigning job duties to her assistant managers, she is organizing. In working with her chef on reducing food cost, she is directing. In each of these examples, she is controlling how the restaurant or cafe operates.

Yet the line between the two roles becomes somewhat blurred when we consider that a leader can also manage, and a manager can also lead. Conversely, anyone in an organization can be a leader, but not everyone with the title of manager knows how to lead. Thus, anyone with foodservice experience can attest to the unpleasantness of working for or with a manager who does not inspire employees or one whom not everyone considers a leader. One of the more useful approaches to discerning the sometimes-subtle differences is shown in Table 14.2, which builds on Drucker's earlier quotation.

TABLE 14.2   Characteristics of Managers vs. Leaders

Manager	Leader
Administrates	Innovates
Focuses on systems and structure	Focuses on people
Relies on control	Inspires trust
Possesses short-range view	Maintains long-range perspective
Asks how and when	Asks what and why
Watches the bottom line	Watches the horizon
Imitates	Originates
Accepts the status quo	Challenges the status quo
Does things right	Does the right thing

Adapted from Bennis, W. G. "Managing the dream: Leadership in the 21st century." *Journal of Organizational Change Management, 2*(1) (1989): 7.

Leadership Behaviors

Another way to explore the difference between leadership and management is to consider the tasks, behaviors, or functions that are specific to each type. For outstanding leadership, then, we can consider ten behaviors that are suggested by the transformational and in some cases servant leadership theories when applied to the foodservice industry:[5]

1. *Vision.* Outstanding leaders see the future and articulate how employees can play a role in that future, one that aligns with both the organization's and the employees' values.

2. *Passion and self-sacrifice.* Outstanding leaders are passionate in conviction and integrity. They model the behavior of a loyal servant and make extraordinary self-sacrifices for the company and employees.

3. *Confidence, determination, and persistence.* Outstanding leaders show faith in themselves and their employees, as well as confidence that their vision will be attained. They also exhibit strong moral conviction, despite the challenges they pose to the status quo.

4. *Image building.* Outstanding leaders are self-conscious and often insecure about their own image, as they want to be perceived as competent and credible.

5. *Role modeling.* Outstanding leaders build on the aforementioned ideal image so that employees can emulate the associated behaviors, embracing the organization's values and aligning these values with their own.

6. *External representation.* Outstanding leaders act as spokespersons for their foodservice organizations and serve as symbols to those outside of the company. (Think of the pizza chain, Papa John's. As shown in Figure 14.3, the spokesperson in its advertisements and the face on the website is founder "Papa" John Schmatter.)

7. *Expectations of and confidence in employees.* Outstanding leaders continually communicate high performance expectations with the implicit message that employees will realize these expectations.

8. *Selective motive arousal.* Outstanding leaders selectively stimulate employee motives that are instrumental in leading others to achieve the goals of the leader and the organization.

Courtesy Papa John's International, Inc.

Figure 14.3 Papa John's advertisement featuring founder and leader "Papa" John Schmatter.

9. *Frame alignment.* Outstanding leaders persuade employees to implement changes that facilitate the alignment of their personal goals with those of the organization. This congruence also pertains to employees' interests, values, and beliefs with respect to the leader's ideology.

10. *Inspirational communication.* Outstanding leaders often communicate their messages using vivid stories, slogans, symbols, and ceremonies that celebrate the employees' and organizations' success in overcoming hurdles or realizing goals.

The next step in understanding what constitutes effective leadership is identifying the skills that are needed to behave consistently with these ten principles. Fortunately, we have a considerable body of research identifying and analyzing the skills that a high-performing leader should possess:

- Communication skills, including listening
- Cultural flexibility
- People skills
- Problem solving
- Motivating skills
- Goal setting
- Delegating
- Time management

■ Decision making

■ Team building

■ Innovativeness

Note that these skills are behavioral in nature. They are not traits or styles. But they also may seem contradictory. After all, if delegating is important, why is decision making on the list? Can't it be delegated? Notice, too, that there is considerable overlap. For example, people skills are difficult to apply without communication skills. The reason for the apparent paradoxes and redundancies is that effective leaders do not employ any one skill or set of skills independently of the others. Effective leaders adapt their multiple skills to specific situations as appropriate.

Management Functions

Recognizing that leaders can be managers and managers can serve as leaders, we should now consider the functions of management, particularly in light of the behaviors and skills associated with leadership introduced in the previous section. As noted earlier, these functions are generally described as planning, organizing, directing, and controlling. We can break down each of these functions into several components.

Planning. Planning and coordinating apply to all aspects of a foodservice operation. For example, a manager sets goals and objectives for the year. In addition to budgetary goals, these might involve succession planning for various members of the staff. Planning can also include short- and long-term staffing needs. In the short term, say the next two weeks, a manager schedules the staff in terms of who works when. The long-term planning potentially involves comprehensive changes to staffing patterns.

Organizing. Earlier we identified assigning job duties as an organizing function. Another is developing job descriptions (recall our discussion of these in Chapter 13). Organizing also includes managing paperwork, collecting data to generate operating reports, and clarifying roles for supervisory staff members. Finally, organizing also includes bringing all of a foodservice operation's functions together to achieve management goals. This might mean making sure everyone knows how her job contributes to realizing the organization's vision or more specifically how ordering and receiving or recruiting and selecting employees complement one another.

Directing. At first glance, giving direction might seem to involve simply telling an employee what to do, but it also includes decision making and problem solving, as well as motivating and reinforcing positive behaviors. Another function in this area is directing the flow of information. Do the employees know what the manager expects? Do they know what the policies are? Do they know what to do in an emergency? These all pertain to directing.

Controlling. The last function can be somewhat misleading. A manager can't control every aspect of a foodservice operation. Even a small deli has so many small service exchanges and operational issues that it would be impossible for one person to control them all. However, a manager can monitor work and workplace behavior. He can ensure that foodservers are not standing in the kitchen chatting instead of attending to guests. He can also control the processes that are in place. (Recall our discussion of handling food invoices.)

It might seem that a manager's job is difficult to summarize even using the typology discussed here. In truth, the beauty of foodservice management is that no two days are the same. While one day might involve extensive planning, the next might be spent directing, putting out small fires throughout the operation. One group of researchers attempted to assess what managers do during the course of the average day. As shown in Figure 14.4, only a portion of a manager's day is spent doing the traditional functions. It is also interesting, and valuable, to note that the bulk of a manager's activities involves interpersonal skills.

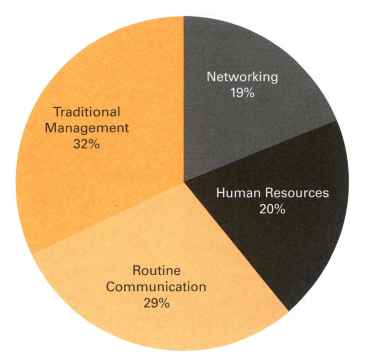

Figure 14.4 Relative distribution of managers' activities.

Adapted from Luthans, F., R. M. Hodgetts, & S. Rosenkrantz (1988). Real Managers. *Ballinger: Cambridge, MA. p. 27.*

▪▫ SUPERVISION

Many foodservice managers begin as supervisors, a management level that is relatively low in responsibility and authority. Supervisory positions are, however, vital to an organization's output. Think of an evening supervisor who oversees the largely part-time staff responsible for feeding patients in a hospital foodservice setting, or a supervisor of a small corner cafe who oversees four baristas. Such supervisors are charged with watching, directing, and often participating in the foodservice operation's primary activities.

To understand the differences between managers and supervisors, it is useful to categorize managerial skills as technical, interpersonal, and conceptual. **Technical skills** are those required to complete a specific job function. For example, a cook requires a range of culinary skills to fulfill his role. An auto mechanic must have the necessary skills to repair cars. The sophistication of the technical skill needed for a particular job function depends on the complexity of that job.

Interpersonal skills involve the ability to interact and communicate with others. The ability to "get along" with others is part of this, but that alone is typically not sufficient for effective communication. In jobs that require strong interpersonal skills (such as manager), the ability to convey ideas and listen to others is critical.

Conceptual skills involve seeing the big picture. In our earlier discussion of leadership, we talked about the importance of seeing how a company fits within an industry and within the global economy; these are conceptual skills. In the foodservice industry, this means understanding how all aspects of a restaurant, cafe, or nightclub fit together, how each is important in maximizing customer satisfaction. Finally, conceptual skills in today's environment include understanding the political, social, and economic forces that might affect a foodservice operation.

Industry leaders require strong conceptual and interpersonal skills. Consider, for example, the ten behaviors associated with outstanding leadership. On the one hand, virtually every one entails some combination of conceptual and interpersonal skills. On the other hand, technical skills are not particularly important to good leadership. Consider the CEO of an automotive company. She needs to appreciate the complexities of designing, building, and repairing a car, but she does not need to know how to replace a spark plug.

Effective managers generally can balance technical and conceptual skills. Especially at lower levels of management, where a kitchen manager might need to fill in for a cook or a bar manager might tend bar for a shift, technical skills are important. Yet these managers also must possess conceptual skills in order to manage a business effectively. As we've demonstrated, the skills that are most important for managers are interpersonal.

The skill set required by supervisors is somewhat the reverse of what leaders must possess. Although interpersonal skills are obviously important because a foodservice supervisor is, primarily, overseeing people, technical skills are more important for supervisors than for managers or leaders because supervisors must understand very clearly how to perform the tasks that his employees perform. On the other hand, supervisors need conceptual skills much less than do managers and leaders; what supervisors need most is an understanding of how the job functions she oversees contribute to the foodservice operation as a whole.

To understand the role played by supervision in foodservice operations, let's consider the following 12 **supervision principles:**[6]

1. *Set unmistakable goals.* No employee can do his job effectively unless he understands what he's supposed to do. Consider, for example, a hospital foodservice supervisor who hires a tray-delivery employee and simply says, "Deliver breakfast trays to patients on the seventh floor." Thanks to a series of phone calls from upset patients, the supervisor learns that the employee failed to fill the empty coffee cups, which were on the trays. In this example, the supervisor did not make the goals clear.

2. *Supervise the work more than the worker.* The supervisor who hovers over the grill cook to ensure she does every little thing perfectly is not going to be effective. Alternatively, the supervisor who monitors the hamburgers that are on the serving line and then thanks the cook for what looks good and makes suggestions on how to improve what doesn't will have a more productive work experience.

3. *Distinguish between essential and nonessential rules.* In any foodservice operation, some rules are more critical than others are. Think of a cook who likes to wear expressive chef pants. No one but the kitchen staff sees him. Still, the policy is for each cook to wear black pants. This is a good example of allowing self-expression within guidelines, and perhaps making all employees feel they have a bit more control. On the other hand, head covers are essential because of health department regulations and cannot be a matter of choice.

4. *Reward sparingly, punish much more sparingly.* As in many industries, the common form of reward is praise and the most common punishment is criticism. In general, public praise is good. However, there may be instances in which praising one employee may be interpreted as a criticism of his peers. In such situations, praise should be withheld until the appropriate supervisor can deliver it without unintended effects. On the other hand, public criticism is unnecessary. A supervisor's public criticism of an employee undermines the employee's position in the workgroup, reducing that person's capacity to perform and lowering the morale of those around her.

5. *Give credit where credit is due*. Success should be credited to an entire work group, say the entire kitchen staff. After all, the supervisor has asked everyone to work together, so everyone should be credited when things go well. However, the supervisor should assume responsibility for failure. This is easier said than done, perhaps, but blame and excuses must stop with management. It is a manager's responsibility to ensure employees' success, not to blame them (or anyone else) for his failure.

6. *Listen to complaints sympathetically; never complain in turn*. This follows from number 5. Sometimes employees just want to know that their supervisor cares about how they feel. By listening respectfully, the supervisor conveys a sense that she does indeed care about what the employees have to say and how they feel. Employees, however, do not want to listen to the supervisor complain—ever.

7. *Defend the faith*. The supervisor represents management and, as such, he should take the employees and the foodservice operation more seriously than anyone else does. A supervisor, like a leader, has the opportunity—and one that should not be wasted—to instill pride in the very nature of the job.

8. *Develop an inner circle*. When a supervisor has a wide **span of control**—that is, a large number of people that she supervises—it is advisable to identify a handful of top performers and share some of the supervisory responsibility with them. This does not mean abdicating authority—having an informal team of lieutenants can make everyone more successful. When there are few employees within the span of control, however, this strategy could be seen as playing favorites, which harms morale.

9. *Protect the status of subordinates*. A supervisor might work under several layers of management, all with arguably greater stakes in her foodservice operation's success. Some managers will not respect a supervisor's role and may be inclined to discipline a line employee who reports to that supervisor. In such a case, the supervisor must intervene. For example, say a supervisor instructs hostesses to make every effort to seat guests as quickly as possible. The operation's normal policy dictates that only hostesses may seat people. However, the supervisor asks a server whether, if there are no hostesses staffing the podium at a particular time, he would seat one or two parties. When the general manager observes this server seating a group at a table, he immediately disciplines the hostess for breaking policy. Here, the supervisor must intercede and assume responsibility, protecting the subordinate.

10. *Retain final control*. Despite the earlier discussion about the importance of delegating and working with employees, the supervisor must have the last word in making important decisions. A supervisor will inevitably have to make unpopular decisions, but failing to make such decisions when she deems them necessary is not meeting the responsibilities of the job.

11. *Innovate democratically*. Even in the simplest foodservice operation, there are nearly always multiple ways of doing things. A supervisor who asks employees about how to improve things (and embraces good suggestions) will be far more successful than one who has all the answers and forces changes unilaterally. This may seem contrary to the previous principle, but in fact, they are complementary.

12. *Take infinite pains*. This is arguably the most important principle and is probably the hardest to learn. Some people come by it naturally, while others need to acquire the habit by experience and practice. Supervisors must strive, as Drucker said, to "do things right."

■□ LEADERSHIP DEVELOPMENT

We have worked our way from the top of the managerial ladder to the bottom in the preceding sections. We now consider the importance of moving back up the ladder. Supervisors are often the best sources for operations needing new managers. Everyone has met someone who knows someone who started as a dishwasher and worked his way up to dining room supervisor and who is now a general manager. As we observed in Chapter 13, this type of promotion from within works best when coupled with a thoughtfully executed management development program.

Management development begins with succession planning. For a high-performing supervisor, for example, this involves identifying the skills and knowledge she needs in order to develop into a successful manager. This is likely different for each person. With the needs identified, the foodservice organization can then create training programs for its supervisors. In some cases, formal education is needed. Here, many foodservice operations offer tuition reimbursement to help employees attain promotions within the company. Not surprisingly, a manager who begins as a supervisor and credits the organization for providing the tools he needs to move up will be grateful and most likely very loyal.

In the course of succession planning, a foodservice organization must identify its short- and long-term management needs. For example, a rapidly growing chain restaurant can calculate how many managers and supervisors it needs at the various levels according to its growth plans. Since effective management is the leading success factor in the foodservice industry, such a chain must have a plan for filling upcoming vacancies. Often, the general manager of an existing, profitable restaurant is transferred to help open a new unit, while the assistant general manager from the existing unit is promoted to the general manager's position (or is also transferred to another unit as its new general manager). As you can see, this natural succession of management positions creates opportunities at the various management levels.

Such an approach to development can also be applied to filling supervisory positions. Many foodservice employees can be great supervisors and managers, given the right tools, training, and opportunities. Thus, foodservice managers should take the time to identify employees who have such potential, and such aspirations. This requires understanding employees' career goals, strengths, and areas of opportunity. To complete this process, a manager must communicate with employees. If opportunities exist, a manager should provide likely employees with several options and, as we noted earlier, clear the path so they can realize their career goals. Such communication should include a frank discussion of what is required, what is expected, and how long it will take to achieve the goal.

■□ ETHICS

We conclude this chapter with a lengthy discussion of ethics. And while you may note that we've already considered ethics when discussing purveyors, we address it here because of the reality that hospitality managers today face more ethical dilemmas than ever in this industry. Moreover, we seem to be experiencing a shortage of leaders with high ethical standards.

Drucker's quotation about doing the right thing has been extended by many to form the following principle: *Do the right thing, at the right time, for the right reasons.* This integrates ethics into the management process, but it is no easy task. Several authors have suggested that a stronger sense of ethics is needed; yet, as some have noted, discussing and fostering ethics is like "nailing Jello to a wall."[7]

Despite this challenge, researchers have proposed an **ethics check** for managers.[8] They contend that every manager, in making a decision, should ask three questions:

1. *Is it legal?* (Will I violate the law or company policy?)

2. *Is it balanced?* (Is it fair to all concerned?)

3. *How will it make me feel about myself?* (Will it make me proud? Will I fear that others might learn of my decision?)

Using this as a framework, we consider ethics in terms of the guest and the employee.

Ethics and the Guest

Guests should expect to be treated fairly. Yet we see all too often in our industry instances in which this simply doesn't happen. For example, on April 1, 1993, 21 Secret Service agents entered a Denny's Restaurant in Maryland. They were rather striking in appearance, dressed in uniforms common to the presidential detail: black shoes, black pants with wide gold stripes on the sides, white shirts with narrow black ties, gold badges, gun belts, and the official seal of the president of the United States.

At the time, Denny's was offering an All-You-Can-Eat Breakfast. Customers could choose five items and eat all they wanted for a fixed price. Each item was cooked to order.

Many of the agents ordered the All-You-Can-Eat Breakfast. Even considering the complexity of the order, it became obvious eventually that the table of African-American officers was still without food, while other tables seated at roughly the same time (including those occupied by similarly garbed white Secret Service agents) had already received additional servings. After 45 minutes, the African-American men still had not received their orders while guests who had entered the restaurant a half hour after the agents did had already been served. The unfortunate event resulted in a lawsuit. Late-night comedian Jay Leno later made the following joke on national television: "Denny's is offering a new sandwich called the Discriminator," he said in May 1993. "It's a hamburger, and you order it; then they don't serve it to you."[9]

While not intended to make an example of Denny's to imply that it is more discriminatory than any other restaurant, the case illustrates the most basic of potential ethical violations. (We should note that the Denny's chain and its parent company were very responsive to alleged ethical breaches and engaged in considerable training and education efforts to eliminate such practices. In 1994, it also paid $54 million in settling two class-action lawsuits related to race discrimination.[10]) Again, there is no room for even one guest to feel any form of discrimination.

If the individuals involved in the Denny's example had applied the ethics check to themselves, the answers would have surely indicated a better course of action. It is management's job to ensure that such events as those described do not happen, but it is often difficult to avoid. It is possible that until the Secret Service agents spoke to the manager (which they did on their way out of the restaurant; they were never served), he didn't even know of the problem. Thus, returning to our earlier discussion of supervisory roles, we see again an example in which a manager or supervisor is unable to control everything.

Ethical Treatment of Employees

Ethical violations regarding employees are likely more commonplace than violations related to guests. Unfortunately, the foodservice industry has a poor record when it comes to the three types of ethical breaches that we will address: sexual harassment, pay and promotion discrimination, and employee privacy violations.

Sexual harassment in the foodservice industry can be defined as unwelcome sexual advances, requests for sexual favors, or other verbal or physical conduct of a sexual nature. In particular, the most current guidelines state that such activities constitute illegal sexual harassment when they involving making sexual behavior, either explicitly or implicitly, a condition of employment; when submission to or rejection of such conduct is used as a basis for employment decisions (e.g., promotion or demotion); and when such conduct unreasonably interferes with an individual's work performance or creates a work environment that is intimidating, hostile, or offensive.

The foodservice industry has ingredients that lend themselves all too readily to a recipe for sexual discrimination. For example, the busiest times are typically at night. When employees end their shifts, most people are asleep. This is a people business, and requires mostly extroverted, gregarious employees. The very nature of the business is seductive. Although no single one of these conditions encourages—or should encourage—sexual harassment, in combination they create an environment that is conducive to its occurrence.

In order to minimize sexual harassment in the workplace, management can and should be proactive. First, every foodservice operation should have a clear policy that prohibits sexual harassment and ensure that every employee is familiar with it. The procedure should have a clear outline of steps employees should take to file complaints with supervisory staff. The policy should ensure confidentiality and call for prompt remedial action against an offender if the foodservice management's investigation reveals wrongdoing. Finally, management must be consistent and vigilant in enforcing the policy.

Pay and promotion discrimination is another problem of particular concern in the foodservice industry because of the large numbers of women and minorities in employee ranks. Discrimination based on these and other factors, such as age or religion, are not only unethical and immoral; they are also illegal. Moreover, the **Equal Pay Act** was passed in 2003, yet the gap in median annual wages between men and women is still staggering. Although things are slowly improving, the number of women and minorities in upper management remains sadly low.

A similar form of discrimination may affect parenting and dual-career families. Statistics suggest that fathers whose wives have jobs make substantially less money than fathers whose wives stay at home to take care of the children. Adding the reality that women make less than men do, this means that dual-income families are taking two needless hits to family income. The wife makes less because of the **glass ceiling** effect (organizational bias in the workplace that prevents minorities and women from advancing to leadership positions) and the husband makes less because his wife is working.

The final form of ethical breach we consider pertains to **employee privacy** issues. Recent developments, largely in technology, have implications for employee privacy. For example, a civil lawsuit was filed in 2004 after a Hooter's restaurant manager was caught secretly videotaping job applicants as they changed into the required Hooter's uniform consisting of orange shorts and a tank top. The manager was later sentenced to five years in prison.

Computer technology also makes it easier to gather information on potential or prospective employees. A 2010 CareerBuilder survey of hiring managers found that 45 percent reported using social media in their background checks of prospective employees. While there is no case law restricting employers from using social networks such as Facebook, a restaurant manager could unwittingly violate antidiscrimination or employee privacy laws as a result. Nevertheless, this type of screening will undoubtedly increase. The message is that employers should use caution when contemplating using information gathered in this way. For instance, employers would be breaking the law if they screened out applicants, even before interviewing them, based on racial or ethnic details gleaned from social media sites. Applicants need to be aware that such information, pictures, and videos, even if not intended for public consumption, may complicate or undermine their efforts to land a job.

It is important to note, too, that technological advances create new ethical questions. For example, should managers be included as "friends" in social networks such as Facebook? This question becomes even more complicated when a line employee is promoted to a supervisory position. Information previously included on the employee's social network site may not be appropriate when those previously connected as friends are now subordinates. However, if one continues to follow the general ethical principles outlined here, associated ethical behavior should be apparent.

In addition to accessing databases that contain all types of personal information, employers find another avenue to violating employee privacy in monitoring employee communications. Although employees typically use passwords to protect e-mail and voicemail messages, they are not wholly safe from prying eyes and ears. A *Macworld* survey found that supervisors in 21 percent of the 301 companies surveyed had examined employees' computer files, e-mail, or voicemail in an effort to assess employee productivity or investigate potential thefts.[11] The **Electronic Communication Privacy Act** makes employers potentially liable for this type of employee-privacy invasion. The best advice to foodservice managers is to establish a policy that restricts employees' nonbusiness use of the Internet or e-mail and to inform employees that their computer use will be audited to ensure adherence to this policy.

A similar privacy-related issue arises in connection with drug testing. Many foodservice companies require drug tests of job applicants. Some conduct random or periodic tests of existing employees. Is this illegal? Is it unethical? Answering the former question is easy. There is current legislation on the books that specifically addresses drug testing. The ethical question is answered by considering if such a practice violates an employee's right to privacy. For foodservice managers who require drug tests, ethical concerns can be mitigated if they provide reasons, which in most cases are rational, for carrying out such a practice. For example, drug tests might be required because an employer is concerned with employee and guest safety.

Again, we return to the ethics check. When it comes to sexual harassment, pay and promotion discrimination, and employee privacy issues, it is easy to determine whether a given behavior is right or wrong. It is up to every foodservice management professional to maintain high standards of personal and professional ethics. After all, as the saying goes, integrity is its own reward.

MANAGERIAL IMPLICATIONS

Organizing people and allocating resources has always been important in the foodservice industry, but in today's business environment—featuring rapid globalization, accelerating innovation, and relentless competition—how an operation manages these tasks bears directly on success or failure. Our industry is particularly challenging because it relies so heavily on human capital. Thus, every foodservice professional should be well versed in leadership and management.

Early views of leadership focused on leaders' traits, even physical and personality traits. Behavioral theories were later applied to understand the differences between effective and ineffective leaders. More recently, contingency theories have been developed that recognize that successful foodservice operations adapt their leadership approaches to the situation at hand. The latest approach to foodservice leadership, termed servant leadership, suggests that leaders lead best by serving others.

We must understand the difference between leadership and management because each can be associated with a specific set of appropriate behavioral practices. Some of these behaviors are common to both, while others are unique to leadership and management, respectively. Both also require certain skills. Again, some of these are common to leadership and management. Management, however, is distinct because it involves the necessary functions of planning, organizing, directing, and controlling.

Many of the skills needed by leaders and managers are also needed by supervisors, while some are required of supervisors to a greater extent. For example, while leaders need strong conceptual skills, supervisors require stronger technical skills. We introduced a set of supervision principles to explain the role of supervision in foodservice management.

Leadership development is important, especially in growing foodservice organizations. Such operations need to groom their personnel and create opportunities for upward mobility. This involves identifying an organization's future needs and employees' needs and aspirations. The organization can then develop training methods or provide educational support to help employees grow and realize collective personal and organizational objectives.

Leaders and managers share a common need for integrity and ethics. The notion of doing the right thing, at the right time, for the right reasons underscores this well. This principle applies to guests and employees alike. To meet their obligations to guests, foodservice managers must prevent any form of discrimination from occurring. To meet their obligations to employees, they must take a strong ethical position regarding sexual harassment, pay and promotion discrimination, and employee privacy violations. Finally, foodservice managers must ensure that policies related to these areas are in place and are applied conscientiously to ensure a safe, enjoyable, and principled workplace.

INDUSTRY EXEMPLAR

Jack's Oyster House

The sign could be in any urban setting, with a slightly faded hue that reflects a century of exposure to Northeast weather. It reads, simply, "Jack's." The moniker evokes images of a dark-wood interior, with peevish, gray-haired waiters sporting white gloves. Even the financial-district setting, filled with modern buildings and new businesses, suggests the establishment exists only as a remnant of long-dead halcyon days.

Jack's Oyster House is as different from such images as the moon is from the sun. Upon entering the restaurant that's been called "Albany's Greatest Restaurant Legend" and "Best Restaurant of the Century," customers are greeted by an enthusiastic staff. The décor, with evidence of its mahogany-walled past, includes impressionistic art and contemporary place settings. The menu, too, combines the rich history of traditional American favorites with adventures in contemporary haute cuisine.

But the differentiating factor—one that separates this operation from almost any other restaurant in existence today—is the service. When guests arrive, they are treated warmly and openly as though they were regulars, even on their first visit. Servers exude passion for service, which is apparent in everything from their meticulously careful method of pouring the wine to their suave introduction of the dessert menu. In fact, service at Jack's is almost indescribable; it's friendly without being invasive, warm yet professional, comforting but not condescending.

Is this service style a functional recipe for success? The restaurant's numbers speak volumes. Annual sales in 1994 hovered around $1.4 million. In 2002, this number exceeded $3.25 million. Today sales are approaching $4 million.

The impulse for service—and success over the decades—stems from a single person, an individual who embodies the service ethic he preaches. Brad Rosenstein is a third-generation restaurateur who was in the business even before graduating from the Cornell University School of Hotel Administration in 1983. During his tenure in the industry, he has developed a reputation as a pioneer in service-model development that encompasses every aspect of foodservice operations.

More than anything, it's his approach to leadership that sets him apart as a foodservice icon. For example, he doesn't separate the restaurant into "front-of-the house" and "back-of-the house" units. Rather, he views one as the heart of the operation and the other as its soul. In training, he prompts the wait staff to respond to a guest's expression of thanks not with "you're welcome" but rather, by saying, "It was my pleasure."

Are these examples subtle? Of course. But they serve to underscore the approach of a true leader, one who

@ Rebel Creative Marketing Concepts.

understands that this is a service industry and, as such, requires an absolute focus on the customer experience.

Under Brad's leadership, Jack's Oyster House has garnered several awards. It earned DiRoNA certification in 2007 by achieving the highest distinction from the Distinguished Restaurants of North America, a non-profit organization that serves as the premier authority for recognizing and promoting excellence in dining. The restaurant earned the Wine Spectator Award for excellence, given to restaurants whose wine lists offer interesting selections appropriate to the cuisine and with a wide range of appeal, every year since 2007. Again owing to Brad, Jack's is also the winner of The Ivy Award, one of the most coveted industry accolades and one shared with other famous restaurants such as the French Laundry, Charlie Trotter's, Emeril's, and the "21" Club.

KEY TERMS

▪▪▪□ Case in Point ▪□▪□▪■▪□▪□▪□▪□▪□▪□▪□▪□▪□▪□▪□▪□▪□▪□▪□▪□▪□▪□▪

Daphne's Dilemma

Daphne had an outstanding internship with a managed-services company while she was in college. It allowed her to shadow the medical center's management dietitian and observe the leadership and management skills that made her successful. So, when Daphne earned her registered dietitian credentials, she was thrilled that the same managed services company made her an offer to be the clinical dietitian at Holy Family Hospital. That was five years ago.

Since then, Daphne has honed her skills well and is now considered one of the better managers in the company. She communicates well, delegates when appropriate, and most find her to be very likable. Her manager, Joan, who has run the foodservice department, has been hugely successful in her 25 years on the job. She has also served as Daphne's mentor. Now the time has come for Joan to retire, in two months. She plans to move to her country cottage and enjoy her leisure time with the grandkids.

Today, Joan has suggested that Daphne consider two positions that are open in the company. The first

and the one that Joan is clearly urging Daphne to take is the one she, Joan, is about to vacate. The other position is good, too. It is at a medical center of similar size but is in a nicer part of town and, according to all accounts, is in a better position financially. There has been a lot of turnover at the other hospital and the last foodservice director was just fired; he'd been there for only six months. The salary, which would be a nice increase from what Daphne currently earns, would be the same at either location.

Daphne is thrilled to be considered for this promotion, but truly doesn't know what to do. She tends to obsess over such decisions, and this one is no exception. She spent hours last night drafting a list of the advantages and disadvantages (of which she can think of very few) corresponding to each location. Then, she remembered a table that she had seen in one of her college textbooks. She can't remember exactly, but recalls that it pertained to selecting jobs with differing criteria. After a short search of her shelves, she finds the book and, with little effort, finds the table (see Table 14.5). She smiles that she

Case in Point *(continued)*

used her favorite highlighter on the table headers, indicating that this was something she needed to remember.

1. If you were Daphne, what would you list as positives for staying at Holy Family? What are the negatives?

2. Make the same list for the other opportunity.

3. What would you do?

TABLE 14.5 Chances of Success in Various Types of Managerial Succession

	Strong Predecessor	Weak Predecessor
Inside Successor	Chances unfavorable	Chances uncertain
Outside Successor	Chances moderately favorable	Chances very favorable

REVIEW AND DISCUSSION QUESTIONS

1. Why is focusing on a leader's personal characteristics insufficient for understanding leadership?

2. In a foodservice context, what would be the likely result if a leader were to embrace the laissez-faire leadership style?

3. What is the difference between transactional and transformational leadership?

4. Using the managerial grid, identify the optimal coordinates for a manager, and describe why this is so.

5. In terms of leader-member exchange theory, is it better to be in the *in-group* or the *out-group*? Why?

6. How is servant leadership dramatically different from earlier leadership theories?

7. Using the four traditional elements of management, provide an example illustrating each that draws from a foodservice setting (do not use the examples included in the chapter).

8. From the ten leadership behaviors listed in the chapter, what are the three most important to you, and why?

9. What skills are critical to supervision? Provide an example of each.

10. What is meant by *span of control*?

11. Why is leadership development important?

12. Describe a situation in which you might have found the ethics check useful, and then apply it.

13. Using your choice of search engine, find a report of an ethical breech in a foodservice setting, describe it, and suggest how things should have been handled.

ENDNOTES

1. Moore, B. B. "The May Conference on Leadership." *Personnel Journal* 69(1) (1927): 122–135.

2. Drucker, P. F. "Management's New Paradigms." *Forbes* 162(7) (1998): 152–169.

3. Kerr, S., and Jermier, J. M. "Substitutes of Leadership: Their Meaning and Measurement." *Organizational Behavior and Human Performance* (December 1978).

4. For a thorough discussion on servant leadership, see Brownell, J. "Leadership in the Service Industry." *Cornell Hospitality Quarterly* 51(3) (2010): 363–378.

5. House, R., and Podsakoff, P. M. "Leadership Effectiveness: Past Perspectives and Future Directions for Research." In J. Greenberg (ed.), *Organizational Behavior: The State of the Science*, Hillsdale, NJ: Erlbaum, 1994, 58–64.

6. Adapted from Caplow, T. *Managing an Organization*. Fort Worth, TX: Holt, Rinehart, and Winston, Inc., 1983.

7. Herman, F. A., and Cullen, T. P. "Still Needed: Ethics in Business Instruction." *Cornell Hotel and Restaurant Quarterly* 27(2) (1986): 49–52.

8. Blanchard, K., & Peale, N. V. *The Power of Ethical Management*. New York: Fawcett Crest, 1988.

9. Adamson, J. *The Denny's Story*. New York: John Wiley & Sons, 2000.

10. Ibid.

11. Smith, L. "Whose Office Is This Anyway?" *Fortune* (August 9, 1993): 93.

PART 5

ADVANCED MANAGEMENT

We have set the stage for the final section in this introduction to foodservice management by reviewing the roots of the foodservice industry and introducing the essential concepts in Part 1, explaining the overarching role of the menu in Part 2, analyzing the food service product cycle, including menu and recipe development and costing, in Part 3, and describing general management functions in Part 4. We conclude the text by considering the fundamentals of advanced management. We present more advanced techniques for conducting operational analyses, integrate integrate the beverage management component, and conclude with a look at the future of the foodservice industry.

INTERNAL CONTROL

LEARNING OBJECTIVES:

After becoming familiar with this chapter, you should be able to:

1. Explain why internal controls are necessary and why they are particularly important in the foodservice industry.

2. Describe the conditions that lead to employee theft.

3. Understand the general principles of internal control.

4. Appreciate the various ways in which employee theft can be identified.

5. Identify how employees can themselves serve as the best deterrents to employee theft.

It has been suggested that one out of every two employees steals. In the foodservice industry, it has been calculated that 90 percent of all financial losses are the result of internal theft. The National Restaurant Association estimates that employee theft accounts for about 75 percent of a foodservice operation's inventory losses, equaling more than 3 percent of annual sales.

■□ WHY IS INTERNAL CONTROL NECESSARY?
□■

The aforementioned statistics lay the foundation for answering this question. The primary purpose of internal control is to safeguard the assets of a business against losses that result from error or fraud. Put another way, internal control is the management function that deals with fraud and embezzlement prevention.[1] In the foodservice industry, the unique nature of the business and its employees create a particularly critical need for such control.

Foodservice Characteristics

Foodservice operations feature several unique characteristics that can be managed successfully only with strong internal control. First, in many segments, foodservice is still primarily a cash business. Not only is there plentiful cash on hand, there are also ongoing cash transactions. The presence of cash exposes an operation to mismanagement or misconduct. This explains why security in banks is so tight. Every transaction provides an opportunity for error or theft.

Decades ago, foodservice operations had mechanical cash registers that did only what the name implies—they recorded how much cash was deposited (see Figure 15.1). A cashier would therefore need to calculate any change due to the customer. It might be argued that errors in calculation led to unintentional losses in equal proportion to losses from theft. Even the simplest electronic cash register today all but eliminates the problem of mistaken calculations. As shown in Figure 15.2, many are designed also to facilitate internal control by displaying, for example, the total due back to customers (lest the employee put the money in the register without recording it only to remove it later for personal gain). However, these are still machines and the routine exchange of cash continues to be a source of revenue loss.

Another unique characteristic of the foodservice business is that all products used, regardless of segment, are consumable or easily usable by the average person. Thus, food, liquor, tablecloths, silverware, glassware—all the things used in a restaurant—have practical value to just about anyone. Even cleaning supplies can be used just as easily in an employee's home as they can be in a restaurant kitchen.

The experience of an onsite foodservice provider that recently won a contract to provide meals at an automotive-assembly plant serves as a case in point. The contract foodservice provider had excellent internal controls for cash and food. After the first three months of operation, its managers found that sales and food cost were equal to or better than budgeted. For some mysterious reason, however, they had lost almost 5,000 plastic trays—the amount normally lost or ruined over the course of about two years. As is the case in most cafes, these trays served a single purpose: To provide customers with a means of transporting food to tables. The management team was at a complete loss. After a lengthy investigation, they discovered two things. First, many of the plant's employees repaired cars on the weekends (not surprising, given their profession). Second, the trays had become very popular among these weekend mechanics to protect floors or driveways from the oil that naturally drips or spills while repairing cars. Although the move was unpopular, the foodservice company had no choice but to switch to cardboard trays, which are typically more expensive because they are disposable, but are also absorbent—so are therefore not useful as oil pans.

© iStockphoto.com

Figure 15.1   Cash register, circa 1950.

Employee Characteristics

There is no reason to believe that foodservice workers are by nature more inclined to cheat or steal than anyone in the general population is. Unfortunately, the circumstances in which most find themselves, combined with other factors that come with the job, make it easier to engage in such behavior in foodservice than in most other industries. First, most line positions are relatively low-skilled jobs and therefore relatively low in pay and social status. Most lineworkers are trained on the job. Thus, a person with no experience waiting tables but a good service mentality can be readily trained without advanced education. Such employees may not be terribly proud of their positions; many view them as temporary way stations on their career paths (which might have nothing to with foodservice) or as stepping-stones to a better career in foodservice. Such line-workers therefore often lack the strong sense of loyalty to the operations for which they work that might deter them from stealing. Furthermore, unless unemployment in a given geographic area is very high, people with experience at one foodservice operation can usually find a similar job at another. Thus, the risk of being fired for stealing does not strike the same fear in the hearts of these workers as it might for others.

Figure 15.2 Basic modern electronic cash register.

We should note that companies that suffer egregiously from embezzlement or theft often seek legal action. When employees are found guilty of such ethical and legal breaches, they often serve prison time. However, it is unusual for a foodservice company to recover profits lost to such crimes.

CONDITIONS CONDUCIVE TO FRAUD AND EMBEZZLEMENT

Armed with an understanding of factors unique to the foodservice industry that might dispose workers to commit theft or fraud in the workplace, we now consider the three conditions that, added to these factors, make theft of a foodservice operation's assets possible: opportunity, need, and failure of conscience.

Opportunity

The most important enabling condition for theft in foodservice operations is **opportunity**. Simply stated, if there is no opportunity, there is no theft. Fortunately, opportunity is the one condition over which management has the greatest influence. This is the foundation of internal control.

Need

Need arises from the economic or psychological conditions that drive people to steal. Thus, personal financial struggles can drive an otherwise honest person to steal. Many view foodservice operation as merely a place to work, giving no thought to those who have invested time and money into creating a business (and an opportunity for otherwise unemployed people to work). Such employees don't view themselves as stealing from and therefore harming an individual but rather as taking what they do not have themselves from an operation that won't miss it. (We discuss this rationale at greater length in the next section.)

Addiction may also drive an employee to steal. Drug abuse, for example, can lead people to make poor personal decisions, especially where money or goods are needed to support addictive drug use. Gambling is another addiction that often leaves people in (sometimes urgent) financial need, and where such people see an opportunity in a foodservice operation to support their habit they are likely to seize it.

Aside from exercising as much prudence as possible during the selection process (as discussed in Chapter 13), there is little managers can do to anticipate this condition of fraud or embezzlement. Even when drug screening is required as a condition of employment, a drug habit might easily form after an employee has been hired. And even if drug screening is conducted during a term of employment, there are many other addictions that no testing method can detect.

Failure of Conscience

The final condition of theft or fraud, **failure of conscience**, is one that allows a thief to rationalize stealing food, money, or other assets. Consider the fry cook who eats a single french fry during a shift. The actual cost is likely less than one cent. Yet this is still stealing. Some managers take the stance that a french fry is a lot cheaper than a fried scallop, so it is just better to let it go. However, stealing any asset is still stealing. It sets a dangerous precedent not to respond to such incidents, even if only with a mild reprimand. A foodservice manager should not differentiate between stealing and not stealing based on some minimum food cost threshold.

It is only human nature, unfortunately, that people are able to convince themselves all too easily that they are somehow justified in stealing. Consider the following rationalizations:

- I deserve this dessert because I work harder than everyone else does.

- We go through so many pounds of shrimp that they won't miss a few.

- The last piece of cake is too small to serve. Someone will throw it away if I don't eat it.

- The manager eats for free—why shouldn't I?

- I haven't eaten any employee meals lately; therefore, it's okay to grab a few things from the walk-in on my way home.

This kind of thinking can do serious damage to the foodservice industry.

■□ GENERAL PRINCIPLES

In light of these three conditions that are conducive to theft or fraud, it is critical that foodservice managers understand the general principles that, if followed thoughtfully and consistently, minimize the likelihood of employee theft and fraud.

Divide Duties

The notion of division of duty was introduced in Chapter 9. Dividing duties means assigning roles such that no one person takes an order, creates or obtains the ordered item, and then collects payment. As we noted, many bars illustrate exactly how this principle is violated as a matter of course. In such cases, the bartender takes the order, makes the drink, and then collects for it. Every one of these functions is within the bartender's reach, and, given the limited space in most bar areas, it is impractical to pay three people to do what the bartender does.

In table-service operations, maintaining this division of duties is much easier. For example, in the typical service sequence in a restaurant, a server takes a guest's food order and enters it into a point-of-sale system. The order is then relayed to the kitchen, and the cooks then prepare the meal. This creates a paper trail that managers can follow if they suspect that funds or other assets are being diverted. It also provides a framework within which employees work: Cooks do not prepare items that are not shown on the point-of-sale (POS) printout or screen and employees can take items from the kitchen only if they have been previously entered into the POS terminal.

Yet even in these circumstances, breaches occur. For example, many restaurants pre-plate desserts, thereby expediting service. In theory, the server enters the order in the system and then obtains the item from the kitchen. Because there is no division of duties in this respect, however, there is no required process to ensure that the item has been documented or that payment has been made. Thus, a server could provide friends with free desserts or offer a free dessert to a customer, hoping for a larger gratuity. In either situation, the employee is stealing.

Another example in which an operation fails to apply division of duties involves two or more employees who collude in order to steal. Consider our earlier example of the cook and the server. If a dishonest server approached a cook and said, "I have a customer who always orders the same thing and always pays in cash; if you make it but I don't enter it into the POS system, we can split the cash." That's theft.

Breaches of this type are often accidental. Sometimes circumstances take workers out of their ordinary routines, making it difficult to carry out the proper procedures that prevent theft or fraud. Imagine, for example, a very busy bar. The cocktail server enters a drink order for a large party. The bartender receives the printed order and begins making the drinks. Just then, the server remembers that she forget to enter one of the drinks. She yells over to the bartender, "I forgot to enter a Cape Cod (cranberry juice and vodka)—just make it now and I'll enter it after I deliver the drinks." Owing to the hectic pace in the bar, both employees forget about it. In this case, the customer was never charged since the printed bill did not include the Cape Cod. While neither the server nor the bartender benefited personally from this mistake, the bar owner did not receive compensation for the beverage and the resulting loss in assets is the same as it would have been had the two workers conspired to prevent payment for that drink.

Fix Responsibility

A correlate to dividing duties is fixing responsibility. Fixing responsibility means not only separating the component functions of a transaction but also making exactly one individual in an organization responsible for each component function, such as handling cash. A breach of this principle is evident in a bar where two bartenders share a single cash register. In the event that the cash drawer is short at the end of the night, management has no way to identify who is responsible for the error. Fortunately, almost all electronic cash registers and POS systems now feature multiple cash drawers for a single terminal.

Some restaurants still use paper checks to take food orders. Each check has multiple copies so that cold food orders can be left in the cold prep area while hot item orders can be left with the appropriate kitchen station. In order to ensure that responsibility for each check is fixed with a single person, such checks should be numbered. Moreover, in an operation that uses this system, management should record the check numbers as they are given to the servers. This practice prevents a dishonest employee from placing an order in the kitchen without remitting payment for it at the end of the night. In that case, management need only compare copies of checks in the kitchen with what is submitted by the front-of-house staff at the end of the night in order to identify possible breaches.

Limit Access

We have in previous chapters recommended limiting access to areas of an operation in which food and beverage inventory are stored. As noted, not everyone needs access to dry goods or the liquor room. In the past, some foodservice managers focused exclusively on securing expensive menu items such as alcohol and meats. Dry goods, such as condiments, were kept in areas accessible to any employee. To be sure, while a bottle of ketchup costs less than a bottle of fine wine does, it is an asset nonetheless, one that management must protect.

Similarly, liquor rooms and wine storage areas that are locked are not always as secure as they may seem to be. Management must supervise distribution of keys to such locks very judiciously. An operation should change all its locks whenever managers are replaced.

Figure 15.3 Drop safe.

It is worth noting that the principle of limiting access pertains to everything. Some restaurant operators place empty beer kegs on the loading dock to make it easier for the beer distributor to collect them. Nevertheless, empty kegs are worth something and might be coveted by an unscrupulous employee. Even cleaning supplies and trash liners must be secured. As we noted earlier, these can be used by anyone off-site.

Finally, access to cash handling areas must be strictly limited. Cash rooms, where employees count their cash at the end of a shift before depositing it, should be secure. They should also feature drop safes—safes that allow for deposits but not withdrawals by employees (see Figure 15.3). These serve a dual purpose: as a protection against internal theft and as a deterrent to robbery.

Minimize Cash Banks

A large foodservice operation, say a large cafe in a medical center, might conduct hundreds of cash transactions at multiple cashier stations during a busy lunch. In order to ensure that every cashier has enough cash in bills and coins in every denomination, some foodservice managers will reason that by maintaining a large bank the operation can avoid having to replenish cash supplies at cashier stations during busy shifts. This practice is not advised.

When an operation sends out a cashier to begin his shift with a large amount of money, it is creating an opportunity for loss. For example, in a worst-case scenario a dishonest employee could conceivably take the full amount and vacate the premises. It is management's responsibility to minimize such exposure. Moreover, requiring cashiers to count out large sums of money—they must count their cash both before and at the end of every shift—is highly inefficient since it consumes a lot of time.

A related issue is that of cash drops. Just as there is no need to start a shift with a large sum of cash in the register, so there is no reason to let cash accumulate unnecessarily. Thus, management should require cash drops whereby employees package bills in prespecified amounts, say, $500; management then collects the money, checks the amount for accuracy, signs a receipt that the cashier places in the cash drawer, and then drops the money in the drop safe.

Minimize Inventory

Much as cash on hand should be kept to a minimum, so should inventory on hand be kept as low as possible. As noted in our discussion of inventory management in Chapter 9, food inventory should be sufficient to ensure that no menu item is unavailable, but there is little or no advantage in storing large amounts of any item. Remember that items in inventory are nonperforming assets until associated menu items are sold. The goal is to maximize return on related inventory investments by holding them for as short a time as possible.

In addition to the financial advantage of keeping inventory low, there is also a psychological dimension. Think, for example, of an almost-empty tube of toothpaste. In order to get enough toothpaste to brush your teeth, you must gently but repeatedly squeeze along the entire length of the tube. While this produces only a modest amount of toothpaste, you subconsciously determine that it is adequate. Now imagine a brand-new tube of toothpaste. Unconcerned about running out, like most people you will likely use a far greater amount than you would with the nearly empty tube. In a large kitchen a similar phenomenon occurs. The kitchen manager tells the cook to be very careful when trimming a roast because it needs to produce the maximum number of portions for the evening and the next delivery won't arrive until the next day. If, by contrast, roasts have been delivered by the case on a given day, a cook who sees all that meat will likely not apply the same care to the trimming process since there is no risk of running out of the product.

Conduct Random Audits

When an employee, particularly a cashier or bartender, steals cash, there are likely times during her shift when the sum of the cash drawer contents will not coincide with the actual sales figure. Suppose, for example, a cashier sees a group of four nurses enter a hospital cafe. The nurses are talking and are clearly in a hurry. The cashier casually turns the POS display away from the main aisle where customers pass as they pay for their food. As each nurse offers payment, the cashier, who knows all the prices by heart, collects the amount appropriate for each order but rings up that amount less $5.00. After the four nurses have paid for their food, the cash drawer is then $20 over the amount that is recorded. She waits for a moment when no one is watching and pockets the $20.

In this simple example, there are several breaches of internal control principles, but it is possible to deter dishonest employees from sneaking cash out of the register by instituting random audits. If the cashier in our example had known that the dining room manager might show up at any time to count the cash in her drawer, she would have been much less likely to attempt her thievery. Such random counts might not deter all employees—determined thieves will eventually try—but they also help management identify cashiers who, owing to carelessness rather than maliciousness, should not be handling cash.

Finally management must be sure to include every employee who operates a register when conducting random counts. Bartenders and cashiers need to know that random counts are performed routinely. The biggest mistake (as our Case in Point at the end of the chapter illustrates) is taking it for granted that star employees can be exempted from routine monitoring.

Maintain Accurate Records

While accuracy is a tenet of any sound approach to financial accounting, the principle of maintaining accurate records lies at the foundation of internal control. After all, an inaccurate income statement serves no useful purpose. Similarly, inventory records, including valuation information, must be accurate. There is no room for approximations or error.

In the often-hectic foodservice business, it is easy to take shortcuts in seemingly unimportant areas or to put off non-customer-related tasks until later. The problem is that an invoice for three cases of lettuce that goes unrecorded artificially decreases food cost. Such a little thing might not seem important, but when a vendor does not deliver enough lettuce the next month because no payment was made, it will have a dramatic effect.

Routinely Upgrade Firewalls and PCI Standards

Data and records might not seem like assets on a par with food or liquor, but they must be protected just as effectively with firewalls or virus scanners. This is readily apparent when considering that customer information is often used for marketing purposes. Moreover, many foodservice systems hold customers' credit card information. Inadequate firewall protection leaves such information vulnerable to being hacked from an operation's computer system, potentially opening it to liability issues.

Payment card industry (PCI) data security standards, which specify credit card processing procedures, must similarly be routinely upgraded. Maintaining these standards will continue to grow in importance as more and more customers use credit or debit cards instead of cash. This trend is desirable in most foodservice settings as it means less cash handling and therefore lower exposure to theft.

Rotate Managers

The foodservice business is anything but routine: Any experienced manager knows that no two days are alike. Nevertheless, such duties as counting inventory should be rotated among responsible managers and employees (in Chapter 9 we described how physical inventory should be tallied, noting that using two people expedites the process).

Dishonesty can be found among managers as well. Indeed, a dishonest assistant manager, for example, can easily hide theft—at least in the short term—by falsifying inventory records. Consider a manager who steals a case of frozen lobster tails. At the end of the same month, instead of recording two cases on hand (the actual amount in the freezer), he writes "three cases" on the inventory record sheet. On paper, then, there is no variation in food cost as the ending inventory is artificially inflated. (For a review of food cost calculation, refer back to Chapter 9.) The following month, he steals another case of frozen lobster tails, confident that he can hide his actions by repeating the false recording. Indeed, at the end of the month, there is only a half case of frozen lobster tails on hand; however, he records "2½ cases." At some point, someone will discover that there is a problem. After all, if additional lobster is not ordered, there will not be an adequate supply to prepare menu-item orders. This will bring the error to light. However, depending on inventory levels and the frequency of falsified reporting, revealing the fraud could conceivably take months.

The solution, of course, is to rotate responsibility. Rotating responsibility also means that more people take an interest in important operational concerns and more people share the labor involved in applying internal controls. Counting physical inventory, for example, is a labor-intensive activity that is performed generally only during off hours, when a foodservice operation is closed. Many operations conduct inventory on the evening of the last day of the month. Needless to say, few managers relish the thought of performing such a task on, say, New Year's Eve. Rotating responsibility for inventory creates a perception of fairness among the management team while also enhancing internal control if for no other reason than that those responsible bring a stronger sense of commitment to the task.

Keep the Customer in Mind

These principles of internal control all contribute to protecting the financial viability of a foodservice operation. This last, customer-oriented principle is intended to ensure that effective internal control does not detract from the customer experience. For example, say a large restaurant with 350 seats has an expansive wine list. The wine is secured in one of two wine storage units, one for white wine and one for red (at correspondingly appropriate storage temperatures). For the sake of internal control, the storage units can be accessed only by the general manager. With such a system in place, it would be difficult to fill multiple wine orders during a busy shift without substantial delays in delivery to tables. Although such a system would minimize opportunities for theft, guest satisfaction and wine sales are likely to suffer (a very different approached is shown in Figure 15.4).

Another example of a well-intended internal control strategy is the practice of blind receiving described in Chapter 8. Blind receiving requires the receiver to compare what is delivered with an invoice or with a purchase order that displays no quantities (forcing the receiver to add the quantity of each item to the purchase order). This practice ensures that the operation is charged only for what was delivered. This practice can, however, lead to shortages in the event that the amount received is far less than what was ordered.

The lesson is to ensure customer satisfaction and use common sense when applying internal control. The manager who performs a surprise cash count at the height of the lunch rush

Courtesy the Purple Café and Wine Bar, Seattle, Washington.

Figure 15.4   The Purple Café and Wine Bar in Seattle features more than 600 wines from around the world.

may have the best intentions, but the people in line who are then unable to eat lunch because they stood in line too long will not be happy. Similarly, a customer who has to wait needlessly for an entrée to be delivered because cooks have no access to a meat refrigerator do not care that management is trying to protect its assets. Ultimately, management must weigh the benefits of internal control against both the financial costs and potential compromises in customer service.

IDENTIFYING EMPLOYEE THEFT

Thus far, we have discussed why internal controls are necessary, described the conditions in which theft is most likely to occur, and reviewed several key principles designed to prevent such thefts. However, even with the best customer-friendly internal control practices and policies in place, thefts will happen. Here, we discuss what to watch for and how to generate trust. We then consider how technology can be used innovatively as part of the internal control process. We conclude by suggesting that, while many employees steal, honest employees often represent the best form of internal control.

What to Watch For

Many of the financial ratios discussed in Chapter 10 as well as the advanced analytic techniques we present in Chapter 16 effectively indicate potential losses due to theft. For example, spikes in food cost or beverage cost may be direct effects of inventory theft. Similarly, variances in sales can indicate that food is being served but that payment is either not being collected or is being pocketed by servers. Dramatic changes or unexplained patterns in inventory-turnover-analysis data are also good indicators that something is wrong.

In addition to auditing cash registers, managers should also look at cash and credit card tips. In the bar, management might ask the bartender to count her cash tips while the manager counts the cash in the drawer. If tips are 50 percent of sales, there is likely a problem. Similarly, management can readily monitor gratuities recorded through credit card transactions. Servers who routinely receive inordinately large gratuities may be giving away food or drinks, or may be defrauding the customer by altering the tip amount on the credit card receipt.

Indeed, the practice on the part of foodservers of altering tip amounts or adding tips when none was indicated by the customer has become distressingly widespread. The most affected customers are business travelers, perhaps because servers assume, probably correctly, that business travelers are paying against expense accounts and do not compare receipts with credit card records.

Consider this scenario: Dinner at a restaurant was $46.40. The service was extremely slow and the waiter rather surly, so the business traveler decides on a gratuity of about 10 percent, or $4.60. The total amount for dinner and gratuity is then $51.00. The unscrupulous waiter, feeling cheated by the ungrateful guest, adds a "1" to the left of the tip amount making the new tip $14.60. He then changes the "5" on the total line to a "6". (This is particularly easy in some foodservice operations where the foodserver processes such gratuities and management doesn't even look at actual credit card vouchers. Of course, this is in itself a breach of good internal control.)

To prevent servers from adding extra gratuity dollars, some savvy customers have adopted systems that can flag such fraud without the need to compare actual receipts with monthly credit-card statements. One such approach, borrowed from the computer industry, is referred to as **checksum**. It involves adjusting the gratuity amount slightly so that the last digit equals the sum of the digits to the left of the decimal point of the total check and gratuity amount. Using our earlier example, for example, the guest adjusts his tip to $4.66. The new total is $51.06 (i.e., 5 + 1 = 6). When she looks at her credit card statement, she ensures that all restaurant charges have been similarly recorded. If the waiter had altered the amount as described, the total charge on the statement would be $61.06, highlighting the overcharge. She then calls the credit card company and has the charge reversed. We also hope that she calls the restaurant to report the incident.

Customer complaints—such as the one we have just imagined—provide another indication of employee theft. Some complaints that would seem to have little to do with internal control might actually support such control. For example, customer complaints about high prices or inconsistent pricing might signal overcharging on the part of servers and warrant management intervention.

Mystery Shoppers

An approach that provides external, objective information involves using **mystery shoppers** (see Chapter 11, where we noted the role played by mystery shoppers in improving customer service and generating customer loyalty). As we have seen, mystery shoppers pose as normal customers but actually dine in order to gather data, and some companies offer dedicated mystery shopping services. Thus, using mystery shoppers can play a dual role not only by helping a foodservice operation improve customer relations but also by indicating breaches of internal control. We know that some mystery shopping services work with chains or individual foodservice units to create checklists or evaluation forms that are then used by mystery shoppers to evaluate their experiences. Some of these firms contract with individual foodservice outlets to provide one mystery shopper per month. Others provide services on an as-needed basis. The point is to recognize the potential of mystery shoppers for internal control. For example, a manager who suspects a bartender of stealing might hire a mystery shopper to monitor the situation.

Some foodservice operators simply invite friends and family members to serve as mystery shoppers, with payment in the form a free meal. Here, the operator provides the volunteer mystery shopper with a gift certificate, one that any customer might have. The operator then meets with the friends to discuss what they experienced, rate the food, and review the interactions between guest and server.

Larger companies are also creating their own mystery shopping services rather than outsourcing. These firms use the same employees and send them to the various units. The advantage is that the shoppers can make comparisons across units. They are also more likely to be familiar with company standards and expectations.

Trust

Former President Ronald Reagan made the following saying famous: "Trust, but verify." This is probably the best single piece of advice for foodservice managers when instituting internal control. This underscores, too, some of the principles discussed earlier. Conducting random audits and rotating managers help to verify that employees are behaving honestly. Similarly, mystery shoppers are not brought in just to trick employees; they are intended to verify that food and service are being delivered properly and honestly.

Trust in the foodservice industry sometimes means that foodservice managers must trust their instincts. If an employee's lifestyle seems inconsistent with his job description (as it might be with a busser who drives to work in an expensive car or with a prep cook who wears expensive jewelry), the employee might have some other means of income, but he might also be supplementing his income at the foodservice operation's expense.

Trust can also be built, and when it is, it helps to deter theft. The most important way to build trust is to treat employees ethically and with respect, which, in turns, means being sensitive to their needs. For example, making information regarding gambling or drug addiction available might indicate to employees that management cares about their health and welfare, thus increasing trust. Employees are more inclined to trust managers they see as caring about them.

Technology

Technology represents another front in the war against theft. For example, more and more foodservice operations are integrating **closed-circuit television (CCTV)** systems to monitor cash handling. This is evident in operations ranging from small ice-cream parlors to cavernous nightclubs. As we noted earlier, management cannot be everywhere and see everything. However, CCTV allows managers to see much more from a single position. Of course, we are not advocating that a foodservice manager simply sit in his office and monitor the CCTV screens. Rather, CCTV can help managers observe employee behavior. And in most larger operations, the register is tied to a camera system that records both the transactions and the cashier. Thus, a manager suspecting theft can review the recorded images. Of course, It makes sense that employees who know the camera is trained on them will be less likely to try something dishonest or detrimental to the operation.

Technology also makes it possible to report and track information about employee behavior that requires little time and uses already available data. For example, most POS systems can readily generate server sales reports. These can be used to observe servers' productivity and potential glitches (low sales on a busy night) that might raise red flags for management. Other reports related to inventory turnover, cash-versus-credit sales, and credit card gratuities as a percentage of sales by server (discussed earlier) are also important guideposts for managers seeking to maximize internal control.

▗▖ THE BEST DETERRENT

Foodservice managers implement internal control practices knowing that such practices work only if employees follow them. Ultimately, the best deterrent to theft, fraud, and error is also a foodservice operation's most valuable asset—its employees.

That is, internal control works best when employees have integrity. The search for employees with integrity begins with the screening process. Employees who change jobs frequently or who can't account for large gaps in their employment histories may be more difficult to manage. Thus, in a sense internal control can begin by following the steps outlined in Chapter 14 for recruitment and selection.

Next, internal control practices must be included in the training process. For example, cooks should be taught (if they don't already know) about the financial impact of adding an extra meatball to every order of spaghetti and meatballs. Such a lesson can be imparted dramatically by annualizing what such seemingly trivial losses can cost an operation. For example, suppose the cost of one meatball is calculated for a particular cafe at $0.50. This might not seem like much money, and a cook might hope to create added value for a customer by "beefing up" an order. However, if our cafe typically sells 100 orders of the meatball-based entree per month, adding that extra meatball to every dish would equate to a loss of $600!

The same approach can be used with front-of-the-house staff. For example, say the policy for serving iced tea at a small beachside restaurant calls for adding a single lemon slice to each glass. Management calculates that the cost of a lemon slice is $0.08. Iced tea is very popular; the restaurant sells about 5,000 glasses per month. An extra lemon slice added to every glass would equate to an annual loss of $4,800.

These potential losses can also be emphasized by placing them in the context of employee benefits. During an employee's orientation period, a manager might describe her operation's annual employee holiday party or summer picnic, which is held to celebrate the operation's success and thank employees for their service. The manager might add that putting an extra lemon in every iced tea could force the operation to cancel such events, a sure way to help drive the point home.

Finally, employee theft is often contagious. If an honest employee watches his peers stealing, whether this entails eating food without purchasing it or stealing mustard from dry storage—and also sees management turning a blind eye—he might find similar behaviors irresistible. Thus, management must be vigilant and consistent in ensuring and enforcing internal control practices and policies. Ultimately, if an employee steals from a foodservice operation, it is management's fault for providing the opportunity in the absence of effective internal control.

MANAGERIAL IMPLICATIONS

Theft in the foodservice industry is a substantial problem, one that leads to significant financial losses every year. The nature of the business, one that involves many cash exchanges and consumable ingredients such as food and liquor, contributes to the problem. The prevalence of low-skilled, low-paying jobs does not help.

Three conditions exist that may lead to fraud and embezzlement and necessitate thorough internal control practices and policies: opportunity, need, and failure of conscience. The one most within management control is opportunity. If there is no opportunity for theft, there is no theft. Need leads to theft insofar as an employee's economic or psychological problems, such as an addiction, can drive her to steal. The final condition, failure of conscience, is facilitated by the human tendency to make excuses—thieves are always quick to rationalize stealing food, money, or other assets.

Following several general internal control principles can minimize the likelihood of employee theft. For example, dividing duties such that no employee is responsible for taking a customer's order, filling that order, and then collecting for it can ensure against some incidents of theft. Fixing responsibility with one individual for such things as cash handling is also advisable.

A seemingly obvious principle of internal control, but one that is often breached, involves limiting access to a foodservice operation's assets such as food and liquor. Even cleaning supplies should be secured. Access to cash must also be extremely limited and systems for collecting and depositing money must be securely in place.

Cash bank stores, which are usually located in the bar or in a cashier's cash register, should be kept to a minimum. Begin with the smallest amount of cash possible when a shift begins. As cash is collected, employees should make cash drops. Similarly, the amount of food and beverages in inventory should be adequate to ensure that all menu items can be prepared when ordered; excessive inventory simply increases the likelihood of theft and overuse.

If a cashier or bartender is stealing by collecting money, placing it in the register, but not recording it, then inevitably the sum of cash in the drawer will on some occasions fail to match the sum shown on the sales registry. Therefore, random audits of all cash registers should be performed. These should apply to all employees, not just those whom management suspects of fraudulent activity.

Accurate records are an absolute necessity for monitoring operations. Inaccurate records defeat internal control by preventing management from taking corrective actions for problems they do not know about. Even small errors in financial accounting or operational shortcuts can lead to much larger problems.

Computer firewalls must be routinely upgraded in order to protect vital data. Such data may include customers' credit card information. Similarly, current PCI security standards must be followed.

Managers should be rotated not only to create workload equity but also to prevent possible breaches of internal control. For example, the same manager should not record the physical inventory every month. Not only is the inventory process very labor intensive, it can be exploited to hide theft. In other words, a manager could steal something but then record it as being in inventory. Such a theft might not be discovered for months.

The last principle of internal control reminds us that the customer is paramount. Implementing internal control measures that cause delays in menu-item delivery or lengthy guest-check processing is self-defeating because eventually they will turn customers away. Thus, it is management's responsibility to balance the benefits of any internal control approach against the potential costs or compromises in customer service.

Even in an operation that follows all these principles, employee theft will occur. To detect it, managers should monitor operating ratios such as food-cost and labor-cost percentages. They should look for variances in sales or unexplained patterns in inventory-turnover statistics. Managers should also monitor cash tips collected by bartenders. Large tip totals relative to sales might indicate theft. Credit card tips should also be monitored and compared against credit card sales. Repeated occurrences of excessive gratuities may be a sign that a foodserver is altering credit card payment vouchers.

There are methods other than internal bookkeeping to acquire information that is relevant to preventing fraud. Mystery shoppers, for example, can provide invaluable information, not only about customer service issues but also about internal control violations. Technology can also be used to monitor operations. Such tools as closed-circuit television systems can enhance management's view of an operation.

It is management's responsibility to trust its employees but also to verify that what should be happening is happening. Managers should also trust their instincts. While it would be unethical to fire an employee who might be suspected of stealing without strong evidence, it is appropriate to monitor such an employee closely. Trust also can be enhanced by offering information and guidance in dealing with addictions or other health- or safety-related issues.

Perhaps the best deterrent to theft is treating employees as part of the solution. This includes hiring employees with high moral standards. It means training them to implement proper internal control practices and to understand the magnitude of financial costs when such practices are breached. Finally, management must support honest employees by enforcing internal control practices and policies equitably and uniformly.

A.H., Inc.

On May 25, 1939, Anthony and Isabel Hesch established a company that focused on providing its customers with quality products and dependable services. The vending industry was still in its infancy, but Mr. and Mrs. Hesch thought that it could be a viable one, particularly for a family business. At first, they had only a few machines in Arlington Heights, Illinois.

The company, still based near Arlington Heights, today installs and services thousands of vending machines in the greater Chicago area. It operates numerous cafes, many offering well-known signature brands such as Chef's Expo, Maxwell Street Grill, and Brickman's Deli. The company also provides coffee service to many businesses and corporate headquarters.

A.H. is today a major regional onsite foodservice company that offers a variety of full-line foodservices that satisfy customer sets of all sizes. For example, the firm:

- Designs, manages, and operates cafeterias for many of the market's most prestigious businesses
- Provides new and reliable vending equipment with quality products and full-line service

- Operates its own state-of-the-art, fresh-food production facility, providing excellent vending items and catering services
- Provides new and reliable equipment to deliver complete service of coffee, water, and breakroom supplies

With more than 65 years of experience, knowledge, and commitment to its customers, A.H. provides professionalism, impeccable service, and top-quality products. Its goal is to represent a true employee benefit to its clients by providing excellent lunchroom solutions at affordable pricing. Its commitment to excellence is reinforced by its loyal and talented people as well as a company-wide commitment to providing total customer satisfaction.

Given its ability to offer such a wide range of services, it is no surprise that A.H.'s internal control practices are advanced compared with most found in the industry. Thus, even as the company focuses outwardly on providing quality service, it focuses inwardly on efficiently managing its diverse range of products and equipment.

KEY TERMS

Case in Point

Pennies, Nickels, and Dimes

Bridget had the best job in the world—she managed one of the most popular nightclubs in New Orleans. There was a line to get in every night, the club was profitable, and the owners were pleased with her performance. Moreover, she had a great staff with almost no turnover. Why would anyone not want to work at Stubblefield's?

Stubblefield's featured two levels, an upper story with pool tables, air hockey, electronic darts, and several large television screens. Food was also served on the upper floor. Offerings included the usual bar fare but its chicken wings were by far the most popular items and included variations such as Sweet and Spicy, Asian, and Atom Bomb—the hottest one.

© iStockphoto.com

The lower floor was designed around a large dance floor. There were two separate bars; the larger of the two was staffed by two bartenders while the smaller was designed for one bartender and was used primarily on Friday and Saturday nights. Typically, there were three or four cocktail servers, with up to five on busy nights. Opposite the two bars was the DJ booth.

On a slow Monday night, the head bartender, John, was scheduled for his break at 11:00 P.M. However, Bridget was trying to finish her annual performance reviews and wanted to complete Katie's review when her shift ended at 11. So, Bridget went behind the bar around 10:30 and asked John if he would mind taking his break then, rather than waiting. Bridget was puzzled by John's hesitation; she couldn't figure out what difference it would make if he took his break a little earlier. After a moment, John left to go to the employee break room.

Bridget hadn't been a full-time bartender since college, but she could still cover for her employees (so long as it wasn't too busy). Mondays weren't usually very busy, so she had no qualms. She looked around and noticed that everything was clean. John had obviously been using the idle time provided by the slow night well. Just then, a customer ordered a draft beer. Bridget served the guest and made change from John's register. She noticed that three nickels were in the pennies slot in the register. It struck her oddly because John was her best bartender and was meticulous about money handling. He was never over or short when it came time to count the money in his register at the end of the night.

On a whim, Bridget got a reading from the register for cash sales for the night using her code key. (Only managers could generate such information.) She found that the drawer had an excess of $15. She thought it odd, but figured it must be a mistake.

At the end of John's shift, he counted the money in his cash drawer while seated in the manager's office, which was the practice for every bartender. Bridget casually sat at her desk, which was positioned across from where John was sitting. She then accessed the total sales for John's shift on her computer. He submitted the exact amount that was due.

What happened to the $15? Given that John was her best bartender and very proud of his cash handling, Bridget just let it go.

On another Monday night a few weeks later, Bridget decided that, while she trusted John, the prior event deserved attention. So, around 9 P.M., she asked John to take a break for a quick inventory in the beer storeroom.

As John commonly did this (but usually before his shift) when it was time to place an order, John thought nothing of the request and promptly left the bar. Bridget immediately checked the cash sales and then opened the cash drawer. This time, there was a quarter in the penny slot and three pennies on top of the quarters. Bridget did a quick cash count and found the drawer had an excess of $28. Yet when John finished his shift, his cash deposit was exactly correct.

Is there something wrong here? What should Bridget do?

REVIEW AND DISCUSSION QUESTIONS

1. Describe three factors that are especially common in the foodservice industry that make it ripe for employee theft. Provide concrete examples.

2. Bottled condiments, such as ketchup and mustard, used in foodservice operations often carry a label that says, "Not for Individual Sale." Part of the reason is that these items are sold as part of discounted cases and manufacturers do not want the items sold individually (which is also illegal). What is another reason?

3. Using your choice of search engine, look for reports of theft in the foodservice industry. Identify a statistic regarding employee theft in foodservice that is not cited in this chapter. Be sure to include the reference site.

4. Which condition for fraud and embezzlement is easiest for management to control? Which one is the most difficult? Explain your answer completely.

5. Review the rationalizations offered that employees might use to justify stealing food. Name three others.

6. Drawing on your experience or observation, describe a foodservice operation in which the duties are not divided in a way that provides effective internal control.

7. A bartender, working alone, is scheduled for a 20-minute break. The manager fills in for her while she is gone. Since there is little time to change cash banks, the manager simply uses the bartender's cash register and cash drawer. It this good internal control? Why or why not?

8. What is a "drop safe"? Describe how it might be used in a foodservice operation.

9. The bar manager and head bartender have taken the liquor inventory for the last several months. There has been no significant variation in the inventory valuation data from month to month, and both sales and costs are in line. At the end of the fourth month, the bar manager is on vacation but shows up to take inventory, explaining that he doesn't want to saddle anyone else with the hassle. Should the general manager be concerned? What actions should she take?

10. What are three financial ratios that if monitored could indicate problems associated with internal control violations? Explain fully.

11. A server who has worked at a particular midscale restaurant is considered a star employee. He has been with the restaurant for two years and routinely receives customer compliments. Last week, his charge tips averaged 40 percent. Should management be concerned? If yes, what steps should they take?

12. What is a good reason to use a mystery shopper? Why might a foodservice operation choose not to use one?

13. Apply the notion of "trust but verify" to a foodservice situation other than those provided in the chapter.

14. Describe an internal control practice that would effectively safeguard a given category of assets but would have a negative impact on customer satisfaction. Then, offer a better approach.

ENDNOTE

1. Geller, A. N. *Internal Control: A Fraud-Prevention Handbook for Hotel and Restaurant Managers*. Ithaca, NY: Cornell University, 1991.

OPERATIONAL ANALYSES

LEARNING OBJECTIVES:

After becoming familiar with this chapter, you should be able to:

1. Describe how revenue management can be applied to foodservice operations and explain the interrelationship of sales, expenses, and profit.

2. Apply a range of cost-analysis techniques, which ultimately lead to more effective pricing.

3. Explain how operational productivity is quantified and how such assessment differs by segment.

4. Understand the Pareto principle, identify management functions to which it applies, and understand the alternative strategies for carrying out these functions that it suggests.

The discussion of internal control in Chapter 15 leads naturally into our next advanced management topic—operational analyses. There are several techniques available for analyzing any foodservice operation. We addressed the most basic of these in Chapter 10. We begin here with the overarching topic of revenue management, and then discuss an analytic technique that demonstrates how expenses function relative to varying revenue dollars. This leads to a consideration of price elasticity. Next, we look at cost-analysis techniques. We then consider two extremely useful operational analysis techniques and conclude with an important note on how to regard all operational issues.

■□ REVENUE MANAGEMENT
□■

Referred to as *yield* management in years past, **revenue management** lies at the core of any business. Without revenue, expenses cannot be covered and the business cannot operate. Successful revenue management results in selling the right product or service to the right customer at the right price through the right channel, thereby maximizing revenue.[1] Applying basic economic principles, then, revenue management must address situations in which there is excess demand, which acts like a lever that pushes prices higher, or excess supply, which may force a manager to lower prices.

Revenue management produces optimal results when a company has accurate historical information. Such a company must also adopt robust forecasting tools and dedicate resources to the entire revenue-management process. Companies implementing revenue management effectively report up to 5 percent greater revenue than do those that forgo such techniques.

Revenue Management in Restaurants

Applying our general definition to the foodservice industry, we define revenue management as selling the right seat in the right place to the right customer at the right price and for the right duration.[2] Here, determining what counts as *right* involves generating the highest revenue figures possible while also delivering the greatest value (as described in Chapter 2). Note that this is not merely a case of balancing supply and demand. The goal here is to profit but also to provide an experience that the guest will want to repeat.

Foodservice operators cannot approach revenue management in the same way that related industries such as airlines or even hotels do. Airlines often offer tickets at discounts for flights booked well in advance. A customer who books at the last minute has been conditioned to expect a premium for her lack of planning. Hotels, too, charge more for a guest who arrives without a reservation and is desperate for a room. This premium on tardiness means that revenue management is easier for airlines and hotels because reservations are usually made well in advance, and often, particularly with airlines but also for a growing number of hotels, payment is made when reservations are placed. Airlines have the added benefit of being able to change departure and arrival times. In the foodservice industry, it is unreasonable to charge a premium for customers without reservations, and few would be willing to pay for a dinner at a fine-dining restaurant well in advance of eating the food.

On the other hand, foodservice shares one major commonality with airlines and hotels as well as cruise ships and even the car rental industry. That is, the product is perishable. If a flight departs with empty seats, the lost revenue associated with each empty seat cannot be recaptured, and a hotel with empty beds on a given night cannot recoup those lost sales. Similarly, a foodservice operator cannot recover the revenue lost to an empty seat at lunch.

Despite the unique nature of the foodservice industry, however, operators can practice revenue management successfully as long as they adjust to the business requirements that apply exclusively to their industry. We address these differences in light of the definition presented earlier: the right seat in the right place to the right customer at the right price and for the right duration.

The right seat in the right place to the right customer: This is perhaps the most difficult piece of restaurant revenue management. Obviously, the ideal approach would be for a foodservice company to implement a series of concepts, each of which uniquely corresponds to a given segment (e.g., QSR, theme, onsite) in every market. This, then, would provide opportunities for customers to self-select and maximize revenue. However, few foodservice companies are capable of operating successfully in every segment (although perhaps such an approach can be found in food courts in malls, airports, and universities, where a variety of concepts at slightly differing price points maximize participation).

Another way to achieve this goal is marketing. As noted in Chapter 12, one of the goals in marketing a foodservice operation is communicating the value proposition to potential customers, drawing them to the operation, and, as we've put it, putting them in the right seats.

The Right Price

A more malleable revenue-management lever is price. This is achieved initially by applying the appropriate pricing technique (as discussed in Chapter 5). Prices can be manipulated in order to maximize revenue. For example, a restaurant might offer early bird specials—specially priced menu items—from 4 P.M. until 6 P.M., a traditionally slow time. This can raise revenue incrementally by filling otherwise empty seats. Similar pricing applications include happy hour specials during low-demand periods and late-night appetizer discounts. These strategies are intended to shift demand, increasing it during traditionally slow dayparts.

Another price manipulation strategy involves offering discount coupons and premium pricing—for example, charging more (often using specialized menus) for peak dining times or days (such as Valentine's Day). Time-limited coupons can entice customers who might not otherwise patronize a foodservice operation. The widespread use of couponing was particularly evident during the economic downturn that hit the foodservice industry in early 2008. While a worthy revenue management technique in the short term, couponing can create long-term problems. For example, if a customer routinely sees advertisements that include a 20 percent coupon discount, he may decide to patronize that particular restaurant only when he can benefit from the discount. This, then, negatively affects revenue in the long term.

Specialty menus (see Figure 16.1) offer a number of advantages. Menu items can be priced at a premium and the number of items can be reduced to allow for faster preparation. Also, because customers are less likely to resist paying a premium when dining on holidays, there are few if any negative effects on short- or long-term revenue management.

We should note that some of the revenue-management strategies employed in the airline industry have been implemented by foodservice operators. The thought is that customers are willing to pay higher prices as demand increases. Thus, a popular restaurant, say in New York City, might charge $30 for an entrée in the 5 P.M. to 7 P.M. daypart, raising it to $34 during the restaurant's busiest time, from 7 until 10 P.M., and then lower it to $28 from 10 P.M. until closing, the slowest daypart. Such practices have not been received well, however, and are difficult to manage. For example, imagine a guest who arrives at 6:58 P.M. and receives the blue discounted menu and another who is seated at 7:01 and is handed the premium-priced red menu. If these two parties are seated next to each other, the red-menu guest, upon seeing that the other party is being charged less for the same menu items, is likely to be very unhappy.

The Right Duration

The last piece of an effective revenue-management strategy involves managing meal duration, which is a bit more complicated. In hotels, there is a check-in time and a check-out time. Rental car companies benefit because the duration of the car rental is a contractual matter; if a customer keeps the car longer than expected, he pays more. This is not the case in foodservice operations. A guest might consume three courses in an hour or eat an appetizer while occupying the table for two hours. Moreover, in North America, foodservice operators have yet to embrace a practice common in many European countries of a cover charge, paid by every guest, which is used to help cover the cost of dining amenities like bread, olive oil, butter, and so on.

"*The Heights Cafe and Grill is surely among Ithaca's very finest. Imaginative cuisine, beautifully presented. Sophisticated atmosphere. World class wine list. Attentive service.*"

– Mark Finkelstein
Ithaca Times

Courtesy of Heights Cafe

Figure 16.1 Heights Cafe menu.

DINNER

APPETIZERS

Crispy Calamari
Fra Diavlo Sauce
11.

Fresh Mozzarella
Stuffed with Feta, Jalapeño Peppers & Basil
Roasted Peppers, Greek Olives, Mint Infused Extra
Virgin Olive Oil
Grissini
12.

Sicilian Cauliflower
Pine Nuts, Raisins & Red Onions
8.

Lemon-Crab Risotto
Little Neck Clams, Asparagus, Parmesan Cheese &
Lardons
10.

Braised Beef Hash
Poached Egg, Dill Crème Fraiche & Port Demi Glace
12.

Fried West Coast Oysters
Pulled Pork, Red Cabbage Slaw & Sweet Corn Salsa
Smoked Tomato Tartar Sauce
13.

House Smoked Salmon & Panko Crusted Brie
Orange-Caperberry Salad & Local Goat Cheese Wonton
Lingonberry Preserve & Wasabi Maple Reduction
14.

Pine Nut & Wild Mushroom Ravioli
Veal Bolognese & Chianti Demi Glace Drizzle
Shaved Pecorino
11.

Oven Roasted Beets
Parsnips, Carrots, Red Onion & Gorgonzola Cheese
Extra Virgin Olive Oil
8.

Old School Meatball
Marinara, Parmesan, Fresh Mozzarella, Ricotta & Basil
9.

Soup of The Day
Chef's Homemade Delight

The most effective way in which foodservice operations can manage dining duration is not by forcing a guest to limit her time at a table, which would obviously have detrimental effects, but by streamlining the efficiency with which food is prepared and served. While a customer does not want to receive an entrée while she is still enjoying the starter course, she doesn't need to wait a long time between courses. The same is true of handling payment. During peak times, payment processing can take a substantial amount of time because servers are busy waiting on other guests. However, if the time spent in offering the check and then collecting payment can be reduced, seat turnover can be increased.

Break-even Analysis

In discussing financial management in Chapter 10, we illustrated the relationship between fixed and variable expenses and revenue. Here, we introduce a quantitative method for examining this relationship, one that can aid in measuring the effectiveness of revenue-management strategies. The objective is to use break-even analysis (sometimes referred to as cost-volume-profit analysis) to identify a **break-even point (BEP)**, which is the volume of sales at which revenue covers fixed and variable costs but does not yet produce a profit.

The key assumptions underlying this calculation are that fixed costs remain constant while variable costs change at a constant rate with sales. Moreover, the technique requires addressing costs with both fixed and variable components accordingly. This same approach can be applied using total revenue, number of orders, or number of covers.

The BEP is expressed as follows:

$$\begin{aligned} \text{BEP} &= \text{Net income \$0} \\ &= \text{Revenue} - \text{Fixed costs} - \text{Variable costs} \end{aligned}$$

Before we apply BEP, we should mention that variable costs, which as we discussed in Chapter 10 include food cost, and the portion of labor and direct operating expenses that vary in direct proportion, must be computed with reasonable accuracy. Recall, too, that we view total labor expenses and to a lesser extent (because a large percentage is variable) direct operating expenses as semivariable since they consist of both variable and fixed components. Thus, we can use this information to calculate the contribution margin, which is the contribution to profit resulting from revenue less variable expenses.

A related calculation is the **contribution rate**, which is expressed as:

$$\frac{\text{Profit} + \text{Fixed costs}}{\text{Total sales}} = \text{Contribution rate}$$

An alternative calculation is:

$$\frac{\text{Total sales} - \text{Variable costs}}{\text{Total sales}} = \text{Contribution rate}$$

The application of break-even analysis is apparent in the following example: Consider a fast-casual restaurant that has an average check of $10.00. The sales and costs are:

Sales	$1,500,000	100%
Variable Costs	$1,125,000	75%
Fixed Costs	$300,000	20%
Profit	$75,000	5%

First, let's calculate the contribution rate:

$$\frac{\$75,000 + \$300,000}{\$1,500,000} = 0.25$$

Now, the easiest approach to calculating BEP is to use the following formula:

$$\frac{\text{Fixed costs}}{\text{Contribution rate}} = \text{BEP in sales}$$

So,

$$\frac{\$300,000}{0.25} = \$1,200,000$$

This means that after sales reach $1,200,000, every $10 check (the average amount spent per customer) contributes $2.50 to profit, since all fixed costs are now covered. This can also be depicted graphically, as shown in Figure 16.2.

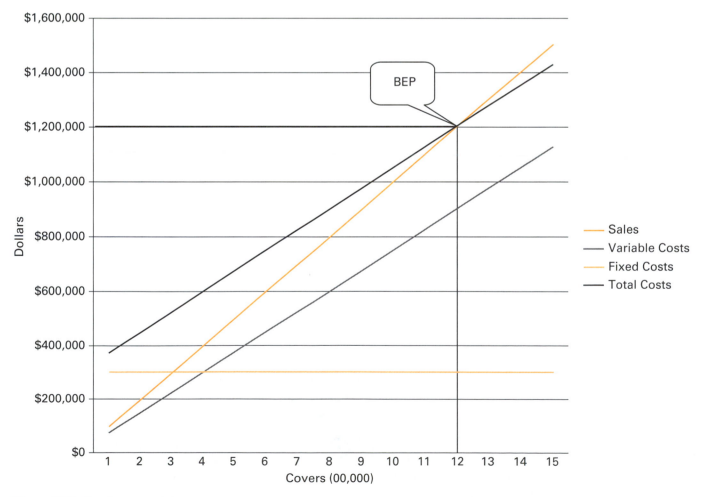

Figure 16.2 Break-even point.

The operator wants to determine the number of covers required to reach the BEP. This can be calculated in a number of ways, but the easiest way is to use the BEP sales calculations and divide by the average check. Thus, $1,200,000/$10 = $120,000. Note the relationship as shown in Figure 16.2.

Break-even analysis, as you can see, offers tremendous utility. A foodservice manager can use it to better understand how volume, cost, and profit are related. He can use it to forecast profit based on sales volume and consider the effects of changes to fixed costs. He can also test alternative pricing strategies to facilitate price optimization and menu engineering (as introduced in Chapter 5).

Price Elasticity

This review of the various components of break-even analysis underscores how important menu prices are in determining profitability. However, there is another useful concept that we have waited until now to address: **price elasticity**. This concept provides a means that foodservice operators can use to assess customer sensitivity to menu prices. For example, when the price of an item is increased, and especially if this increase is dramatic, one would expect demand for that item to decline. Similarly, if we reduce the price of an item, we likely expect to increase the number sold.

The associated demand for a menu item can be described as elastic or inelastic. Every foodservice manager hopes that there is an inelastic demand for her menu offerings. That is, when menu prices are increased, the percentage reduction in the number of items sold is less than the percentage of the price increase. If raising prices leads to a disproportionate reduction in demand, the operator knows that demand is indeed elastic.

The following formula can be used to calculate an item's elasticity:

$$\frac{\text{Change in quantity ordered}}{\text{Quantity ordered prior to change}} \Big/ \frac{\text{Change in price}}{\text{Original price}} = \text{Price elasticity}$$

If the result is less than 1, demand is considered to be inelastic since the percentage change in price is less than the percentage change in demand (number of orders sold).

For example, say a foodservice operator promotes a nightly special in addition to the usual menu offerings. For the past several weeks, he has offered the same special on Wednesday nights for $19.95. This week, he's decided that the popularity of the item justifies a price increase to $22.95. In essence, he thinks there is an inelastic demand for the special. In the past few weeks, he has sold 100 orders of the special on a given Wednesday. Following the price change, he sold 88 orders.

We can then calculate the elasticity as follows:

$$\frac{13}{108} \Big/ \frac{\$3.00}{\$19.95} = 0.80$$

Since 0.80 is less than 1, we see that he was correct. (In this simplified example, we assume that all other operational factors are equal and that the one night of sales at the higher price is indicative of future sales.) Applying our earlier discussion of the BEP, we can also conclude that, if the previous price produced even a small profit, indicating that all fixed and variable costs were covered, the $3 increase is all profit.

In segments such as onsite foodservice where multiple dining options exist, demand is generally elastic. Similarly, in markets where many restaurants compete for market share, demand is elastic. For the fortunate foodservice operator who has little competition (imagine a fine-dining restaurant with no competition in a strong economy) demand is relatively inelastic—at least to a point.

◼◻ COST-ANALYSIS TECHNIQUES
◻◼

As we noted in discussing financial management in Chapter 10, several finance-related ratios are effective tools for operational analysis. The most basic of these, food cost percentage and labor cost percentage (and the aggregated prime cost percentage), are widely used as simple methods for analyzing individual foodservice operations as well as comparing same-segment operations. However, these simple ratios do not tell the whole story. Borrowed from the manufacturing sector, a conceptual method that has only recently been applied to foodservice appears to offer considerable utility. Another that dates back decades but deserves mention is the application of potential costs. Both are discussed here.

Activity-based Costing

The application of BEP analysis illustrates that even in businesses where the majority of expenses are variable, fixed costs must still be covered. In the foodservice industry, this is readily apparent, particularly when fixed expenses in urban centers where rent is high are disproportionately greater than in locations where land cost is low. To this end, **activity-based costing (ABC)**, which has been applied in manufacturing, healthcare, and banking, can be effective because it allows managers to trace fixed costs to individual menu items. In essence, ABC assigns fixed costs to output, which in this case is food. Put another way, it allows us to view fixed expenses as a direct function of a foodservice operation. Given the problems associated with pricing models that do not include fixed costs, this is particularly valuable.[3]

In applying ABC, the first step is to identify areas that are responsible for fixed costs. For example, in most foodservice operations, fixed costs can be allocated largely to either the front of the house or the back of the house. Using the Uniform System of Accounts for Restaurants (cited in Chapter 10) and recalling our discussion of financial management regarding semifixed costs, these costs include, in whole or in part, salaries and wages, employee benefits, direct operating expenses, music and entertainment, marketing, utility services, occupancy costs, repairs and maintenance, depreciation, and general and administration expenses. Thus, we examine each of the fixed expenses and apportion them to specific front-of-the-house or back-of-the-house activities.

This apportionment also requires us to categorize the expenses into four distinct **cost drivers**. The first is a **direct cost driver** expense that increases whenever a specific food item is prepared. This expense, then, is allocated to the appropriate menu item and can be treated as wholly variable in the traditional sense (i.e., it varies in direct proportion to the number of items sold). A **batch cost driver** is an expense incurred for a batch of food items. Such a cost is therefore allocated across menu items to which these expenses relate. The third category, **product-level cost driver**, arises in the course of activities related to menu-item production and is therefore allocated across menu items in proportion to the raw cost of each specific menu item. Similarly, a **facility-sustaining cost driver** (e.g., building insurance) is an expense that is necessitated by a foodservice operation's general processes and is allocated again in proportion to the raw cost of each menu item.

As you may note, ABC involves a tedious process and is, to a certain extent, subjective in terms of cost allocation. However, it does make it possible to allocate all expenses. If these expenses are then built into the pricing models used for food and beverage items, there is a greater likelihood that the operation will be profitable. Moreover, it forces management to look at every expense as a function of sales, and allows for identification and reduction of activities that cost more than they add in value.

Potential Food Cost

In the past, a common practice in foodservice management was the calculation of the **potential food cost**. The potential food cost is the cost of food under perfect or ideal conditions. Consider a chicken entree that includes a five-ounce chicken breast. The chicken used is packaged in cases of 24 5-ounce breasts, at a case cost of $36. The *potential* cost of chicken for one entree, then, is $1.50 ($36/24). Assume, however, that not all the chicken is used and four of the chicken breasts must be discarded. The *actual* food cost for the chicken portion of the entree for that period is then $1.80 ($36/20).

Applied on a larger scale, a foodservice operator could calculate the potential food cost for an entire period (say, one week). This would require multiplying the number of menu items sold by the potential food cost for each of the corresponding items. This results in the potential food cost dollars for the week. Dividing this number by the revenue for the week provides the potential food cost percentage. Next, the manager calculates the actual food cost and divides that number by the revenue. The potential food cost approach suggests that any negative variance greater than 1 percent indicates a problem.

Justification for this approach is related to forecasting difficulties, the perishability of food, and the inescapable fact that any type of food production nearly always results in at least a small amount of waste. Moreover, the notion of a 1 percent allowance provides wiggle room for the kitchen staff. However, it also suggests that the budgeted food cost is ideal and perhaps not realistic. Current advances in food tracking, the availability of preportioned items, and greater culinary expertise, however, have largely eliminated the need for this practice. Also, proper costing and pricing methods should provide for any allowance previously integrated into the potential food cost approach. Most foodservice managers today, therefore, treat the budgeted food cost as both the potential food cost and the true basis of comparison with actual costs (and accept only positive variances).

OPERATIONAL ANALYSIS TECHNIQUES

As was noted in an earlier chapter, it is often said in management that you improve only what you measure. With this in mind, we now consider two operational analysis techniques. Both involve measuring a foodservice operation's productivity.

In its most general application, **productivity** is a performance measure and can be defined as *the effective use of resources to achieve operational goals.*[4] Based on this definition, the basic industrial model defines productivity as output divided by input. Extending this notion, productivity can be represented by the following equation:

$$\frac{\text{Goods} + \text{Services}}{\text{Labor} + \text{Materials} + \text{Energy} + \text{Capital}} = \text{Productivity}$$

Partial-factor Productivity Analysis

Productivity can also be expressed as either a **partial-factor statistic** or a **multiple-partial-factor statistic** by selecting at least one of the listed variables from both the numerator and the denominator. Some partial-factor productivity statistics can be very meaningful and can be useful as indicators of operational performance, most commonly in labor management. Poorly formulated or misunderstood measures can be damaging, however, and, if relied on as the primary indicators of performance, disastrous. The key is to select outputs and inputs that indicate which operational areas are most in need of scrutiny.

The first such measure of productivity was applied in the QSR segment. Given that food production is reasonably standardized in this segment, the focus was on sales and labor, with the measure being **sales per labor hour**. Sales are treated as total sales net of sales tax. Labor hours are calculated using productive hours only, which include regular time, overtime, on-call hours (if worked), and hours spent in training and orientation. Salaried positions are accounted for based on eight hours per day per person (even if a manager worked substantially longer shifts).

This partial-factor statistic is also useful in midscale and theme restaurants because, as we have observed in previous chapters, labor currently outpaces food cost as the largest expense item in many foodservice segments. However, its application in fine dining is limited. Here, labor hours are proportionately greater than in other segments owing to the focal emphasis on service. Thus, reducing labor with the intent of maximizing the ratio can have undesirable effects because doing so could compromise service delivery.

Nevertheless, the sales-per-labor-hour statistic has also been used in the onsite business and industry (B&I) segment. However, three operational issues that separate B&I operations from their traditional-restaurant brethren make this measure less than ideal. First, some B&I operations are subsidized. Thus, sales of one operation cannot be compared with those of another with a different or no subsidy built into the price structure. A second, less apparent, problem is the existence of satellite outlets. Satellites, which range from small coffee kiosks to fully functional eateries, are generally considered financially viable, because they maximize distribution and food-production economies yet require very little labor in terms of actual sales. They can, as a result, wreak havoc on sales-per-labor hour statistics.

The third challenge in using this fast-food-borne, partial-factor productivity statistic relates to catering activities. Some B&I operators include catering sales in the sales-per-labor-hour productivity measure. Others keep catering sales separate but cannot always separate the labor used for catering activities. For example, when an entrée is prepared en masse for both a catering function and sales in the main cafe, it is difficult to determine how much of the cook's preparation time should be attributed to the catering activity. Similarly, how should managerial hours be distributed between catering and routine operations when one manager oversees both?

In the corrections, education, and healthcare onsite foodservice segments, **meals per labor hour** is a common partial-factor productivity measure. In corrections, this is a reasonable statistic, at least for determining labor productivity, since the number of meals served is a direct function of the number of inmates. Moreover, the number of distinct types of meals is limited, although this is changing today as greater emphasis is placed on meeting prisoners' dietary restrictions and preferences.

In the case of schools, however, which are largely government subsidized, this measure is fraught with problems. First, a school meal is typically considered the equivalent of an entrée, two side dishes, and a beverage; à la carte items are not often considered (although they arguably constitute a small percentage of total sales). Second, subjective meal equivalents are used in tallying sales from business generated outside the central school. Since operators are increasingly seeking add-on business—from child daycare centers, adult daycare centers, preschools, and private schools, whereby meals are sold at a reduced cost to reflect the efficiencies attained in volume food production—meals-per-labor-hour can be greatly, albeit artificially, inflated.

Colleges and universities face similar problems with this meals-per-labor-hour statistic. Meal-plan configurations are so diverse that rarely are any two school plans alike. This is problematic since each meal plan specifies what constitutes a meal; some colleges base this on a specific dollar amount while others equate it to preassigned menu combinations. Moreover, where vending has replaced traditional foodservice facilities to any significant extent, the quantification of meals is rather arbitrary.

This latter problem also raises issues in healthcare foodservice. Counting meals—the essential component in calculating meals per labor hour—is surprisingly complex here, even more so than in education. The problems with healthcare catering are the same as those mentioned earlier related to B&I foodservice. The issue of quantifying patient meals, however, dwarfs such problems. Rarely do patients eat three meals a day. This is unfortunate, since it would otherwise be easy to calculate meals—simply take the number of patients and multiply by three. In addition, some patients are on tube feedings, which require varying amounts of time to prepare and deliver (tube feedings can also be very expensive in terms of product cost). Should a tube feeding count as a meal?

Another problem associated with accounting for patient meals is caused by the typically diverse patient mix. Pediatric patients, for example, generally eat smaller meals than their adult counterparts do. At the other end of the continuum are psychiatric patients, some of whom are in recovery from addiction or related illnesses and may require double portions at every meal. Should a tray for pediatrics with a three-ounce hamburger, two ounces of potatoes, and juice be considered equivalent to a tray sent to a psychiatric wing with two servings of lasagna, garlic toast, two salads, two large milks, and two desserts? These same differences are also seen in the consumption habits of outpatients—one might reach satiety with a cup of broth, while another enjoys a multi-item meal.

Three other important components of patient meals also strongly influence the meals-per-labor-hour determination. Floor stocks, such as juices, coffee, and crackers, which are maintained at par levels on various floors, augment a patient's intake of calories. These must be routinely replenished, adding labor hours. Dietary supplements, used in a variety of healthcare settings to dramatically boost patients' caloric intake, are difficult to translate into meals yet are a real cost to the department (with some costing only pennies per serving and others costing several dollars). Finally, between-meal snacks are a big part of many patients' meal service.

Many healthcare foodservice managers have addressed their revenue management issues by using an **equivalent meal value (EMV)**, calculated as the food cost corresponding to a typical midday meal. (Most operators consider a "typical" meal as an entree, two side dishes, a beverage, and a dessert.) While the EMV varies according to the user, most agree that it is somewhere around US$1.80. This factor can be used for patients, catering, and public eateries.

The obvious problem with using an EMV is that no consideration is given to variations in menu mix, the positioning of the institution, or sales strategies. An EMV's appropriateness is particularly questionable when applied to catering. Is a lobster dinner prepared and served to 12 board members the same as 65 boxed lunches served at an orientation meeting? Using an EMV, these two events would equate to the same number of meals. Is that accurate? Finally—and this applies to restaurants in other segments, too—onsite operators struggle with another aspect of EMV, which is created by the customer who comes to the cafe or university bistro with his bag lunch from home and purchases only a drink and dessert. All of these problems can be overcome, but the key is for foodservice managers to use meaningful data to calculate the EMV and apply it appropriately.

A minority of operators have combated some of the problems associated with using an EMV by replacing it with a **floating equivalent-meal-price factor** (EMP). An EMP is the average price of a complete meal specific to the daypart, catered event, or patient meal. To be effective, the EMP must be calculated repeatedly. The frequency of such calculations is dictated by variations in sales, catered events, and patient eating patterns. Thus, an operator will very likely use several EMPs during any one day, with each corresponding to the daypart and outlet. Without benefit of moderately sophisticated financial tracking systems, such a task is extremely burdensome, and may require so many management hours that this in itself saps the operation's productivity.

Regardless of segment, partial-factor productivity statistics can be useful. They may not, however, be good indicators of overall performance since they serve only as measures of isolated aspects of an operation. Similarly, problems arise when managers analyze partial-factor productivity measures as indicators of overall operational performance without considering the effects of related variables. For example, partial-factor productivity is often used as a surrogate for profitability, since it follows, ostensibly, that optimal utilization of labor, materials, energy, or capital would equate to increased profits. Effective treatment of any one of these, however, does not ensure overall performance. This is easily demonstrated by considering a kitchen manager who replaces labor-intensive food items with preprepared products in order to decrease labor costs. Such an approach would surely increase sales per labor hour. However, the cost of the prepared items might exceed the labor cost reduction. As a result, labor productivity is improved at the cost of weakening the financial viability of the operation. In this case, if productivity had been measured by dividing sales by the combined cost of labor and food, the wisdom of the operational change, at least in short-term financial terms, would have been accurately deduced. Thus, when total operation-wide productivity is the target of analysis, aggregate measures that integrate the majority of operational inputs are appropriate. (We discuss this in greater detail in the following section.)

Before moving on, we pause to note that single-factor productivity statistics can be particularly useful. For example, if used for **intertemporal analysis** of a single aspect of an onsite operation (which involves comparing the same statistic over time), they can demonstrate unwanted or unexpected variations. Such analyses, using meals per labor hour, for example, also offer the advantage that no adjustments are needed for inflation, assuming the EMV is adjusted accordingly each year. Intertemporal analysis using dollar-based statistics (such as those pertaining to labor costs) must, however, be adjusted to reflect constant-dollar values.

Total-factor Productivity Analysis

As noted, expanding the number of factors in evaluating productivity substantially increases the measure's usefulness. Obviously, food cost is a critical element here, since it often has a reciprocal effect on labor productivity and always has an effect on the price-value equation. In addition, labor cost (as opposed simply to hours) can be more useful since hours worked do not necessarily correspond proportionately to labor costs.

In essence, the greater the number of variables included in a productivity statistic, the more accurate it is in assessing the foodservice operation's actual efficiency. For example, consider the following aggregate, total-factor productivity statistic:

$$\frac{rev_i}{fc_i + lc_i + doe_i + mp_i} = \text{Productivity}$$

where

- rev_i = revenue for period i
- fc_i = food cost for period i
- lc_i = productive labor cost for period i
- doe_i = direct operating expenses for period i
- mp_i = apportioned minimum profit

Note that productive labor and direct operating expenses are treated as entirely variable for convenience purposes here. Fixed costs (e.g., occupancy, depreciation) are not included since they will conceivably not vary over the short term. This allows for comparison across units where fixed costs such as occupancy expenses or administrative overhead may differ. Finally, it includes profit, which is a function of productivity.

While this is a much more robust statistic than the partial-factor productivity statistics discussed earlier, it still fails to account for an important operational concern. Consider, for example, a productivity statistic commonly used in many hotels' housekeeping departments: Rooms cleaned per hour. A housekeeper who cleans more rooms per hour is considered more productive. However, there is no measure of quality. This is problematic because a housekeeper could conceivably save a lot of time by, say, not vacuuming the entire room or only partially cleaning the bathroom. This will likely lead to guest dissatisfaction and ultimately reduced profits.

Applying this concern to foodservice productivity assessment, an emerging practice is to integrate two critical measures of quality in foodservice: customer satisfaction and employee satisfaction. These measures are also not simply being integrated as variables in a ratio statistic but instead are integrated into highly sophisticated computer models.[5] Although explaining the statistical techniques used for such analyses is beyond the scope of this text, we note that the trend in foodservice productivity analysis will continue to force operators in every segment to expand their understanding of operational productivity, measured accurately only through holistic productivity indices.

THE PARETO PRINCIPLE

We conclude this chapter by considering a management principle based on work done in the late 1800s by the Italian economist Vilfredo Pareto, who asserted that 80 percent of the effects of any event or factor stem from only 20 percent of the causes. The principle emerged from Pareto's observation that 80 percent of the land in Italy was owned by 20 percent of the population. He later surveyed other countries and found similar results. The **Pareto principle**, which is also referred to as the 80–20 rule, the law of the vital few, and the principle of factor sparsity, can be found in many domains. For example, software developers have noted that fixing 20 percent of a software program's bugs would reduce errors and crashes by 80 percent. It also has several applications in foodservice management, including human resources, sales, and marketing.

In managing people, most foodservice managers note that 80 percent of their time is spent dealing with 20 percent of their employees. This 20 percent is likely to be the worst-performing employees, which is why the demand on a manager's time is so great. Many have asserted that this is a problem across industries and creates a self-fulfilling situation. That is, good employees note that management's attention is devoted to dealing with problems rather than rewarding positive behavior. This leads to decreased motivation on the part of the good employees to perform well. Ultimately, you get job dissatisfaction and unnecessary turnover. Management research indicates that effective managers should instead focus 80 percent of their time on the top 20 percent of their employees in order to increase job satisfaction, workplace performance, and operational productivity.

In analyzing sales for many businesses, it is often concluded that 80 percent of sales is driven by 20 percent of customers, and this happens in the foodservice industry. Here, the 20 percent are the loyal customers who bring repeat business and thereby provide 80 percent of revenue. These customers are sometimes referred to as *barnacles*, because they tend to stick to a restaurant or chain without fail. The 80 percent are the *butterflies* who flit around in indiscernible patterns.

This sales information applies to marketing as well. Most marketing is targeted at the butterflies. While marketing strategies sometimes succeed in converting butterflies into barnacles, marketing dollars devoted to this effort have been diverted from helping to retain loyal customers. Thus, foodservice marketers now look to appeal to loyal customers through advertising that shows new items in addition to long-time favorites. Targeted at untapped customers, they seek to create an exciting image, perhaps underscoring what makes a particular foodservice operation unique in a given market.

The lesson from the Pareto principle is that foodservice managers should identify the 20 percent of employees, customers, or issues that require 80 percent of their time. Then, they need to adjust processes so that this time can be spent more effectively. Ultimately, the goal is to turn the 80–20 issue upside down so that the manger's time is spent more productively.

MANAGERIAL IMPLICATIONS

The concept of revenue management, widely used by airlines, hotels, cruise lines, and rental car companies, can readily be applied to the foodservice industry. For foodservice operators, it involves selling the right seat in the right place to the right customer at the right price and for the right duration. However, foodservice operations lack some of the advantages that other industries enjoy relative to revenue management. For example, foodservice customers would not likely be willing to pay for a meal months in advance. Foodservice operations do share, however, the common issue of product perishability. Lost revenues from an empty hotel room or from an empty restaurant seat cannot be recouped.

The primary levers foodservice operators can use to manage revenue are prices and dining duration. Prices can be adjusted, coupons might be offered, and special menus can be used to manipulate prices in order to maximize revenue by shifting demand. Foodservice managers can also maximize revenue by making all guest-related processes, such as taking payment, more efficient, thus reducing dining duration.

To understand how fixed costs, variable costs, sales, and profit are related, a foodservice operation can manage revenue using break-even analysis, which involves calculating a break-even point. At the BEP, all variable and fixed expenses are covered. Sales beyond that point must cover only the variable costs; the remaining contribution is profit.

Understanding price elasticity is yet another way to discern the effectiveness of a foodservice operation's pricing approach. Foodservice managers hope that there is inelastic demand for their menu offerings. That is, when menu prices are increased, the percentage reduction in the number of items sold is less than the percentage of the price increase. If demand is elastic, then, as prices are raised, the number of corresponding menu items ordered is disproportionately lower.

In terms of cost analysis, one technique that offers considerable utility is activity-based costing, which essentially allocates all fixed expenses to associated menu items. This apportionment requires that these expenses be categorized as one of four distinct cost drivers, ensuring that all expenses are considered and optimal pricing is achieved. It also draws management's attention to every expense, viewed as a direct function of sales.

Productivity can be assessed using a variety of partial-factor statistics in order to measure specific aspects of a foodservice operation. These are most useful when applied in specific ways depending on the segment. In order to get an accurate picture of overall operational productivity, a more robust model is required. Such a model should include sales and expenses that are not wholly fixed as well as projected profit. An emerging practice is to integrate measures of quality and to create complex models that are intended to paint a highly accurate picture of operational efficiency.

The final operational consideration is referred to as the Pareto principle. The lesson here for foodservice managers is to focus the majority of their time on optimizing the customer experience as opposed to focusing that time on "putting out fires." The Pareto principle can be applied to human resources, sales, and marketing.

INDUSTRY EXEMPLAR

Benihana

The Benihana story has its roots in Japan immediately following World War II. At that time, Yunosuke Aoki, a samurai descendant and a popular Japanese entertainer, opened a small coffee shop in Tokyo with his wife, Katsu. A red safflower they noticed in the neighborhood streets gave the Aokis the inspiration for the restaurant's name—Benihana—which in Japanese means "red flower."

Yunosuke's show-business background taught him that the public loves new products and new experiences. This little Benihana coffeehouse soon became known for serving and using real sugar. Yunosuke would have to pedal his bicycle more than 20 miles to purchase the sugar.

The family's four sons grew up with the coffee shop, which later became a full-service restaurant. Each of them understood the restaurant business from the ground up— the importance of absolute cleanliness in the kitchen and of using the freshest ingredients and the very best cooking tools money could buy.

The eldest son, Hiroaki, also grasped the importance of offering guests something out of the ordinary, and he had inherited his father's appreciation for the theatrical. There was something magical about this combination, and the thought stayed with him as he completed college in Japan. Meanwhile, Hiroaki's athletic ability earned him a spot on the Japanese Olympic wrestling team. This team membership would eventually bring him to America.

By the time Hiroaki arrived on US soil in 1960, he had already begun forming the idea that America might be ready for a different kind of food presented with an entertaining flair. Adopting a name that would be easier for Americans to pronounce, "Rocky" Aoki set off to make his dream a reality. He worked seven days a week selling ice cream in New York City and studied restaurant management at night. Through saving and borrowing, Rocky scraped together enough money to finance his first four-table restaurant on New York's West 56th Street.

Based on an authentic Japanese farmhouse interior, the Benihana dining concept gradually came into focus. Food would be prepared at the table "teppan-yaki" style (*teppan*, meaning "steel grill" and *yaki*, meaning "broiled") with highly trained chefs creating dazzling effects while slicing, dicing, and flipping food in the air and twirling and spinning razor-sharp knives and cleavers. Rocky also believed that, because the restaurant was near Broadway, the showmanship of the chefs was extremely important. Beef, chicken, and shrimp would be the stars of the menu, all prepared "hibachi-style" (an American term for teppanyaki cooking). Guests would sit at communal tables and place their orders directly with the chef and watch in amazement as he worked his magic. Cooking time for the various ingredients was a critical element in the presentation (we have more to say about cooking time later), because they all had to be ready to be deftly deposited onto the guests' plates simultaneously.

(continued)

Courtesy of Benihana Inc.

In 1964, even after all the preparation and planning, Benihana of Tokyo was serving only one or two guests a day. Aoki family members moonlighted at other restaurants just to pay the bills. Six months after the restaurant opened, however, an enthusiastic review by Clementine Paddleford, the legendary *New York Herald-Tribune* restaurant critic, reversed the trend for good. New Yorkers flocked to the four-table Benihana, and Rocky Aoki suddenly found himself having to turn dining guests away.

The first Benihana of Tokyo restaurant paid for itself in six months. Rocky opened another Benihana in New York just three blocks the east of the original, then moved on to Chicago to build his third just four years later. The second restaurant paid for itself in less than a year. Chicago proved extremely successful, making greater profits than both New York restaurants combined. By 1972, Rocky Aoki had opened six Benihana of Tokyo restaurants, using company profits to invest in the new locations.

Rocky Aoki passed away in 2008, but his legacy lives on in the global brand and cultural icon he created, as generations continue to enjoy the Benihana experience in restaurants worldwide. Today, the publicly traded company has more than 6,000 employees and is the largest operator of teppanyaki restaurants in the country.

Besides its colorful history, Benihana is also noteworthy for managing pricing and dining duration. The menu features various cuts of steak and seafood items, each at a different price point. It also offers combinations, such as Rocky's Choice, which include its trademark Hibachi steak and chicken breast. Most entrees are bundled with side dishes, including Benihana onion soup, Benihana salad, a shrimp appetizer, hibachi vegetables, homemade dipping sauces, steamed rice, and Japanese hot green tea, which substantially increases the perceived value.

Customers dine at Benihana for the great food *and* the experience. This creates both a challenge and an opportunity. Since many will rate the experience based on how long it lasts, a dinner that is perceived as too short may result in poor return business. If a dinner takes an unusually long time, however, seat turnover, revenue, and profits will be reduced.

Benihana has a recipe for managing the associated dining duration. In fact, the company's formulaized approach creates a dining experience that is robust but not necessarily long. For example, after guests are seated, beverage orders are taken and menus offered. Beverages are quickly delivered, often with the first course. Food orders are then taken. While guests enjoy their beverages and occasionally additional appetizers, the kitchen assembles the food items for the table's chef. The chef then appears and entertains the guests but also cooks the food. Owing to this well-honed operational efficiency, actual food preparation often takes less time than in other theme restaurants. Yet the perception of exceptional service is greater because the guest is taking part in the process. The result? Happy customers and a profitable foodservice company.

KEY TERMS

Case in Point

Sales and Labor

Heather was excited about her new job. She had never thought about working in a senior-living facility with a large assisted-living area. In fact, she had thought that "nursing homes" were places where old people lived and where the employees were old, too. So, when the recruiter called, she was somewhat surprised. However, after the initial interview with the facility administrator, Karl, and the subsequent tour, she had a completely different view of this healthcare segment. The residents were amazing and not everyone was "old." Moreover, the other managers and employees seemed fun and energetic; they also seemed to really like what they did for a living. Thus, at only 29 years old, Heather had an opportunity to manage the upscale cafe as well as the patient services in the facility. It sounded like there might also be some opportunities to cater events.

Rolling Hills was part of a huge chain of assisted-living facilities. Heather viewed this as another advantage. It meant that there would be opportunities for upward mobility—although she wasn't sure what these opportunities might be. Karl had said only that, in terms of organizational structure, she reported directly to him but would also have a dotted-line relationship (called such because that is how it appeared on the organizational chart) with the regional dietitian.

The first few months were challenging but satisfying. Heather managed 22 employees, most of whom worked full time. In her second month, she fired an employee who complained incessantly. Apparently, this employee had other problems, including stealing food from the storeroom. Other than that, things were shaping up nicely. She had also found a great replacement for the fired employee.

During a staff meeting that included all the managers in the facility, the nursing director complimented Heather on the recent cosmetic changes in the cafe. She then posed a question to Heather: "Why doesn't the cafe offer cold food to go, such as pizzas that can be cooked at home or precooked chickens? It would be much more convenient for employees to buy food in the cafe for dinner instead of having to stop at the supermarket."

Heather put the same question to her staff the next morning. Their response was overwhelmingly positive. It turns out that this had been requested many times over the last few years. Unfortunately, the former foodservice director had vehemently opposed the idea.

Heather also had the opportunity to meet Suzanne, the regional dietitian. Suzanne seemed very nice and during their few short meetings told Heather that she was there to support her and that she was available by phone at any time. Suzanne also mentioned that they would review the operating statistics for the foodservice department in the near future.

After six months, it was time for Heather's mid-year review, which was conducted by both Karl and Suzanne. The review began with several compliments, one again about the cafe. Then, Suzanne explained that corporate had noted a major red flag that deserved Heather's immediate attention. According to a corporate report that compared foodservice operations at all of the Rolling Hills facilities, Heather's foodservice operation was using more labor hours per patient bed than any other was. Suzanne explained that this productivity statistic was monitored closely because it was a good indicator of labor management. After all, it was reasonable that foodservice directors of larger facilities would require more labor, but any differences should be proportional to the number of beds.

Heather let out a sigh of relief. She quickly explained that she had added an FTE three months earlier. This position was responsible for making the numerous "to go" items now available in the cafe. The items included, just as the nursing director had requested, pizza and roasted chickens, but the choices didn't stop there. They also offered side dishes such as whipped potatoes with garlic and macaroni and cheese. These were packaged in microwavable containers so people could buy the precooked food and quickly assemble a family meal when they got home. The cafe had even begun offering cakes and pies, which were extremely popular. Sales in the cafe had skyrocketed.

Suzanne smiled, but then said: "It's great that you're doing such wonderful things. Karl tells me that the staff really likes the convenience, too. That being said, we are measured on labor hours per patient bed. You are going to have to figure out some way to show the impact of this 'take home' program on your organization. Without this, you will not be meeting the company productivity standard. And if you can't get your labor hours below the company standard, we will be forced to find a new foodservice director."

What should Heather do?

REVIEW AND DISCUSSION QUESTIONS

1. How does revenue management differ, say, between foodservice and hotels?

2. Identify the three components of foodservice revenue management and provide an example of how each can be ensured.

3. Using the following data, calculate the BEP, assuming an average check of $24. What is the BEP in terms of covers?

Sales	$2,000,000	100%
Variable Costs	$1,500,000	75%
Fixed Costs	$400,000	20%
Profit	$100,000	5%

4. Describe one situation in which demand for a menu item is inelastic and another in which it is elastic (and provide the numbers and calculations).

5. Name two advantages and two disadvantages of activity-based costing.

6. Why isn't potential food cost used as much today as in the past?

7. Define *productivity* using the general ratio described in the chapter. For each of the variables, provide an example.

8. Identify a foodservice segment and a partial factor productivity statistic (other than those discussed) that might be appropriate to that segment. Be sure to explain why you think this is a good partial-factor measure.

9. Why should some measure of quality be included in a holistic measure of productivity?

10. Apply the Pareto principle to something in your life. Explain fully.

ENDNOTES

1. Smith, B. C., Leimkuhler, J. F. & Darrow, R. M. "Yield Management at American Airlines." *Interfaces* 22 (1) (2001): 8–31.

2. Kimes, S. "The Basics of Yield Management." *Cornell Hotel and Restaurant Quarterly* 45 (1) (1989): 68–84.

3. Raab, C., Shoemaker, S. & Mayer, K. J. "Activity-based Costing: A More Accurate Way to Estimate the Costs for a Restaurant Menu." *International Journal of Hospitality & Tourism Administration* 8 (3), (2007): 1–15.

4. Reynolds, D. "Productivity Analysis." *Cornell Hotel and Restaurant Administration Quarterly*, 39 (3) (1998): 22–31.

5. For example, see Reynolds, D., & Biel, D. "Incorporating Satisfaction Measures into a Restaurant Productivity Index." *International Journal of Hospitality Management* 26, (2007): 352–361.

CHAPTER 17

BEVERAGE MANAGEMENT

LEARNING OBJECTIVES:

After becoming familiar with this chapter, you should be able to:

1. Appreciate the history of the beverage industry and understand how prohibition affects today's beverage operations.

2. Understand the effects of alcohol on health and the legal issues that affect the sales and service of alcoholic beverages.

3. Explain how managing foodservice operations and pricing food for sale differ from managing alcohol sales and service.

4. Determine training requirements based on a foodservice operation's location and unique features.

In foodservice management, the term *beverages* denotes beer, wine, and spirits, as well as nonalcoholic **mocktails**, beverages that simulate alcoholic beverages but lack alcohol (often with "virgin" in their names, as in the Virgin Mary, a Bloody Mary without vodka). Products such as soda (commonly called "soft drinks") and coffee are stocked and served, at least for accounting purposes, as food. Although there are a number of reasons, the primary one is economics. The significance of beverage sales to the foodservice industry is easy to calculate: The average net profit from food sales is between 2 and 10 percent; the typical net profit from beverages is closer to 40 percent. That means that every $1 in beverage sales at 40 percent profit equates to something like $8 in food sales at 5 percent profit—no wonder new restaurants celebrate when they hang a liquor license on the wall!

© iStockphoto.com

Figure 17.1   Sales in sporting venues are substantial.

While beverage management is important in traditional restaurants, it is also essential in onsite foodservice segments. Consider sports and entertainment. Beer sales generate huge revenues in sports arenas (see Figure 17.1). Even in the healthcare segment most foodservice operations provide events catering, which usually means offering beverages with hors d'oeuvres and wine with dinner—some even offer beverages to patients with the physician's permission. Thus, understanding beverage management is important to foodservice managers in all industry segments.

In this chapter, we consider first the beverage industry itself, covering both its history and the landscape today. We then introduce beverage control, much as we discussed food management in the previous chapter. Next, we address the moral and legal responsibility involved in serving beverage alcohol. Finally, we tackle issues associated with staff training for beverage service.

▪▫ BEVERAGE INDUSTRY OVERVIEW
▫▪

Throughout history, beverage alcohol has functioned both spiritually and socially in human activity. It supplied vital nutrition in prehistoric human culture, and found widespread use for its medicinal, antiseptic, and analgesic properties. Its capacity to alter states of consciousness gave it an important place in early religious rituals, a practice that continues in many religions today. It has fueled economies, trade, and cross-cultural interactions.

For centuries, people have included alcohol in celebrations of momentous occasions such as anniversaries and weddings. Consider the source of the word *bridal*—centuries ago, a woman, upon becoming engaged, would make a special ale to celebrate the upcoming wedding, referred to as "bride ale." Even the word *honeymoon* likely has a lineage related to alcohol. Long before honeymoons involved travel to exotic destinations, the term referred to a month or cycle of the moon immediately following the wedding when the couple would drink mead—which is made from fermented honey—every night.

A Brief History

Dating back as early as 10,000 BC and most likely the result of an accident, humans discovered that food with natural sugar and enough moisture content would ferment into an alcoholic beverage. The discovery of Stone Age beer jugs confirms that intentionally fermented beverages were part of our early diet. The oldest wine jars discovered thus far date back to 5400–5000 BC. The Old Testament (Genesis 9) asserts that Noah, upon exiting the ark, planted a vineyard in what is now eastern Turkey. There are also records that beer and wine were used for medicinal purposes as early as 2000 BC.

The Greeks, having learned to make wine from the Egyptians, are cited as being the first to age wines, sometime around 1500 BC. The ability to age wine was tied to the creation of airtight clay cylinders. In fact, the Greeks' study of **viticulture**—the cultivation of grapes—was referred to as *oinos logos* (wine logic), which is the origin of **enology**—the study of wine.[1]

For the next several centuries, beer, ale, and wine were staples in the human diet, sometimes representing up to 50 percent of one's daily caloric intake. While the beverages' caloric content fueled the body for the hard labor in which most engaged, beer and wine were in many places the only beverages safe to consume because most water sources were polluted. (Note, too, that coffee and tea were not introduced into Europe until the mid-seventeenth century.)

Moving on to the Middle Ages, the most important innovation regarding alcohol was **distillation**. Although distillation was likely practiced to some extent in earlier ages—distilled liquids seem to have been used for medicinal purposes in China as early as 800 BC where a distilled spirit was made from rice beer, and in the fourth century BC Aristotle apparently observed that "seaweed can be made potable by distillation; wine and other liquids can be submitted to the same process"—the modern distilled beverage industry likely originated much later.

It was Albertus Magnus (1193–1280) who first clearly described the process of manufacturing distilled spirits as a beverage.[2] As Magnus noted, distilling wine by successive evaporation and condensation of the alcohol resulted in aqua vitae, or "water of life." This is what became known as *brandy*, derived from the Dutch word *brandewjn*, meaning burnt (or distilled) wine.

It is worth digressing to note that distillation without modern equipment must have been difficult to achieve. Since alcohol vaporizes at a lower temperature (173°F) than does water (212°F), the distiller had to carefully control the heating process lest the wine simply boil. Once the alcohol is vaporized, it had to be recondensed into liquid form (see Figure 17.2). Moreover, the resulting liquid would have been rather unpalatable without aging in barrels or added flavoring.

By the sixteenth century, spirit drinking was still practiced largely for medicinal purposes. Beer consumption, however, was quite high in some parts of the world. Polish peasants consumed up to three liters of beer per day.[3] Swedish beer consumption may have been 40 times higher than in modern Sweden. English sailors received a ration of a gallon of beer per day, while foot soldiers received two-thirds of a gallon. In Denmark, the usual consumption of beer was purportedly a gallon per day for adult laborers and sailors.[4]

In the following century, thanks to a now-famous winemaker in a French abbey, sparkling wine appeared. Around 1668, Dom Perignon used strong bottles and a corking system that he invented and began bottling wine that preserved the carbonation produced during fermentation.

In seventeenth-century Russia, grain spirits were not flavored and were called "life water" or *vodka*. In other areas, however, juniper berries were used to flavor distilled spirits, resulting in a beverage known as *junever*, the Dutch word for "juniper." The French changed the name to

Courtesy of Dry Fly Distilling, Inc.

Figure 17.2   Example of a modern still by dry fly.

genievre, which the English changed to *Geneva*, later modified to the familiar *gin*. Gin was originally used as a medicine. In 1690, England passed the Act for the Encouraging of the Distillation of Brandy and Spirits from Corn, and within four years the annual production of distilled gin reached nearly 1 million gallons.

At the same time, the Virginia colonists brought to the New World the practice of brewing beer and continued their tradition of including beer as part of a typical meal. They also established the nation's first distillery on what is now Staten Island. Soon after that—most likely, the work of European settlers in the West Indies who had mastered the distillation of fermented molasses, a byproduct of sugar cane—a rum distillery was operating in Boston.

By the eighteenth century, the English government was actively promoting gin production to utilize surplus grain and to raise revenue. In 1727, official (declared and taxed) production of gin reached 5 million gallons; six years later, the London area alone produced 11 million gallons.[5] The proliferation of gin had some unfortunate consequences for English society. Gin's abundance, coupled with the public policy encouraging its consumption during a time when there was little stigma attached to drunkenness and the number of poor people was reaching epidemic numbers, created what is referred to as the **Gin Epidemic**—a period of extreme drunkenness that provoked moral outrage and governmental intervention.

The situation leading to the Gin Epidemic was not unique to England. With a profusion of inexpensive spirits, many countries began to experience problems with alcohol abuse, particularly when economies were unfavorable or the devastating effects of various wars were taking their toll. In the United States, the response was a **temperance movement**, a social movement in which the consumption of alcohol is discouraged and even openly combated. Those who supported the movement, known as *dries*, worked to prohibit alcohol sales and consumption.

Prohibition

By the late nineteenth century, the abundance of bars in every US town created an unprecedented competitive environment. As a result, many bars—in an attempt to drum up more business—promoted prostitution and gambling. Not surprisingly, such practices were not viewed as friendly to what we now call family values.

The situation was creating religious, ethnic, and gender antagonism. Many church leaders saw the emerging practices as the end to morality. The aforementioned associations between alcohol, prostitution, and gambling didn't help. In fact, many religious leaders referred to saloons as moral voids and drinking as a personal sin.

Already problematic ethnic tensions also divided those who believed alcohol to be evil and those who viewed it as integral to many honorable—or at least longstanding—cultural beliefs and practices. For example, "dries" of white, Northern European descent stereotyped "wet" Irish, German, and Italian immigrants who brought their alcohol drinking traditions with them as hedonists and social undesirables. This was particularly difficult for Germans, who at the time represented a large percentage of new immigrants, because many were brewers and beer-hall owners hoping to assimilate into the social mainstream.

Finally, many women supported the anti-alcohol sentiment. At the time, women had very few rights. To make matters worse, they were also not allowed in saloons, where many political discussions were taking place. Thus, women's opposition to alcohol dovetailed nicely with the objective of achieving their civil rights, including the right to vote. The most well-known temperance activist was Carrie Nation. Ms. Nation earned her reputation in Kansas, which was the first state to outlaw alcoholic beverages. She singlehandedly enforced the law by entering saloons, screaming at customers, and destroying liquor bottles with her hatchet.

The hostility against saloons and the alcohol industry at large, along with the political forces on both sides of the temperance movement and a shift in the balance of power in Congress (where the prohibitionists far outnumbered those who opposed such regulation), resulted in the passing of the **Eighteenth Amendment** to the United States Constitution— the **National Prohibition Act** in 1920. Referred to as the **Volstead Act**, prohibition was first regarded as **The Noble Experiment** whose intent was to protect American family values. The act made the manufacture, sale, and transport of alcohol illegal. (Interestingly, it did not prohibit the consumption of alcohol.)

The law was, however, very hard to enforce. Moreover, even though public saloons were closed, demand for alcohol was met by the advent of speakeasies—establishments that sold alcohol secretly and illegally. To enter a speakeasy, one often had to utter a password through a small slot in the door—if you spoke the right word, you got in easily. In New York City alone, it is estimated that there were as many as 100,000 speakeasies.[6] While prohibition likely reduced alcohol consumption somewhat, it did little to reshape the moral landscape. Instead, it created a huge underground trade in alcohol that was controlled mainly by organized crime, as well as thousands of private criminals tending their personal stills.

As many predicted prohibition was repealed on December 5, 1933, with the ratification of the **Twenty-First Amendment**. The Eighteenth Amendment was later referred to as the government's best **failed experiment**. The amendment pushed the right to legislate alcohol down to the state level, which explains the presence of state-by-state differences in the distribution and promotion of alcohol across the country. For example, Mississippi did not repeal prohibition until 1966; many areas are still dry. Conversely, consumers in Texas and other states can purchase beer through drive-through stores that operate similarly to QSR drive-throughs.

Alcohol's nonbeverage uses only added to the social problems spawned by the Prohibition era. Since many industries used alcohol as a cleaning agent (primarily ethyl alcohol), **bootleggers** (a term coined during Prohibition that refers to those who hid a flask in their boot filled with alcohol) quickly learned that making beverages from still-available ethyl alcohol was a quick way to supply their customers. This led the government to order the poisoning of industrial alcohol, which was accomplished by the addition in some cases of deadly methyl alcohol—used today in antifreeze. Neither bootleggers nor their customers were aware of the danger of consuming the tainted alcohol. It is estimated that as many as 10,000 people died from drinking the deadly cocktails.[7]

On a lighter note (depending on your theory of choice), several terms that were coined during prohibition are still used in the foodservice industry today. The most notable of these is the term **86'd**. Today, if a restaurant runs out of a menu item, the chef will tell the foodservers that the item is 86'd, meaning that no more are available for sale. Similarly, a bar might "86" a customer, cutting him off from being served any more drinks. Although we know the term emerged from the Prohibition era, we do not know with certainty when or how it was first used. Many believe that the term came from a speakeasy in New York City at 86 Bedford Street, at which the cry "We're 86'd!" would be heard at the first sign of a police raid. This was a call for everyone to throw their glasses in the fireplace and run.

Another theory stems from the organized crime that emerged with prohibition. When a gang leader ordered someone who opposed organized crime's liquor sales killed, he told the hitmen to "86" the unfortunate victim, which meant that person was to be killed and then buried 80 miles outside of town and six feet underground. (A similar theory holds that the executed person would be buried in a grave eight feet long and six feet deep.) A more plausible explanation may be associated with the restaurant Delmonico's in New York City (which, as you recall from Chapter 1, featured the first printed menu). Every item on the menu was numbered; the most popular steak was number 86, which would frequently sell out. Still others have suggested that, in the early days of the Great Depression (and during Prohibition), soup kitchens were limited to 85 patrons. To be the 86th was undesirable. Similarly, the standard soup kettle at the time was believed to serve 85 ladles of soup. Finally, the 86th floor of the Empire State Building leads to an observation deck, from which as many as 30 people committed suicide by leaping to their deaths. Given the macabre implications of some of these stories, perhaps we in the foodservice industry should embrace the "Delmonico theory"!

Today's Beverage Industry

The landscape of today's beverage industry has changed dramatically since those post-Prohibition days. Although in the current climate the promotion of alcohol through advertising—especially distilled liquors—on network television and other media is to some extent in retreat (note that many chains have changed their names from "bar and grill" to "grill and bar"), actual sales of alcoholic beverages remains robust. According to the National Restaurant Association, commercial restaurant sales in 2010 totaled approximately $530 billion (with onsite foodservice adding another $41 billion). Of this $530 billion, approximately 15 percent came from beer, wine, and spirits sales, which equates to $79.5 billion. Given that the typical cost of beverage alcohol is less than 25 percent of sales, this means that beverage sales contributed some $60 billion in gross profit.

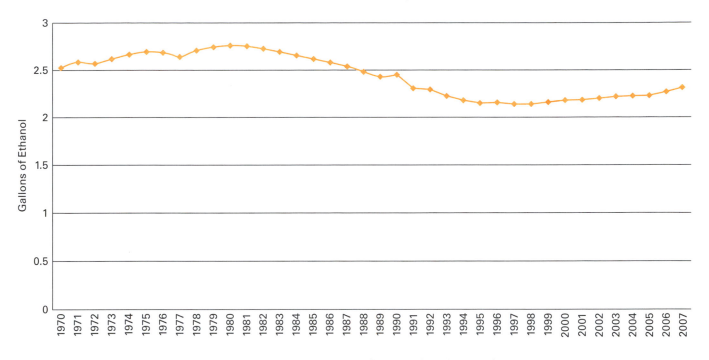

Figure 17.3   Per capita alcohol consumption in the United States (people of drinking age), 1970–2007.

Despite the financial benefit of beverage sales, foodservice operations are subject to trends and lifestyle changes—and this includes the role of beverage alcohol. If you combine the recent trend toward healthier lifestyles with greater sensitivity to substance abuse, you would expect beverage alcohol consumption to be lower today, but the reality is that US consumption per adult has not changed dramatically over the last several decades (see Figure 17.3).[8] In fact, in 2009, the average American of drinking age consumed seven bottles of spirits, 12 bottles of wine, and 230 cans of beer. Such statistics cannot help but hearten foodservice managers, particularly as about 30 percent of adults drink no alcohol. This doesn't mean, though, that we are a nation that imbibes more than most; the United States ranks fortieth in the world in alcohol consumption per person.

Although overall alcohol consumption has changed very little, consumption patterns have shifted in recent years. For example, Americans drink more than two-and-a-half times more wine today than they did in 1960 (see Figure 17.4), driven largely by greater awareness of the science and pleasure of fine winemaking as well as dramatic increases in wineries throughout the world, which produce wines that have broad appeal. At the same time, beer consumption has decreased over the last 50 years but has remained relatively static since 1994 (see Figure 17.5).[9]

RESPONSIBLE BEVERAGE ALCOHOL SERVICE

Now that we understand the financial opportunities represented by the considerable magnitude of consumption, we turn to the service of beverage alcohol. More specifically, we address the responsibility associated with serving alcohol in the face of formidable health-related and legal issues.

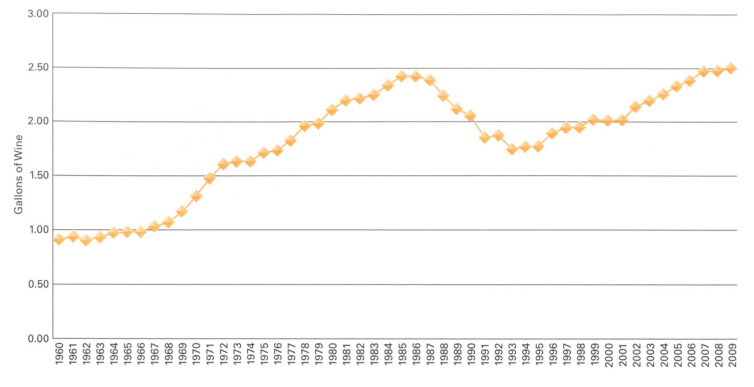

Figure 17.4 Per capita wine consumption in the United States (people of drinking age), 1960–2009.

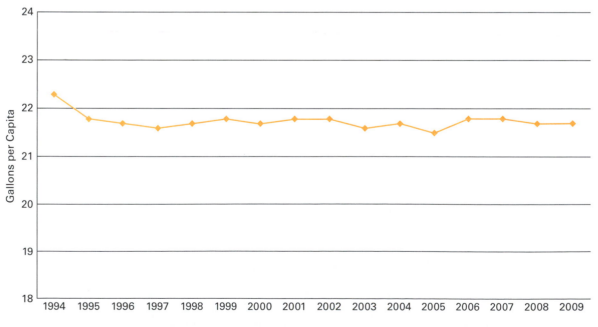

Figure 17.5 Per capita beer consumption in the United States (people of drinking age), 1994–2009.

Alcohol and Health

As noted earlier, the alcohol responsible for the intoxicating effects of beer, wine, and spirits is **ethanol**. (Note in Figure 17.3 that we measure ethanol consumption per adult.) To help put this into context, it is useful to compare the ethanol content in various beverages. For example, a 12-ounce domestic beer, a 4.5-ounce glass of red Bordeaux wine, and a 1.25-ounce shot of 80-proof vodka each contains approximately one half-ounce of ethanol (see Figure 17.6).

The differences in serving size under comparison stem from differences by volume and percentage in the ethanol content. Still, the comparison is useful. It is a common misconception that drinking three or four beers is not the same as downing three or four shots over the same period; in reality, the amount of ethanol is the same.

With this in mind, consider that most health professionals agree that moderate drinking is not only consistent with a healthy lifestyle but may actually enhance it. Moreover, the **French paradox**, which arises when one juxtaposes low rates of coronary heart disease with the high dietary cholesterol and saturated fat intake that is characteristic of French cuisine, suggests that the French habit of drinking wine (especially red wine) with meals is healthy. For example, wine contains **phenolic compounds**, which are antioxidants that protect humans against various diseases and the effects of aging (**resveratrol** is the primary antioxidant in wine). Moreover, ethanol in any form contains an enzyme, the **t-PA antigen**, which helps prevent chronic internal blood clots.

Drinking alcohol also yields subjective or aesthetic benefits for most people, particularly as it applies to food. The pairing of food and beverages can enhance the overall dining experience.

One mixed drink with
• 1.5 fl oz (44 mL) of 80-proof liquor (such as vodka, gin, scotch, bourbon, brandy, or rum)

5 fl oz (148 mL) of wine

12 fl oz (355 mL) of beer or wine cooler

Figure 17.6   The amount of ethanol in each of these beverages is approximately the same.

© iStockphoto.com

Figure 17.7 Wine served with a meal.

Moreover, alcohol may increase the appetite, again making for a more enjoyable meal. Finally, an evening meal at a restaurant with beer, wine, or spirits creates a festive atmosphere (see Figure 17.7).

So why doesn't everyone promote drinking? The challenge is the "moderation" mentioned earlier. The latest report from the USDA notes that alcohol consumption can have beneficial or harmful effects, depending on the amount consumed and a person's individual characteristics. The government agency notes that the lowest all-cause mortality occurs with an intake of one or two drinks per day but also adds that morbidity and mortality are highest among those drinking large amounts of alcohol. Alcohol is also an addictive substance, and as such, can interfere with one's family life and career. The National Institute of Alcohol Abuse and Alcoholism provides corresponding guidelines for moderation and defines "low-risk" drinking (i.e., drinking that does not lead to abuse) as consisting of no more than 14 drinks a week for men and 7 drinks a week for women, with no more than 4 drinks on any given day for men and 3 drinks a day for women.

This notion of moderation also pertains to how the human body processes alcohol. The first effect is a pleasant feeling that provides for the relaxation that is associated with "having a drink." However, since the typical person can process the equivalent of only one drink (as defined earlier) per hour, consuming alcohol at a greater rate creates other less-felicitous physical effects. As intoxication begins to influence brain functions, the alcohol can impede muscle coordination, judgment, and eyesight. To the risk of addiction and other health issues associated with heavy drinking we must also add the problem of drunk driving, which kills thousands of people every year. At what point does drinking alcohol become a problem? It varies by individual, but the definition of intoxication in most states is a **blood alcohol concentration (BAC)** of 0.08 percent. The problem is that BAC can increase even after a person stops consuming alcohol. Common approaches that include drinking coffee or combining spirits with stimulant-laden mixers do not help the body process the alcohol. Similarly, walking or engaging in other exercise does not help the body expel alcohol. Thus, the best way to avoid intoxication is to limit one's alcohol intake.

Legal Issues

In addition to the health aspects surrounding alcohol, foodservice managers must be aware of a host of legal issues. We live in a litigious era in which many are quick to blame others rather than assuming personal responsibility for their behavior. Thus, a customer who orders multiple drinks while at a bar and then makes a poor decision such as driving while intoxicated or provoking a fight might blame the operator. Truth be told, today a foodservice operation that serves alcohol *is* held partly responsible for the behavior of its customers. While the bartender did not force the customer to consume alcohol, she (and everyone working in the foodservice operation) must nevertheless observe **duties of care**. These duties include serving alcohol responsibly.

These duties also vary considerably from one foodservice operation to the next and carry an undeniable moral dimension. However, **dramshop laws** (*dram*, meaning a small drink of liquor; *shop*, meaning the place where the drink is served) make it a legal issue as well. In essence, such laws assign liability for damages—say, in a drunk-driving accident—to both the driver who caused the accident and the foodservice operation that provided the drinks. While the terms of these laws vary from state to state, they require operators to take special care in serving beer, wine, and spirits.

In many cases, legal liability is related to **foreseeability**, which is the reasonable anticipation that a particular course of action will likely result in harm or injury. For example, if a bartender serves a guest six drinks over a 30-minute period, it is foreseeable that the guest will soon have a considerable BAC. Foodservice operators therefore must take **reasonable care** to prevent potential harm or injury. Failure to take reasonable care may result in needless injury, lawsuits, and business losses. (We will talk more about this later in reference to staff training.)

As a consequence of these legal and moral issues, the beverage alcohol industry is heavily regulated. All states require foodservice operators who serve alcohol to obtain state-issued licenses. The regulations and policies that govern such licenses vary from state to state, resulting in differences in how many licenses are granted, the days on which and times at which alcohol may be served, the manner in which it can be sold (for example, a state may require that beer be sold in bottles only), how taxes surrounding beverage alcohol are collected and paid, and the terms of particular licenses. Some states provide licenses for liquor to be served both in a restaurant and to go, while others strictly prohibit transporting alcohol off premises. Still other regulations govern how and from whom foodservice operators may purchase alcohol. For example, some states allow a restaurant to purchase wine only from a distributor, not directly from a winery. Some states allow microbreweries to serve food while others dictate that no food may be served on premises if beer, wine, or spirits are made there. Thus, every foodservice manager must be familiar with her particular state's laws, regulations, and policies. Failure to follow these may result in fines, license revocation, and even imprisonment.

▪▫ BEVERAGE CONTROL
▫▪

With such a wide array of laws and regulations, it should not be surprising that controls surrounding beverage alcohol are perhaps even more stringent than those discussed earlier pertaining to food. In this section, we cover the general guidelines for beverage control. We then address purchasing, receiving, storing, and issuing. Finally, we conclude with a discussion of pricing considerations.

General Guidelines

While all of the food management techniques covered in Chapter 9 apply to managing beverages, the strong demand for beer, wine, and spirits make controlling these products even more complex. For example, theft of beverage alcohol is an even greater problem than theft of food. Given the opportunity, employees may be unable to resist stealing bottles of liquor or wine. More problematically, in many bar operations, there is no division of duty (which we introduced in Chapter 9 and discussed in terms of internal control in Chapter 15). In other words, the person who takes the beverage order from the customer also produces that order and collects the payment. In almost every other service sector, these duties are clearly demarcated. In the front of the house, for example, the foodserver takes the guest's order and enters the order into the computer system for transmission to the kitchen. The kitchen staff then produces the menu item. In this example, the foodserver cannot obtain the menu item without creating a record of the order.

This is not the case in a bar. A bartender could conceivably take a drink order and provide the drink without charging for it (intending either to pocket the money if the patron leaves cash when he departs or to provide a free drink in anticipation of a larger gratuity). Similarly, a bartender could serve a high-priced drink, collect the appropriate payment from the guest, and then enter a lesser-priced item in the register, stealing the difference. Even with some division of duties in place, a foodservice worker could order a beverage from a bartender and collect payment from a guest, splitting the "winnings" between the two colluding employees. These examples underscore the ease with which operations that serve alcohol can be defrauded (as you should recall, we discussed internal control in greater detail in Chapter 15).

Beverage control can be made easier with the use of a par system (also referred to as a **par stock** system). As introduced in Chapter 8, a par stock is a predetermined level of inventory for each beverage item. Typically, the par stock level is one-and-a-half times the amount sold during a typical shift. (For bars with particularly high sales during certain periods, the par stock is one-and-a-half times the amount sold during the busiest days or nights.) For example, say a bar has a par stock of 12 bottles of vodka. At the end of a given shift, the bartender requisitions eight bottles and delivers eight empty bottles to the person responsible for filling liquor requisitions (typically the bar manager). Thus, the inventory in the bar returns to the par level of 12 full bottles. This approach expedites the physical inventory process and aids in internal control. Of course, par levels should be reviewed periodically to ensure that the operation is not carrying excessive inventory or routinely running out of a given product during a shift.

Additional general controls include managing the ordering process, maintaining consistency in recipes, and keeping the bar supplied with glassware and ice. A critical step in managing the ordering process is recording beverage sales properly. Typically, a bartender takes an order, fills the order, and then documents the order. In a busy operation and even with the intent of maximizing service quality, a bartender may wait to enter drinks until he has served several customers. This is not advisable as he may forget to document one or more orders.

Much as standardized recipes are vital in food production, standardized beverage recipes are critical in beverage cost control. The impact of just an extra quarter-ounce of liquor for each drink made during a shift could be very detrimental to profit and create undesirable expectations on the part of guests. Standardization also pertains to glassware. If a recipe calls for an eight-ounce glass for, say, a screwdriver, the item is costed for 1¼ ounces of vodka and 3½ ounces of orange juice (the remaining volume is taken up by ice). However, if the bartender erroneously uses a 12-ounce glass, the cost of the ingredients rises, especially if she maintains the same vodka–orange juice ratio. Imagine, too, the difference if fresh-squeezed orange juice is used.

Ice may be a humble ingredient—after all, it's just frozen water—but it also figures into control calculations. As seen in the previous example, ice takes up considerable space in a glass. If an adequate amount of ice is not used, more alcohol or mixer is needed to fill the glass. Similarly, even the shape of the ice makes a difference when placed in glasses of various sizes and shapes (smaller ice cubes take up more volume in the glass, crushed ice still more).

Purchasing, Receiving, Storing, and Issuing

As it is in food management, the primary purpose of purchasing, receiving, storing, and issuing controls of beverage items is to ensure that every item is purchased at the optimal price, received to match specifications, stored in its proper storage area, and sufficiently stocked in the service area.

Purchasing

The laws in a given state may to some extent regulate management of the purchasing process. For example, in **control states**—those states where the foodservice operator must buy liquor from state stores—available items are dictated largely by the associated control board. In **license states**, the buyer is typically allowed to purchase from licensed wholesalers and, in some states, licensed distributors and manufacturers. As we noted earlier, however, every state is unique and in some states regulations differ for spirits, beer, and wine.

With that in mind, the remaining purchasing decisions are the same as they are with food—initially shaped by the menu and the associated menu item recipes. For spirits, this includes the selection of house or **well brands**. These are the basic spirits used unless a customer requests a specific brand of alcohol. The well brands are so named because the bottles typically reside in a well or speed rail within the bartender's immediate reach. Next come **call brands**, so named because customers call for them by brand name. Above this we now have both **premium brands** and the emerging category of **ultra-premium brands**. (Ultra-premium brands include very expensive spirits that typically adorn the top shelf of the bar. A good example is Rémy Martin Louis XIII cognac, with a typical retail price per bottle of $1,800 to $2,500. See Figure 17.8.)

The same decisions must be made for beer and wine. Many operators today understand the advantage of featuring local microbrews and local wines. Of course, whether a foodservice outlet includes local offerings depends on its location, but featuring items known to the local market is always good.

In terms of order quantities, the forecasting models discussed in Chapter 8 can be easily applied to beverage service. With beverages, however, it is extremely important to treat each category differently. On the one hand, because freshness matters to beer quality, beer inventory should turn over quickly through frequent restocking. On the other hand, there may be quantity discounts on spirits and since spirits do not degrade with time, it may be worthwhile to benefit from such discounts at the cost of carrying a larger inventory.

Wine purchasing can be the most problematic. When an entire vintage has been sold, a new vintage takes its place. Thus, operations with elaborate wine lists that include vintage information must ensure that enough stock is on hand. High-end wines, while nice to include on the menu and very desirable to the operator owing to their profitability, are undesirable to keep in large quantities.

Receiving

As in the case of food management, receiving beverages involves four basic steps:

1. Confirm that the delivery matches the purchase order.
2. Confirm that the invoice matches the purchase order.
3. Make accept-or-reject decisions.
4. Complete the paperwork.

Figure 17.8 Rémy Martin Louis XIII Cognac.

Courtesy of Rémy Cointreau USA.

While receiving food involves checking for freshness along with quantity, receiving beverages includes checking vintages, bottle sizes, brand, and varieties. Furthermore, beverage receiving must take place in a secure environment. Publicly accessible loading docks needlessly expose the operator to theft.

Storing

Due to the extended time involved, the key to storing beverages is security, and the techniques for achieving security are similar to those used in securing food stocks. With security ensured, the next concern is temperature, light, and humidity. Keg beer should be kept below 38°F and bottled beer should be kept at temperatures between 40°F and 50°F; bottled beer should be protected from sunlight. Wines should be stored on their sides within a temperature range of 52°F to 57°F. (There is considerable argument about the "ideal" temperature for storing wine. Some wine makers argue that wine keeps best when stored at specific temperatures for specific regions and varietals. Unfortunately, in the foodservice context wine storage with multiple temperature zones is impractical for most operators.) Humidity in the wine storage area should be kept above 70 percent.

Finally, spirits should have dedicated space in the storage room and be grouped by type—vodka with vodka, gin with gin, and cordials with cordials. While some argue that it is acceptable to leave whole cases in their original boxes, current practice involves removing all spirits from their boxes when they are initially placed in storage. This technique is adopted as a security precaution, preventing dishonest employees from removing bottles and resealing the boxes, which not only reduces profits but also creates errors in inventory management.

Issuing

The last leg in the cycle ensures that products are available to fill customers' orders. Beverage items are typically issued directly from the beverage storage areas to the bar. As in other areas of food and beverage management, issuances must be recorded and responsibility assigned at each control point.

For spirits, issuing is best facilitated using a one-empty-for-one-full approach as described in the earlier discussion of par stocks. Once full bottles have been issued at a quantity matching the empty bottles, the empty bottles can be recycled. In catering operations, empty bottles are sometimes used to assess sales levels and customers are simply charged for the amounts of alcohol served. Controlling beverage service at this juncture can be accomplished by stamping bottles as they are issued with a unique symbol, perhaps the restaurant logo. This helps to inform management of possible fraudulent activity, evidence of which is an empty bottle that is not stamped.

Most bars use a par system for bottled beer. Thus, at the end of every shift, the bartender requisitions the appropriate amount of each brand to ensure the bar is stocked for the following shift. Keg beer is typically changed as each keg is emptied (which too often happens at the peak of a busy night). Whenever an empty keg is changed, it should be marked and stored securely.

A similar par system approach can be used for wine in operations in which frequent-selling wines are stored in the bar. However, many foodservice operations find that it is best simply to requisition wine as needed. During busy periods, however, customers may have to wait while the appropriate person (usually a manager) can be found to fetch the wine from the storage area. At least one operator has turned this into an advantage. In the Mandalay Bay Hotel in Las Vegas, the

American-style restaurant Aureole features a visual trademark: a four-story wine tower with its very own Wine Angel Stewards, who gracefully ascend the tower to retrieve bottles as they are ordered (Figure 17.9).

Pricing

The final aspect of beverage control is pricing. While the pricing methods discussed in Chapter 4 generally apply to beverage pricing, it has its own special challenges. For example, suppose a customer orders a shot of bourbon "neat" (meaning without ice) and that 1¼ ounces of well scotch costs $0.44. If we use the factor method, and expect an 11 percent beverage cost, we can readily calculate the price as follows:

$$\frac{\$0.44}{11} = \$4.00$$

Depending on the local market and foodservice segment, this might be an appropriate price. Moreover, it produces a gross profit of $3.56.

However, if we apply the same approach to a super premium spirit, say the Rémy Martin Louis XIII Cognac discussed earlier, we find that a 1¼-ounce serving costs approximately $66 (assuming the wholesale price is $1,320). Using the factor method, the price calculation would be:

$$\frac{\$66}{0.11} = \$600.00$$

The gross profit would then be $534! While this might sound irresistibly profitable to the foodservice operator, the reality is that she will have very few customers willing to spend that much. More to the point, even if she reduces the price by half, the gross profit is still $234! One would have to sell 91 shots of scotch at $4.00 to capture as much gross profit. The point here is, however, that in some cases the foodservice operator must use her own judgment when pricing beverages. No simple calculation will provide a definitive answer.

The same problem is seen in bottled wine pricing. It is a common practice to price house wines served by the bottle at twice the wholesale price. Thus, a bottle that a guest might buy at a retail store for $12 is priced at the restaurant at $18 (twice the wholesale price of $9). The typical guest will think the higher price is justified because someone else is serving the wine and washing the dishes, not to mention that the beverage enhances the overall dining experience. However, even if a guest knows that his favorite bottle of French wine sells for $200 in the local wine shop, he will be unlikely to spend $300 (twice the wholesale price of $150) in a restaurant for the same wine. This again illustrates the principle that no single pricing strategy is appropriate for all beverages.

In very general terms, the cost percentage on draft beer is the lowest among beverage products, followed by the cost percentage for spirits. Bottled beer's cost percentage is the next highest, and bottled wine typically has the highest beverage cost percentage.

A final thought on beverage pricing pertains to operations that follow the trend towards offering wines by the glass. Many restaurants have boosted wine sales by adopting this practice. Still, too many operators offer a very limited number of wines by the glass because they fear that, if a bottle is opened but only two glasses of that wine are ordered, the result is a net loss. In truth, however, the gross profit on a glass of wine is proportionately greater than it is on a full bottle. Why? A bottle of wine yields between 4½ and 5 glasses. Let's assume the bottle costs the operator $38 and is listed for $50. If she prices the wine by the glass at $15 and sells five glasses, the gross profit is $37—that's $25 more than if she sold the bottle as a unit. And, even if fewer than five glasses are sold, the remaining wine can be used in staff training.

Figure 17.9   Aureole Restaurant, Mandalay Bay Hotel, Las Vegas, which features a four-story wine storage staffed by Wine Angels.

An additional practice that can, with creative pricing, boost sales and profits is the emerging practice of selling wine by the half glass. In an effort to drink responsibly and in moderation, a guest may enjoy a glass of wine with the first few courses but then want a little more for a different varietal to go with the entrée as the meal lingers. Selling this guest a half glass creates revenue that would not have existed because the guest would not have ordered another full glass. This practice also communicates the message that the restaurant is sensitive to overservice of alcohol. The common approach to pricing wine by the half glass is to charge 60 percent of the price of a full glass. Again, customers are willing to pay a premium for this.

Finally, the recent trend to offer flights of beer or wine is yet another way to market alcohol and increase sales. A *flight* is usually the equivalent of a single full serving (say four three-ounce servings of beer), but the price for this assortment is generally slightly more than a single full serving. The rationale is that customers are willing to pay a little extra for the variety.

STAFF TRAINING

As alluded to in the earlier discussion of health and legal issues surrounding alcohol, training staff members is paramount. We discuss the full training cycle, from orientation through employee development, in Chapter 13, but it is worthwhile focusing here on several key beverage-related issues that must be emphasized and managed as part of the training process. These include making sure employees understand the basic laws governing alcohol service as they pertain to servers and bartenders, and making sure they know something about reducing liability exposure.

The Basics

As we noted earlier, laws regulating alcohol vary considerably from state to state. Nevertheless, there are basic guidelines that require servers everywhere be trained. For example, licensing affects the available legal product set. Some licenses allow only beer sales; others allow an operator to sell beer and wine only while still others allow for the sale of all legal liquor categories. As mentioned, some even allow beer, wine, and spirits to be purchased for consumption at home.

The nuances involved in this regulatory landscape are very complex and important. For example, many customers who purchase a bottle of wine do not want to drink the entire bottle and would like to save it for the next day. In some states, no unfinished wine can be removed from the premises. Servers in these states or localities must be trained to apply some finesse when reminding customers of this regulation while avoiding advising them to drink more than they can manage. In other states, unfinished wine can be taken home by the customer so long as the server replaces the cork and wraps the bottle in a sealed package. The notion here is that customers must leave the package sealed until safely at home. Yet other states are very lax and customers can take unopened bottles home as long as they are transported beyond the reach of the driver (preferably in the trunk).

Another practice that a foodservice manager might face is that of customers bringing their own wine to a restaurant. Where allowed by state and local law, most foodservice operations charge a **corkage fee** for this customer choice. Although this practice is common in restaurants that have not yet been granted or do not have the proper beverage license, even restaurants that sell wine sometimes must decide whether to accommodate customers wishing to bring their own wine or beer. The corkage fee allows the server to open and serve the wine, while it allows customers perhaps to save money or simply to drink their favorite wine. Some restaurants allow this on the condition that they don't already carry the wine in question (for obvious reasons). In some states this practice is permitted but servers are not allowed to open or serve the beverage. Here, the server must be trained to provide glassware but never, under any circumstances, to open or pour the beverages.

Beverage servers also need training to help them manage legal serving hours. Most people are familiar with "closing time," after which no more alcohol may be served (usually preceded by a **last call**—a final offer to fill beverage orders). Many states also regulate how early in the day beverages may be served, and some still forbid the sale of liquor on Sundays or specific holidays (for example, Election Day and Christmas).

The final basic training issue, and one that is the same for all 50 states and the District of Columbia, involves the minimum age for buying and consuming alcohol, which is 21 years of age. The legal drinking age is intended to curtail drinking by college-age students and to reduce drunk-driving accidents involving those under 21. There is no leniency in this area, and the fines for violating such regulations can be sizable.

Minimizing Liability

While these basic training points are important, a more complex issue relates to minimizing liability and helping to ensure public safety. While again applicable laws differ from state to state, servers should never serve intoxicated customers. This may seem like an obvious precaution, but the truth is that it is not always easy to distinguish the intoxicated from those who are merely pleasantly disposed or mellow.

For example, it is reasonable to expect a bartender to monitor a patron sitting at the bar. It is reasonable to expect that bartender to ensure that no guest is overserved and, should it appear that such a guest has requested more alcohol than is reasonable given the situation, the bartender must cut off the guest from further drinking. If the guest is obviously intoxicated, restaurant employees also must advise the person not to drive, offer to call a cab, or—if the situation warrants it—notify the police that the person is or may be driving while intoxicated.

However, in busy nightclubs and restaurants at peak hours, monitoring each patron's consumption can be difficult. Many a customer enjoys two drinks at a bar and appears completely sober—even though he has been drinking heavily at another bar yet is showing no effects. Thus, training is necessary so that foodservers, bartenders, cocktail servers, bouncers, and managers all watch for signs of intoxication. While this type of training is beyond the scope of this text, there are many server-training programs available, including one from the National Restaurant Association Educational Foundation.

Finally, we must address the issue that is underscored in this chapter's case in point: the fake ID. One of a foodservice or bar operator's chief protections against liability is the right to ask every customer to prove that she has attained legal drinking age by showing identification with her date of birth. If an ID appears upon close inspection to be valid, a server can serve a customer knowing he has taken reasonable care. However, if a server, bartender, or bouncer who is responsible for checking IDs sees bumps, alterations, or a photograph that does not resemble the customer, then she should confiscate the identification and refuse service. One of the best tools available for such purposes is the **I.D. Checking Guide**, which includes every valid driver's license and ID card format, from the United States and Canada to worldwide, in full size and color, including state IDs.

MANAGERIAL IMPLICATIONS

Alcohol undeniably plays a major role in the foodservice industry. It has served as a **social lubricant**, fueling economies and stimulating cross-cultural interactions for centuries. Its roots date back to 10,000 BC when it was one of the few safe beverages, providing caloric content to our ancestors. Moreover, its ties to culture and religion remain active today.

Problems with overindulgence, however, have engendered temperance movements around the world. In the United States, such a movement led to legislation that made the manufacture, sale, and transport of alcohol illegal. The Eighteenth Amendment to the United States Constitution—the National Prohibition Act—was enacted in 1920. It proved almost impossible to enforce effectively, and it spawned an underground trade in alcohol that benefited organized crime more than ordinary citizens. Prohibition was lifted in 1933 when the Twenty-First Amendment was passed. This legislation pushed much of the responsibility for legislating laws on alcohol production and sales to the state level.

Today, the beverage industry represents almost $80 billion in foodservice sales. Even in the onsite foodservice segment, alcohol service is routinely included in catered functions. Alcohol use is very popular in the United States, with the average American adult in 2009 consuming seven bottles of spirits, 12 bottles of wine, and 230 cans of beer (including restaurant and bar sales and in-home consumption). Some 30 percent of American adults do not drink at all, however. The United States ranks fortieth in the world in alcohol consumption per person.

The alcohol responsible for the intoxicating effects of beer, wine, and spirits is ethanol. A 12-ounce domestic beer, a 4.5-ounce glass of red Bordeaux wine, and a 1.25-ounce shot of 80-proof vodka each contains approximately one-half ounce of ethanol. In any type of beverage, ethanol contains an enzyme, the t-PA antigen, that helps prevent chronic internal blood clots. Other possible health benefits include the antioxidant effects of red wine's phenolic compounds. Alcohol may increase appetite as well, making for a better restaurant experience.

When not consumed in moderation, however, alcohol can have very harmful effects. The typical person can process the equivalent of one drink per hour, but consuming alcohol at a greater rate creates a host of mostly deleterious physical effects. As intoxication begins to influence brain function, alcohol can impede muscle coordination, judgment, and eyesight. The definition of intoxication in most states is a blood alcohol concentration (BAC) of 0.08 percent. Chronic alcohol abuse involves physical addiction and contributes to a host of costly social and health-related problems.

Foodservice operators have duties of care that require them to provide alcohol service responsibly. Dramshop laws add a legal component to this obligation. While such laws vary from state to state, they require foodservice operators to take special care in their service of beer, wine, and spirits.

The strong demand for beer, wine, and spirits makes controlling these products especially complex. This includes the frequently occurring failure to maintain a proper division of duties and the potential for financial gain to employees who steal from a foodservice operation. These risks can be minimized through such control measures as the use of a par system and a comprehensive approach to managing the ordering and standardization at all points in the beverage control sequence.

The purchasing process is regulated in every state to greater or lesser extent, and the corresponding laws must play into managing that process. Yet there are many other issues to consider in purchasing alcohol. Receiving alcohol, too, poses challenges but still requires the four basic steps for receiving that apply to receiving food. The key to storage is security, followed in

INDUSTRY EXEMPLAR

M. J. Barleyhoppers

Located in northern Idaho, M. J. Barleyhoppers is the area's largest microbrewery. Besides offering great food and entertainment, what sets this microbrewery apart from others is its location—it's in a hotel. The Red Lion Hotel in Lewiston offers a host of amenities, including large, flat-screen televisions in its 181 guestrooms, indoor and outdoor pools, and a convenient location.

The microbrewery produces seven year-round hand-crafted ales in styles ranging from a light wheat to a stout, and seasonals such as Octoberfest, Snake River Porter, and Bock at the Moon, a Maibock style. In addition to these great beverages, M. J. Barleyhoppers is also known for its food. Naturally, it tempts customers with the usual bar fare, such as wings and burgers, but the offerings don't stop there. Appetizers include crab cakes and ahi tuna, seared rare with a signature wasabi sauce. The Mango Salad is a great second course, which is drizzled with pomegranate dressing. Entrees include a crab and

Courtesy of M. J. Barleyhoppers.

importance by temperature, light, and humidity. Issuing, as is the case with pricing, must be handled differently for each product category.

Training staff members is paramount for any foodservice operation that hopes to provide efficient and consistent beverage service. Employees lacking the proper training inevitably run afoul of the laws that regulate what types of alcohol can be sold at what types of outlet, when it can be legally sold, and the age at which customers may be legally served. Properly managing such issues minimizes liability and fosters public safety (not to mention good will).

Swiss sandwich, a steamboat stout burger (marinated in stout beer), and a ribeye steak served with garlic Idaho mashed potatoes and vegetables.

The entertainment, too, differentiates the operation from the typical microbrewery, offering specials every night including Two-Step Tuesdays with live music and comedy night on Wednesday. It is a popular place to hold a bachelorette or bachelor party, and if you can't have the party in the bar, you can always order kegs of their specialty beers and ales to serve at home.

KEY TERMS

mocktails   371

viticulture   373

enology   373

distillation   373

Gin Epidemic   375

temperance movement   375

Eighteenth Amendment   375

National Prohibition Act   375

Volstead Act   375

The Noble Experiment   375

Twenty-First Amendment   375

Failed experiment   376

bootleggers   376

86'd   376

ethanol   379

French paradox   379

phenolic compounds   379

resveratrol   379

t-PA antigen   379

blood alcohol concentration (BAC)   380

duties of care   381

dramshop laws   381

foreseeability   381

reasonable care   381

par stock   382

control states   383

license states   383

well brands   383

call brands   383

premium brands   383

ultra-premium brands   383

corkage fee   388

last call   389

I.D. Checking Guide   389

social lubricant   390

The Fake ID

When Josh's older brother Jake went to college, he quickly found someone who could obtain a fake driver's license for him, enabling him to get into bars near campus. Jake, now in his 30s (the two boys are 15 years apart in age), frequently tells stories of his college shenanigans that were made possible by his premature entry into the bar scene. Jake often adds, at the end of every story, an observation to the effect that using a fake ID "was no big deal. Everyone had one, and if you got caught they just slapped your wrist."

It was no surprise, then, that when Josh started college he thought it would be a good idea to get a fake ID.

Times had changed, though, and Josh found that asking around did not produce positive results. In fact, most people to whom he mentioned the idea discouraged it. "Why do you want to get a fake ID?" "Why risk getting kicked out of school?" "We have lots of functions around the college that are fun—why do you need to drink just to have fun?"

These questions made him rethink the whole idea. Still, he kept coming back to his brother's hysterical stories. Josh wanted to have the same kind of college experience that his brother had enjoyed. So he did some online searching and found a site that, for a mere $500, would deliver a falsified driver's license that, according to the site, "even fools trained experts."

Before the first semester was barely under way, Josh got his dream answered in the yellow envelope with no return address. Sure enough, there it was. It didn't look very authentic. It was from another state, however, and since Josh had never seen a driver's license from that state, he assumed it was a good rendition.

Friday night came around, and Josh headed out to the best-known pub near campus. He'd never been in the place and was nervous, but he wanted to experience his own stories to tell his friends just as Jake had told him his.

The large, somewhat intimidating bouncer stood at the bar's entrance and when Josh's turn in line finally came, said only: "ID please." Josh was ready with his new ID in hand. It took the bouncer all of three seconds before he responded, "This looks fake. Are you sure you want to use it?"

Josh was crushed. What did he mean, fake? He had spent his entire summer savings on the ID; it couldn't look fake! Then the bouncer told him he would call the police to double-check. He then gave Josh a choice: "Look, you aren't the first one to try to use a fake ID. And, yes, I'm going to confiscate it. However, if you just walk away, I'll forget I ever saw you and simply put the fake ID in the box with the other hundreds of them that I've collected since I started working here. Or you can wait for just a minute and the police will take care of it."

Josh was so sure that the ID was the real deal that he hadn't thought about what to do if this happened. He was so thunderstruck that he did nothing. He simply stood there. It seemed like only seconds had passed when two police officers began asking him questions. He was then escorted to their patrol car and taken to the station. There, he was booked for a felony.

While in some states using a fake ID is still a misdemeanor, other states have equated it to identify fraud and treat it as a felony offense, meaning more jail time, higher fines, and years-long suspensions of driving privileges. Over the long term, a felony weighs down the offender with a criminal record that might limit his or her career choices (a felon cannot qualify for a liquor license, for example). In addition, the offender might be prohibited from owning a gun or voting. Unfortunately, the state where Josh was going to college fell into this latter category.

As a result of the conviction, he was kicked out of school.

What would you have advised Josh to do before he got the fake ID? What lessons can you learn from this? (Unfortunately, this is a true story—only the names have been changed . . .)

REVIEW AND DISCUSSION QUESTIONS

1. What is a *mocktail*? Give two examples.

2. Provide two examples of alcohol's role in history.

3. What is the difference between fermentation and distillation?

4. Why was Prohibition called *The Nobel Experiment*? Did it work?

5. What is your favorite explanation of how the term *86'd* came into use?

6. Using your choice of search engine, identify the five leading countries in terms of per capita alcohol consumption.

7. What is the *French paradox*?

8. A person drinks an excessive amount of alcohol well into the late hours of the night. He then gets up early in the morning and drives. Is it possible that his BAC is over the legal limit? Explain your answer.

9. Why are issues of foreseeability and reasonable care important in the foodservice industry?

10. Explain the notion of *division of duty*. Provide an example of where this may be missing in the foodservice industry (cite an example not already provided in the chapter).

11. You've just been hired as a bar manager and your first task is to replace the ice-making machine. What are some considerations?

12. What is the difference between a *control state* and a *license state?*

13. Again using your choice of search engine, name three examples of ultra-premium spirits.

14. Why do temperature, humidity, and light matter when storing the various categories of alcohol?

15. The price for a glass of Chateau Ste. Michelle Cabernet Sauvignon is $13.25. What should you charge for a half glass?

16. Why would a restaurant charge a high corkage fee? On the other hand, a new restaurant in San Francisco is charging a corkage fee of only $1. What is their strategy?

ENDNOTES

1. For related information, see Katsigiris, C., and Thomas, C. *The Bar & Beverage Book* (4th ed.). Hoboken, NJ: John Wiley & Sons, 2007.

2. Patrick, C. H. *Alcohol, Culture, and Society.* Durham, NC: Duke University Press, 1952. Reprint edition by New York: AMS Press, 1970.

3. Braudel, F. *Capitalism and Material Life, 1400–1800.* Translated by Miriam Kochan. New York: Harper and Row, 1974.

4. Austin, G. A. *Alcohol in Western Society from Antiquity to 1800: A Chronological History.* Santa Barbara, CA: ABC-Clio, 1985.

5. French, H. V. *Nineteen Centuries of Drink in England: A History* (2nd ed.). London: National Temperance Publication Depot, 1890.

6. "Teaching with Documents: The Volstead Act and Related Prohibition Documents." United States National Archives. 2008-02-14. www.archives.gov/education/lessons/volstead-act/.

7. Blum, D. "The Chemist's War: The Little-Told Story of How the US Government Poisoned Alcohol during Prohibition, with Deadly Consequences." *Washington Post* (February 2010).

8. National Institute on Alcohol Abuse and Alcoholism. www.niaaa.nih.gov/Resources/DatabaseResources/QuickFacts/AlcoholSales/consum03.htm.

9. Beer Institute, www.beerinstitute.org/statistics.asp?bid=200.

CHAPTER 18

THE FUTURE OF THE FOODSERVICE INDUSTRY

LEARNING OBJECTIVES:

After becoming familiar with this chapter, you should be able to:

1. Apply lessons learned from past changes in the foodservice industry to enhance your understanding of the issues facing managers today.

2. Appreciate the forces that affect and that are in many ways shaping the future of foodservice management.

3. Identify likely changes that we will see in each of the foodservice segments.

4. Conceptualize how devices and applications that are typical of today's technology might evolve in tomorrow's foodservice industry.

Having considered the vital internal control function, advanced analytic approaches, and the complex issues associated with beverage management, we conclude this section, and the text, with a look ahead. We begin by considering past predictions to see which did or did not come true. We then discuss the forces for change that will undoubtedly shape the future of our industry.

We extend the consideration of these forces to make our own segment-by-segment predictions for the future. Finally, we consider the role of technology in the foodservice industry, both today and tomorrow.

■□ LESSONS FROM THE PAST

In Chapter 1, we discussed the evolution of the foodservice industry from its earliest days. We considered the public houses of France, the forerunners of our current restaurant format. We observed the progression in hospitals from serving beer and bread to now being part of the healing process by offering tasty and nutritious food. We also considered how business and industry (B&I) food was first introduced to increase productivity but provided the added benefit of increased employee satisfaction. Moreover, we noted earlier that, in the past, onsite foodservice was considered a completely different kind of organization, both philosophically and organizationally. Understanding these developments helps us appreciate the foodservice business today.

In 1988, the National Restaurant Association identified the following nine basic functional areas of a foodservice manager's job:

1. Cost control and financial management

2. Supervising operations

3. Organizing and planning each shift

4. Communicating with other managers and staff

5. Customer relations

6. Motivating employees

7. Developing employees

8. Communicating with outside sources

9. Monitoring and maintaining facility equipment

As you can see by comparing this with the managerial functions and supervision principles discussed in Chapter 14, the basic elements of foodservice operations have not changed dramatically.

A later study conducted in 1993 set out to predict the skills that managers in the year 2000 would need.[1] It predicted that foodservice managers in the future would likely:

■ Need greater computer proficiency

■ Supervise a more culturally diverse staff

■ Find that service will become a more competitive point of differentiation

■ Need better teaching and training skills

■ Need better skills for managing people

■ Need excellent interpersonal skills

■ Play an increased role in waste management and recycling

■ Deal with customers who are more educated about nutrition

■ Need to cater to the service demands of a more diverse customer base

■ Empower front-of-house employees to render better service

eaders from the Past

Figure 18.1   Square watermelon.

All of these predictions seem to have come true, even more so when applied to the present than in 2000. These are, however, general trends, which are far easier to predict than the advent of specific products and services. Let's consider, then, some specific prognostications that have been made. A prognosticator of 1900 predicted the following for the next millennium: "Strawberries as large as apples will be eaten by our great-great-grandchildren for their Christmas dinners a hundred years hence. Raspberries and blackberries will be as large. One will suffice for the fruit course for each person. Cranberries, gooseberries, and currants will be as large as oranges."[2]

Well, this prediction of super-sized berries didn't come true. Then again, who would have predicted that in 2001 Japanese farmers would begin growing square watermelons that fit conveniently and precisely onto refrigerator shelves (see Figure 18.1)? The intent was to maximize space in the typical Japanese refrigerator, which is smaller than those found in the United States and Europe. Of course, this convenience came at a cost. When they were first marketed, the average price per square watermelon was $82.

A 1950 issue of *Modern Mechanics* made some interesting food-related predictions for the year 2000. Consider three noteworthy examples:[3]

Cooking as an art is only a memory in the minds of old people. A few die-hards still broil a chicken or roast a leg of lamb, but the experts have developed ways of deep-freezing partially baked cuts of meat. Even soup and milk are delivered in the form of frozen bricks.

This expansion of the frozen-food industry and the changing gastronomic habits of the nation have made it necessary to install in every home the electronic industrial stove, which came out of World War II. In eight seconds a half-grilled frozen steak is thawed; in two minutes more it is ready to serve. It never takes more than half an hour to prepare an elaborate meal of several courses.

In the middle of the 20th century statisticians were predicting that the world would starve to death because the population was increasing more rapidly than the food supply. By 2000, a vast amount of research has been conducted to exploit principles that were embryonic in the first quarter of the 20th century. Thus sawdust and wood pulp are converted into sugary foods. Discarded paper table "linen" and rayon underwear are bought by chemical factories to be converted into candy.

FORCES FOR CHANGE

As entertaining as it is to consider what people in the past expected in the foodservice industry of the future, the reality is that predicting that future is no easy task. Let us consider changes that would have been almost impossible to predict in a related industry. In the early 1800s, the US farming and agriculture industry had not changed dramatically in a thousand years. Later in that century and over the course of the early 1900s, however, everything changed. With the rapid rise of mechanization, particularly in the form of the tractor, farming tasks could be done at a speed and on a scale that was previously inconceivable. In fact, between 1700 and today, the total area of cultivated land worldwide increased almost 500 percent.

Mechanization's effects were sweeping. For example, in 1810, agricultural products represented 75 percent of total US exports; as of 2010, this number was less than 15 percent. In 1890, farmers represented 49 percent of the US workforce. Today, they represent less than 2 percent. Indeed, today the services sector (including foodservice) has overtaken agriculture as the economic sector employing the most people worldwide. This sector is now responsible for 90 percent of all new jobs in the United States.

What can we learn from this? The world is changing, and at a rate of change that is faster than at any other time in history. As foodservice managers, you need to embrace these changes. First, however, you must understand the forces that drive them.

Globalization

For the foodservice industry, the world is shrinking. As regional economies and cultures have become more integrated through a global network of communication, transportation, and trade, the effects are undeniable: We are now part of a global society. This creates a wealth of opportunities for foodservice operators. For example, many of yesterday's foodservice entrepreneurs understood that in order to protect the business from economic decline in certain parts of the country, they could expand into growing markets elsewhere, as sales in restaurants or cafes in regions with booming economies would compensate for potential financial shortfalls in operations located in regions with weak economies. This strategy is even more effective when applied globally. Thus, financial downturns in a country's economy can be covered by operations in other parts of the world.

McDonald's has become emblematic of **globalization**; some people call it **McDonaldization**. *The Economist* magazine uses the "Big Mac index" (the price of a Big Mac) as an informal measure of purchasing power parity among world currencies. It has even been suggested that, should the world end tomorrow, discoverers from a distant planet would assume Earth shared a common worship of a deity portrayed by golden arches.

The term *McDonaldization* was originally intended to be derogatory. Perhaps this judgment deserves a second look. McDonald's hires about 1 million people annually, more than any other American organization, public or private. It is the largest purchaser of beef, pork, and potatoes. It also offers more playgrounds than any other private entity in the United States.

In a study titled *Golden Arches East*, a group of anthropologists looked at the impact McDonald's has had on East Asia, and Hong Kong in particular.[4] The findings indicated that McDonald's had solved the problem of losing face for many customers. Owing to cultural norms, it can be a source of embarrassment in some parts of Asia when one person orders a more expensive meal than another does. This causes the person ordering the less expensive meal to lose face. Since items on a McDonald's menu are all similarly priced, this has ceased to be an issue. Moreover, when it opened in Hong Kong in 1975, McDonald's was the first restaurant to consistently offer clean restrooms, driving customers to demand the same of other restaurants and institutions. By popularizing the idea of a quick restaurant meal, the study suggested, McDonald's also contributed to breaking down several taboos, such as one on eating while walking in Japan. In most cases, McDonald's was quickly accepted, after which it was no longer seen as a foreign institution.

We focus here on McDonald's largely because of all the attention the foodservice icon has garnered over the years in connection with its global growth. Yet globalization can be seen in every sector. For example, of the three leading managed services companies on the planet, only ARAMARK is based in the United States. (As noted earlier, Compass Group PLC is based in the United Kingdom and Sodexo is based in France.)

Globalization creates opportunities for a better understanding of other cultures, but it will also require greater management expertise to manage an increasingly diverse workforce. On the upside, globalization provides economic opportunities for businesses looking to expand, translating into untold opportunities for future foodservice managers.

Social Responsibility

We have mentioned social responsibility routinely throughout this book. We recognize it here as a force for change because it is no longer a fad that companies grudgingly adopt as a marketing vehicle; it is now a common operating practice. Corporate social responsibility, or the obligation of an organization to behave ethically, stems from ethical behavior at the individual level. Current concerns related to social responsibility include protecting the environment (discussed at greater length in the following section), promoting worker safety, supporting social issues, and investing in the community. Other examples of corporate social responsibility include building Habitat for Humanity homes, organizing corporate teams to participate in charity runs and street fairs, and establishing nonprofit charitable foundations to which employees and the corporation can contribute.

Social responsibility carries with it a myriad of financial implications for business organizations. First, people like to work for companies that share their values. Thus, an organization will naturally attract employees to whom socially responsible business practices are appealing. Second, investors often choose to put their money into companies that share their values and ethics. (This has created a new category of investments called **green stocks**.) Finally, communities are more welcoming to organizations that are socially responsible, resulting in a mutually beneficial relationship.

Returning to McDonald's, it is interesting to note that the QSR giant has been engaging in socially responsible practices for years. For example, when environmentally damaging packaging and waste produced by the company's restaurants became a public concern, McDonald's started a joint project with the non-profit environmental organization Friends of the Earth to eliminate the use of polystyrene containers and to reduce the amount of waste produced. McDonald's Europe invests in similar business practices. The company buys all of its coffee from the poorest farmers in the world at fair trade prices and from farms sanctioned by the Rainforest Alliance, a nonprofit organization that promotes sustainable farming. It also buys most of its beef locally in an attempt to support local communities.[5]

Sustainability

By definition, *sustainability* means the capacity to endure. For our purposes, however, it denotes business practices that contribute to or preserve rather than deplete natural resources. In Chapter 3, for example, we introduced the notion of food miles. Foodservice operators who reduce the number of food miles associated with each product used contribute to the health of the environment. This is related to another issue introduced in the same chapter, the carbon footprint. As individuals and organizations, we need to reduce greenhouse gases emissions.

Steps that take foodservice operations toward a sustainable, green future include managing energy, adopting simple practices such as recycling, composting, and reducing water consumption, adopting environmentally friendly packaging for take-out items, and communicating related efforts to customers. Organizations that undertake such practices can positively impact the environment while increasing customer satisfaction and growing the bottom line. For example (as depicted in Chapter 10), National Restaurant Association research shows that the typical foodservice operation incurs utility costs that equal 3 to 4 percent of total sales. Too few foodservice operators bother to manage this expense.

Two foodservice functions—purchasing and usage—provide the best opportunities to reduce carbon use while lowering energy costs. Some states allow foodservice operators to buy electricity from third-party suppliers, but too few consider this even though it is typically cheaper. Moreover, many operators assume that electricity and natural gas meters are foolproof or are read correctly each month. Savvy operators will take the time to ensure that they are being billed accurately. Similarly, some landlords bill foodservice operators for utilities as part of the monthly rental cost or as an added expense. This should be negotiated like any other term in a contract.

On the usage side, many operators think that utility costs are driven up primarily by the kitchen, which requires gas and electricity for cooking. However, statistics from the US Environmental Protection Agency illustrate that cooking is responsible for only 23 percent of total utility expenses in foodservice operations (see Figure 18.2). Thus, foodservice managers should follow trends in lodging such as using LED and compact fluorescent bulbs, which immediately reduce energy use. Even simple, low-cost additions such as a digital thermostat can produce savings. Other changes require capital expenditures, but can also produce considerable energy savings. Many new dishwashing machines, for example, are designed to use less energy (and less water), which may justify replacing old equipment.

Many foodservice operators think that recycling involves only beer and wine bottles. However, robust recycling programs that include glass, plastics, metals, papers, and cardboard can reduce garbage and the associated refuse removal expense by 50 to 70 percent. Even cooking oil can be recycled. In fact, many operations now sell their used oil, which can be burned as biofuel, for a profit. Composting, too, is a form of recycling. While composting might be impractical in many operations, those that are able to compost waste find that the impact on the environment is extremely positive.

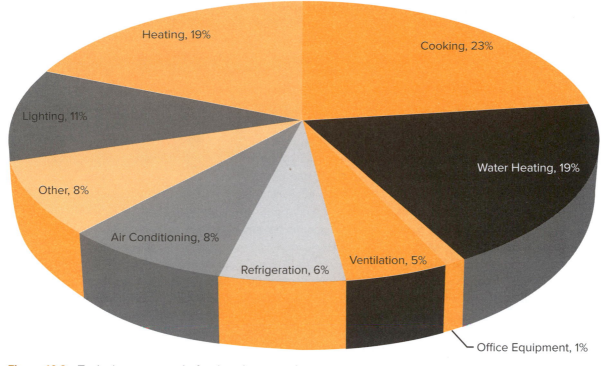

Figure 18.2 Typical energy use in foodservice operations.

The cost of water in many municipalities is high and continues to rise. As we mentioned earlier, replacing equipment is one way to reduce the associated expense. It is also possible to save through operational changes. For example, many onsite operators are going "trayless." Eliminating trays not only does away with the expense of purchasing them, but also eliminates the cost of washing them. The reduction in water use is substantial.

Foodservice operations with large takeout components should review their packaging practices. Intelligently managing packaging can result in cost savings while protecting the environment. For example, many operations routinely include napkins, condiments, and utensils with every order. By simply asking customers whether they would prefer not having such items packed with their food, foodservice operators could reduce the needless waste that results from including unwanted items. Biodegradable packaging, such as containers made from corn, can also reduce disposable trash and in some cases packaging costs.

In addition to saving money and reducing negative environmental impact, these green practices can also provide competitive marketing advantages. The National Restaurant Association reports that 62 percent of adults will likely choose a restaurant based on its environmental friendliness and 44 percent say they are likely to choose where to dine based on a given foodservice operation's energy and water conservation practices. In addition, a foodservice operation's sustainability practices can help attract and retain good employees who want to work for companies that care about the environment. So, foodservice operations should not only engage in sustainable practices—they should also make these efforts known.

Because we have noted the call for sustainable practices in previous chapters, we will limit the discussion here. In essence, foodservice managers should embrace sustainability because it is good for the Earth and good for business. As leaders of this global industry, you, the next generation of foodservice professionals, must strive to satisfy customers' current desires without compromising the ability of future generations to meet their own needs—that is sustainability.

Quest for Quality

Consumers today want quality in everything. This includes clothing, cars, and foodservice. This applies to all industry segments—a QSR, a corporate headquarters cafe, and a fine-dining restaurant are all expected to deliver excellent products. Although the expected standards vary with price and setting, people want value, which includes product and service quality.

This is a force for change because, in concert with the highest level of competition ever seen in this industry, it will force foodservice operators to rise to unprecedented standards. Onsite cafes that use locally produced, sustainable products are no longer the exception. Foodservice operations that pride themselves on quality service will need to do more to ensure quality in all areas. Healthcare foodservice provides a fitting example. By its nature, the hospital kitchen is far away from its customers, who often suffer from illnesses requiring major restrictions in their diets. In the past, it was assumed that quality food and service could not be attained under these conditions. But as patients and their families became better educated about the possibilities, they began to demand this quality.

This quest for quality also translates into changing the value equation introduced in Chapter 2. During the height of the recent economic recession, about 23 percent of foodservice operations generated customer traffic through deals or bundled offerings. The National Restaurant Association reports that 75 percent of adults say they would patronize full-service restaurants and 66 percent would go to QSRs more often if they offered discounts during slower dayparts or days. This is, of course, a two-edged sword. Most consumers are hesitant to pay $5 for an item that they know will sell for $4 tomorrow. Thus, foodservice operators must be extremely savvy in promoting such discounts. Furthermore, customers expect the same quality when receiving discounts. This means that operators must carefully maintain portion size and product quality lest they disappoint the guest.

To meet this customer-driven quest for quality, foodservice operators must understand consumers' changing attitudes, behaviors, and dining preferences more than ever. This will blur lines between dayparts, service levels in any given segment, and promotion strategies. QSR leader Jack in the Box realized this some time ago when it eliminated the common practice of featuring breakfast menus in the morning and lunch and dinner menus later in the day. Now, customers can get a breakfast sandwich at 5 P.M. or tacos and onion rings at 8 A.M. The change increased same-store sales without increasing costs. Again, this was in response to customers' changing dining preferences.

Finally, this new era in foodservice that is shaped by diverse forces of change creates opportunities and challenges. Foodservice professionals who are bold and willing to take risks on innovative promotions will likely realize huge returns. The challenge, however, is to innovate in ways that are in concert with the changing business landscape. This means, in essence, seeing into the future. As we will see next, however, not every crystal ball offers the best advice.

◼◻ PREDICTIONS BY SEGMENT

As we noted earlier, it is easy to poke fun at predictions that have not come true. It is also more difficult than ever to prognosticate, given the forces for change discussed earlier that add more variables to the mix. Nonetheless, we offer here some short- and long-term predictions by segment.

Quick Service

The easy prediction for QSRs based on current trends is that fat will continue to fall out of favor. Americans will increase their demand for healthier foods. Look for menu offerings at current concepts to reflect this trend, but also expect new concepts to emerge that balance taste and health even when serving hamburgers and fries. (A good example is this chapter's industry exemplar, Five Guys Burgers and Fries.)

With obesity in America reaching epidemic proportions and local municipalities looking to regulate the industry into removing trans fats and other harmful foods, look for the QSR segment to try to get ahead of the curve. Local municipalities also have waded into the regulatory waters, waging campaigns to reduce trans-fat consumption.

In its 2009 State Legislative Review,[6] the National Restaurant Association noted that ". . . major menu-labeling actions in 2008 spurred more interest in the issue in the first half of 2009. These included New York City's menu-labeling mandate, the enacting of California's menu-labeling law, and Congress' introduction of a bill that would create a national nutrition-disclosure standard." The article identifies problems that restaurant chains might experience with as many as 30 or 40 states issuing menu mandates. In some ways, this actually underscores the importance of one national set of rules, which (as we discussed in Chapter 3) are now part of the 2010 Patient Protection and Affordable Care Act that requires foodservice operations with 20 or more locations to list calorie content information for standard menu items on restaurant menus and menu boards. Moreover, New York City has already banned trans fats. Several other states and many cities and municipalities are considering such laws, all of which further complicate the issue for any food-service group, whether national or regional.

It should be noted that the trend towards greater nutrition disclosure is well under way, the ban on trans fats is spreading nationwide, and the next big target for nutrition groups will almost surely be salt, or sodium, to be precise.[7] One author notes that, among other companies, Au Bon Pain and Uno Chicago Grill have been working to address salt content "rather than waiting for legislation to force their hands." Many national food producers, such as Campbell's, are already conducting advertising campaigns noting the reduction of sodium content in their soups by the use of sea salt (sea salt has a stronger flavor, enabling less to be used, thereby reducing the sodium content). Future targets for disclosure activities could be gluten and other forms of fat, supported by comparison systems to help consumers determine which foods to choose as healthier options. Such legislation is very well intended, but can involve some very complex information, not easily addressed on a food label, package, or menu.

We can also predict that hiring good employees will become even more difficult in the future. Perhaps one reason for this is indicated by a recent announcement made by McDonald's. The chain recently informed federal authorities that it will be forced to discontinue its healthcare offerings unless part of the new healthcare reform law is dropped. A provision in the new law requires employers to spend 80 to 85 percent of premium revenues on medical care. McDonald's, which offers "mini-medical" plans to nearly 30,000 employees, said that it would not reach those figures in 2011 and would have to eliminate health coverage unless something changes. Other QSR chains are preparing to make similar announcements.

Finally, we predict that pricing models will increasingly differentiate. As customers demand higher quality, some QSRs will answer with ultra-premium menu offerings that approach mid-scale-restaurant prices. Others will seek to attract value-minded customers who make the purchasing decision based wholly on price. The outcome will be positive for customers as more choices will be available across a range of price points. For QSR operators, however, such decisions can shape the associated brand image for an entire generation.

Fast-Casual

The fast-casual segment will continue to grow and will be influenced strongly by cuisines of various cultures. The earliest ethnic chains, such as Baja Fresh (see Chapter 3) and Rubio's, easily distinguished themselves with good-quality Mexican fair. In the future, we will see growth in fast-casual concepts not only featuring cuisines found commonly in other segments but also some that venture into new fast-casual concepts, such as Middle Eastern and Korean-influenced chains.

The lines that separate the QSR, fast-casual, and midscale segments will continue to blur. Fast-casual chains will expand into other dayparts, particularly breakfast, and will offer pricing that will likely capture customers who might have stopped at a McDonald's or a Denny's before going to work. Similar trends will be seen in late-night offerings.

The last prediction for the fast-casual segment pertains to service. In its original manifestations, the only difference in service between fast-casual restaurants and QSRs was that, in the fast-casual segment, food was delivered to the customer's table. In the future, service will increase as a differentiating factor, with greater emphasis on customer-employee interaction during food delivery. However, human interaction at the point of sale will be reduced as technology emerges in the order-taking process. (We talk more about this in the chapter's last section.)

Family/Midscale

The prevailing marketing theme in the family or midscale segment is customer loyalty. At present, some 75 percent of guests in this segment are repeat customers. In the future, midscale restaurants will seek to increase this percentage. This will likely spawn a host of frequent-user programs such as those offered in related industries, especially lodging. Shari's already has a punch card for children offering free items for fully punched cards. Technology will make such rewards programs increasingly seamless in the future, as customers will eventually not need to carry cards with them. Rather, sales will be tracked through credit card tracking systems and rewards will be given automatically.

The thrust here is to turn customers into members. Everyone wants to belong, and midscale restaurants can create membership programs at very little cost. Restaurant operators could, for example, provide free mini-appetizers to members when they arrive. Nonmembers would notice other tables receiving these amenities and ask what they need to do to qualify for something similar. Servers will then become membership stewards, helping customers become members so they feel as though they belong to an exclusive group.

In this segment, as in QSRs, product and price variation will increase. Here again, some chains will focus primarily on price while others will emphasize quality or novelty. This will be evident in food items as well as beverages. Many will expand their wine lists and offer microbrews to further differentiate themselves and, again, build customer loyalty.

Moderate/Theme

Theme restaurants in the future will integrate many offerings typically found only in fine-dining restaurants. These include more-expansive beer and wine lists and personalized service. Other changes will involve comfort foods, but not items associated with American cuisine. Savvy operators in this segment will look to other cultures and cuisines to identify "new" comfort foods, like noodle dishes, for the increasingly diverse customer.

Another change, which relates back to our discussion of the menu as the center of any foodservice operation, will be menu storytelling. Theme restaurants will increase their use of the menu to enhance the dining experience through anecdotes as well as suggestions for menu item combinations and food and beverage pairings. Customers can expect to see more prix fixe dining options in this segment as well.

Dining duration will also increase in this segment. As theme restaurant operators enhance their offerings and emulate service quality traditionally found in fine dining, guests will stay longer, likely ordering more courses consisting of smaller dishes. This will have the added effect of higher check averages. A related trend will see more operations adopting pervasive themes that transcend every aspect of the restaurant. Evidence of this is already emerging. For example, consider the Jekyll & Hyde Club in New York City. The interior is macabre with vestiges of a time long past. Upon entering, guests proceed down a long, dark corridor where dried blood stains the floor. The menu items and drinks are contemporary. The food is so good, in fact, that its servers describe it as "otherworldly."

Fine Dining

Hints regarding how fine dining will change in the future can already be found in leading restaurants. For example, The Bazaar by José Andrés (Figure 18.3), a Beverly Hills, California, bar and restaurant, cost more than $12 million to build but offers no appetizers or entrees. The menu consists entirely of small plates and signature cocktails that are flash frozen using liquid nitrogen

Photo courtesy of SLS Hotel at Beverly Hills.

Figure 18.3   The Bazaar by José Andrés, Beverly Hills, California.

and items created by combining liquids with alginate to form bubbles. It grossed $13 million in its first year.

The small-portions approach is a clever way to manipulate psychological barriers to spending. Research indicates that while many restaurant customers would avoid ordering a $60 entree, they won't bother to add up the cost of several small dishes that equate to the same expenditure.

At a recent conference of Executive Chefs across America, many top chefs commented that smaller portion sizes represent the wave of the future in fine dining. The added benefit of the small-plate format is that it works with many cuisines. The trend will also move into beverages where, instead of a glass of wine, guests can purchase tastes of wine or a flight of various vintages or varietals.

Just as theme restaurants will likely adopt conventions found historically in fine dining establishments, the fine dining restaurant of the future will not necessarily look like its former self. Gone are the white tablecloths and gloved waiters. Instead, we will see more theme-type approaches.

Another major change will draw from the current trend toward offering a chef's table, which has guests dining in a restaurant's kitchen and interacting with the chef while she prepares their food. The future will likely see fine dining chefs replacing waiters, serving the food themselves throughout a restaurant as opposed to doing so only at the chef's table. This will provide a more personal experience for the guest, and arguably a more gratifying one for chefs.

Onsite

The future in onsite foodservice is in some ways very easy to predict. It is almost certain that more and more foodservice operations will be run by managed-services companies. This is just an extension of the global trend toward outsourcing any aspect of a business that is not considered part of the firm's core competency.

Other trends will reflect those in other foodservice segments. For example, the trend toward healthier menu items will also be found in onsite foodservice regardless of setting. In fact, nutrition will play an unprecedented role in this segment. A greater variety of ethnic dishes will also become common. Finally, food offerings will continue to increase in sophistication in tandem with an increasingly sophisticated customer base.

Unique to onsite and particularly relevant to healthcare foodservice, the ongoing trend toward greater customization and more choice in menu items will become even more prevalent. An example of this flexible concept was discussed in a 2010 article in *Food Management* magazine,[8] which outlines a concept developed by Morrison Healthcare Foodservice in which both patient and retail food are served from a small cafe within a patient unit. Equipped with small tablet computers containing all necessary patient information including diet and nutrition, servers visit each patient to take food orders. Ambulatory patients may instead choose to dine in the cafe (but must still observe their dietary restrictions), and may be joined by family members. Patients and guests can select from a wide variety of healthy choices on a bistro-style menu, with items such as quesadillas, pork roast in chipotle-chili broth, and Dijon herb-encrusted tilapia. This concept as described here is a pilot but portends a likely future. It also highlights onsite-specific issues for the future—healthy, sustainable, highly varied foods close to those who will be eating and served by friendly staff soon after it is ordered.

When predicting the future of foodservice, we should also discuss vending. Because vending is found in so many onsite operations, it is appropriate to address it in this section, although the trend will spill into other segments. Visions of what vending will look like in the future may already be found in big cities in Japan where there is one vending machine for every 23 residents. There, one can find anything from eggs to DVDs behind a little door. The idea is simple. Vending is the ideal way to offer a greater variety of products in greater quantity and at reduced prices. Without the human element in the service end of dining, price points drop.

Another refreshing change in vending will be a trend toward healthier vending machine offerings. Future vending machines will offer a wider range of food items, including items cooked to order. Cashless vending will also facilitate greater sales.

Technology will also help shape changes in vending. There are already prototypes of machines that feature flat screens instead of the glass cases traditionally used to display a machine's contents, and the next trend will see touch screens replacing buttons. Thus, the front of a vending machine might display four categories of food items. A customer first clicks on a category, then on the specific item she is considering. On screen the item, price, and nutritional information are all displayed. This makes the experience more interactive and allows for informed buying decisions. It also aids in managing the vending business because changes to the menu can be made remotely.

TECHNOLOGY IN 2050

In some respects, we have made relatively safe predictions based on industry trends that have been under way for years. It is far more difficult to make predictions about the use of technology and electronics in the foodservice industry. The pace of technological change is dizzying, and accelerating. To frame our discussion, then, we will first imagine extensions of today's technology into the future and then speculate on a distant future in which technology is even more omnipresent than it is now.

Extending What Is "New" Today

Considering that Internet use was almost nonexistent outside of academic or government circles 25 years ago, who would have predicted that most people today would be carrying around communication devices that connect them to others anywhere on the planet, not only making conventional phone calls but also text messaging, blogging, social networking, and surfing the Web? Yet today, the use of cell phones throughout the civilized world is a multibillion-dollar business, one that has changed how we communicate, socialize, and conduct business. We can even make calls, receive texts, and send e-mails from airplanes. In the foodservice industry, this technology has changed how foodservice is marketed. For example, some chains issue sweeping text messages to advertise a new product. Many have developed applications that allow customers to place their orders from their phones

Early in 2010, Apple launched yet another new technological innovation. The iPad has attracted a lot of attention in foodservice, as enthusiasts see multiple possibilities for the 9.5-by-7.5-inch device in restaurants: a consumer product that accommodates a seemingly endless range of commercial applications. For example, Au Bon Pain is piloting a new iPad app as a **linebusting** (reducing waiting times in lines) solution. When the restaurant is busy, the staff uses two iPads to take customer orders and payments. Managers each carry an iPod Touch—which has the same responsive touchscreen—loaded with the same app to help with additional linebusting. Early results are encouraging.

Human resource specialists see the iPad as a training platform. For example, a foodservice operator could offer portable training videos for employees, and the iPad's larger screen improves the experience. The iPad also can handle e-learning software, which the iPod cannot; this would assist foodservice companies that offer both types of training, achieving their training objectives with only the one device as opposed to purchasing both a PC and an iPod.

Another innovative use of such technology in the foodservice industry ties into our earlier discussion about customer loyalty. For example, Pandini's—a fast-casual restaurant operated by

Figure 18.4   Pandini's.

the Retail Brand Group (a Sodexo subsidiary)—wants to create an atmosphere in which families can eat dinner together while giving kids an opportunity to access tutoring or homework assignments online. (See Figure 18.4.) Thus, the company launched an iPad program whereby parents can borrow an iPad (the restaurant requires only a driver's license in deposit) and their children can use the device to do homework .

This is but one example illustrating how the new technology of today is shaping the foodservice industry of tomorrow.

Singularity

Serious futurists have borrowed from physics the concept of a **singularity** to envision the future of technological advancement. Some believe that, within 40 years, the pace of technological change will become so rapid that, in a life-altering event known as the singularity, our bodies and our brains will ultimately merge with machines, or in some other way a super intelligence will emerge, making it impossible for mere human intelligence to predict the post-singularity future. Other interpretations of the concept of a singularity have been the subject of science fiction for years. Some depict machines with artificial intelligence that seek to eradicate the human race. Others present scenes in which the human brain is made smarter and has greater capacity for learning through an embedded chip.

Some proponents of the singularity concept argue that the ever-shortening gaps in technological innovations make such an event inevitable. Others assert that dramatic and irreversible changes to paradigms and worldviews are accelerating in frequency; the inventions of writing, mathematics, and the computer are past examples of such changes. Supporters of a positive singularity cite that such an event would lead to a civilization that has achieved mastery of its planetary resources. Those that view the prospect of a singularity as the end of human life as we know it and the beginning of domination by artificial life forms suggest that this would be as natural a development as any other evolutionary milestone.

We mention the concept of a singularity largely as an example of how uncertain we are about the effects of technology on the foodservice industry (and on society for that matter). Consider, for example, the attention-grabbing robotic cook that was unveiled at the 2000 National Restaurant Show. Shown in Figure 18.5, Flipper the Robocook was previously employed by IBM to assemble computers but was redesigned to work in restaurant kitchens. (It is now marketed by AccuTemp Products, Inc.)

Many expected the new technology to transform the restaurant industry. Some thought it would be the single solution to the global shortage of workers in QSRs. Some labor unions regarded it as an atrocity and a violation of the right to work. In reality, however, the machine was more a novelty than a practical replacement for hourly employees. Still, it is an example of new technology that years ago would have been considered pure science fiction.

So what will technology in the foodservice industry of 2050 look like? We can say with confidence that some degree of automation in at least some segments will occur. In the back of the house, many of the ordering and invoicing processes will surely become paperless and seamless. Similarly, the payment processes used in foodservice operations, from QSRs through fine dining, will be conducted very differently from the way they are today. The cash sale will become a thing of the past.

In addition, we expect nutritional analyses to be even more automated than today, with nutritional information disseminated much more conveniently and expansively. Similarly, we expect foodservice customers to be much more aware of the importance of nutrition. Successful foodservice operators will have evolved to meet the associated demands for healthy, tasty cuisine.

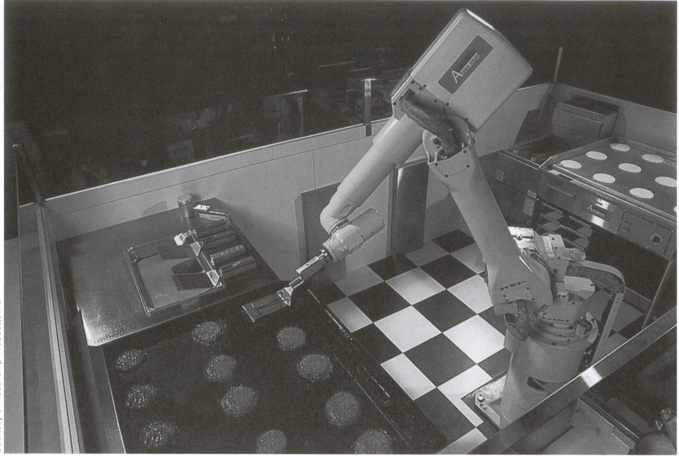

Courtesy of AccuTemp Products, Inc.

Figure 18.5   AccuTemp's Flipper the Robocook.

Final Thought

We conclude our discussion by acknowledging that some of our predictions will likely come true in our lifetimes while others, including this notion of a singularity, may remain fodder for the dreams of future generations. Nonetheless, the future of foodservice management appears bright and filled with opportunities. The future leaders of this exciting, global industry must, however, embrace the popular science fiction writer Isaac Asimov's advice:

> No sensible decision can be made any longer without taking into account not only the world as it is but also the world as it will be.

INDUSTRY EXEMPLAR

Five Guys Burgers and Fries

Jerry Murrell is considered by many the restaurateur of the future. A former stocks and bonds trader, he once noted that Ocean City, Maryland, had 50 places selling boardwalk fries, but only one place, Thrashers, always had a long line. Why? Because while Thrashers sells nothing but fries, it serves a great product using high-quality potatoes and peanut oil. Murrell also knew of J. W. Marriott, who had an A&W stand that he converted and built into the Hot Shoppes chain. Marriott said that anyone can make money in the food business as long as she has a good product, reasonable prices, and a clean place. Murrell thought that by using this formula he could be successful at running a good hamburger and fry place. Since he had five sons to help him, "Five Guys" seemed like a perfect name.

New entrepreneurs enter the QSR segment every day. So what makes Five Guys a model of the future? It integrates many of the best practices mentioned throughout this book. The company focuses on quality, a focus exemplified by its practice of buying only potatoes grown north of the 42nd parallel because they grower more slowly and are therefore denser (the company buys about 8 percent of the Idaho baking potato crop). The beef used to make Five Guys hamburgers is 80 percent lean and never frozen (there are no freezers in any Five Guys restaurant). Buns are browned on a grill as opposed to the faster and cheaper toaster method, to provide a caramelized taste. This notion of a single focus

on the menu offerings is also seen in the simple décor, consisting mostly of red and white tiles. There are no frills. It's all about the burgers and fries. Five Guys also understands marketing. It figures its best salespeople are its customers.

The company offers no drive-through service. The burgers are made to order, which takes too long for a drive-through component. There are over 250,000 possible burger combinations at Five Guys! In one of the first Five Guys restaurants, there was a sign that read: "If you're in a hurry, there are a lot of really good hamburger places within a short distance from here."

The first Five Guys opened in Arlington, Virginia, in 1986. Over the next five years, Murrell and his family opened five more locations around the DC metro area. In 2002, the company began franchising in Virginia and Maryland. In 2003, all the franchise territories in those states had been bought, leading the company to expand nationally. As of this writing, there are 625 locations in over 40 states and four Canadian providences.

KEY TERMS

globalization 398
McDonaldization 398

green stocks 399
linebusting 407

singularity 409

Case in Point

The Traditional Family-style Restaurant

Edward had seen it all. When he got his first foodservice job in college, things were simple. The foodserver took the customers' orders, entered them in the POS terminal by the condiment station, and then delivered the food when the cooks finished preparing it. Some 40 years later, Edward couldn't even remember the last time he had hired a foodserver. In place of the traditional dining-room manager was now a woman with a degree in information systems and a minor in business. Most of her days were spent ensuring that the automated order system embedded in the surface of each

table was functioning within expected parameters. The system was responsible for changing menu items and the associated holographic display (along with prices) depending on the level of business, the demographic of the customers seated at a particular table, the time of day, and the cost of items calculated in real time as they arrived in the kitchen.

Edward looked over the dining room and thought, "What has happened to the food*service* business?" The food at his typical family-style restaurant was delivered to each table via a series of belts and sophisticated automated robotics once found only in automotive assembly plants. The bar still featured an attractive display of fancy liquor bottles, but the actual beverages were made by a machine and delivered in the same way as the food. Guests didn't even expect a person to clear their dishes; they had long become accustomed to using the "back window," a hatch of sorts found at each table through which dirty dishes were deposited by the customer and then automatically sanitized and returned to the kitchen for reuse.

Missing the days of old, Edward espied a table of older customers and decided to surprise them by personally delivering their food. He thought they would be thrilled. He couldn't have been more wrong.

When he arrived at the table, the guests looked at him as if he was some sort of thief, or perhaps someone who might have tainted their food. The woman closest to Edward said, "Thank you, but we'll wait for our food to be delivered the usual way." She then resumed her conversation with her friends.

Edward returned to his office. He had originally gone into the foodservice business because he liked serving people. He always had a great feeling when guests were pleasantly surprised by a creative dish or a wine that they had never had, but thanks to the sommelier's suggestion would now be their new favorite. This was a people business.

He couldn't help but wonder, "Would things ever return to the way they were in the good old days?"

REVIEW AND DISCUSSION QUESTIONS

1. Look at the nine basic functional areas of a foodservice manager's job. How do these compare with the supervision principles discussed in Chapter 12? In particular, what is unique to each of the lists?

2. Did any of the three predictions drawn from the 1950 *Modern Mechanics* article come true, at least to a limited extent? Explain your answer fully.

3. Identify and explain two positive and two negative effects of globalization as they pertain to the foodservice industry.

4. It was noted that *McDonaldization* was originally used in a derogatory manner. Why?

5. Visit the websites for ARAMARK, Compass Group PLC, and Sodexo. What were the annual revenues for each? In how many countries does each company operate?

6. Why might someone invest in green stocks rather than in others?

7. Create a list of ten sustainable practices that a foodservice operator can introduce. Define each one in terms of both the cost and the benefit.

8. For each of the six foodservice segments, make your own predictions about what we might see in the future (distinct from those already offered).

9. Using your choice of search engine, find and describe three themed restaurant chains that are differentiating themselves in unique ways.

10. Why will more companies outsource their foodservice in the future?

11. Describe a technology that your grandparents would likely not have envisioned, and then describe a technology that doesn't exist today but that you might expect to become a reality.

12. We noted that cash transactions will likely no longer occur in the future. What are three ways in which this is already happening today?

ENDNOTES

1. Mills, S. F., & Riele, H. "Foodservice manager 2000." *Journal of Hospitality & Tourism Research*, 17 (1993): 147–159.

2. Watkins, J. E. "What May Happen in the Next Hundred Years." *The Ladies Home Journal* (December 1900).

3. Kaempffert, W. "In the Next Fifty Years." *Modern Mechanics* (February 1950): 112–123.

4. Watson, J. L. *Golden Arches East*. Palo Alto, CA: Stanford University Press, 1998.

5. Capell, K. "McDonald's Offers Ethics with Those Fries." *Business Week* (January 9, 2007).

6. National Restaurant Association. "2009 State Legislative Issue Review: Menu Labeling Legislation." www.restaurant.org.

7. Frumkin, P. "Nutrition Groups Set Sights on Sodium as Next Menu Battleground." *Nation's Restaurant News* (June 30, 2008).

8. "Morrison Debuts Room Service/Retail." *Food Management*. www.food-management.com/book_review/morrison-debuts-room-service-0510.

INDEX